Impacts of Military Spending on Economic Growth

Gerardo Reyes Ruiz
Center for Naval Higher Studies, Mexico

IGI Global
Scientific Publishing
Publishing Tomorrow's Research Today

Vice President of Editorial	Melissa Wagner
Director of Acquisitions	Mikaela Felty
Director of Book Development	Jocelynn Hessler
Production Manager	Mike Brehm
Cover Design	Jose Rosado

Published in the United States of America by
IGI Global Scientific Publishing
701 East Chocolate Avenue
Hershey, PA, 17033, USA
Tel: 717-533-8845
Fax: 717-533-7115
Website: https://www.igi-global.com E-mail: cust@igi-global.com

Library of Congress Cataloging-in-Publication Data

Names: Reyes Ruiz, Gerardo, 1971- editor
Title: Impacts of military spending on economic growth / [edited by] Gerardo Reyes Ruiz.
Description: Hershey, PA : IGI Global Scientific Publishing, 2026. | Includes bibliographical references and index. | Summary: "This book aims to show multiple examples based on the military spending of a country or region, but, above all, to show real studies where you can see the consequences, inequalities, and all kinds of results associated with military spending"-- Provided by publisher.
Identifiers: LCCN 2025022714 (print) | LCCN 2025022715 (ebook) | ISBN 9798337334561 hardcover | ISBN 9798337334578 paperback | ISBN 9798337334585 ebook
Subjects: LCSH: Military readiness--Economic aspects | Economic development | Armed Forces--Appropriations and expenditures
Classification: LCC HC79.D4 I47 2026 (print) | LCC HC79.D4 (ebook) | DDC 338.9--dc23/eng/20260126
LC record available at https://lccn.loc.gov/2025022714
LC ebook record available at https://lccn.loc.gov/2025022715
British Cataloguing in Publication Data
A Cataloguing in Publication record for this book is available from the British Library.

Table of Contents

Detailed Table of Contents

allowing for increased public investment in infrastructure, education adjusting for inflation, and demonstrates how well a country is utilizing its resources—including labor, capital, technology, and natural resources—to produce more and better goods and services over time.The importance of economic growth cannot be overstated, particularly for developing nations striving to overcome poverty, unemployment, and underdevelopment. Growth provides governments with greater fiscal resources, allowing for increased public investment in infrastructure, education, healthcare, and other essential services.

This paper examines the evolution of India's defence expenditure, focusing on its historical trends, structural composition, and long-term relationship with GDP. From post-Independence reliance on British defence supplies to the development of a public sector-led industrial base, India's defence strategy has responded to major geopolitical events such as the 1962 Sino-Indian war and the Kargil conflict. Analysis of data from 1970–71 to 2024–25 reveals a shift toward capital-intensive spending, driven by modernization goals and initiatives like Atmanirbhar Bharat. Although defence spending has risen in absolute terms, its share in GDP has declined from over 3% in the 1980s to below 2% in 2024–25. A cointegration analysis confirms a stable long-run link with GDP, but elasticity of 0.901 suggests sub-proportional growth. Despite growth in indigenous production and exports, issues persist in R&D, procurement, and quality control. The study underscores the need for sustained fiscal support, efficient governance, and technological advancement to meet evolving security needs.

This study is devoted to assessing the relationship between the dynamics of defense spending in countries worldwide and their economic growth. This problem is becoming increasingly relevant as geopolitical conflicts in the modern world intensify. Within the framework of this chapter of the book, global defense spending and key channels of influence of defense spending on the development of individual national economies are assessed, the main structural and dynamic changes in defense spending in the context of an unstable geopolitical situation are shown, and aspects of increasing defense spending in the context of the economic problems that developed countries are currently facing are demonstrated.

This paper reinterprets military expenditure in the South China Sea not as a deviation from economic rationality, but as a historically consistent strategy of statecraft. Challenging the conventional "guns versus butter" dichotomy, it contends that militarization is embedded within the political economy of development. Defense spending becomes a dual-purpose asset: projecting power while stimulating industrial capacity and reinforcing state authority in contested maritime zones. Building on the concepts of the security-growth nexus and Military Keynesianism, the paper argues that defense expenditure functions as strategic rent-seeking in a fragmented order marked by legal ambiguity and institutional fragility. In the absence of enforceable regimes, military infrastructure substitutes for law, and presence replaces treaty-based legitimacy. Through an analysis of military spending and its geopolitical implications, this study examines how China, the United States, ASEAN, and claimant states convert defense budgets into tools of strategic accumulation.

This study explores the relationship between military expenditure and economic growth in 10 MENA countries using a country-specific time-series approach. Employing advanced empirical techniques—namely the Bootstrap Fourier-Kruse Unit Root Test and Bootstrap Fourier-Shin cointegration analysis—it accounts for structural breaks and data nonlinearity. The findings reveal a heterogeneous and context-dependent relationship: while countries such as Algeria, Egypt, Israel, Morocco, and Oman exhibit a positive association between military expenditure and growth, others like Saudi Arabia and Tunisia show limited or no significant impact. These results challenge assumptions of panel-based analyses and underscore the importance of methodological rigor and contextual nuance. The study concludes military expenditure can act as either a catalyst or a constraint for growth, depending on national conditions. Policy recommendations stress defense efficiency, fiscal balance, diversification, and regional stability for sustainable development in MENA.

The intricate relationship between defense and security expenditures and economic growth has long been a subject of debate among economists, policymakers, and political scientists. In a world where geopolitical tensions, national security concerns, and international conflicts shape the policy priorities of states, the allocation of resources to defense and security has become a vital aspect of economic planning. While some argue that defense spending is a necessary investment in maintaining stability, sovereignty, and global influence, others contend that excessive military expenditure can divert crucial resources away from social and economic development, potentially stifling long-term growth.Historically, nations have justified large-scale defense and security expenditures on the grounds of safeguarding territorial integrity, maintaining internal stability, and deterring external threats. In doing so, governments aim to create a secure environment conducive to economic activity and foreign investment.

Military spending has increased substantially across the globe over the last few decades. The Stockholm International Peace Research Institute (SIPRI) states that the 2024 global military expenditure accounted for almost 2.5% of the global GDP. All regions of the globe have increased their military spending regardless of the difference between developed and developing countries. The NATO members determined to increase their military spending to 5% of the GDP by 2035. It will force other nations to also engage in the battle of spending more on the military. Although the military spending is increased on the grounds of national security, it puts forward only a restrictive vision without prioritizing the people's genuine concerns, interests, and security. A people-centered understanding of national security is essential for guaranteeing a sustainable future that allocates the benefits

of Sri Satya Sai Institute of Higher Learning to acquire a better knowledge of how integral education works.

Preface

INTRODUCTION

Economic growth remains one of the most studied yet complex phenomena in modern scholarship. Traditionally understood as a quantitative measure, growth has been linked to myriad factors—from education and health to sustainability and artificial intelligence. Over the past decades, various models have emerged to explain and justify the progression of nations or regions in economic terms. However, a recurring limitation in much of the existing literature has been its narrow focus, often excluding the realities of Third World countries due to data constraints and systemic biases toward First World contexts.

Among the many variables influencing economic growth, military spending stands out as one of the least explored yet most debated. While commonly analyzed through the lens of national security, the economic ramifications of military budgets have not received equal scholarly attention. In some instances, statistical models suggest a weak or nonexistent correlation between defense expenditures and GDP growth; in others, strong positive associations are found. Such inconsistencies underscore a central truth: economic growth is multifactorial, and any singular explanation must be approached with caution and critical nuance.

This edited volume, *Impacts of Military Spending on Economic Growth*, seeks to address this gap by bringing together a diverse range of case studies, empirical analyses, and theoretical reflections. Our primary aim is to illuminate how military expenditure affects economies—both positively and negatively—across different regions and contexts. More importantly, we endeavor to present real-world data and practical applications that serve not only academic interests but also pedagogical innovation.

Each chapter included in this volume offers a distinct perspective on the complex intersection of defense spending and economic development. Whether through statistical modeling, comparative analysis, or exploratory research, the contributions collectively broaden the discourse and offer new ways of understanding economic behavior in the presence of military investment. The book is not meant to serve as traditional instructional material, nor does it propose a singular framework for interpreting growth. Instead, it is an invitation to reimagine how we teach, study, and apply economic theory in real-world contexts.

This book is especially valuable for researchers, instructors, and students who already possess a foundational understanding of economics and are seeking new insights or applications. Instructors will find within these chapters opportunities to enhance their classroom dynamics, using real case studies to foster deeper student engagement. Researchers are invited to use these findings as a springboard for further inquiry, potentially leading to the development of innovative models and frameworks. Students, in turn, are offered access to contemporary discussions that go beyond textbook generalities and delve into the intricate, often controversial, terrain of military economics.

What distinguishes this work is not only its thematic focus but its educational potential. The integration of practical cases and advanced statistical approaches makes it an adaptable resource across levels of instruction and fields of inquiry. It bridges the gap between research and learning, encouraging knowledge transfer in a way that is dynamic, contextual, and deeply relevant.

In presenting this book, we hope to spark critical dialogue, inspire fresh pedagogical approaches, and contribute to a more comprehensive understanding of economic growth through the lens of military spending. We trust that the readers—whether they be scholars, educators, or policy analysts—will find in these pages a meaningful addition to their intellectual pursuits.

ORGANIZATION OF THE BOOK

This volume opens with a case study on Mexico's economic growth from 2010 to 2024, exploring how military expenditure has intersected with macroeconomic indicators such as GDP, employment, and foreign direct investment. In Chapter 1, the authors investigate how increases in military budgets—largely justified by efforts to combat domestic violence—have coincided with other economic shifts, allowing readers to reflect on the nuanced relationship between defense spending and Mexico's broader development trajectory.

Chapter 2 presents a foundational exploration of econometric models used to explain economic growth, emphasizing how real output—adjusted for inflation—serves as a key measure of national performance. The chapter reinforces that for developing nations, understanding and modeling economic growth is more than theoretical—it has practical implications for public investment, poverty reduction, and long-term resilience.

In Chapter 3, the discussion turns to India's defense expenditure, tracing its evolution from post-independence strategies to the current era of self-reliance and capital-intensive modernization. With a detailed review of data spanning from the 1970s to 2024–25, this chapter offers rich insights into structural changes in spending patterns, GDP linkages, and the enduring policy challenges India faces in research and procurement despite growing indigenous capabilities.

Chapter 4 broadens the scope by analyzing global defense expenditures and their interrelationship with national economic growth. This chapter is especially timely given the current rise in geopolitical tensions. Through a comparative lens, the authors unpack the determinants and transmission channels that define how defense budgets affect the economic stability of diverse countries, particularly in an era of economic uncertainty and evolving military needs.

Chapter 5 provides a unique geopolitical perspective in its examination of the South China Sea, arguing that military spending should not merely be seen through the lens of sacrifice or trade-offs but as a strategic act of state-building. The chapter challenges the conventional "guns versus butter" debate by framing militarization as a form of strategic accumulation, essential for asserting sovereignty, especially where legal and institutional frameworks are ambiguous or absent.

In Chapter 6, a rigorous empirical approach is adopted to study 10 countries in the MENA region, offering country-specific analyses through advanced econometric techniques. The findings emphasize a heterogeneous landscape: while some nations benefit from a positive link between military and economic growth, others show negligible or even adverse effects. This chapter highlights the importance of tailored policy frameworks and refined data interpretation when navigating regional defense economics.

Chapter 7 revisits the age-old debate on defense versus development, scrutinizing how national security budgets either support or undermine economic aspirations. This chapter situates military spending within broader debates on sovereignty, global power dynamics, and developmental priorities, illustrating that the impact of defense expenditure is often context-specific, shaped by both domestic and international pressures.

Chapter 8 brings a critical eye to the global escalation in military expenditure, drawing on recent data to assess how rising defense budgets may sideline human development goals. The chapter calls for a people-centered approach to national security, one that integrates economic inclusivity and sustainability alongside traditional defense imperatives. It questions whether current spending trajectories are aligned with the broader welfare of societies.

In a novel take, Chapter 9 delves into the encryption technologies employed in Mexican customs and ports, highlighting how military-grade information security systems can facilitate economic modernization and regional growth. It positions information protection as a cornerstone of national security, arguing that successful economic reforms—particularly in high-volume trade environments—depend on robust digital infrastructure supported by defense innovations.

Finally, Chapter 10 returns to the critical topic of human capital, offering a deep dive into India's experience linking education and economic development. Through econometric analysis and a case study of Sri Satya Sai Institute of Higher Learning, the authors demonstrate that while military spending plays a key role in national strategy, investments in education and values-based learning are foundational for sustained and equitable economic progress.

Together, these chapters offer a multifaceted understanding of how military expenditure shapes, supports, or hinders economic development across different national and regional contexts. The insights presented here are not only academic but also pedagogical, offering tools for teaching, research, and informed policy-making in a rapidly evolving global landscape.

CONCLUSION

As this volume draws to a close, it becomes evident that the relationship between military spending and economic growth is neither linear nor universally applicable. The chapters presented in this edited collection reveal a dynamic and multifaceted interplay shaped by national priorities, geopolitical realities, technological capacity, and fiscal strategy. From the modernization of defense industries in India and the encryption of critical infrastructure in Mexico, to the strategic militarization of maritime zones and the contested development paths in MENA countries, each contribution underscores the importance of context, methodology, and interpretation.

What unites these diverse studies is a shared commitment to understanding military expenditure not as an isolated budgetary item, but as an influential force embedded in the broader political economy of growth. The research included here challenges us to reconsider the traditional boundaries between security and development, between national defense and public welfare. Indeed, several chapters illustrate that defense spending can serve as both an enabler of innovation and stability, and a potential diversion from urgent social investments—depending entirely on how such funds are managed, measured, and aligned with a country's long-term vision.

This book also seeks to bridge the gap between academic inquiry and practical application. By incorporating real-world case studies, empirical modeling, and critical theoretical perspectives, we offer a body of work that is as valuable in the research lab as it is in the classroom. It is our hope that scholars, educators, and students alike will use these findings to foster deeper debates, create more inclusive models, and design more responsive policies that reflect the complex trade-offs at play in defense economics.

Ultimately, the study of military spending and its economic implications is not just a question of balance sheets—it is a reflection of national values, global responsibilities, and the future we envision for societies at large. We invite our readers to engage with these insights critically and constructively, as we continue to explore the evolving terrain where security meets growth.

Chapter 1

Factors That Interact With Military Spending During Mexico's Economic Growth 2010–2024

Gerardo Reyes Ruiz
https://orcid.org/0000-0003-0212-2952
Center for Advanced Naval Studies (CESNAV), Mexico

ABSTRACT

Mexico's economic growth over the last twenty years has seen major changes and significant challenges in its domestic policy decisions. Consequently, Military Expenditure (ME) has increased in order, among many others, to counteract violence. However, some micro and macroeconomic indicators that favor Mexico's global perspective and positioning have also been recorded. The review of some economic variables, such as GDP, foreign direct investment (FDI), and employment, among other indicators, allows us to reflect on the pre-existing interaction between these factors that explain Mexico's good economic performance. Therefore, this research analyzes the interaction that ME has had with other national and international indicators, and that, in turn, helps us understand its relationship with national economic growth

INTRODUCTION

The word "economics" has its origin in the composition of two Greek words: "oikos" and "nomos," which together form "oikonomia," which can be translated as "household management" (Mankiw, 2012). For their part, Samuelson and Nor-

DOI: 10.4018/979-8-3373-3456-1.ch001

dhaus (1948) defined Economics as "the study of how society manages its scarce resources." These authors argued that economic resources, particularly natural resources, are limited, whereas the desires and needs that human beings construct are comparatively unlimited. In other words, Economics, as one of the main Social Sciences in the world (Fourcade, Etienne and Yann, 2015), studies the activities of men who live in society insofar as said activities, applied to obtaining goods or resources aimed at satisfying their material needs, presuppose a peculiar relationship between man and the means he uses to achieve his ends (Porter and Ross, 2003). That is to say, the economic implies a special connection between humans and the nature that surrounds them (Kanbur, 2002; Bögenhold, 2021). Undoubtedly, in any country or region, there are needs, generated by its society, that must be met to survive -such as food or progress- and are indicative of a better quality of life overall (Backhouse and Fontaine, 2010). However, as mentioned above, the resources that nature offers us are limited and even scarce, for this reason, people, based on their needs -whether individual or group- have to work to increase both the resources and the goods that are produced through them and, in this way, manage to satisfy, in the best way possible, their most basic needs (Schumpeter, 1954; Backhouse and Fontaine, 2010). Of course, if there were no needs at all or if the means/resources to satisfy them were unlimited, then the economy would have no reason to exist, because, under this assumption, it would be useless to search for the most economic "objective" to adapt it to the necessary means that, in turn, satisfy material needs. If we now assume that our daily lives are filled with economic decisions, then every one of those decisions we make, especially those geared toward the efficient use of resources and -in particular- the satisfactions we obtain from them, impact on our current and future capacity in life, which plays a preponderant role in our society as a whole. Thus, the study of economics helps us understand and evaluate the decisions we make as economic agents and, above all, to identify their impact at the national and even international levels (Schumpeter, 2021; Kates, 2020).

The economy is also known as the entire set of decisions made by individuals, companies, and governments, which gradually impact a large number of activities related to production, distribution, and consumption, which will define how all these resources will be distributed within a country or region (SEDEMA, 2025). In other words, the economy of a country or region is the setting of all the activities carried out, precisely, within that country or region, with the main purpose, among many others, of generating wealth. The evolution of economics has been transformed over time. For example, for the German Karl Marx, economics is the science that studies the social relations of production (Escudé, 2021). That is, based on the concept of historical materialism, Marx studied the relationship between his concept, which he called "labor-value." His proposal established that value has its origin and objective according to the amount of labor necessary to obtain a good.

From there Marx deduces that Economics studies the set of phenomena derived from the relationship established between human needs and their satisfactions obtained through production, distribution and exchange (Wang, 2019).

Without a doubt, the study of economics helps us better understand certain phenomena, even those of a global nature, such as poverty, informality, loss of purchasing power, and wealth distribution, to name just a few. These can impact social stability and even constitute risks and threats to the national security of a country or region (Neu and Wolf, 1994; Murphy and Topel, 2013; Chimits et al., 2024). For example, let us recall that very few countries were able to withstand the serious financial and banking problems of the 1990s. Moreover, since 1920, these problems emerged when Latin America began to experience foreign capital flows like never before in its history. However, the following question makes sense: What is the cause or causes of financial instability from that time to the present in that part of the world? Undoubtedly, the answer is not trivial, but economics could help us better understand this problem. Continuing with the previous scenario, some phenomena currently persist that can be associated as a consequence of the global COVID-19 pandemic (Ibn-Mohammed et al., 2021), because there are political, economic, social, security, among other variables, that were aggravated by, and during, this health crisis that was experienced throughout the world (McKibbin and Roshen, 2023). Given this scenario, the global economic deficit observed since the beginning of 2019 stands out, given that the nature of this global pandemic continues to represent a great risk to the National Security of a country or region (Rothwell et al., 2024; Choi, Kim, and Lee, 2022). Undoubtedly, the consequences of this problem were of a diverse nature and multiple consequences, which is why, on the one hand, continuous actions must be taken against possible or potential pandemics and, simultaneously, efforts must be combined to continuously strengthen any economic system. Hence, the importance of studying Economics to establish the analysis of all those variables that serve to recover both the growth and economic development of a country or region (Teng et al., 2022; Sunge, Mudzingiri and Mkhize, 2024).

At this point, it is important to highlight that economic growth is not the same as economic development (Dragoi, 2020; Colombatto, 2006). Many researchers agree that these concepts, while closely related, should not be considered synonymous. Let us examine the convergence of this concept for some authors (Welch and Welch, 2016; Wiesmeth, 2022; Novales, Fernández and Ruiz, 2022; Dragoi, 2020; Becker, 2017):

- Economic growth is represented by the increase in goods and services produced within a country's or region's economy over a period. Achieving greater and constant production of goods and services within a country's economy can be due to improvements in the quality of education, technology, or the added value of goods and services obtained within certain sectors of the economy. Economic growth is generally expressed as a percentage of Gross Domestic Product (GDP), which can be adjusted for inflation. In very general terms, GDP represents the market value of the final goods and services produced within a country's or region's economy.

- Economic development, for its part, is defined as a process focused on growth expressed both qualitatively and quantitatively in the economy of a country or region. In general terms, economic development seeks to measure all aspects related to the population of a country or region and addresses, from multiple perspectives, issues related to wealth, health, education, access to quality housing, among other factors. In other words, economic development, broadly speaking, involves providing better options in education, health, employment, and environmental conservation, among others, which is expected to lead to an increase in the per capita income of a country or region.

A fairly brief explanation for differentiating these two concepts can be made as follows: economic growth addresses the origins of a booming economy, while economic development focuses on analyzing the consequences of a growing economy, generally associated with the well-being of a population (Akar, Saritas and Kizilkaya, 2021). Therefore, it makes sense that continued and sustained economic growth remains an unmet aspiration for many countries around the world due to, among many other factors, prolonged and far-reaching political uncertainties (Rahman and Alam, 2021). What should be clear is that economic growth refers to an increase in an economy's productive capacity, through which the economy must be able to produce additional quantities of goods and services to meet the needs of its population. In this sense, generally, our standard of living is measured by the quantity of goods and services available to us, so economic growth should be considered as a synonym for the increase in the standard and quality of life of a country or region (Gürler and Özsoy, 2019).

On the other hand, and for this work, it is also important to mention that Economics is divided into two main branches: Microeconomics (Parkin, 2018; Nicholson and Snyder, 2016; Case, Fair and Oster, 2019), which focuses on the study of individual units (companies and families); and Macroeconomics (Williamson, 2017; Thomas, 2021; Chugh, 2017), which focuses on the study of the Economy at a global level based mainly on economic policy in its fiscal and monetary aspects, in the development of its main indicators such as GDP, inflation, unemployment, etc., through which its influence can be analyzed, directly or indirectly, even with an international character. Therefore, as well stated in Blanco and Aznar (2004), Economics "seeks to provide concepts, theoretical elements and analytical categories that allow a rigorous understanding of the issues it addresses and the laws that govern them", which is why they recommend:

- You must follow an appropriate method to understand and solve them, and based on this, establish the best predictions for certain future situations.
- To act, as much as possible, rationally, to transform the economic conditions under which we carry out our social life. As a consequence of this:
- Economics must be considered a social practice. Therefore, economics must be capable of:
- Address all economic problems, placing them in either a social or political context, and then providing the best possible solution.

Thus, economics, being a social science, also focuses on the behavior of individuals, their interaction with everyday events, and the effect they have on their environment (Kanbur, 2002). For example, the effect that the prices of goods or services, production, wealth, or consumption have on individuals, just to mention a few. In this sense, it is considered a social science because it studies both human activity and behavior. The latter attracts a lot of attention from behavioral sciences, mainly because it is considered a dynamic "object" of study: Humans are unpredictable (SEDEMA, 2025). Thus, for the Mexican government, economics is a social science that studies how to manage resources and their availability to satisfy, to the best extent possible, the human needs of Mexicans. Therefore, this social science analyzes everything from behavior to decisions and considers the actions of human beings in a country or region (COMECSO, 2025). There is no doubt that economics is a complex phenomenon, and scholars approach it through multiple models, all of which attempt to offer an explanation based on economic theories. Furthermore, when interpreted by human beings, economics is bound to be influenced by both the vision and ideology of the people who interpret it, usually economists. Consequently, there are different interpretations of the same economic phenomenon. Economics has developed within this context of multidimensional opinions, which has led to the evolution of its explanations, but, above all, this evolution has necessarily been more convincing. For all the reasons mentioned above, it is understandable that economics, due to its great social and historical influence, but particularly due to its strong theoretical foundation, has been, and continues to be, the scene of great debates among scholars of its various subjects. As can be seen, the study of economics is as broad as human activity itself. However, despite modern science, there are still some theories that, from an economic perspective, cannot be validated or, on the contrary, refuted. For all these reasons, scholars on the subject, the vast majority of whom are economists, continue to formulate and propose principles that help us understand economic phenomena and, of course, find the best way to resolve them.

BACKGROUND

The term growth generally carries a connotation of quantitative increase (Alenda-Demoutiez, 2022). In this sense, multiple theoretical models of economic growth have emerged over time (Piętak, 2014). For example, in the second half of the 20th century, theoretical models emerged to justify the economic growth of a country or region through education (this period even came to be known as the knowledge economy) (Hanushek and Wößmann, 2010). Among the large number of these proposed models, which are based on the concept of education, the most notable are those of Nelson and Phelps (1966), Lucas (1988), Becker, Murphy and Tamura (1990), Rebelo (1991) and Mulligan and Sala-I-Martin (1992), which argued and emphasized the role of human capital in the form of educational achievements. Likewise, other empirical studies of growth, based on indirect indicators of human capital, have been proposed for a wide range of countries, such as those by Romer (1990), Barro (1991), Kyriacou (1991), and Benhabib and Spiegel (1992). However, most of these studies were hampered by the limited educational information available at all levels systematically for a large number of countries, particularly those considered to be in the Third World, since much of this research focused on countries known as the First World.

In addition to education, the economic growth of a country or region has been associated with multiple factors such as climate change (Chandy, 2023), people's happiness (Easterlin, 2013), health (Sarwar, Alsaggaf and Tingqiu, 2019), human capital (Barro, 2001), employment (Haider et al., 2023), supply and demand (Raisová and Ćurþová, 2014), Foreign Direct Investment (FDI) (Baiashvili and Gattini, 2020), energy use (Rahman and Alam, 2021), sustainability (Wang et al., 2023) and, of course, Artificial Intelligence (AI) (Gonzales, 2023). Without a doubt, economic growth is a multifactorial component, as there are other factors than those mentioned here (some of which have not yet been studied in depth) that can be associated with this economic behavior. Based on the premise that the planet's resources are scarce and limited, and also because, unfortunately, not everyone has access to all of these resources, we are forced to manage and even optimize these goods and services to satisfy our needs, even the most basic ones. It is precisely at this intersection that economic science makes sense, primarily because it encompasses individual decision-making, the positioning of organizations/companies, and the major decisions made in a country or region regarding the allocation and distribution of those resources, even when some of them are scarce at a given time. In this context, it is necessary to reflect on the increasing importance of economic concerns, especially those that transcend and affect the global sphere. In a globalized world, information is increasingly accessible and disseminates with surprising speed and efficiency, and traditional media such as books, newspapers, magazines, newsletters, television, etc.

have had to adapt to current technological changes to provide us with information, commentary, criticism, and all kinds of innovations related to the economic context (Trattner, Jannach, Motta et al., 2022; Newman, 2024). Thus, we read or hear daily about the high cost of certain goods or services, housing shortages, inadequate transportation, rising electricity rates, crop yields, strikes, and so on. The aforementioned manifestations of our economic life, in turn, indicate a nation's economic outlook, which is part of the entire historical development process of each country or region. These economic manifestations, just as they provide a perspective of the national economic landscape, also allow us to glimpse the international environment of that country or region. In other words, these two perspectives allow us to appreciate the relationships, economic ties, positioning, and problems that each country or region faces within its environment.

One of the factors that has been little analyzed concerning economic growth is the budget allocated to Military Spending[1] in a country or region. Typically, this budget is analyzed from the perspective known as National Security and its implications (Tsitouras and Tsounis, 2024; Retter et al., 2019; Giraldo Martinez et al., 2023; Chimits et al., 2024). Likewise, many of the econometric models used to explain economic growth through the defense budget consider, a priori, a causality between all the variables involved in these models (Dunne and Tian, 2020). Furthermore, it has been detected, for some countries or regions, that there is no statistical significance when explaining the endogenous variable of economic growth through the exogenous variable called Military Expenditure (Gavilanes and Michael, 2020). However, there is also statistical evidence, for some countries or regions, that these two variables are positively correlated (Raifu and Aminu, 2023). In this divergence of results, it is important to mention that causality or statistical significance will depend on the information involved in the statistical models, since, as mentioned above, economic growth is multifactorial (d'Agostino, Dunne and Pieroni, 2018). In other words, and by way of analogy, when attempting to explain economic growth using the education of a country or region, it is important to consider the disaggregation of the information and, above all, the group of countries being considered. Mainly because the results found have shown that education, in itself, generates absolutely nothing; that is, this variable alone is not a cause of economic growth, but, on the contrary, economic growth does imply a level of education above international standards for a country or region (Bils and Klenow, 2000). Furthermore, to achieve economic growth, as well as an excellent educational level, various factors must necessarily interact simultaneously so that this economic growth can be achieved in a perfectly defined period (Moon and Hio Gum, 2006).

MILITARY SPENDING IN THE INTERNATIONAL ENVIRONMENT

In the section called The independent resource on global security of the Stockholm International Peace Research Institute, Military Expenditure is considered to be all current and capital expenditure (SIPRI, 2025):

a) the armed forces, including peacekeeping forces;
b) defense ministries and other government agencies involved in defense projects;
c) paramilitary forces, when deemed trained and equipped for military operations;
d) military space activities.

In addition, this should include expenses on:

i. staff, including:
   a. salaries of military and civilian personnel,
   b. retirement pensions for military personnel, and,
   c. social services for personnel,
ii. operations and maintenance,
iii. procurement,
iv. military research and development,
v. spending on military infrastructure, including military bases, and,
vi. military aid (in the donor country's military spending).

- SIPRI's estimate of military aid includes financial contributions, training and operating costs, replacement costs for stockpiles of military equipment donated to beneficiaries, and payments to purchase additional military equipment for the beneficiary. However, it does not include the estimated value of the stockpile of donated military equipment.
- Civil defense and current expenditures on prior military activities, such as veterans' benefits, demobilization, conversion, and weapons destruction, are excluded.
- In practice, it is not possible to apply this definition to all countries, and in many cases, SIPRI simply uses the national data provided. Therefore, priority is given to choosing a uniform definition for each country to achieve consistency over time, rather than adjusting figures for individual years according to a common definition. Considering these difficulties, military expenditure data are best suited for comparisons over time and may be less suitable for detailed comparisons between individual countries. Finally, when comparing data from different countries, it is always recommended, where appropriate, to make use

of the footnotes and special notes accompanying those countries' data, which indicate some differences in the SIPRI definition.

In this context, there are currently multiple studies addressing the economic effects of military spending on a country or region; however, there are also diverse opinions regarding what these effects or relationships might be (Dunne, Smith and Willenbockel, 2005). Benoit's (1973, 1978) early analyses, which examined the correlation between these two variables across countries, allowed for the study of a wide variety of econometric models, which facilitated an understanding of different theoretical perspectives. From this perspective, four theoretical approaches have been developed to address the economic effects of military spending: neoclassical, Kcynesian, institutional, and Marxist (Dunne, Smith and Willenbockel, 2005). These multiple approaches allow for the identification of several factors through which military spending affects the economic growth of a country or region (Dunne and Coulomb, 2008). However, the most recent contributions on this topic have focused mainly on some exogenous or endogenous form of the neoclassical growth model. However, since there is currently no economic theory of economic growth associated with military spending, we cannot yet speak of a theoretical framework within which the military spending of a country or region can be classified (Dunne, Smith and Willenbockel 2005). What we can be certain of is the association of certain factors, which interact simultaneously with military spending, to justify or understand the economic growth of a country or region (Riveros Gavilanes, 2020). Next, let's analyze some relevant data associated with military spending at the international level.

Figure 1 shows the behavior of Military Expenditure from 1960 to 2023 (World Bank Group: https://data.worldbank.org/indicator/MS.MIL.XPND.CD?end=2023&start=1960&view=Figure). A sustained growth in Military Spending worldwide is clearly seen during this period, reaching USD 2.39 trillion (current prices) by 2023. Figure 2 reflects the accumulated Military Spending by country during 1960-2023 (constant 2022 USD) (SIPRI, 2025).

Figure 1. Military expenditure in the world 1960-2023

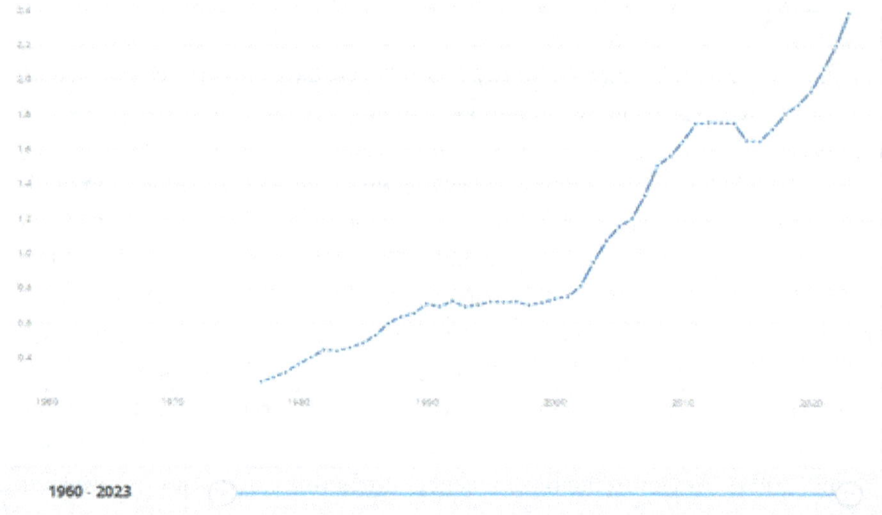

Figure 2. Military expenditure in the world by country 1960-2023

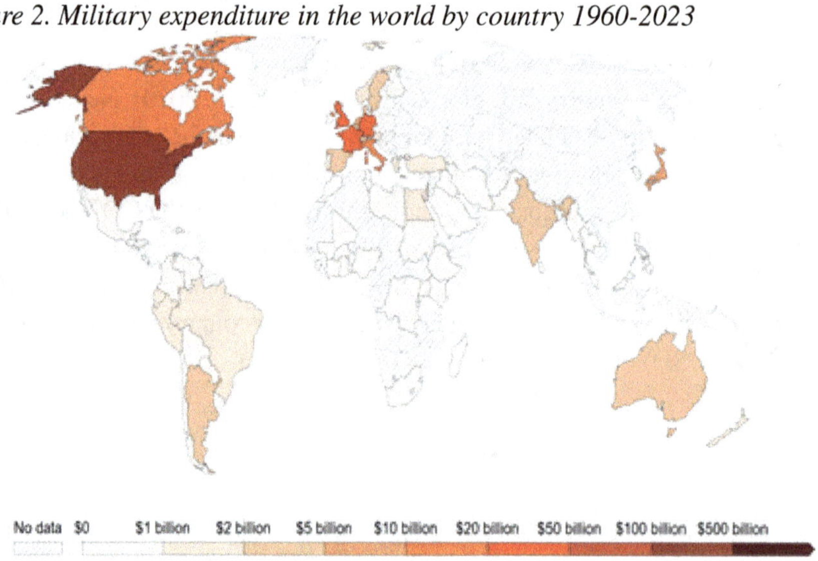

Military spending has undoubtedly grown considerably, as shown in Figure 3. This figure increased overall, even by region, from 1988 to 2023 (SIPRI, 2025). The Americas region's share stands out. This region includes the following subregions (SIPRI, 2025: https://www.sipri.org/databases/regional-coverage):

- **Central America and the Caribbean:** Antigua and Barbuda, Aruba, Bahamas, Barbados, Belize, Cuba, Costa Rica, Dominica, Dominican Republic, El Salvador, Grenada, Guatemala, Haiti, Honduras, Jamaica, Mexico, Nicaragua, Panama, Saint Kitts and Nevis, Saint Lucia, Saint Vincent, Trinidad and Tobago.
- **North America:** Canada, USA.
- **South America:** Argentina, Bolivia, Brazil, Chile, Colombia, Ecuador, Guyana, Paraguay, Peru, Suriname, Uruguay, Venezuela.

Figure 3. Military expenditure by region 1988-2023

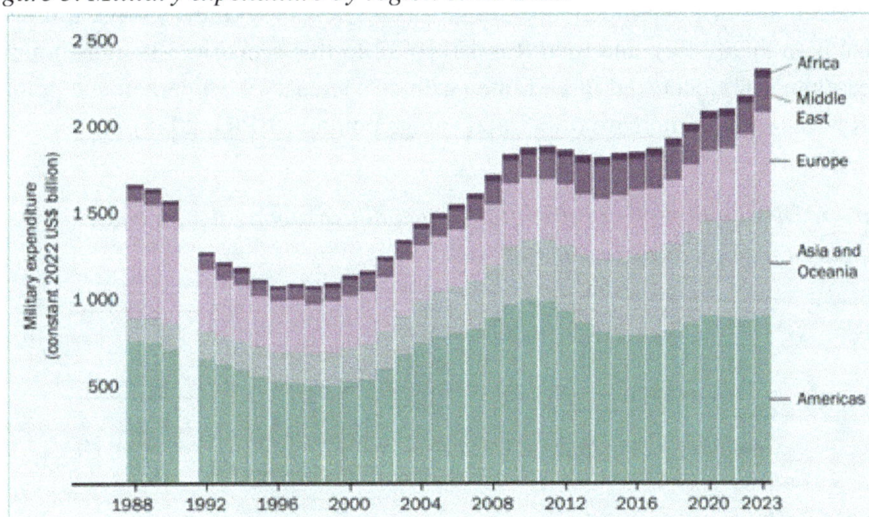

In this region -the Americas- military spending reached $1,009 billion in 2023, 2.2% more than in 2022 and 10% more than in 2014. This concept rose to $943 billion in 2023, 2.4% more than in 2022 and 11% more than in 2014 for North America: With $27.2 million in 2023, that is, Canada's military spending was 6.6% more than in 2022 and 49% more than in 2014. In other words, Canada's military spending in 2023 represented 1.3% of its GDP for that year, which is still below the target currently set by the North Atlantic Treaty Organization (NATO) for military spending, which is 2% of GDP. (SIPRI, 2025).

Global military spending is concentrated in a relatively small group of countries or regions. The top two spenders, the United States and China, accounted for about half of global military spending in 2023 (see Figure 4). Furthermore, the top 10 spenders in 2023 accounted for almost three-quarters (74%) of the global total; that is, the top 10 countries increased their military spending in 2023 (SIPRI, 2025). Of this latter group of countries, the largest percentage increase occurred in Ukraine, where its military spending increased by 51%, catapulting it from 11th place in 2022 to 8th place in 2023 (SIPRI, 2025). For the 10 countries leading the world in military spending, it is a fact that this item registered an increase from 2022 to 2023: The largest increase in this item occurred in Ukraine, where military spending, as a percentage of GDP, increased by 11 percentage points to 37%. Next came Russia, with a 1.2 percentage point increase in military spending, reaching 5.9% of GDP. Military spending as a percentage of government spending, which can well be considered a measure of government priorities, increased in nine of the top 10 spenders in 2023 (SIPRI, 2025). Among the top 10 countries, military spending, as a percentage of government spending, was highest in Ukraine (58%), followed by Saudi Arabia (24%), and then Russia (16%). In this scenario, the most notable increases in 2023 occurred in Ukraine (with an increase of 19 percentage points) and Russia (with an increase of 3.2 percentage points) (SIPRI, 2025).

Figure 4. Distribution of world military expenditure among the 15 countries with the greatest participation in 2023

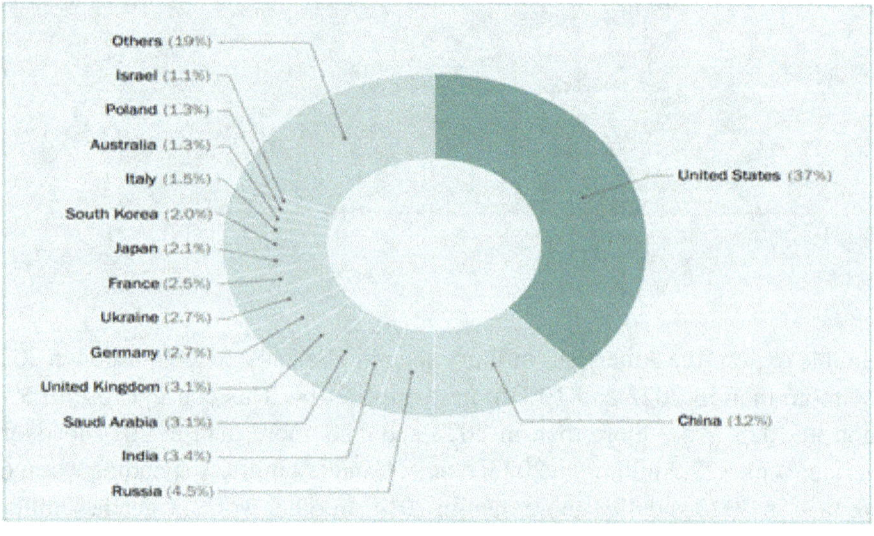

Continuing with this analysis, the United States Military Spending was 916 billion USD in 2023, which implied an increase of 2.3% compared to 2022 and an increase of 9.9% compared to 2014. This performance positioned the United States as the country that allocates the most money in the world to the item known as Military Spending (in 2023, the United States allocated 3.1 times more than China in the concept of Military Spending). It is important to highlight that, in 2023, the largest percentage increase of all categories considered in the United States Military Expenditure was that of "Research, Development, Testing and Evaluation" (RDT&E): Thus, by 2023 the United States spent 9.4% more on RDT&E than in 2022 (in real terms), that is, this country has prioritized spending on RDT&E over all other categories of its Military Expenditure since 2014 (SIPRI, 2025).

For its part, China -the world's second-largest military spender- allocated approximately USD 296 billion to its military in 2023, a 6.0% increase over its military expenditure in 2022. As shown in Figure 4, China's military expenditure accounted for 12% of global spending and 50% of spending in Asia and Oceania. Moreover, China is the main driver of spending trends in other parts of the region, as many of its neighbors perceive China's growing military power as a reason to enhance their own military capabilities. China's military expenditure has increased significantly over the past 29 years (this uninterrupted trend is the longest recorded by any country in the SIPRI Military Expenditure Database). However, the growth rate of China's military spending has slowed over the past 10 years: China recorded a 60% increase from 2014 to 2023, which, compared to other periods, was far from the 150% recorded for the periods 2004-2013 and 1994-2003. Undoubtedly, this performance also reflects China's economic slowdown over the past decade. Despite this latest result, China recorded a single-digit increase in its military spending for the eleventh consecutive year through 2023, which was in line with its annual GDP growth over the same years (SIPRI, 2025). The world continues to invest more and more money in military spending, due to a 6.8% increase in 2023 compared to 2022 (see Figure 5). For the same years, the subregion that showed the greatest growth in this concept was the one known as North Africa (Algeria, Libya, Morocco, Tunisia) with 38%, followed by the subregion known as Eastern Europe (Abkhazia, Armenia, Azerbaijan, Belarus, Georgia, Moldova, Ukraine, USSR -until 1991-, Russia) with 31%. In contrast, the subregion that showed the greatest contraction in its Military Spending was the one known as Central Asia (Kazakhstan, Kyrgyzstan, Tajikistan, Turkmenistan, Uzbekistan) with -5.3%, followed by the subregion known as Southeast Asia (Brunei, Cambodia, Indonesia, Laos, Malaysia, Myanmar, Philippines, Singapore, South Vietnam -until 1975-, Thailand, Timor-Leste, Vietnam) with -1.6%.

Figure 5. Main changes in military expenditure by subregion, 2022-2023

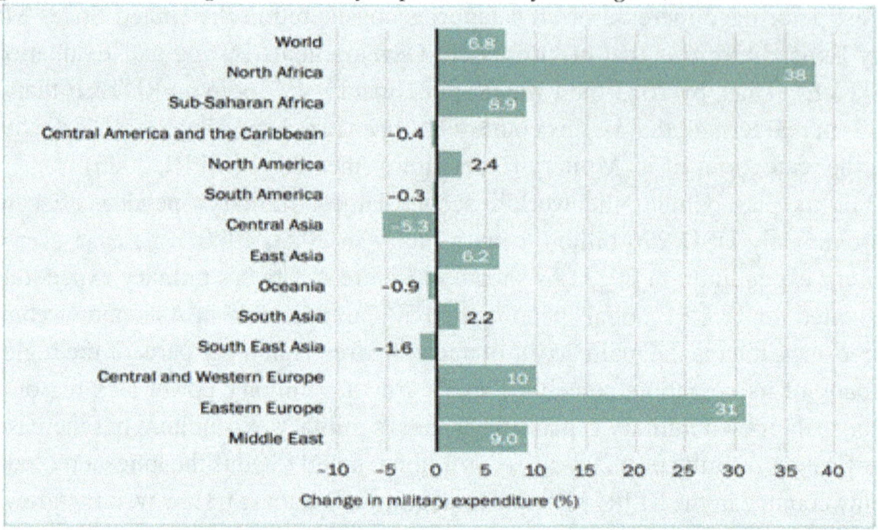

Por su parte, el Gasto Militar de un país como porcentaje de su PIB refleja, grosso modo, el costo económico de las fuerzas armadas para el país. Se estima que este comportamiento presentó, a nivel mundial, un incremento, ya que pasó del 2.2% en 2022 al 2.3% en 2023. En promedio, los estados de Oriente Medio tuvieron la carga militar más alta en 2023, con un 4,2% del PIB, seguidos de los estados de Europa (2,8%), África (1,9%), Asia y Oceanía (1,7%) y las Américas (1,2%). En 2023, el Gasto Militar promedio aumentó sustancialmente para los estados de Europa (+0,5 puntos porcentuales), Oriente Medio (+0,5) y África (+0,2): El Gasto Militar promedio se mantuvo sin cambios para los estados de las Américas y Asia y Oceanía. El mayor aumento del Gasto Militar en 2023 se produjo en Ucrania (+11 puntos porcentuales). Otros aumentos notables de la carga militar en Europa fueron los de Polonia (+1,6 puntos porcentuales), Armenia (+1,4), Rusia (+1,2), Finlandia (+0,8), Azerbaiyán (+0,8), Estonia (+0,7) y Dinamarca (+0,6). Líbano (+6,0 puntos porcentuales), Israel (+0,9) y Arabia Saudita (+0,7) tuvieron los mayores aumentos del Gasto Militar en Oriente Medio. El mayor aumento del Gasto Militar en África se registró, con gran diferencia, en Argelia (+3,5 puntos porcentuales) (SIPRI, 2025).

Figure 6. Military expenditure by country as a percentage of its GDP in 2023

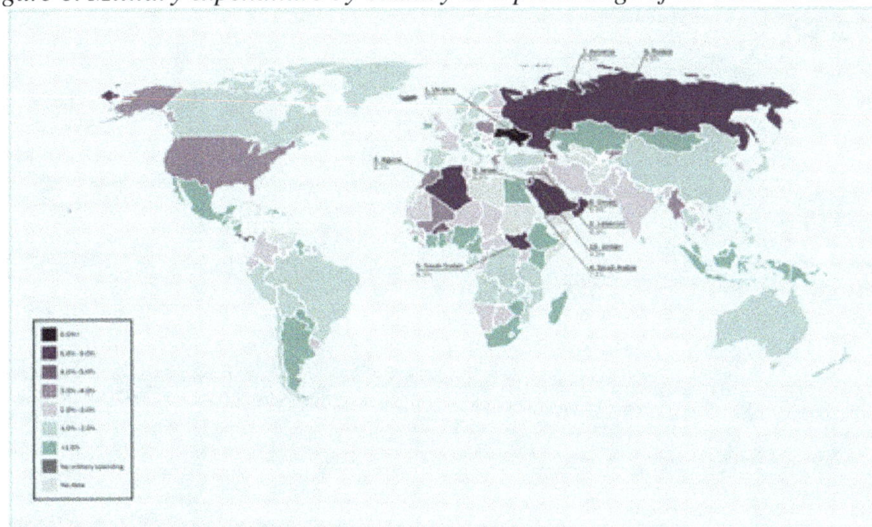

MAIN FOCUS OF RESEARCH

Military Spending in Mexico and its Main Associated Indicators

This section identifies the main national and international indicators that converge simultaneously to facilitate understanding of Mexico's economic growth over a period. This is done in order to understand the impact of economic policies implemented in Mexico through military spending, which, in some way, are in line with the spending and investment policies of the Mexican State. To begin this section, in Figure 7, the World Bank (https://datos.bancomundial.org/indicador/MS.MIL.XPND.GD.ZS?end=2023&locations=ZJ&start=1960&view=Figure) reports military spending for Latin America and the Caribbean for the period 1960-2023. It is striking that the behavior for this region is contrary to that found for the world's Military Spending (see Figure 1), that is, while the latter showed sustained growth from 1960 to 2023, the behavior of this concept for Latin America and the Caribbean decreased considerably for the same period.

Figure 7. Military expenditure (% of GDP) in Latin America and the Caribbean 1960-2023

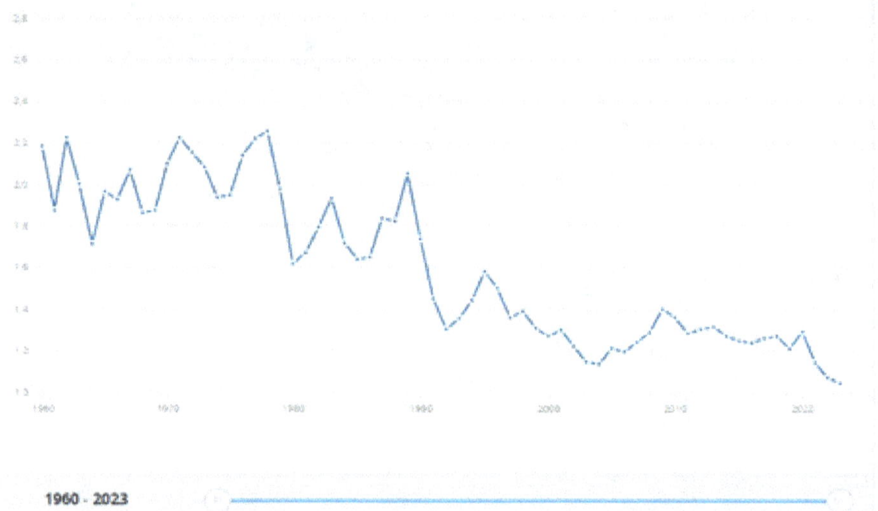

In this context and based on information reported by Statista (https://es.statista.com/), in 2023, Brazil was the country that allocated the most money to military spending in Latin America and the Caribbean, with more than USD 22 million (current prices converted at the exchange rate for the year in question). In second place was Mexico with almost USD 12 million, followed by Colombia with almost USD 11 million (see Figure 8).

Figure 8. Military spending in Latin America and the Caribbean in 2023 (millions of USD)

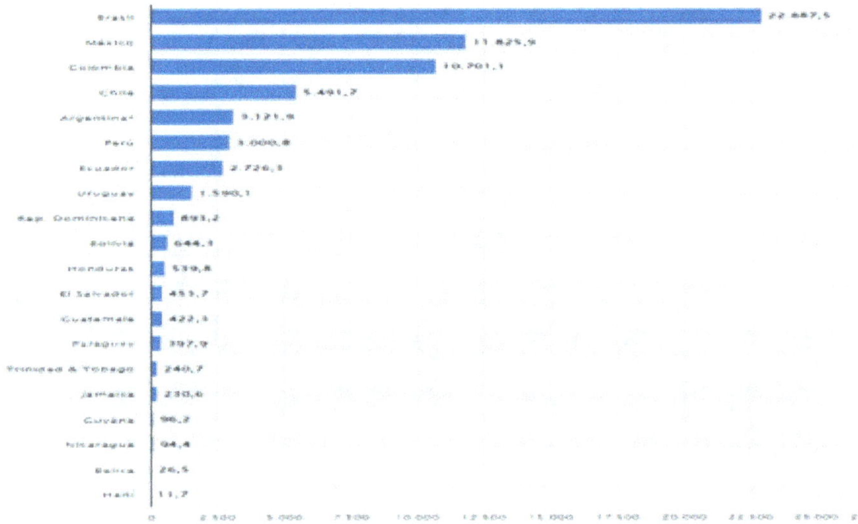

In 2023, Mexico was the country with the second-highest military expenditure in the Latin American and Caribbean region. In that year, spending on defense and armed security in Mexico amounted to USD 11.8 million, which represented an 18% variation compared to the figure reported in 2022 (see Figure 9) (Statista; https://es.statista.com/). Furthermore, it is observed that, in general terms, Mexico's military expenditure has shown sustained growth during the period 2008-2023.

Figure 9. Military expenditure in Mexico from 2008 to 2023 (millions of USD)

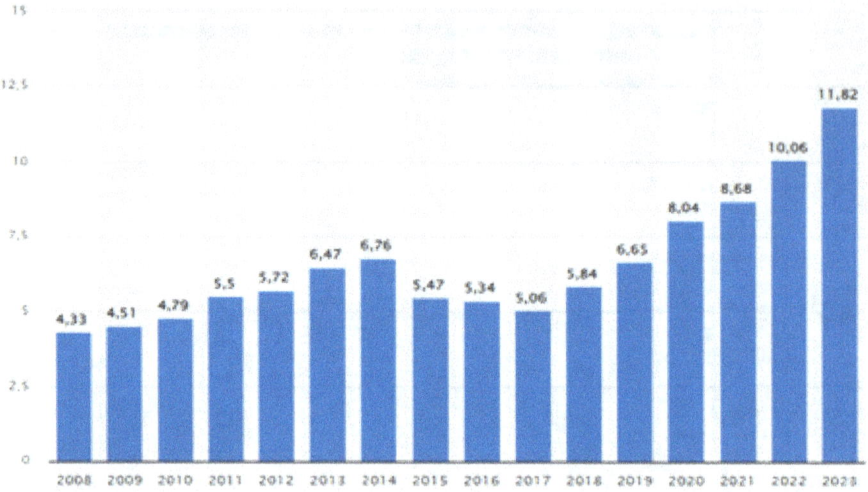

Some Indicators of Interest for Mexico

Military spending for Mexico reached USD 11.8 million in 2023, 55% more than in 2014 (but with a lower share of 1.5% compared to 2022). Simultaneously, allocations to the National Guard -a militarized force used to curb the country's criminal activity- increased from 0.7% of Mexico's total military spending in 2019 to 11% in 2023, when this internal force was formalized (SIPRI, 2024). In this scenario, military spending in Mexico -as a percentage of its GDP- showed a generally stable trend until 2023. However, it is noteworthy that, starting in 2020, a slight downward trend has been seen for this item (see Figure 10). What is clear is that Mexico's military spending is far below the minimum standard established by NATO for this concept, which is 2% of GDP.

Figure 10. Military expenditure in Mexico from 1960 to 2023 (% GDP)

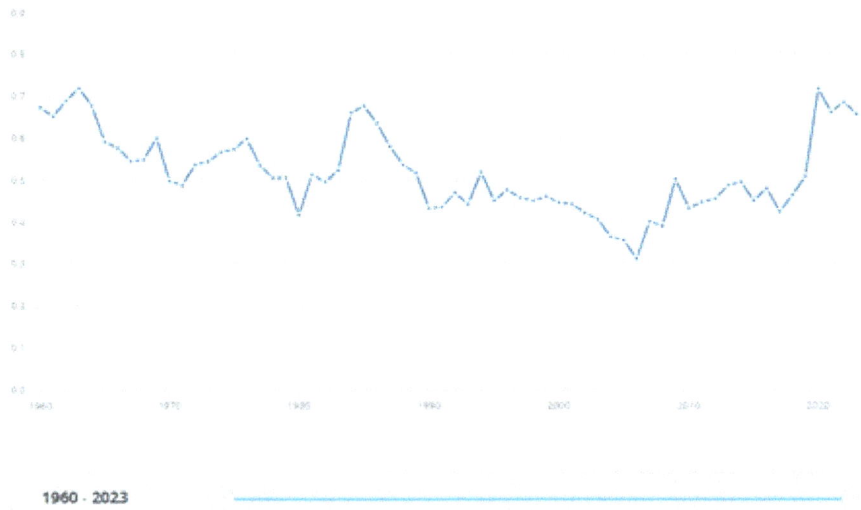

Mexico's growing military spending has had a positive impact on Mexicans since 2018. This is because, based on historical data from the Urban Public Security Survey (ENSU) (https://www.inegi.org.mx/programas/ensu/) and presented in the Second Semi-annual Report of the Permanent Armed Forces on Security Tasks (https://infosen.senado.gob.mx/sgsp/gaceta/65/3/2024-02-01-1/assets/documentos/2do_Informe_Semestral_Fuerza_Armada_Permanente.pdf), the number of Mexicans who considered it dangerous to live in their city gradually decreased: In September 2018, this citizen perception was 74.9%, while in September 2023 it was 61.4%.

Figure 11. Perception of insecurity in the population aged 18 or over

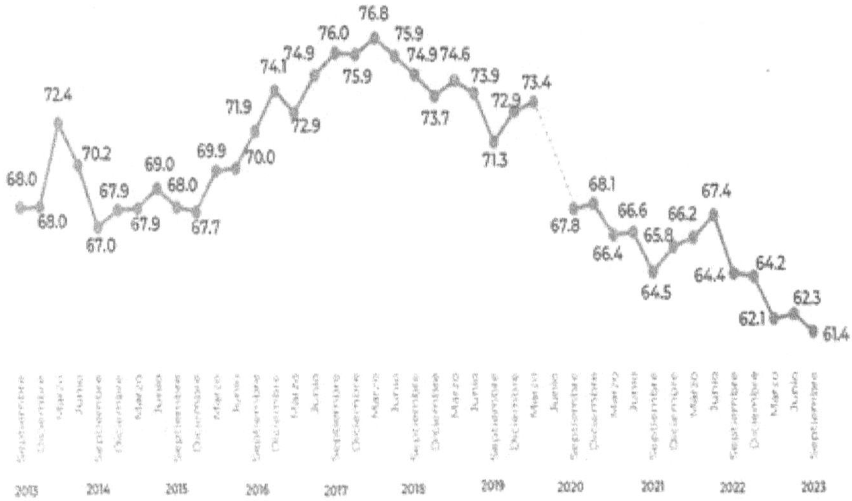

This positive change in the insecurity of Mexicans was also accompanied by an increasingly positive perception of the performance of the Permanent Armed Forces (FAP), that is, Mexicans recognize both the performance and the commitment of these FAP concerning public security tasks. Based on the results of the ENSU 2023, 85.4% of the Mexican population considered, in September 2023, the performance of the members of the Secretariat of the Navy (SEMAR) to be effective, while, for the same date, 82.8% of Mexicans surveyed considered the performance of the members belonging to the former Secretariat of National Defense (SEDENA) to be effective (see Figure 12).

Figure 12. Performance of the Army and Navy (ENSU, 2023)

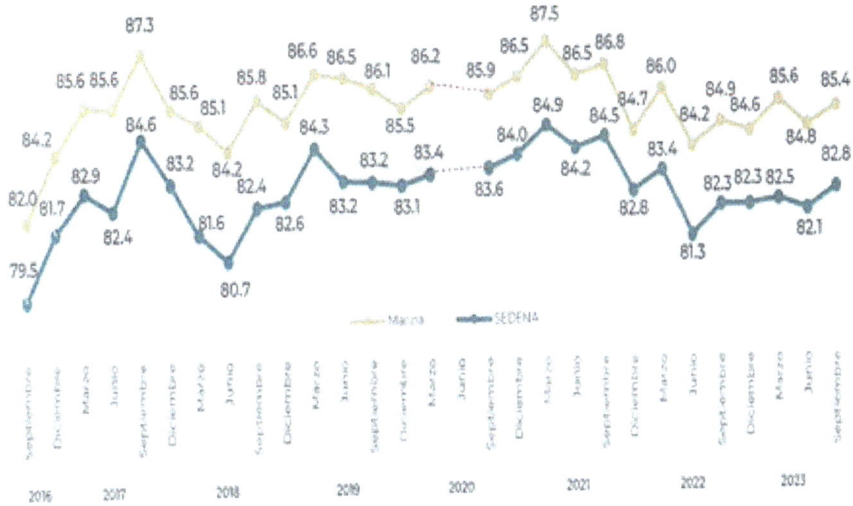

The results of the 2023 ENSU cannot be taken as casual, since through the national statistics obtained by the 2023 National Survey on Victimization and Perception of Public Security (ENVIPE) (https://www.inegi.org.mx/programas/envipe/2023/), presented in the Second Semiannual Report of the Permanent Armed Forces in Security Tasks, it was verified that 87.8% of the Mexican population aged 18 and over considered the performance of the SEMAR elements to be effective, while for the previous SEDENA (now DEFENSA) this percentage rose to 85.5% (see Figure 13).

Figure 13. Performance of the Army and Navy (ENVIPE, 2023)

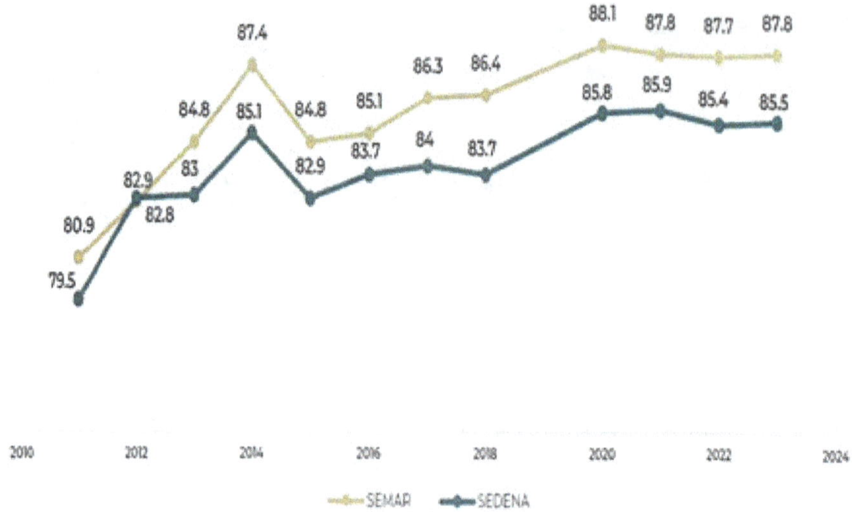

Confidence in the Armed Forces in Mexico was validated by ENVIPE 2023 by recognizing the work carried out by soldiers and sailors in matters of public security, that is, 90.1% of the Mexican population aged 18 and over recognized the SEMAR as the authority that inspires the greatest confidence, while 87.2% of the Mexicans interviewed believed that the current DEFENSA is the second national institution that inspires the greatest confidence (see Figure 14).

Figure 14. Level of perception of trust of Mexican society in authorities (ENVIPE, 2023)

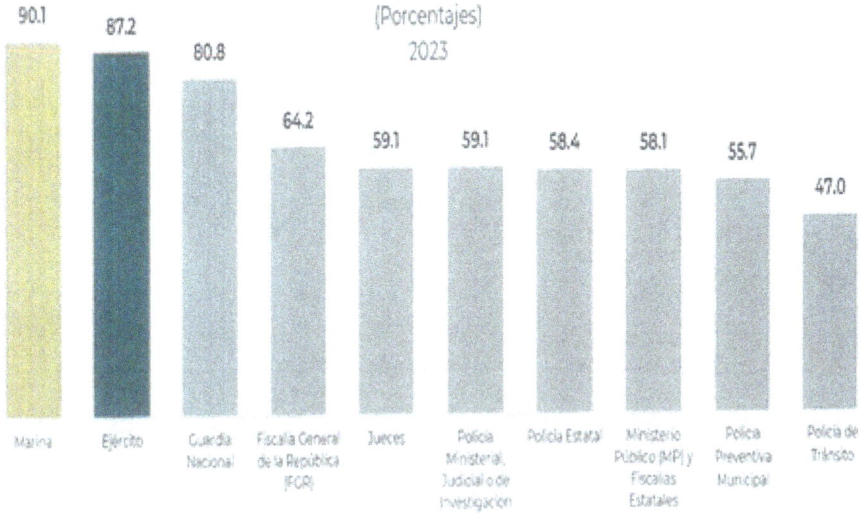

An important indicator obtained for Mexico, during the period 2018-2024 (October), is the one related to the unemployment rate (https://www.proyectosmexico.gob.mx/por-que-invertir-en-mexico/mercado-potencial/sd_historico-tasa-de-desempleo-en-mexico): Figure 15 shows that this concept registered 3.6% of the Economically Active Population (EAP) registered in 2018, while in October 2024 this percentage rose to 2.8%. Without a doubt, this indicator is a reflection of multiple efforts made through Mexican domestic policy, including increasing the EAP during this period (see Figure 15) (https://www.inegi.org.mx/temas/empleo).

Figure 15. Historical unemployment rate in Mexico 2006-2024

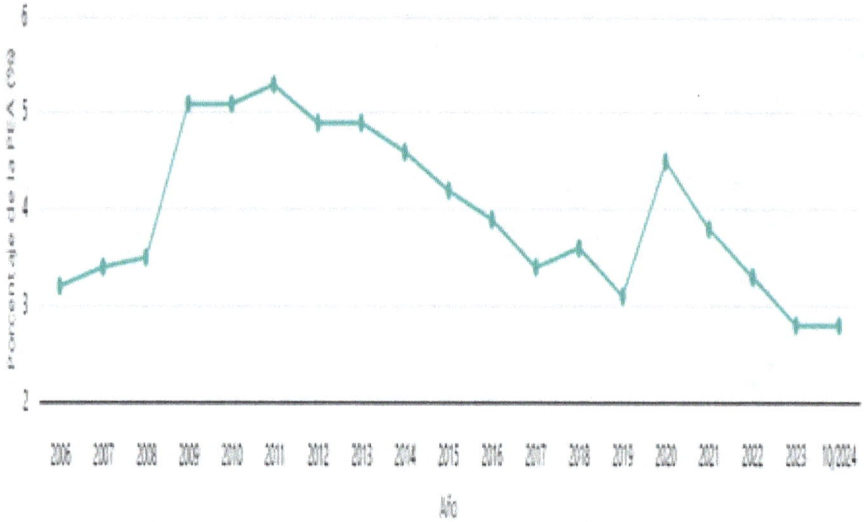

Figure 16. Economically active population 2005-2024

The interaction of several factors related to the Mexican economy managed to impact the so-called informal employment rate (as a percentage of the population aged 15 and over), which registered 56.6% in the first quarter of 2018, while for the fourth quarter of 2024 this participation was 54.5% (see Figure 17).

Figure 17. Labor informality rate (seasonally adjusted series) 2006-2024

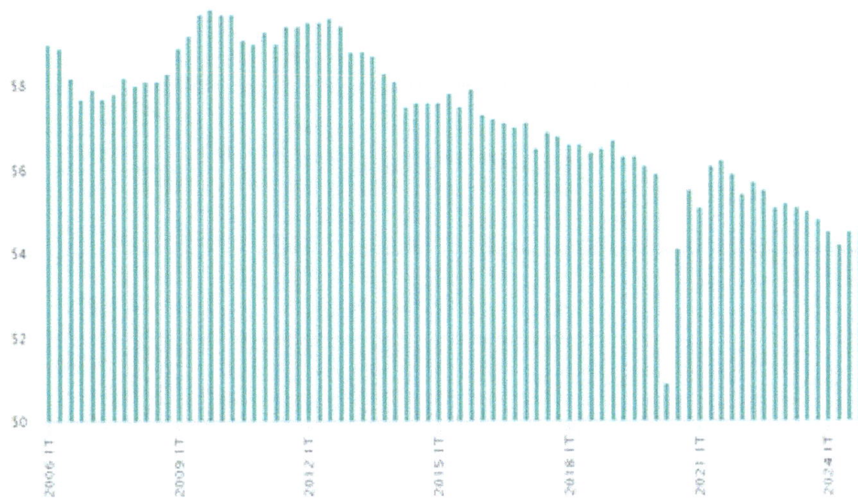

This positive behavior was also reflected in the average monthly labor income, since from the first quarter of 2018 to the third quarter of 2024, sustained growth was seen for this concept: By the third quarter of 2024, the average labor income was $10,088.7 pesos, with an annual real growth rate of 6.57% (https://mexicocomovamos.mx). Likewise, when disaggregated by employment status, an important result was obtained, that is, while in a formal job the average monthly labor income was $13,612.97 Mexican pesos, simultaneously in an informal job it was $7,009 Mexican pesos, which implied that the average income of a formal job almost doubled the average income of an informal job (see Figure 18). Regarding the gap in average labor income between men and women, for men this amounted to $10,819.91 Mexican pesos, while for women it was $8,996.83 Mexican pesos: As of the third quarter of 2024, the average monthly labor income of men was 1.2 times higher than that of women. This dynamic, referring to the average monthly labor income between men and women, was observed in both formal and informal employment: The average monthly labor income of men in formal employment was 1.14 times higher than that of women in the same situation, while, in the case of informal employment, the average monthly labor income of men was 1.31 times higher than that of women (see Figure 19).

Figure 18. Average monthly labor income by employment status 2010-2024

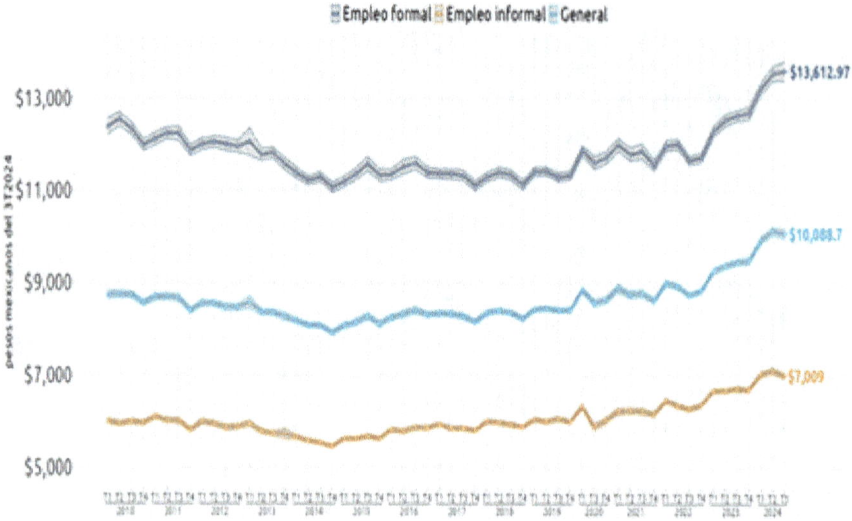

Figure 19. Average monthly labor income

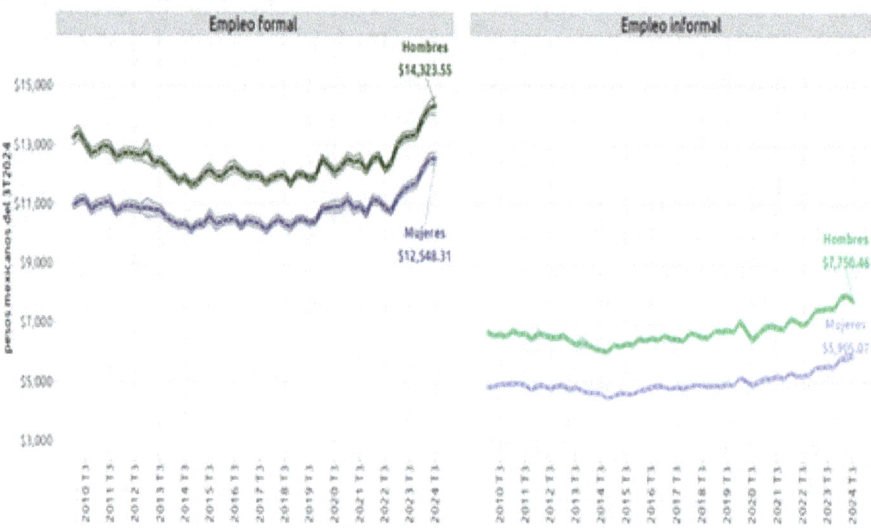

Without a doubt, these positive dynamics were because the minimum wage (geoFigureic zone A: Mexico City) gradually increased since 2018, going from 88.3 in 2018 to 248.9 Mexican pesos in 2024. Based on these data, provided by the National Commission of Minimum Wages (https://www.gob.mx/conasami), it can be stated that this increase was historic because it presented a variation of 181.9% for this period mentioned (see Figure 20).

Figure 20. Minimum wage (pesos per day in zone A) 2010-2024

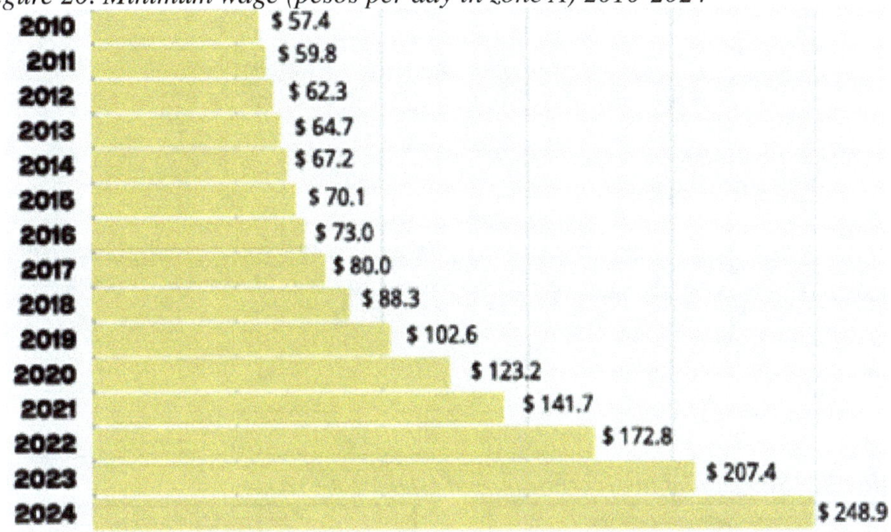

This increase in the minimum wage, since 2018, also benefited tax collection in Mexico, since based on information from the SAT (https://www.sat.gob.mx) and INEGI (https://www.inegi.org.mx), it can be seen that throughout the period 2018-2023, Mexico's tax revenues grew gradually (see Figure 21). This growing trend may even extend into the fourth quarter of 2024 (see Figure 22), where growth, albeit slight, in budget revenues is also perceived for the period 2018-2024 (Reports on the Economic Situation, Public Finances and Public Debt as of the fourth quarter of 2024, https://www.gob.mx/shcp).

Figure 21. Net tax revenue (% of GDP) 2010-2023

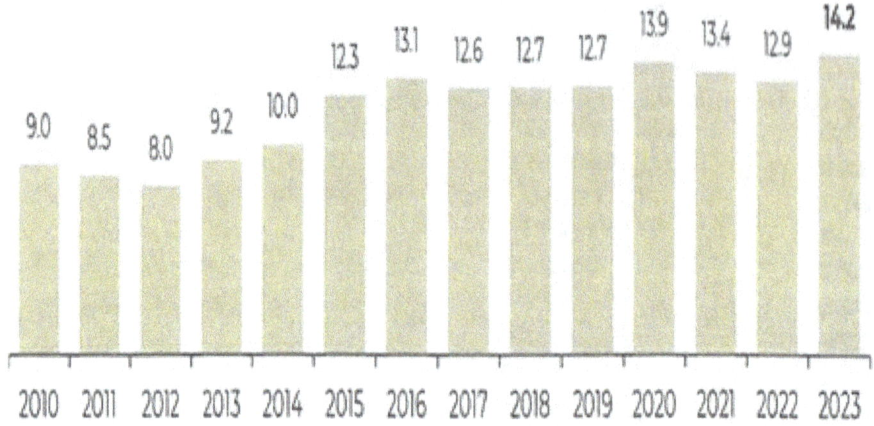

Figure 22. Budget and tax revenues (% of GDP) 2000-2024

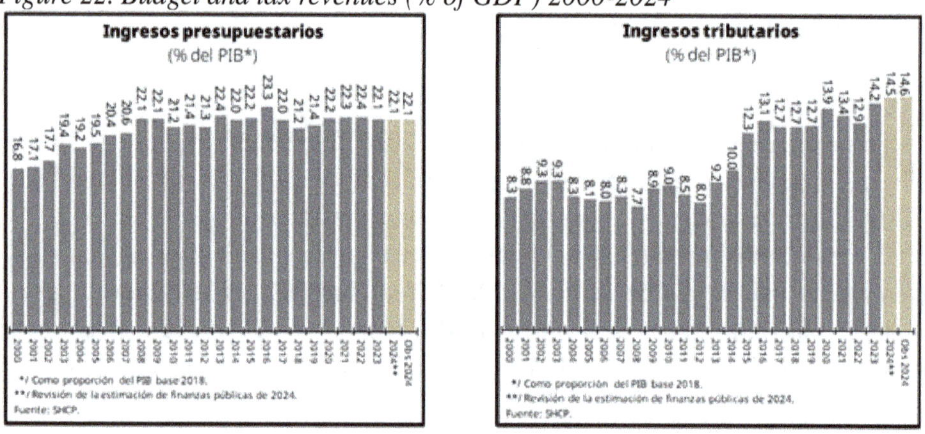

A Favorable Economic Environment for Mexico

The globalized economic environment remains a challenge for Mexico, especially in terms of external variables that may influence our economic growth. However, Mexico continues to demonstrate economic maturity both internationally and domestically. As a first indicator, Mexico's GDP grew 0.6% in the fourth quarter of 2024 compared to the same period in 2023, according to the timely estimate published by INEGI (https://www.epdata.es).

Figure 23. Interannual variation of Mexico's GDP (quarterly timely estimate) 2018-2024

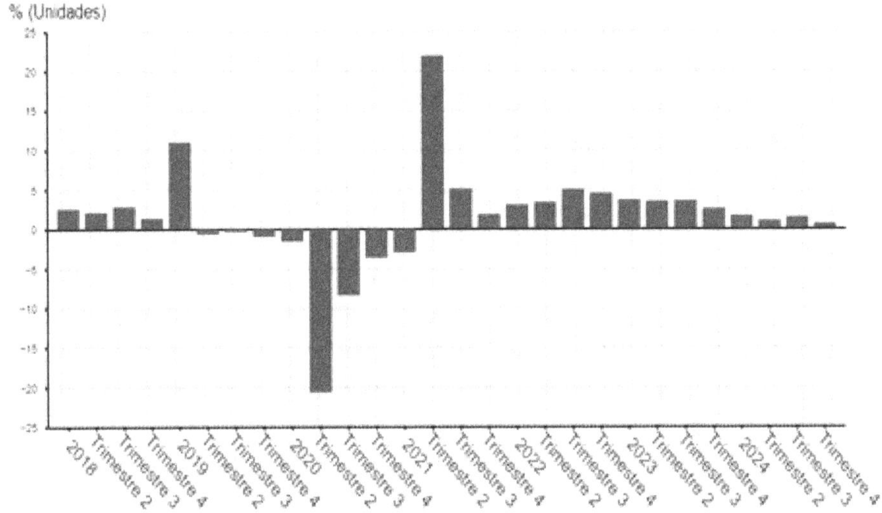

Strengthening GDP has been a priority for Mexico: Figure 24 reflects the efforts of multiple actors and factors converging simultaneously, leading to a gradual increase in Mexican exports to the United States of America (USA) since the beginning of the 21st century. Furthermore, Mexican exports to the USA, during the fourth quarter of 2024, surpassed Chinese exports to that same country for the first time (https://www.epdata.es).

Figure 24. Performance of Mexican exports to the USA 1997-2024

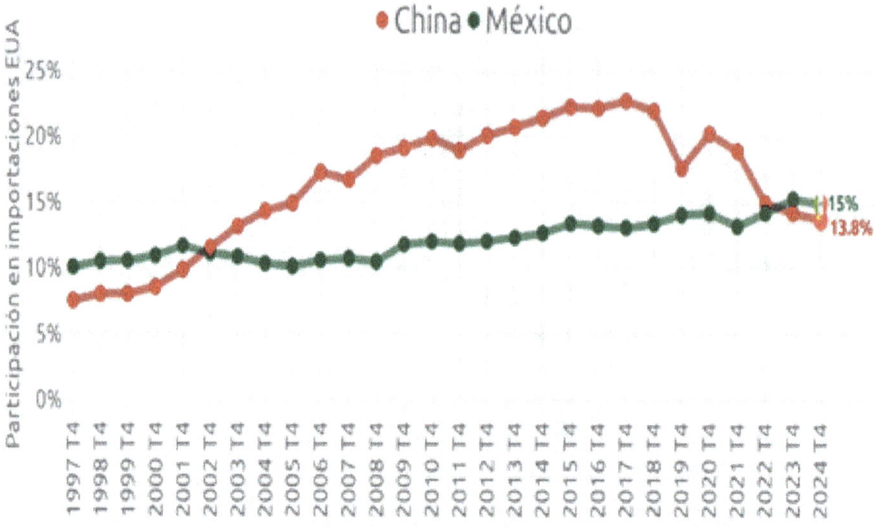

On the other hand, it is undeniable that Mexico's economy is strengthening with an increase in Foreign Direct Investment (FDI), which, broadly speaking, is defined as “an operation that involves a long-term relationship in which a natural or legal person resident in one economy (direct investor) has the objective of obtaining a lasting stake in a company or entity resident in another economy” (https://www .cepal.org/es): At the end of 2024, a new historical maximum of FDI was registered in Mexico with 36 thousand 872 million dollars, this being the highest figure since records have been kept for this concept (see Figure 25).

Figure 25. Foreign direct investment in Mexico (millions of current USD) 2012-2024

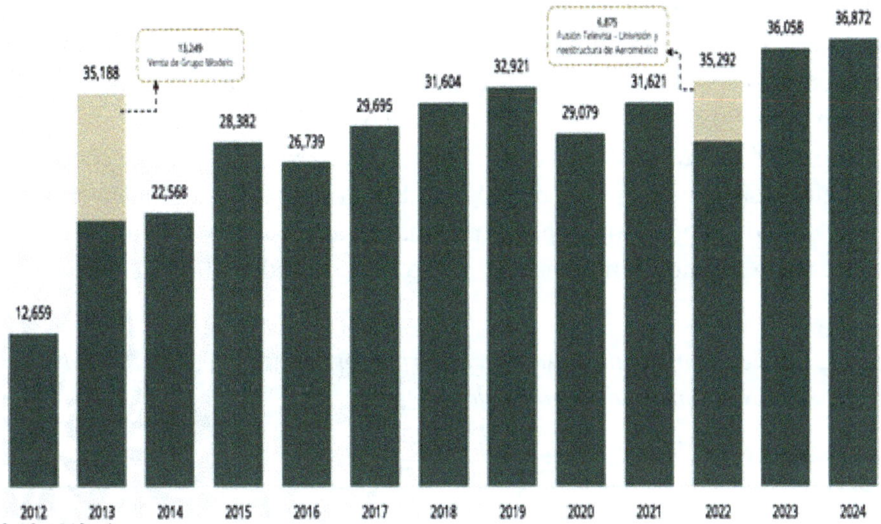

Likewise, and based on the latest Mexico Migration and Remittances Yearbook 2024 (https://www.gob.mx/conapo), it is notable that remittances, as a % of GDP, continue to grow worldwide and that this growing trend is also observed in Mexico (see the blue line on the left side of Figure 26): In 2018, USD 34.4 billion were recorded, while in 2023, remittances totaled USD 63.3 billion (see the right side of Figure 26). These data allow us to affirm that the remittances received by Mexicans in 2023 represented almost double the remittances received in 2018. Therefore, the total number of remittances sent to Mexico has been growing since 2018 and by 2022 even surpassed FDI (see the orange line on the left side of Figure 26).

Figure 26. Remittances to Mexico (as a % of GDP left -blue line- and billions of USD right) 2000-2023

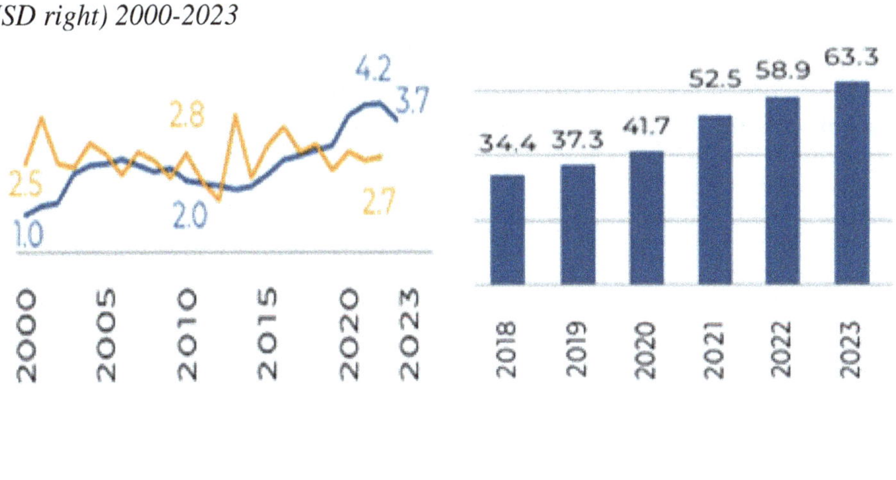

Mexico shares a large border with the United States, making it the main destination for our country's migratory flow and, therefore, the main source of our remittances. In this scenario, it is worth highlighting that international remittances showed significant changes for Mexico in 2023: From 2019 to 2023, India remains the main recipient of remittances, and its share of total remittances increased from 11.5% to 14.5%. In Mexico's case, by 2023, it displaced China from second place, and its global share increased from 5.4% to 7.8%. Furthermore, it is noteworthy that Nigeria moved from 7th to 9th place, and that Guatemala appeared among the 10 countries with the most remittances received in the world in 2023 (see Figure 27).

Figure 27. The 10 main destination countries for remittances, 2019 and 2023e (millions of US dollars and % worldwide)

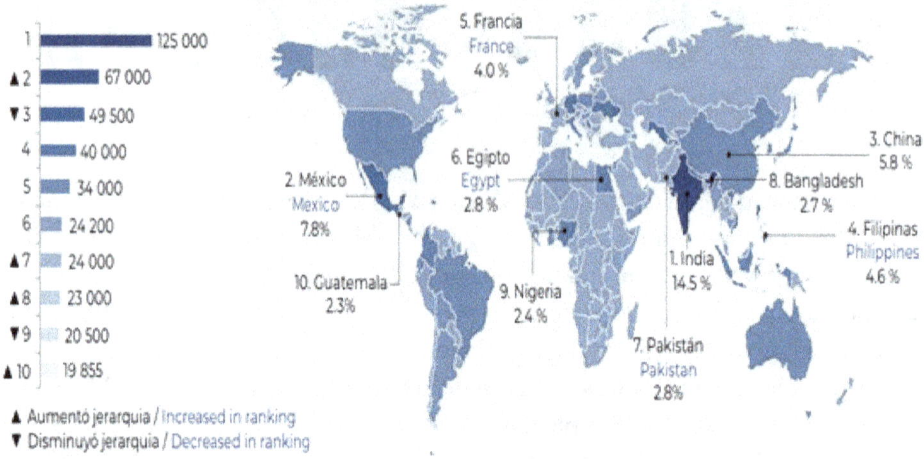

All of these factors were boosted by the confidence foreign investors perceived in Mexico's economic climate. Undoubtedly, one of the factors that strengthened this confidence is inflation (see Figure 28), as inflation was recorded at 3.59% in December 2024, compared to 4.83% in December 2018 (https://www.epdata.es). This reduction undeniably confirms the Mexican authorities' commitment to maintaining economic stability and sound finances during the 2018-2024 period.

Figure 28. Annual inflation rate in Mexico 2010-2024

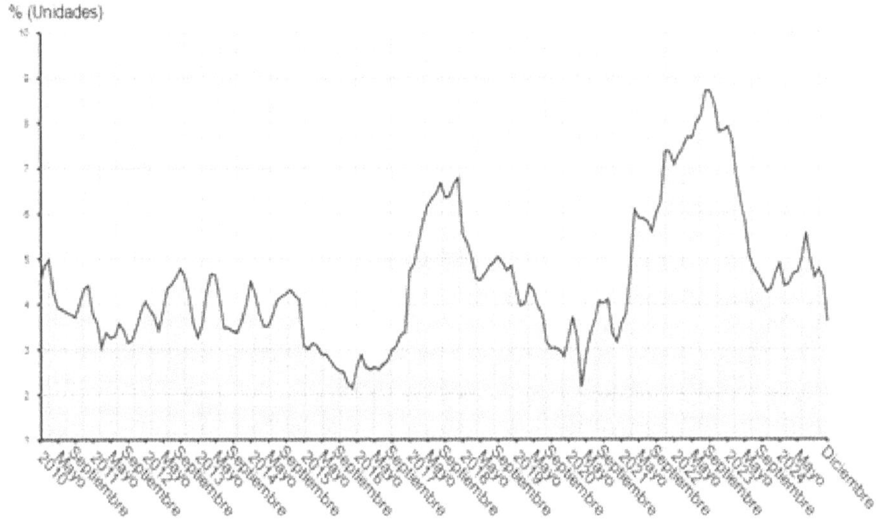

Thus, Figure 29 confirms the above, as the exchange rate between the Mexican peso and the USD remained stable during the 2018-2024 period. The convergence of all the factors outlined in this section allowed for the strengthening of the national economy, as reflected in Figure 30: working poverty showed a slight change in 2024, rising from 35.0% to 35.1% between the second and third quarters of that year. Furthermore, for the same period, working poverty remained at similar levels in urban areas, rising from 30.9% to 30.7%, while in rural areas it increased from 47.6% to 48.5%, an increase of 0.9 percentage points. Finally, it is important to mention that real per capita labor income -using first-quarter 2020 prices between the third quarter of 2023 and the third quarter of 2024, the purchasing power of average real per capita labor income increased by 7.1%, from $3,124.26 to $3,346.45 real pesos per month. This change in labor income represented an increase of approximately $222.19 real pesos compared to the third quarter of 2023.

Figure 29. Daily historical series of the peso-dollar exchange rate 2000-2025

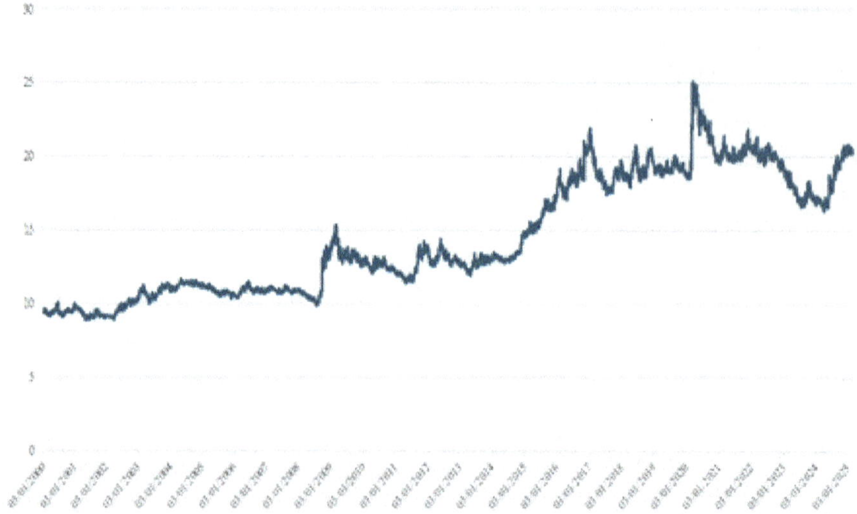

Figure 30. Percentage of the Mexican population with labor income less than the cost of the food basket 2007-2024

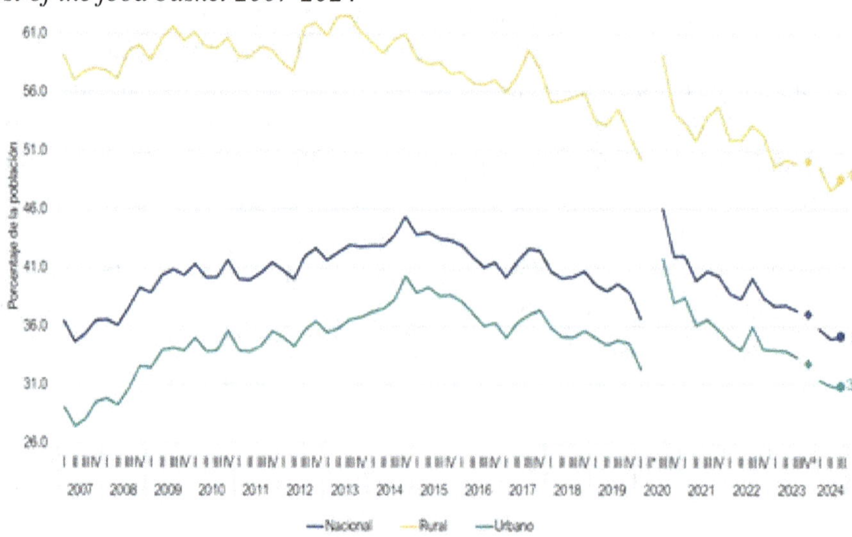

CONCLUSIONS

Based on the latest data reported by SIPRI, as of April 22, 2024, global military spending reached $2.44 trillion in 2023. This figure represents a 6.8% increase in real terms compared to 2022, which, in turn, represents the largest year-on-year increase since 2009. The 10 countries that spent the most in 2023 -led by the United States, China, and Russia- increased their military spending, establishing new scenarios, but, above all, new challenges for maintaining world peace. New challenges for economic growth are also looming in all regions of the planet. One of these challenges is the association of a country's or region's economic growth with its military spending, since military spending is generally associated with national armed conflicts or even with an international escalation. This work has shown that the latter is not entirely true, since the factor known as Military Spending is related, directly or indirectly, to multiple factors that, when interacting simultaneously, can lead to positive results for the economy of a country or region.

The study of military spending is undoubtedly important for multiple areas of knowledge, primarily because its effects and implications, as well as its benefits, must be understood at all levels of public spending, particularly those related to economic growth. Currently, there is research that emphasizes the negative aspects of military spending; however, there is also research that highlights the positive aspects associated with military spending in a country or region. In this bijection of opinions, it is important to mention that the positive or negative aspects associated with a factor will always depend on how it is measured or, at best, on the variables involved in its measurement. What is clear is that the multiple factors that coexist to explain economic growth must interact simultaneously to achieve the objectives set forth in a country's or region's economic policy. That is, the efforts made in a country's or region's productive sector should not only be the result of good decisions but also the result of excellent foresight into possible scenarios, even at the international level. In this regard, and to meet all previously established commitments related to a country's or region's military spending, it is very important to have budgetary support. In this context, Mexico has a major commitment to allocate 2% of its GDP, the minimum currently established by NATO, to meet all the demands a country or region needs in an increasingly globalized world. Undoubtedly, the current commitments are multiple; however, the current environment for Mexico, including at the international level, demands an approach that prioritizes military spending to ensure not only economic stability but also world peace.

REFERENCES

Akar, G., Saritas, T., & Kizilkaya, O. (2021). The Impact of Human Development on Economic Growth: An Application on Transition Economies. *Business and Economics Research Journal*, *12*(2), 307–318. DOI: 10.20409/berj.2021.323

Alenda-Demoutiez, J. (2022). From economic growth to the human: Reviewing the history of development visions over time and moving forward. *Third World Quarterly*, *43*(5), 1038–1055. DOI: 10.1080/01436597.2022.2042680

Backhouse, R. E., & Fontaine, P. (2010). *The History of the Social Sciences since 1945*. Cambridge University Press. DOI: 10.1017/CBO9780511845260

Backhouse, R. E., & Fontaine, P. (2010). Introduction: History of Economics as History of Social Science. In *History of Political Economy* (Vol. 42, pp. 1–21). Duke University Press., DOI: 10.1215/00182702-2009-070

Baiashvili, T., & Gattini, L. (2020). *Impact of FDI on economic growth: The role of country income levels and institutional strength*. Economics EIB Working Paper 2020/02, European Investment Bank. ISBN 978-92-861-4573-5

Barro, R. J. (1991). Economic Growth in a Cross-Section of Countnes. *The Quarterly Journal of Economics*, *106*(2), 407–443. DOI: 10.2307/2937943

Barro, R. J. (2001). Human Capital and Growth. *The American Economic Review*, *91*(2), 12–17. DOI: 10.1257/aer.91.2.12

Becker,G.(2017).*EconomicTheory*(2nded.).Routledge.DOI:10.4324/9781351327688

Becker, G. S., Murphy, K. M., & Tamura, R. (1990). Human Capital. Fertility, and Economic Growth. *Journal of Political Economy*, *98*(5, Part 2), 12–37. DOI: 10.1086/261723

Benhabib, J., & Spegel, M. M. (1992). The Role of Human Capital and Political Instability in Economic Development, unpublished manuscript. New York University, May 1992.

Benoit, E. (1973). *Defence and Economic Growth in Developing Countries*. Lexington Books.

Benoit, E. (1978). Growth and defence in LDCs. *Economic Development and Cultural Change*, *26*, 271–280. DOI: 10.1086/451015

Bils, M., & Klenow, P. (2000). Does schooling cause growth? *The American Economic Review*, *90*(5), 1160–1183. DOI: 10.1257/aer.90.5.1160

Blanco, J., & Aznar, J. (2004). *Introducción a la Economía. Teoría y Práctica.* Editorial Mcgraw-Hill.

Bögenhold, D. (2021). Economics in the Social Science Spectrum: Evolution and Overlap with Different Academic Areas. *Atlantic Economic Journal, 49*(4), 335–347. DOI: 10.1007/s11293-022-09739-4

Case, K., Fair, R. C., & Oster, S. E. (2019). *Principles of Microeconomics* (Global Edition 13th). Pearson.

Chandy, L. (2023). *Economic Development in an Era of Climate Change*. Carnegie Endowment for International Peace.

Chimits, Ch. (2024). *European Economic Security: Current practices and further development*. European Parliament Coordinator: Policy Department for External Relations. Directorate General for External Policies of the Union. PE 754.449-April 2024. Recuperado de https://www.europarl.europa.eu/RegData/etudes/IDAN/2024/754449/EXPO_IDA(2024)754449_EN.pdf

Choi, Y., Kim, H., & Lee, Y. (2022). Economic Consequences of the COVID-19 Pandemic: Will It Be a Barrier to Achieving Sustainability? *Sustainability (Basel), 14*(3), 1629. Advance online publication. DOI: 10.3390/su14031629

Chugh, S. K. (2017). *Modern Macroeconomics* (MIT Press). USA: The MIT Press.

Colombatto, E. (2006). On economic growth and development. *The Review of Austrian Economics, 19*(4), 243–260. DOI: 10.1007/s11138-006-9247-x

COMECSO. (2025). Sitio web del Consejo Mexicano de Ciencias Sociales. https://www.comecso.com/

d'Agostino, G., Dunne, J. P., & Pieroni, L. (2018). Military Expenditure, Endogeneity and Economic Growth. *Defence and Peace Economics, 30*(5), 509–524. DOI: 10.1080/10242694.2017.1422314

Dragoi, D. (2020). Economic growth versus economic development. *Atlantic Review of Economics (ARoEc)*, 4(1), 1-11. https://hdl.handle.net/10419/282275

Dunne, J., & Tian, N. (2020). *Military Expenditures and Economic Growth*. Oxford Research Encyclopedia of Politics., DOI: 10.1093/acrefore/9780190228637.013.1929

Dunne, J. P., Smith, R. P., & Willenbockel, D. (2005). Models of Military Expenditure and Growth: A Critical Review. *Defence and Peace Economics, 16*(6), 449–461. DOI: 10.1080/10242690500167791

Dunne, P., & Coulomb, F. (2008). Peace, War and International Security: Economic Theories. In *Contributions to Conflict Management, Peace Economics and Development*, 6, 13-36. Bingley: Emerald (MCB UP). DOI: 10.1016/S1572-8323(08)06002-5

Easterlin, R. A. (2013). Happiness and Economic Growth: The Evidence. *Discussion Paper Series (University of Southern California)*, IZA DP No. 7187. Recuperado de https://docs.iza.org/dp7187.pdf

Escudé, G. J. (2021). Karl Marx's Theory of Capitalism Exposition, Critique, and Appraisal. *MPRA*, Paper No. 113685, 1-590. https://mpra.ub.uni-muenchen.de/113685

Fourcade, M., Etienne, O., & Yann, A. (2015). The Superiority of Economists. *The Journal of Economic Perspectives*, *29*(1), 89–114. DOI: 10.1257/jep.29.1.89

Gavilanes, R., & Michael, J. (2020). Military Expenditure and Economic Growth: The South American Case. *MPRA*, Artículo No. 98508. https://mpra.ub.uni-muenchen.de/98508/

Giraldo Martinez, G. A., Flórez Zuluaga, J. A., Morante Granobles, D. F., & Escobar Soto, J. F. (2023). Efectos económicos de la inversión en investigación y desarrollo en defensa y su impacto en la productividad en países desarrollados. *Revista Facultad de Ciencias Económicas*, *31*(1), 13–29. DOI: 10.18359/rfce.6223

Gonzales, J. T. (2023). Implications of AI innovation on economic growth: A panel data study. *Journal of Economic Structures*, *12*(1), 13. DOI: 10.1186/s40008-023-00307-w

Gürler, M., & Özsoy, Ö. (2019). Exploring the relationship between life expectancy at birth and economic growth in 56 developing countries. *Journal of Global Health Reports*, *3*, e2019001. DOI: 10.29392/joghr.3.e2019001

Haider, A., Jabeen, S., Rankaduwa, W., & Shaheen, F. (2023). The Nexus between Employment and Economic Growth: A Cross-Country Analysis. *Sustainability (Basel)*, *15*(15), 11955. DOI: 10.3390/su151511955

Hanushek, E. A., & Wößmann, L. (2010). Education and Economic Growth. In Peterson, P., Baker, E., & McGaw, B. (Eds.), *International Encyclopedia of Education* (Vol. 2, pp. 245–252). Elsevier. DOI: 10.1016/B978-0-08-044894-7.01227-6

Ibn-Mohammed, T., Mustapha, K. B., Godsell, J., Adamu, Z., Babatunde, K. A., Akintade, D. D., Acquaye, A., Fujii, H., Ndiaye, M. M., Yamoah, F. A., & Koh, S. C. L. (2021). A critical analysis of the impacts of COVID-19 on the global economy and ecosystems and opportunities for circular economy strategies. *Resources, Conservation and Recycling*, *164*, 105169. DOI: 10.1016/j.resconrec.2020.105169 PMID: 32982059

Kanbur, R. (2002). Economics, Social Science and Development. *World Development*, *30*(3), 477–486. DOI: 10.1016/S0305-750X(01)00117-6

Kates, S. (2020). *Classical Economic Theory and the Modern Economy*. Edward Elgar Publishing. DOI: 10.4337/9781786433572

Kynacou, G. A. (1991). Level and Growth Effects of Human Capital. A Cross-Country Study of the Convergence Hypothesis, unpublished manuscript, New York University, June 1991.

Lucas, R. E. (1988). On the Mechanics of Development Planning. *Journal of Monetary Economics*, *22*, 3–42. DOI: 10.1016/0304-3932(88)90168-7

Mankiw, N. G. (2012). *Principles of Economics*. South-Western Cengage Learning.

McKibbin, W., & Roshen, F. (2023). The global economic impacts of the COVID-19 pandemic. *Economic Modelling*, *129*, 106551. DOI: 10.1016/j.econmod.2023.106551

Moon, Y. J., & Hio Gum, K. (2006). A Model for the Value of Intellectual Capital. *Canadian Journal of Administrative Sciences*, *23*(3), 253–269. DOI: 10.1111/j.1936-4490.2006.tb00630.x

Mulligan, C. B., & Sala I Martin, X. (1992). Some Empirical Evidence on Two-Sector Models of Endogenous Growth. unpublished manuscript, University of Chicago, June 1992.

Murphy, K. M., & Topel, R. H. (2013). Some Basic Economics of National Security. *The American Economic Review*, *103*(3), 508–511. DOI: 10.1257/aer.103.3.508

Nelson, R. R., & Phelps, E. S. (1966). Investment in Humans, Technological Diffusion, and Economic Growth. *The American Economic Review*, *56*, 69–75.

Neu, C. R., & Wolf, Ch.Jr. (1994). *The Economic Dimensions of National Security*. RAND Corporation., https://www.rand.org/pubs/monoFigure_reports/MR466.html

Newman, N. (2024). *Journalism, Media, and Technology Trends and Predictions 2024*. USA: Reuters Institute for the Study of Journalism with the support of the Google News Initiative (GNI).

Nicholson, W., & Snyder, Ch. (2016). *Microeconomic Theory: Basic Principles and Extensions* (12th ed.). Cengage Learning.

Novales, A., Fernández, E., & Ruiz, J. (2022). *Economic Growth. Theory and Numerical Solution Methods*. Springer. DOI: 10.1007/978-3-662-63982-5

Parkin, M. (2018). *Microeconomics* (13th ed.). Pearson.

Piętak, Ł. (2014). Review of theories and models of economic growth. *Comparative Economic Research, 17*(1), 45–60. DOI: 10.2478/cer-2014-0003

Porter, T. M., & Ross, D. (2003). *The Modern Social Sciences*. Vol. 7 of The Cambridge History of Science. Cambridge: Cambridge University Press.

Rahman, M. M., & Alam, K. (2021). Exploring the driving factors of economic growth in the world's largest economies. *Heliyon, 7*(5), e07109. DOI: 10.1016/j.heliyon.2021.e07109 PMID: 34136687

Raifu, I. A., & Aminu, A. (2023). The effect of military spending on economic growth in MENA: Evidence from method of moments quantile regression. *Future Business Journal, 9*(1), 7. DOI: 10.1186/s43093-023-00181-9

Raisová, M., & Ćurþová, J. (2014). Economic growth-supply and demand perspective. *Procedia Economics and Finance, 15*, 184–191. DOI: 10.1016/S2212-5671(14)00476-6

Rebelo, S. (1991). Long-Run Policy Analysis and Long-Run Growth. *Journal of Political Economy, 99*(3), 500–521. DOI: 10.1086/261764

Retter, L. (2019). *Relationships between the economy and national security. Analysis and considerations for economic security policy in the Netherlands*. Santa Monica, Calif., and Cambridge, UK: the RAND Corporation. https://www.rand.org/pubs/research_reports/RR4287.html

Riveros Gavilanes, J. M. (2020). Military Expenditure and Economic Growth: The South American Case. *MPRA*, Paper No. 98508. https://mpra.ub.uni-muenchen.de/98508

Romer, P. M. (1990). Human Capital and Growth. Theory and Evidence. *Carnegie-Rochester Conference Series on Public Policy, 32*, 1990. DOI: 10.1016/0167-2231(90)90028-J

Rothwell, J. T., Cojocaru, A., Srinivasan, R., & Kim, Y. S. (2024). Global evidence on the economic effects of disease suppression during COVID-19. *Humanities & Social Sciences Communications, 11*(78), 1–14. DOI: 10.1057/s41599-023-02571-4

Samuelson, P. A., & Nordhaus, W. D. (1948). *Economics*. McGraw-Hill Education.

Sarwar, S., Alsaggaf, M. I., & Tingqiu, C. (2019). Nexus Among Economic Growth, Education, Health, and Environment: Dynamic Analysis of World-Level Data. *Frontiers in Public Health*, *7*, 307. DOI: 10.3389/fpubh.2019.00307 PMID: 31709219

Schumpeter, J. A. (1954). *A History of Economic Analysis*. Oxford University Press.

Schumpeter, J. A. (2021). *The Theory of Economic Development (Routledge Classics)* (1st ed.). Routledge. DOI: 10.4324/9781003146766

SEDEMA. (2025). Glosario. Definiciones. Recuperado de http://data.sedema.cdmx.gob.mx:9000/datos/glosario-definicion/Econom%C3%ADa

SIPRI. (2024). Comunicado de prensa. EMBARGO: https://www.huffingtonpost.es/uploads/files/2024/06/17/Milex%20Press%20Release%20ESP.pdf

SIPRI. (2025). Sitio web del Stockholm International Peace Research Institute. https://www.sipri.org/

Sunge, R., Mudzingiri, C., & Mkhize, N. (2024). The COVID-19 pandemic and economic recovery: The mediating role of governance, a global perspective. *Heliyon*, *10*(22), e39869. DOI: 10.1016/j.heliyon.2024.e39869 PMID: 39584076

Teng, B., Wang, S., Shi, Y., Sun, Y., Wang, W., Hu, W., & Shi, C. (2022). Economic recovery forecasts under impacts of COVID-19. *Economic Modelling*, *110*, 105821. DOI: 10.1016/j.econmod.2022.105821 PMID: 35261424

Thomas, A. M. (2021). *Macroeconomics: An Introduction*. Cambridge University Press. DOI: 10.1017/9781108764919

Trattner, C., Jannach, D., Motta, E., Costera Meijer, I., Diakopoulos, N., Elahi, M., Opdahl, A. L., Tessem, B., Borch, N., Fjeld, M., Øvrelid, L., De Smedt, K., & Moe, H. (2022). Responsible media technology and AI: Challenges and research directions. *AI and Ethics*, *2*(4), 585–594. DOI: 10.1007/s43681-021-00126-4

Tsitouras, A., & Tsounis, N. (2024). Military Outlays and Economic Growth: A Nonlinear Disaggregated Analysis for a Developed Economy. *Peace Economics, Peace. Science & Public Policy*, *30*(3), 341–391. DOI: 10.1515/peps-2024-0010

Wang, G. (2019). Marx's monetary theory and its practical value. *China Political Economy*, *2*(2), 182–200. DOI: 10.1108/CPE-10-2019-0026

Wang, W., Wei, K., Kubatko, O., Piven, V., Chortok, Y., & Derykolenko, O. (2023). Economic Growth and Sustainable Transition: Investigating Classical and Novel Factors in Developed Countries. *Sustainability (Basel)*, *15*(16), 12346. DOI: 10.3390/su151612346

Welch, P. J., & Welch, G. F. (2016). *Economics: Theory and Practice* (11th ed.). Wiley.

Wiesmeth, H. (2022). *Environmental Economics: Theory and Policy in Equilibrium*. Springer. DOI: 10.1007/978-3-031-05929-2

Williamson, S. (2017). *Macroeconomics (The Pearson Series in Economics)* (6th ed.). Pearson.

1 The concepts of military expenditure and defense of a country or region, although different, will be considered equivalent in this study, mainly because the concept of military expenditure encompasses, in very general terms, the concept of defense.

Chapter 2

Econometric Models to Explain the Economic Growth of a Country or Region

Roop Raj
https://orcid.org/0000-0001-9606-8031
Hemvati Nandan, Bahuguna Garhwal University, Srinagar, India

Rajat B. Hubballi
https://orcid.org/0009-0008-3017-8260
New Horizon College of Engineering, Bangalore, India

K. Lavanya
https://orcid.org/0009-0001-5929-0212
Jain University, Bangalore, India

P. Selvakumar
https://orcid.org/0000-0002-3650-4548
Department of Science and Humanities, Nehru Institute of Technology, Coimbatore, India

Sachin Chavan
https://orcid.org/0000-0002-3588-8068
Balaji Institute of International Business, Pune, India

T.C. Manjunath
https://orcid.org/0000-0003-2545-9160
Rajarajeswari College of Engineering, Bangalore, India

S. Gokila
Karpagam Institute of Technology, Coimbatore, India

ABSTRACT

At its core, economic growth represents the increase in the real output of an economy, adjusting for inflation, and demonstrates how well a country is utilizing its resources—including The importance of economic growth cannot be overstated, particularly for developing nations striving to overcome poverty, unemployment, and underdevelopment. Growth provides governments with greater fiscal resources,

DOI: 10.4018/979-8-3373-3456-1.ch002

allowing for increased public investment in infrastructure, education adjusting for inflation, and demonstrates how well a country is utilizing its resources—including labor, capital, technology, and natural resources—to produce more and better goods and services over time.The importance of economic growth cannot be overstated, particularly for developing nations striving to overcome poverty, unemployment, and underdevelopment. Growth provides governments with greater fiscal resources, allowing for increased public investment in infrastructure, education, healthcare, and other essential services.

INTRODUCTION OF THE UNDERSTANDING OF ECONOMIC GROWTH

At its core, economic growth represents the increase in the real output of an economy, adjusting for inflation, and demonstrates how well a country is utilizing its resources—including the importance of economic growth cannot be overstated, particularly for developing nations striving to overcome poverty, unemployment, and underdevelopment. Growth provides governments with greater fiscal resources, allowing for increased public investment in infrastructure, education adjusting for inflation, and demonstrates how well a country is utilizing its resources—including labor, capital, technology, and natural resources—to produce more and better goods and services over time. The importance of economic growth cannot be overstated, particularly for developing nations striving to overcome poverty, unemployment, and underdevelopment. Growth provides governments with greater fiscal resources, allowing for increased public investment in infrastructure, education, healthcare, and other essential services. As economies grow, businesses tend to expand, generating employment opportunities and raising household incomes. This, in turn, boosts consumer spending and fosters a virtuous cycle of economic activity. Furthermore, sustained economic growth helps nations improve their international standing, attract foreign investment, and integrate more effectively into the global economy. It allows countries to transition from agrarian or resource-based economies to more diversified and industrialized economic structures, enabling them to compete more effectively in the global marketplace. From a regional perspective, economic growth can have a profound impact on reducing disparities between different areas within a country. (Ahmed et al., 2019)It enables lagging regions to catch up with more developed urban centers, encouraging balanced regional development. Infrastructure development, job creation, and better access to services can significantly improve the quality of life in rural or economically disadvantaged areas. Moreover, when growth is inclusive and equitable, it promotes social cohesion and reduces the likelihood of conflict or political instability. Thus, policymakers often prioritize strategies that stimulate regional growth, recognizing its role in national unity and long-term prosperity. by enabling workers to produce more output with the same amount of labor. Human capital development, through education and training, is equally vital, as a more skilled workforce can adopt new technologies and innovate more effectively. Technological advancement is perhaps the most powerful engine of long-term growth, in which businesses and individuals can thrive. Trade and globalization further enhance growth by allowing countries to specialize in their comparative advantages, access larger markets, and benefit from the exchange of ideas and innovations.

Rapid or unbalanced growth can lead to environmental degradation, overuse of natural resources, and rising inequality. In many countries, the pursuit of growth has been accompanied by increased carbon emissions, deforestation, and pollution, raising concerns about sustainability and climate change. Uneven distribution of the gains from growth can exacerbate social divisions and fuel discontent, particularly if certain groups or regions are left behind. Therefore, modern approaches to economic growth emphasize the need for it to be inclusive, sustainable, and resilient. Concepts like "green growth," "inclusive growth," and "sustainable development" have gained prominence as frameworks for balancing economic expansion with environmental stewardship and social equity. Economic growth also interacts closely with other dimensions of development. It can enhance health outcomes by providing resources for medical infrastructure, improve education by funding schools and teachers, and promote gender equality by creating more employment opportunities for women. In turn, these improvements contribute to more robust and enduring growth, illustrating the cyclical and mutually reinforcing nature of development. International organizations such as the World Bank, International Monctary Fund (IMF), and United Nations (UN) often support growth-oriented policies in developing countries through financial assistance, technical support, and policy advice, recognizing growth as a central pillar of the global development agenda. Historically, periods of sustained economic growth have been associated with major marked a turning point in human history, propelling Western economies into new levels of productivity and wealth. Similarly, the rapid growth experienced by East Asian economies in the late 20th century lifted millions out of poverty and created dynamic new centers of economic power. These examples underscore how economic growth can reshape societies, improve living standards, and redefine a country's place in the world. At the same time, they highlight the importance of visionary leadership, sound policies, and the strategic mobilization of resources in achieving sustained and inclusive growth. In today's interconnected world, fostering economic growth is more complex and multifaceted than ever before. Global supply chains, technological disruptions, demographic shifts, and climate change present both opportunities and risks for economies (Akbota et al., 2018) seeking to grow.

OVERVIEW OF ECONOMETRIC MODELS FOR ECONOMIC GROWTH

Econometric models of economic growth. These models use statistical methods and mathematical equations to quantify economic relationships and test theoretical hypotheses using real-world data. Econometrics bridges the gap between theory and practice, allowing for more informed and data-driven decision-making. At the heart of most growth-focused econometric models is the attempt to estimate how different productive capacity. One of the foundational frameworks often employed in such models is the Solow-Swan growth model, which posits that economic growth is driven by labor, capital, and technological progress. Econometric techniques can be used to estimate the relative contributions of these factors by analyzing time-series or panel data across different countries or regions. More advanced models, such as endogenous growth models, incorporate elements like (Ali et al., 2022) human capital, innovation, and knowledge spillovers, and econometrics helps validate these theories through regression analysis and model testing. One major application of econometric models in growth analysis is policy evaluation. Governments and international organizations tax policies, or interest rates, economists can identify patterns and causal relationships that inform future policy directions. Structural equation modeling (SEM), vector autoregression (VAR), and computable general equilibrium (CGE) potential outcomes of policy changes, such as investing in education or infrastructure, before those policies are implemented time-series analysis, models can project future GDP growth based on past trends and current indicators. of the economic outlook. While forecasts are inherently uncertain, especially in the face of unpredictable global events, well-designed models offer valuable insights into likely scenarios and potential risks. and identify common determinants of success or stagnation. This comparative approach helps identify best practices and successful development strategies that can be adapted and implemented elsewhere. (Begum et al., 2015) Moreover, econometric analysis can shed light on why some countries experience faster growth than others, even when starting from similar levels of development. Factors such as governance quality, institutional strength, openness to trade, or investment in innovation can be quantitatively assessed using these models. Errors omitted variable bias, and endogeneity problems also pose serious threats to the validity of econometric results. For instance, when a model assumes that education causes growth, it might ignore the possibility that growing economies simply invest more in education—thus reversing the direction of causality. Addressing such issues often requires sophisticated techniques like instrumental variable (IV) estimation or difference-in-differences (DiD) analysis. disasters, and global economic shifts.

These factors may lead to structural breaks or regime changes that standard econometric models are ill-equipped to handle. Moreover, while models are useful for explaining average relationships across large samples, they may not capture unique national or regional contexts, cultural factors, or institutional specificities that influence economic outcomes. Can be informative, they may not always be a reliable guide to the future—especially in rapidly changing environments. The COVID-19 pandemic, for instance, drastically altered economic structures and labor markets in ways that traditional models failed to predict. Similarly, the growing importance of digital technologies and environmental sustainability calls for new models and approaches that can capture emerging dynamics. In response to these challenges, economists are increasingly integrating machine learning and big data techniques with traditional econometrics to improve predictive accuracy and capture non-linear relationships. Moreover, interpreting econometric results requires caution and expertise. A statistically broader analytical toolkit that includes qualitative assessments, expert judgment, and stakeholder input. Policymakers must be mindful of the limitations of models and avoid over-reliance on any single approach when designing growth strategies. and robustness of econometric research. Open data initiatives, better documentation of methodologies, and peer-reviewed validation processes have helped enhance the credibility of growth studies. Moreover, advances in computing power and statistical software have made it easier to handle large datasets, conduct complex simulations, and visualize results in accessible formats. These developments are expanding the use of econometric tools beyond academia to a wider audience, including business leaders, development practitioners, and civil society. In conclusion, econometric models serve as powerful tools for understanding and explaining economic growth. (Begum et al., 2020) They allow researchers and policymakers to empirically test theories, evaluate policies, forecast trends, and uncover the underlying mechanisms that drive economic expansion. While they offer numerous benefits, including objectivity, precision, and the ability to handle complex relationships, they are also subject to various limitations related to data quality, model assumptions, and external shocks. Recognizing these strengths and weaknesses is essential for the responsible use of econometrics in economic policymaking. As global challenges evolve and new data sources emerge, the future of econometric modeling lies in its ability to adapt, integrate interdisciplinary approaches, and

Solow Growth Model

Econometric models are essential tools in economic analysis, providing a structured way to quantify econometric models help isolate the factors that contribute to the long-term increase in output and productivity, enabling policymakers to design effective growth strategies. This overview examines the different types of econometric models used to explain economic growth, with an emphasis on their strengths and weaknesses(Elliott et al., 2012).Endogenous growth theory, developed by economists such as Paul Romer in the 1980s, extends the Solow-Swan model by introducing the idea that technological progress is driven by investments in human capital, innovation, and knowledge creation. (Engle & Granger, 2017)Unlike in the Solow model, technological progress in the Romer model is not exogenous but is instead the result of intentional investments made by firms and individuals. This shift to an endogenous perspective allows for a deeper understanding of the factors behind innovation and knowledge diffusion.: While the model emphasizes the importance of knowledge, it does not fully explain how knowledge is transmitted across firms or how regional or global disparities in knowledge affect growth. Although the model is theoretically rich, empirical tests often find it difficult to quantify the exact impact of knowledge and innovation on growth, especially in non-industrialized nations where institutions and infrastructure may not be conducive to rapid technological diffusion.

These models use data collected across several entities (countries, regions, or sectors) over multiple periods, allowing researchers to control for unobserved heterogeneity (i.e., factors that differ across countries or regions but remain constant over time). Panel data econometrics enables the estimation of dynamic effects of various growth determinants, such as investment, education, trade, and governance. By using data from multiple entities over time, panel data models allow for controlling individual characteristics, such as geographical location, political stability, or institutional strength, which may affect economic growth These models allow for the analysis of both short-term and long-term effects of growth factors, such as the impact of policy changes, technological adoption, or capital accumulation over time. Panel data econometrics can incorporate both time-series and cross-sectional data, making it possible to estimate the impact of growth determinants with a richer, more diverse set of observations.: Like other econometric models, panel data models are susceptible to endogeneity problems, where causality between variables is difficult to establish. For example, while investment may contribute to growth, rapid growth might also lead to increased investment, creating a feedback loop that is hard to disentangle. Panel data models often require advanced statistical techniques (e.g., fixed-effects or random-effects estimation) and can be difficult to interpret without proper understanding of the assumptions behind them. Dynamic Stochastic General Equilibrium (DSGE) models are widely used in macroeconomic analysis to study economic growth, business cycles, and policy impacts.(Gonzalo & Lee, 2018) These models are based on microeconomic foundations, where agents (households, firms, and governments) make decisions based on rational expectations and optimizing behavior. DSGE models allow economists to simulate how an economy responds to various shocks—such as technological changes, fiscal policy, or external shocks—over time.

Endogenous Growth Models

It has become foundational in the study of growth economics and continues to be an essential tool for policymakers and researchers alike. The Solow model's elegance lies in its ability to explain how mechanisms, and implications of the Solow growth model, as well as some of its limitations and critiques. These assumptions serve as the foundation for understanding how economies grow and what factors are most important in driving long-term growth—is a key driver of economic output. Capital is accumulated through investment, and its productivity is enhanced by the existing stock of capital. (Hansen & Phillips, 2010)However, capital is subject to diminishing returns, meaning that each additional unit of capital will contribute less to overall production as the capital stock increases. Technological progress is also exogenous, meaning it occurs independently of economic activity, and is often modeled as a continuous improvement in the efficiency with which capital and labor are combined to produce goods and services., and labor (L) as follows: This functional form reflects the assumption of diminishing returns to capital and labor, where the marginal productivity of each input decreases as the other input increases. by focusing solely on the factors affecting domestic production, investment, and savings. (Isfat & Raihan, 2022)how much of the output is reinvested into the capital stock to ensure that the economy's capital base can expand over time. how much additional capital will be added to the economy's stock. However, capital is subject to depreciation, meaning some of the existing capital is lost over time. Therefore, the net change in capital () is given by the difference between investment and depreciation, meaning that as the capital stock grows, the additional output generated by each additional unit of capital becomes smaller. This is crucial because it implies that while investment in capital will initially lead to high growth, this effect will eventually diminish as the capital-to-labor ratio increases. which capital and labor are used in production, thereby increasing output without requiring additional inputs. Technological progress is often assumed to be exogenous and is represented by an upward shift in the production function over time. and income stabilize. This steady-state is defined by the point at which the net investment in capital is zero, meaning that capital accumulation matches depreciation, and the economy grows at a constant rate driven entirely by technological progress. meaning that additional capital has a smaller and smaller impact on growth. Instead, the model emphasizes that sustained long-term growth is driven by technological progress, which continuously raises the efficiency of production. This has profound implications for policy, suggesting that investments in innovation, education, and research and development (R&D) are critical for fostering long-term economic prosperity. by accumulating capital more quickly, benefiting from higher returns to investment. However, this convergence process may be slow and contingent upon various factors such as institutional quality, human capital, and the global diffusion of technology. higher economic growth in the short run.(Islam et al., 2021) However, the model also suggests that after a certain point, increasing the savings rate will have diminishing returns and will not significantly affect long-term growth unless it is accompanied by technological progress.

Dynamic Stochastic General Equilibrium (DSGE) Models

Endogenous growth models challenge the assumption that technology is an exogenous factor by modeling technological progress as the result of intentional economic activities. The key assumptions underlying endogenous growth theory are as follows: education, and human capital. In other words, technological change is influenced by economic decisions, and firms or governments invest in R&D to create new technologies that drive growth does not face diminishing returns. This feature allows economies to achieve self-sustaining growth, where higher investments in knowledge, technology, and human capital lead to greater growth without the constraints of diminishing (Jaafar et al., 2020) turns, innovate, and adopt new technologies, contributing to the overall growth of the economy. As a result, policies that improve education and training, or foster innovation, can have a direct and positive effect on growth. Productive investment that leads to the generation of new ideas, inventions, and innovations. The returns to R&D are assumed to be non-rivalrous, meaning that once a new technology or idea is created, it can be used by anyone in the economy without diminishing its value. This characteristic creates the potential for increasing returns to scale and sustained growth A key feature of endogenous growth models is the presence of knowledge spillovers. When firms or individuals invest in R&D or innovation, the benefits of this investment often spill over to other firms or sectors, creating broader economic benefits. This creates positive externalities, where the investment of one entity contributes to the overall growth of the economy without the need for direct compensation or payment for those benefits. These mechanisms allow economies to sustain growth without the need for exogenous technological progress or external factors. productivity of labor, and by improving the skills and knowledge of the workforce, human capital boosts technological innovation and economic output. A well-educated labor force can adopt new technologies more efficiently, create innovations, and contribute to R&D efforts, driving the economy toward higher levels of output. they contribute directly to the economy's output growth. Moreover, many endogenous growth models posit that the returns to R&D investments are non-rivalrous: once a technology is invented, it can be shared by other firms, further increasing productivity across the economy. Invest in R&D, the knowledge and technologies they generate can spill over to other firms or sectors, leading to broader economic benefits. For example, a technological innovation in one industry can boost productivity in related industries, contributing to overall economic growth. Knowledge spillovers can also occur between firms, universities, and public research institutions, creating a virtuous cycle of innovation and growth. This characteristic helps sustain long-term growth without reaching a steady-state, as seen in the Solow model. can continue to grow without needing external inputs.

The accumulation of knowledge and capital creates a cumulative growth process, where growth builds upon itself, leading to sustained increases in output and productivity. growth models provide several important implications for understanding the drivers of long-term economic growth, offering a more nuanced and dynamic view compared to traditional exogenous growth models. growth is ultimately limited by diminishing returns to capital. Endogenous growth theory argues that growth can be sustained indefinitely through continuous innovation and knowledge accumulation. (Khan et al., 2019)Technological progress becomes an intrinsic part of the economic system, driven by investments in R&D and human capital.(Jebli & Youssef, 2017) This provides a more optimistic outlook for long-term economic growth, suggesting that economies can continue to grow as long as there is investment in innovation and the creation of new knowledge R&D, and infrastructure development can enhance human capital accumulation and stimulate innovation, driving long-term growth. For instance, public investment in education and training helps develop a skilled workforce that can generate and adopt new technologies. Similarly, tax incentives or subsidies for R&D can encourage firms to invest in innovation, while intellectual property protections ensure that firms can reap the benefits of their investments in technology (Kirikkaleli & Kalmaz, 2020). A skilled and educated workforce is more capable of generating new ideas, adapting to technological change, and contributing to productivity gains, all of which drive economic growth. This insight has led many policymakers to focus on human capital as a central pillar of growth strategy. Collaborate—can lead to significant regional or national growth. The concentration of knowledge and innovation in certain geographic areas can also create agglomeration effects, where the clustering of industries or firms generates additional growth through increased interactions and shared knowledge. Advancements are the result of intentional investments in innovation, globalization can facilitate the spread of technology across borders. Countries that invest in R&D and human capital can more rapidly adopt and adapt technologies from abroad, further accelerating their own growth. Conversely, countries with less investment in innovation may struggle to catch up, creating disparities in economic performance.

APPLYING ECONOMETRIC MODELS TO COUNTRY-SPECIFIC DATA

Dynamic Stochastic General Equilibrium (DSGE) models have become central to modern macroeconomic analysis, particularly in explaining economic growth, fluctuations, and the effects of various shocks on an economy. (Liu & Bae, 2018) Initially developed as a response to both the limitations of earlier macroeconomic models and the need to account for dynamic interactions in economies, DSGE models have evolved into a key framework for policymakers, central banks, and researchers. These models provide a rigorous, forward-looking structure for understanding the behavior of economies over time, taking into account uncertainty (stochastic elements), time lags, and the role of expectations. This section delves into the key assumptions of DSGE models, their mechanics, and their applications in explaining economic growth. about future economic variables (such as output, inflation, and interest rates) based on all available information. (MacKinnon et al., 2019)Agents are assumed to use the best possible forecasting model when making decisions, meaning that they understand the structure of the economy and anticipate the impact of policy changes or external shock—is modeled as a result of optimization problems. For households, this typically involves decisions about consumption and labor supply, while firms optimize production by choosing capital and labor inputs to maximize profits. The aggregation of these micro-level decisions leads to the macroeconomic outcomes that are studied in DSGE models. Future outcomes. For example, households may decide how much to consume or save by balancing current and future utility, while firms decide on investment and production based on long-term profitability expectations. As the name suggests, DSGE models are general equilibrium models, meaning that they assume markets for all goods, labor, and capital clear simultaneously. This means that the supply of goods equals demand, the supply of labor equals demand, and capital markets clear at every point in time. (Madgule et al., 2023) This assumption implies that all economic agents, by optimizing their behavior, contribute to an overall balance in the economy. shocks. These shocks can come from various sources, such as technological innovation, policy changes, or external factors like natural disasters or international crises.

These shocks introduce uncertainty into the economy, which is crucial for modeling the business cycle and economic fluctuations. The random nature of these shocks means that the economy is constantly evolving, and agents must adapt their behavior in response to these unpredictable (Mehta et al., 2025) changes. In other words, if there is excess demand for a good or service, its price will rise, leading to an increase in supply. This flexibility ensures that the economy moves toward equilibrium in response to shocks, although in practice, some models incorporate nominal rigidities (sticky prices or wages) to account for short-run frictions.. The dynamic nature of the models, combined with the stochastic shocks, enables DSGE models to capture a wide range of economic phenomena, from long-term growth to short-term business cycles. that households balance their consumption with their lifetime wealth. Consumption choices are influenced by interest rates (which affect the return on savings) and income expectations, both of which depend on macro-economic conditions and stochastic shocks. which typically exhibits diminishing returns to each input (capital and labor) but increasing returns when combined. In a typical neoclassical framework, firms may also engage in investment to increase their capital stock, which impacts future production capacity. In models focused on growth, technological progress is often a key driver of productivity improvements. either smooth out business cycle fluctuations or, in some cases, exacerbate economic instability. Monetary policy, for example, can influence interest rates and, therefore, consumption and investment decisions, while fiscal policy can affect demand and supply-side factors. While in others, firms invest in new technology to enhance productivity. In these models, technological progress may be exogenous (as in the Solow model) or endogenous (as in endogenous growth models), where innovation and knowledge accumulation (Nguyen et al., 2021) play a direct role in increasing the economy's productive capacity. Equilibrium and can lead to short-term changes in output, consumption, and investment. For instance, a positive technology shock might increase productivity, leading to higher output, while a negative demand shock could cause a recession.

Figure 1. Economic growth

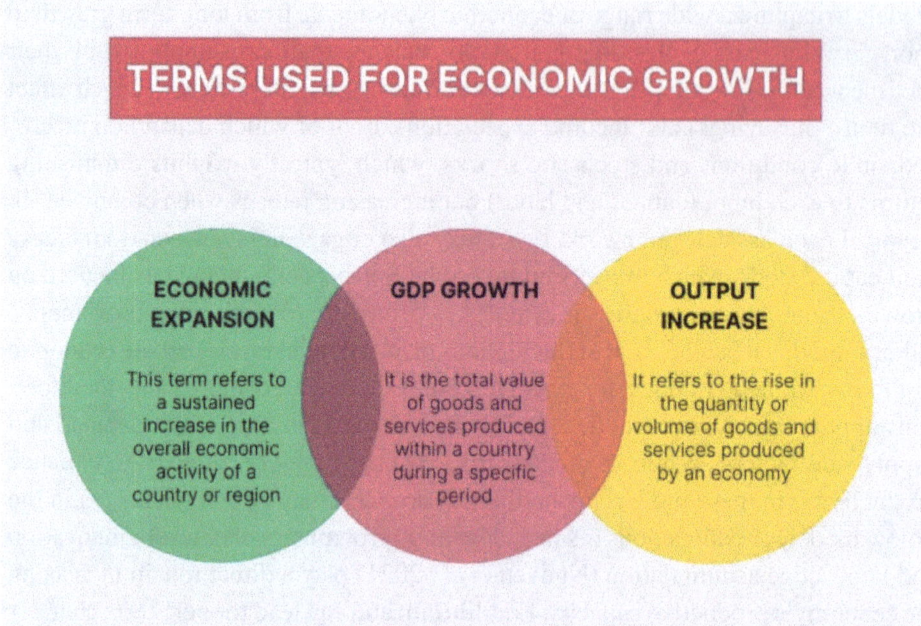

DSGE models also incorporate the idea of propagation mechanisms, where the effects of shocks are amplified and spread over time due to the interactions between agents in the economy. economic growth, the business cycle, and the impact of various shocks. These models provide a flexible framework for analyzing how economies evolve over time and how various factors—such as technology, capital accumulation, and policy—affect growth trajectories. Here are some of the main applications of DSGE models in explaining economic growth: countries grow faster than others. These models can incorporate different sources of growth, such as endogenous technological progress, which depends on factors like R&D and knowledge spillovers, providing insights into how innovation and investments in technology contribute to sustaifluctuations, changes in government policy, or technological breakthroughs—affect long-term growth. For example, a positive technology shock can temporarily boost productivity, leading to higher output and wages, while a negative shock (such as a financial crisis or a pandemic) can reduce economic activity and delay growth. By incorporating these shocks into the model, policymakers can better understand the potential long-term effects of their decisions and the role of policy interventions in stabilizing or stimulating growth. Can use (Nondo & Kahsai, 2020) these models to analyze how changes in taxation or public spending affect aggregate demand and supply. In growth models, fiscal and monetary policies may influence the accumulation of capital and the rate of technological progress, shaping long-term growth patterns. By analyzing how temporary shocks—such as sudden changes in consumer confidence, business investment, or external demand—affect short-term economic fluctuations, DSGE models help explain periods of boom and bust. These models provide insights into how economies self-correct over time, returning to equilibrium after a shock. Furthermore, they can evaluate the effectiveness of stabilization policies, such as interest rate adjustments or fiscal stimulus, in mitigating recessions and boosting recovery.

USING ECONOMETRIC MODELS TO ANALYZE REGIONAL ECONOMIC GROWTH

The application of econometric models to country-specific data is a critical tool in empirical macroeconomics, on linear regressions, vector autoregressions (VAR), cointegration analysis, or more complex dynamic systems, offer a structured methodology for analyzing relationships between key economic variables. This application enables economists and policymakers to make data-driven decisions by testing hypotheses, forecasting future economic outcomes, and evaluating the effectiveness of policies.(Rafiq et al., 2016) However, the application of econometric models to country-specific data comes with several challenges, notably the quality and availability of data, the model's adaptability to the unique economic conditions of each country, and significantly across countries, and this variance can affect the robustness and reliability of the results. However, many countries, especially developing economics, may face challenges in collecting accurate and timely data. Missing or incomplete data can lead to biased estimates and limit the model's ability to capture important relationships. Inaccurate data can result from improper data collection methods, political interference, or underreporting of key economic variables, particularly in countries with less developed statistical agencies. and in some countries, there are significant delays in the release of critical economic indicators. This temporal mismatch between data and the real-time state of the economy can distort econometric estimates, making it difficult to model the current economic situation accurately or to forecast future outcomes with confidences. Different countries may have different methods for calculating GDP, inflation rates, unemployment, or other important economic indicators. (Ramakrishnan et al., 2022) Disparities in definitions, measurement techniques, and reporting standards can make it difficult to compare data across countries, thereby affecting the reliability of the econometric models. Standardizing data across countries is essential for robust and meaningful comparisons, yet this is a complex and often contentious task, particularly when comparing economies at different stages of development or those with diverse economic structures.—may be either unavailable or unreliable.

Subnational data, such as regional GDP, income distribution, or local employment patterns, are critical for understanding disparities within a country and for designing targeted policies.

The lack of such data can significantly limit the scope of econometric analysis and policymaking. However, many countries do not consistently produce high-frequency data on key macroeconomic indicators, limiting the ability of econometric models to capture the dynamics of the business cycle accurately. In some cases, countries may have robust yearly data but lack the fine-grained monthly or quarterly data necessary to understand more rapid economic (Odugbesan & Adebayo, 2020) shifts. to the unique conditions of each country. While econometric models generally rely on a set of core economic principles (e.g., supply and demand, optimization, etc.), their application must consider the specific characteristics of the economy being analyzed. between key economic variables. For example, a model that works well in a developed economy, with stable institutions and a relatively small informal economy, may not be applicable in a developing or emerging market economy, (Pesaran & Timmermann, 2005) where informal sectors play a significant role, institutions are less developed, and there may be more pronounced external vulnerabilities. Models must be carefully calibrated to reflect these structural differences. For instance, the impact of monetary policy on inflation in a small open economy might differ significantly from its impact in a large, closed economy. Econometric models must also account for differences in institutional frameworks, legal systems, and governance structures. For example, countries with stronger financial markets and more developed banking systems may respond differently to interest rate changes or fiscal stimuli compared to countries with weaker institutions. Differences in monetary and fiscal policy regimes, exchange rate systems, and trade openness can also influence the behavior of economic variables, making it essential to tailor models to reflect these country-specific institutional characteristics. For instance, consumption patterns, labor supply decisions, or savings behavior can vary widely across countries due to differences in societal norms, expectations, and institutions. In such cases, econometric models that rely on homogeneous assumptions about consumer behavior or firm decision-making may need to be adjusted to reflect the heterogeneous nature of economic agents in different national contex different countries depends on how well the model's parameters are calibrated. In some cases, global economic relationships may need to be modified to account for unique country-specific circumstances. For example, the parameters related to the elasticity of substitution between labor and capital, or the degree of openness to international trade, may vary significantly across countries. In practice, applying econometric models to country-specific data requires adjustments in model calibration, so the estimated parameters are appropriate for the country's specific economic context.

These breaks can occur due to major policy shifts, financial crises, or changes in the global economic environment. A model that performs well in stable conditions might fail to accurately predict outcomes during periods of abrupt change. Economists must account for such breaks by incorporating mechanisms for modeling nonlinearity, regime shifts, and the potential for discontinuities in economic behavior. For example, a growth model can be used to assess how changes in education policy, infrastructure investment, or technological adoption influence growth. By using country-specific data, policymakers can design more tailored strategies for promoting sustainable development and addressing barriers to growth. unemployment, and other key economic variables. By incorporating country-specific data on historical trends, external shocks, and policy changes, these models can produce forecasts that help policymakers make informed decisions. Scenario analysis can also help assess the potential impact of alternative policy measures or global events, such as changes in trade agreements or global commodity prices. Fiscal stimulus and economic output, or between interest rate changes and investment decisions, economists can determine whether specific policy actions have achieved their intended objectives. This type of analysis helps governments optimize policy interventions to achieve better economic outcomes. Furthermore, the application of econometric models allows for the evaluation of unintended consequences, such as the impact of subsidy removal on vulnerable populations help economists and policymakers understand the forces driving economic fluctuations.(Ranjitha et al., 2025) These models provide valuable insights into the effectiveness of stabilization policies, such as the role of counter-cyclical fiscal policy or interest rate adjustments by central banks valuable in global policy discussions, where countries may look to share best practices or coordinate on issues such as trade, environmental policy, or international aid. Cross-country econometric analysis helps policymakers understand the broader economic environment and identify the policies most likely to lead to growth and stability in their own country.

ECONOMETRIC MODELS FOR FORECASTING ECONOMIC GROWTH

The analysis of regional economic growth using econometric models is an essential area of research within macroeconomics and regional science. By examining economic growth at a more localized level, economists can uncover unique insights that are often masked by aggregate national data. Regional economic growth analysis enables policymakers to design more effective, targeted policies aimed at addressing the specific needs of different areas within a country. However, the use of econometric (Sreenivasulu et al., 2022) models to analyze regional growth presents challenges, especially related to data availability, model specification, and the spatial characteristics of regional economies. The application of spatial econometrics has become increasingly important in this context, this discussion explores the significance of regional data, the role of spatial econometrics, and the challenges involved in applying econometric models to regional economic growth analysis of economic activities and disparities within a country. This disaggregation allows economists to identify patterns of growth, uncover the specific drivers of regional development, and pinpoint areas that require targeted interventions. This data may include information on local GDP, employment levels, industrial composition, regional income distribution, infrastructure, educational attainment, and more. High-resolution data allows for a more precise understanding of what drives economic performance in a specific area. For example, a particular region might be growing due to a thriving tech sector, while another area might be stagnating due to a reliance on traditional industries. Granular data enables these dynamics to be captured and analyzed. Unlike national data, which is regularly published and readily available from institutions such as central banks or national statistical agencies, regional data may not always be as comprehensive or timely. Regional statistics can be scarce, inconsistent, (Sugumaran et al., 2024) or outdated, especially in developing countries or in regions with limited data collection infrastructure. Furthermore, some countries may not have standardized methodologies for gathering regional economic data, making cross-regional or cross-country comparisons difficult. In cases where data are incomplete or of low quality, econometric models must be adjusted or supplemented with other data sources to ensure robustness allows economists to discern persistent patterns and the effects of long-term investments or policy changes. For instance, the impact of infrastructure investments on regional economic growth may not become evident immediately but could unfold over time. (Tang & Tan, 2015) Therefore, having access to panel data (data that spans multiple time periods and regions) is critical for understanding the dynamics of regional growth.

Industry-specific data, such as regional employment in manufacturing versus services or access to education and training in specific fields, can help explain the growth disparities between regions. Models that integrate sectoral data allow for more tailored policy recommendations that take into account the unique economic conditions of each region. where statistical infrastructure may be underdeveloped. As a result, economists often rely on proxies or indirect measures, such as regional electricity consumption, transportation data, or satellite imagery, to approximate economic activity. These alternatives, while useful, introduce additional challenges in terms of data accuracy and comparability across regions. dependencies, where the economic performance of one region may be directly influenced by neighboring regions or spatially distant areas. Ignoring these spatial interactions can lead to biased or inefficient estimates in econometric analysis. Spatial econometrics is a specialized subfield that addresses these concerns by incorporating spatial relationships between observations into econometric models. of its neighboring regions. This correlation can arise from various factors, such as the movement of labor and capital between regions, the spillover effects of technological progress, or the influence of regional policy decisions. For example, an increase in industrial output in a neighboring region might stimulate demand for goods and services in a given region. Econometric models that fail to account for spatial dependence risk underestimating the true relationships between variables, leading to inaccurate conclusions about the factors driving regional economic growth. This allows for the incorporation of spatial spillovers or interactions into the model. For instance, if one region experiences an economic boom, it could have spillover effects on neighboring regions through trade, migration, or shared infrastructure. (Teng et al., 2021). The spatial lag model captures these interactions by incorporating the economic performance of adjacent regions into the analysis, providing a more comprehensive understanding of regional growth dynamicss. These models are used when the unobserved factors affecting regional economic growth are spatially correlated, leading to biased estimates if not addressed. Spatial error models help ensure that the model's error structure appropriately reflects spatial dependencies, improving the reliability of the results allows for the inclusion of spatially lagged explanatory variables, in addition to spatially correlated errors, providing a more flexible approach for modeling spatial interactions.(Vijayakumar et al., 2024) The SDM is particularly useful when regional policies or external factors not only directly affect economic outcomes within a region but also influence neighboring regions. as well as by the performance of neighboring regions. This simultaneity can lead to biased estimates if not properly addressed. To mitigate this, spatial econometricians often use spatial instrumental variables (IV) techniques to identify valid instruments for endogenous variables. This helps to isolate the true causal effect of regional factors on growth while accounting for potential endogeneity issues arising from spatial dependencies. Both time-series and cross-sectional dependencies. By using both spatial and temporal dimensions, spatial panel data models offer a powerful tool for analyzing regional economic growth over time, capturing both the evolution of local economies and their interactions with neighboring regions for a variety of purposes in regional economic analysis. These models help policymakers understand the underlying causes of regional disparities, the effects of regional policies, and the potential for economic convergence or divergence across regions.

THE IMPACT OF MACROECONOMIC POLICIES ON ECONOMIC GROWTH

The empirical evidence on the determinants of economic growth has grown significantly, revealing that multiple variables—ranging from physical capital accumulation to technological progress, from human capital to institutional frameworks—play an integral role in shaping economic outcomes. This discussion explores the key determinants of economic growth as highlighted in the empirical literature, with a particular focus on the roles of institutions, human capital, and innovation, while also examining how these factors interact with each other to foster or impede long-term growth of economic growth. Empirical evidence consistently suggests that the quality of institutions, particularly those that enforce property rights, promote political stability, and ensure legal frameworks, plays a fundamental role in fostering or hindering growth. One of the foundational findings in the literature is the role of secure property rights in fostering economic growth. A study by Acemoglu, Johnson, and Robinson (2001) emphasized that institutions that protect property rights provide the incentives necessary for individuals and firms to invest in human and physical (Voumik et al., 2022a) capital. Without secure property rights, the returns to investment can be undermined by the threat of expropriation, which dampens entrepreneurship and innovation. In countries where property rights are well-defined and effectively enforced, individuals and businesses are more likely to The work of North (1990) also highlighted that countries with strong institutions—those that reduce transaction costs, provide legal certainty, and promote efficient markets—tend to grow more quickly than those with weak institutions.(Wang et al., 2020a) For example, in many Sub-Saharan African countries, weak institutional frameworks have been a key impediment to growth, as they create a poor environment for entrepreneurship, hinder trade, and discourage foreign investment. On the other hand, countries such as Singapore and South Korea, with robust institutional frameworks, have experienced rapid and sustained growth due to the creation of a conducive environment for investment and innovation. stability is another crucial institutional factor influencing economic growth.

The empirical work of Hanushek and Woessmann (2008) found that cognitive skills, as measured by test scores, are more closely related to economic growth than mere years of schooling, suggesting that the quality of education is just as important, if not more so, than its quantity. malnutrition can reduce labor force participation and hinder cognitive development, particularly among children. A study by Bloom and Canning (2000) found that improvements in life expectancy lead to higher economic growth, as healthier workers are more productive and contribute more to economic output. Additionally, better health systems reduce the burden of disease, which in turn improves labor force participation and educational outcomes, creating a virtuous cycle that promotes long-term growth., poor health can be a major drag on economic growth. As a result, investing in public health, sanitation, and access to healthcare is seen as an essential part of fostering sustainable economic growth. The empirical evidence on the importance of innovation in economic growth is overwhelming, and it is widely accepted that innovation is a key factor in explaining differences in growth rates across countries. In this context, innovation—through the development of new technologies and processes—leads to increases in total factor productivity (TFP), which is the residual growth that cannot be explained by changes in capital or laborommunication technologies (ICT) in the late 20th and early 21st centuries has been a major source of growth in developed countries, driving productivity increases in sectors such as manufacturing, services, and finance.(Wang ct al., 2020b). Additionally, foreign direct investment (FDI) often brings in not only capital but also new technologies and managerial expertise that help enhance the productivity of local firms.

CHALLENGES IN ESTIMATING ECONOMETRIC MODELS OF ECONOMIC GROWTH

The interaction of countries in the global marketplace leads to greater resource allocation efficiency, technological diffusion, and enhanced economic welfare. This discussion will explore the role of international trade in economic growth, examining both theoretical perspectives and empirical evidence. It will also delve into the effects of trade liberalization and globalization, highlighting their potential benefits, challenges, and implications for developing and developed economies alike. most efficicntly. Ricardo, building on this, developed the theory of comparative advantage, suggesting that even if a country does not have an absolute advantage in any good, it can still benefit from trade by specializing in the goods it produces most efficiently relative to other goods. This specialization leads to more efficient production, higher output, and greater welfare for trading nations. economic efficiency but also ensures optimal resource allocation within an economy, thereby stimulating growth. The increasing returns to scale achieved through specialization and market expansion can lead to greater productivity and economic growth, especially for small economies that gain access to larger international markets. A significant role in boosting economic growth. The key mechanisms through which trade promotes growth include increased access to markets, technology diffusion, and competitive pressures. economy. As economies open up to trade, they can sell goods and services to a broader consumer base, increasing overall demand and stimulating production. The expansion of markets allows firms to achieve economies of scale, which reduce the average cost of production and increase profitability. This dynamic is particularly important for smaller economies with limited domestic demand, as trade enables firms to expand production and achieve competitive advantages in global markets. Trade also facilitates the diffusion of technology, knowledge, and innovation across borders.

This competitive pressure incentivizes firms to reduce costs, improve quality, and innovate in order to remain viable in the market. This dynamic is particularly beneficial for industries in developing countries, where the introduction of competition can help overcome inefficiencies and foster more efficient production processes, (Zmami & Ben-Salha, 2020). Trade liberalization also leads to more efficient resource allocation by encouraging countries to specialize in the production of goods and services for which they have a comparative advantage. By removing trade barriers and opening up to international competition, countries can shift resources from less efficient sectors to more productive ones, thereby increasing overall output and fostering economic growth and new opportunities for domestic workers. Export-oriented sectors tend to grow as a result of trade liberalization, leading to job creation, particularly in manufacturing and agriculture. However, the impact of trade on employment can vary depending on the industry and skill level of the labor force. While some sectors may experience job losses due to import competition, trade generally leads to net positive effects on employment in the long term by promoting economic, (Pesaran et al., 2001) growth and expanding export sectors. Moreover, the increased demand for skilled labor in export-oriented industries can lead to higher wages and improved living standards, contributing to overall economic welfare. countries. The World Trade Organization (WTO) and various regional trade agreements, such as the European Union (EU) and the North American Free Trade Agreement (NAFTA), have played a significant role in reducing global trade barriers and fostering greater integration into the global economy. Trade liberalization allows countries to exploit their comparative advantage, encouraging specialization in industries where they are most efficient and productive.

THE POTENTIAL OF BIG DATA FOR ECONOMETRIC MODELING OF ECONOMIC GROWTH

Econometric modeling of economic growth has been a cornerstone of economic research for decades, providing valuable insights into the factors that drive national and regional prosperity. However, as the complexity of economies increases and data availability expands, the traditional econometric approaches to modeling economic growth face limitations. In particular, the static nature of many conventional models, their reliance on linear assumptions, and their struggle to handle large datasets with nonlinear relationships create challenges in providing accurate, robust, and timely policy recommendations. In this context, the future of econometric modeling in the field of economic growth lies in embracing newer, more dynamic methodologies, particularly the integration of machine learning (ML) and artificial intelligence (AI). These emerging technologies promise to enhance the predictive power, flexibility, and granularity of economic models, offering new pathways for understanding and forecasting economic growth of constant returns to scale—that may not capture the complexities of modern economies. Additionally, these models often rely on predetermined equations or parameters, which may fail to account for the dynamic and evolving nature of economic systems. One of the key limitations of traditional econometric approaches is their inability to incorporate vast amounts of data efficiently. (Dogan, 2016). As countries and regions collect increasingly large volumes of data across various sectors of the economy, traditional econometric methods—such as ordinary least squares (OLS) regression or fixed-effects models—become increasingly inadequate for managing the scale and complexity of these datasets. This has led to a growing recognition that more advanced, data-driven methods, such as ML and AI, may be needed to complement or even replace traditional techniques for modeling economic growth, (Borlaug, 2007). econometrics, which relies heavily on pre-specified functional forms and assumptions, ML techniques are inherently flexible and data-driven, making them well-suited to tackle the complexities of economic systems. In the context of economic growth modeling, machine learning offers several key advantages: variables, ranging from capital investment and education to technological innovation and institutional quality. As the number of variables and the volume of data increase, traditional econometric models struggle to accommodate the sheer complexity of the relationships between these variables. Machine learning techniques, particularly those involving high-dimensional data, are well-equipped to handle these large datasets. Algorithms such as decision trees, random forests, support vector machines, and neural networks can process and analyze data with numerous variables and nonlinear relationships. These methods do not require explicit specification of a functional form, which allows them to identify complex patterns in the data that might not be apparent using traditional econometric techniques.

Traditional econometric models, such as ARIMA models or structural macroeconomic models, often struggle with forecasting accuracy, particularly during periods of economic indicators. These models can incorporate a wide range of factors, such as interest rates, inflation, trade flows, and financial market activity, to generate more accurate forecasts of GDP growth, productivity, and employment trends. timely and accurate predictions, which is crucial for responding to economic shocks or changes in global conditionstract meaningful information related to economic growth. NLP techniques can be used to assess the tone of news reports, measure public sentiment toward economic policies, or track the frequency of keywords related to economic indicators, such as inflation or investment. By incorporating unstructured data into growth models, AI techniques can provide a richer and more comprehensive understanding of the factors driving economic growth. consumption, and economic growth, adjusting its strategies over time based on feedback from the simulated economy. This iterative learning process allows policymakers to identify optimal policy interventions that maximize long-term growth, based on a dynamic understanding of how economic systems respond to changes data, predict future trends, and recommend policy actions based on economic models. These systems can be used by governments, central banks, and international organizations to support data-driven policy decisions and improve economic planning. from multiple disciplines—ranging from macroeconomics and finance to sociology and political science—AI models can provide more holistic and nuanced policy recommendations.

RECOMMENDATIONS FOR FUTURE RESEARCH AND POLICY

The study of economic growth is one of the most fundamental areas of macroeconomics, and econometric models play a crucial role in understanding the complex mechanisms that drive long-term development across nations and regions. As this book or article has explored, the field of econometrics provides a robust toolkit for explaining, analyzing, and forecasting the dynamics of economic growth. From the foundational models like the Solow growth model to more advanced approaches such as endogenous growth theory, dynamic stochastic general equilibrium (DSGE) models, and recent innovations leveraging machine learning and big data, econometric methods have undergone significant evolution. This conclusion will synthesize the key takeaways from the discussion, providing a cohesive understanding of the importance, limitations, and future directions of econometric modeling in the context of economic growth. and measure the relationships between various economic variables—such as capital, researchers, and institutions to better understand the underlying determinants of growth, test hypotheses, and forecast future trends. These models provide valuable insights into the impact of factors such as investment in infrastructure, education, and health, and the role of institutions in shaping the environment for sustainable growth. Moreover, econometric models offer frameworks for analyzing cross-country and regional differences in economic growth. By controlling for various factors like geography, culture, and historical context, econometric techniques allow for more accurate comparisons and can suggest specific policy interventions that may help lagging regions catch up to more advanced economies.

CONCLUSION

The need for ongoing refinement and testing of assumptions is critical for ensuring that econometric models provide reliable insights, linear assumptions, and relatively small datasets, but the advent of big data has enabled economists to analyze far larger and more diverse datasets, encompassing information from sources such as financial transactions, satellite imagery, social media, and real-time economic indicators. and infrastructure development, which are all critical determinants of regional growth. Moreover, social media data and consumer sentiment analysis can provide an early indication of shifts in economic confidence, enabling economists to forecast changes in demand, investment, and employment more accurately. and explore more complex, nonlinear relationships between economic variables. These algorithms can automatically detect patterns and relationships within vast datasets, offering new perspectives on factors such as technological change, innovation, and human capital development. Furthermore, machine learning techniques such as random forests, support vector machines, and neural networks can capture interactions and complexities between variables that may be difficult to model using traditional econometric approaches. high-frequency data such as financial transactions or labor market activity, economists can generate more timely and accurate predictions of economic growth, inflation, or unemployment, helping policymakers respond more swiftly to emerging economic challenges. The combination of real-time data analytics and advanced machine learning can also allow for the continuous updating of models, thereby improving their robustness over time. will have access to ever more sophisticated tools for understanding the dynamics of growth. The combination of dynamic models like DSGE models with big data analytics promises to offer deeper insights into the short term and long-term drivers of growth. the rationale behind their predictions. The development of explainable AI and transparent algorithms will be crucial for ensuring that policymakers and researchers can trust the insights generated by these models and use them effectively in in economic growth models. In today's globalized world, economic growth in one country or region is often influenced by external factors, such as international trade, foreign direct investment, and global financial markets. As such, future models of economic growth will need to integrate cross-border data flows, policy decisions, and other global phenomena to provide a more accurate depiction of how national economies interact within the broader global economy., and the unique characteristics of different geographic areas. Understanding the dynamics of regional growth is crucial for informing policy decisions that aim to reduce inequalities and promote balanced development across diverse regions., econometric models provide a rigorous framework for evaluating the impact of various policy interventions, whether in the realm of fiscal policy, monetary policy, trade policy, or social policy. By understanding the underlying drivers of growth and quantifying the effects of different policy measures, economists can provide evidence-based recommendations that support economic development. Furthermore, the integration of big data and machine learning into econometric models will allow policymakers to make more informed decisions in real time, respond more effectively to economic crises, and design policies that are tailored to the specific needs of individual countries or regions. For example, by analyzing detailed transaction data or geospatial patterns, policymakers can gain insights into regional disparities, sectoral dynamics, and supply chain vulnerabilities, which are crucial for crafting targeted, timely, and data-driven analyses of economic growth is immense. The future of econometric modeling lies in the effective use of big data, machine learning, and AI, providing researchers and policymakers with powerful tools to understand, forecast, and guide the future of economic growth. Ultimately, the goal is not only to refine our models.

REFERENCES

Ahmed, Z., Wang, Z., & Ali, S. (2019). Investigating the non-linear relationship between urbanization and CO2 emissions: An empirical analysis. *Air Quality, Atmosphere & Health*, *12*(8), 945–953. DOI: 10.1007/s11869-019-00711-x

Akbota, A., & Baek, J. (2018). The environmental consequences of growth: Empirical evidence from the Republic of Kazakhstan. *Economies*, *6*(1), 19. DOI: 10.3390/economies6010019

Begum, R. A., Raihan, A., & Said, M. N. M. (2020). Dynamic impacts of economic growth and forested area on carbon dioxide emissions in Malaysia. *Sustainability (Basel)*, *12*(22), 9375. DOI: 10.3390/su12229375

Borlaug, N. (2007). Feeding a hungry world. *Science*, *318*(5849), 359. DOI: 10.1126/science.1151062 PMID: 17947551

Dogan, N. (2016). Agriculture and environmental Kuznets curves in the case of Turkey: Evidence from the ARDL and bounds test. *Zemedelská Ekonomika*, *62*(12), 566–574. DOI: 10.17221/112/2015-AGRICECON

Elliott, G., Rothenberg, T. J., & Stock, J. H. (2012). *Efficient tests for an autoregressive unit root (No. t0130)*. National Bureau of Economic Research.

Engle, R. F., & Granger, C. W. (2017). Co-integration and error correction: Representation, estimation, and testing. *Econome J Econom Soc*, *55*(2), 251–276.

FAO. (2017). *Food and Agriculture Organization of the United Nations. The future of food and agriculture, trends and challenges*. FAO, FAO.

Gonzalo, J., & Lee, T. H. (2018). Pitfalls in testing for long run relationships. *Journal of Econometrics*, *86*(1), 129–154. DOI: 10.1016/S0304-4076(97)00111-5

Grossman, G., & Krueger, A. B. (1991) Environmental impacts of a North American free trade agreement. National Bureau of Economic Research 1991. working paper 3914, NBER: Cambridge, MA, USA.

Hansen, B., & Phillips, P. C. B. (2010). Estimation and inference in models of cointegration: A simulation study. *Advances in Econometrics*, *8*, 225–24.

Isfat, M., & Raihan, A. (2022). Current practices, challenges, and future directions of climate change adaptation in Bangladesh. *Int J Res Publ Rev*, *3*(5), 3429–3437.

Islam, M. M., Khan, M. K., Tareque, M., Jehan, N., & Dagar, V. (2021). Impact of globalization, foreign direct investment, and energy consumption on CO2 emissions in Bangladesh: Does institutional quality matter? *Environmental Science and Pollution Research International*, *28*(35), 48851–48871. DOI: 10.1007/s11356-021-13441-4 PMID: 33929670

Jaafar, W. S. W. M., Maulud, K. N. A., Kamarulzaman, A. M. M., Raihan, A., Sah, S. M., Ahmad, A., Saad, S. N. M., Azmi, A. T. M., Syukri, N. K. A. J., & Khan, W. R. (2020). The Influence of forest degradation on land surface temperature—A case study of Perak and Kedah, Malaysia. *Forests*, *11*(6), 670. DOI: 10.3390/f11060670

Jebli, M. B., & Youssef, S. B. (2017). The role of renewable energy and agriculture in reducing CO2 emissions: Evidence for North Africa countries. *Ecological Indicators*, *74*, 295–301. DOI: 10.1016/j.ecolind.2016.11.032

Khan, M. W. A., Panigrahi, S. K., Almuniri, K. S. N., Soomro, M. I., Mirjat, N. H., & Alqaydi, E. S. (2019). Investigating the dynamic impact of CO2 emissions and economic growth on renewable energy production: Evidence from FMOLS and DOLS tests. *Processes (Basel, Switzerland)*, *7*(8), 496. DOI: 10.3390/pr7080496

Kirikkaleli, D., & Kalmaz, D. B. (2020). Testing the moderating role of urbanization on the environmental Kuznets curve: Empirical evidence from an emerging market. *Environmental Science and Pollution Research International*, *27*(30), 38169–38180. DOI: 10.1007/s11356-020-09870-2 PMID: 32617821

Leitão, N. C. (2021). Testing the role of trade on carbon dioxide emissions in Portugal. *Economies*, *9*(1), 22. DOI: 10.3390/economies9010022

Liu, X., & Bae, J. (2018). Urbanization and industrialization impact of CO2 emissions in China. *Journal of Cleaner Production*, *172*, 178–186. DOI: 10.1016/j.jclepro.2017.10.156

MacKinnon, J. G., Haug, A. A., & Michelis, L. (2019). Numerical distribution functions of likelihood ratio tests for cointegration. *Journal of Applied Econometrics*, *14*(5), 563–577. DOI: 10.1002/(SICI)1099-1255(199909/10)14:5<563::AID-JAE530>3.0.CO;2-R

Mahadev Madgule, N. (2023). Vinayaka, Yeshwant M. Sonkhaskar, Dhiren Ramanbhai Patel, R. Karthikeyan, P. Selvakumar,(2023). Mechanical properties and microstructure of activated TIG welded similar joints of Inconel alloys by desirability approaches. *Materials Today: Proceedings*, *77*, 528–533. DOI: 10.1016/j.matpr.2022.12.250

Mehta, A. K., Yashoda, L., Selvakumar, P., Mishra, B. R., Das, A., & C. T. C., M. (2025). Teaching Methods: Techniques for Disadvantaged Learners. In S. Hai-Jew (Ed.), *Mitigating Learner Disadvantages in Teaching and Learning* (pp. 181-206). IGI Global Scientific Publishing. DOI: 10.4018/979-8-3693-8623-1.ch007

Nguyen, A. T., Lu, S. H., & Nguyen, P. T. T. (2021). Validating and forecasting carbon emissions in the framework of the environmental Kuznets curve: The case of Vietnam. *Energies*, *14*(11), 3144. DOI: 10.3390/en14113144

Nondo, C., & Kahsai, M. S. (2020). The impact of energy intensity, urbanisation, industrialisation, and income on CO2 emissions in South Africa: An ARDL bounds testing approach. *African Journal of Economic and Sustainable Development*, *7*(4), 307–330. DOI: 10.1504/AJESD.2020.106826

Odugbesan, J. A., & Adebayo, T. S. (2020). The symmetrical and asymmetrical effects of foreign direct investment and financial development on carbon emission: Evidence from Nigeria. *SN Applied Sciences*, *2*(12), 1–15. DOI: 10.1007/s42452-020-03817-5

Pesaran, M. H., Shin, Y., & Smith, R. J. (2001). Bounds testing approaches to the analysis of level relationships. *Journal of Applied Econometrics*, *16*(3), 289–326. DOI: 10.1002/jae.616

Pesaran, M. H., & Timmermann, A. (2005). Small sample properties of forecasts from autoregressive models under structural breaks. *Journal of Econometrics*, *129*(1–2), 183–217. DOI: 10.1016/j.jeconom.2004.09.007

Rafiq, S., Salim, R., & Apergis, N. (2016). Agriculture, trade openness and emissions: An empirical analysis and policy options. *The Australian Journal of Agricultural and Resource Economics*, *60*(3), 348–365. DOI: 10.1111/1467-8489.12131

Ramakrishnan, T., Mohan Gift, M. D., Chitradevi, S., Jegan, R., & Subha Hency Jose, P. Nagaraja, Rajneesh Sharma H.N., Selvakumar P., Sintayehu Mekuria Hailegiorgis, (2022). "Study of Numerous Resins Used in Polymer Matrix Composite Materials", *Advances in Materials Science and Engineering*, vol. 2022, Article ID 1088926, 8 pages, 2022. DOI: 10.1155/2022/1088926

Ranjitha P. K., Selvakumar, P., Anute, N., Manjunath, T., Sureshkrishna, G., & Pougajendy, S.(2025). Transportation Challenges In Islands Tourism. In V. Hassan (Ed.), Navigating MassTourism to Island Destinations: Preservation and Cultural Heritage Challenges (pp. 287-312). IGI Global Scientific Publishing. .DOI: 10.4018/979-8-3693-9107-5.ch011

Sreenivasulu, A., & Manimozhi, T. Satheesh kumar P., Selvakumar P. and Singh P.,(2022). "The Model of Smart Sensing Device For Sensitive Nanoclusters Modification in Sensing Properties," 2022 2nd International Conference on Advance Computing and Innovative Technologies in Engineering (ICACITE), Greater Noida, India, 2022, pp. 1043-1047, DOI: 10.1109/ICACITE53722.2022.9823846

Sugumaran, K. M. D., Pandiyarajan V., Y. B S, Selvakumar P. and M. S, (2024). "Analysis of Electromyography Signals for Control of Mechanical Prosthesis using Machine Learning Techniques," 2024 2nd International Conference on Intelligent Data Communication Technologies and Internet of Things (IDCIoT), Bengaluru, India, 2024, pp. 1059-1067, DOI: 10.1109/IDCIoT59759.2024.10467707

Tang, C. F., & Tan, B. W. (2015). The impact of energy consumption, income and foreign direct investment on carbon dioxide emissions in Vietnam. *Energy*, *79*, 447–454. DOI: 10.1016/j.energy.2014.11.033

Teng, J. Z., Khan, M. K., Khan, M. I., Chishti, M. Z., & Khan, M. O. (2021). Effect of foreign direct investment on CO2 emission with the role of globalization, institutional quality with pooled mean group panel ARDL. *Environmental Science and Pollution Research International*, *28*(5), 5271–5282. DOI: 10.1007/s11356-020-10823-y PMID: 32960445

Vijayakumar, G., Rajkumar, M., Rajiv Chandar, N., Selvakumar, P., & Duraisamy, R. (2024). Muniyandi Rajkumar, Rajiv Chandar N, Selvakumar P and Ramesh Duraisamy, (2024). Environmentally friendly TDS removal from waste water by electrochemical ion exchange batch-type recirculation (EIR) technique. *Environmental Science. Water Research & Technology*, *10*(4), 826–835. https://di.org/10.1039/D3EW00793F. DOI: 10.1039/D3EW00793F

Voumik, L. C., Islam, M. J., & Raihan, A. (2022a). Electricity production sources and CO2 emission in OECD countries: Static and dynamic panel analysis. *Glob Sustain Res*, *1*(2), 12–21. DOI: 10.56556/gssr.v1i2.327

Wang, L., Vo, X. V., Shahbaz, M., & Ak, A. (2020a). Globalization and carbon emissions: Is there any role of agriculture value-added, financial development, and natural resource rent in the aftermath of COP21? *Journal of Environmental Management*, *268*, 110712. DOI: 10.1016/j.jenvman.2020.110712 PMID: 32510446

Wang, Z., Rasool, Y., Zhang, B., Ahmed, Z., & Wang, B. (2020b). Dynamic linkage among industrialisation, urbanisation, and CO2 emissions in APEC realms: Evidence based on DSUR estimation. *Structural Change and Economic Dynamics*, *52*, 382–389. DOI: 10.1016/j.strueco.2019.12.001

Zmami, M., & Ben-Salha, O. (2020). An empirical analysis of the determinants of CO2 emissions in GCC countries. *International Journal of Sustainable Development and World Ecology*, *27*(5), 469–480. DOI: 10.1080/13504509.2020.1715508

Chapter 3
India's Defence Expenditure:
Long-Term Trends, Structural Composition, and GDP Linkages

Sebak Kumar Jana
https://orcid.org/0000-0002-3532-4350
Vidyasagar University, Midnapore, India

Sangshaptak Jana
Vidyasagar University, Midnapore, India

ABSTRACT

This paper examines the evolution of India's defence expenditure, focusing on its historical trends, structural composition, and long-term relationship with GDP. From post-Independence reliance on British defence supplies to the development of a public sector-led industrial base, India's defence strategy has responded to major geopolitical events such as the 1962 Sino-Indian war and the Kargil conflict. Analysis of data from 1970–71 to 2024–25 reveals a shift toward capital-intensive spending, driven by modernization goals and initiatives like Atmanirbhar Bharat. Although defence spending has risen in absolute terms, its share in GDP has declined from over 3% in the 1980s to below 2% in 2024–25. A cointegration analysis confirms a stable long-run link with GDP, but elasticity of 0.901 suggests sub-proportional growth. Despite growth in indigenous production and exports, issues persist in R&D, procurement, and quality control. The study underscores the need for sustained fiscal support, efficient governance, and technological advancement to meet evolving security needs.

DOI: 10.4018/979-8-3373-3456-1.ch003

INTRODUCTION

The interplay between defence expenditure and economic performance has become an increasingly critical area of inquiry, particularly for developing countries like India. Given its position in a geopolitically volatile region, India's military spending not only serves strategic and security objectives but also significantly shapes fiscal policy and broader economic outcomes. As a result, scholarly attention has steadily grown, aiming to unpack the multifaceted impacts of rising defence budgets. This study explores the long-term trends in India's defence expenditure, analyzes the structural composition of military spending, and examines its linkages with GDP and macroeconomic indicators to provide a holistic understanding of its evolving role in national development.

Existing research reveals that the relationship between military expenditure and economic growth is complex and often non-linear. Pieroni (2009) integrates defence and civilian spending within a growth model incorporating endogenous technological progress, concluding that while moderate military spending may support growth, excessive outlays can hinder it by crowding out essential public investment. Similarly, Pradhan et al. (2013) use dynamic panel data models across 22 countries—including India—to demonstrate a significant but sensitive causal relationship, highlighting methodological limitations in earlier studies. Markowski, Chand, and Wylie (2017) emphasize that defence spending trends, particularly in the Indo-Pacific, often reflect underlying economic growth rather than direct security threats, pointing to the need for disaggregated analysis of budgetary shifts and procurement patterns.

Furthermore, fiscal and security dynamics offer additional insights into the broader implications of India's military expenditure. Mukhopadhyay and Das (2018) find that higher defence spending in emerging markets negatively impacts FDI, while Abbas and Wizarat (2018) argue that rising military budgets in South Asia contribute to external borrowing and developmental constraints. Gupta and Sriram (2018) demonstrate that targeted internal security spending can reduce violence in insurgency-prone areas, but poorly allocated resources may exacerbate instability. In terms of employment, Azam et al. (2016) report a complex, elastic relationship between defence spending and unemployment in the SAARC region, suggesting short-term job creation alongside structural economic consequences. Finally, Sasidhar (2024) finds no significant link between India's defence spending and the Global Peace Index, underscoring the need for a balanced approach that integrates military strength with diplomatic initiatives. Collectively, these studies frame the context for a nuanced investigation into India's defence expenditure, emphasizing its diverse impacts across economic, fiscal, and security dimensions.

India's defence expenditure forms a critical component of its national budget, reflecting the country's security needs and strategic priorities. As one of the largest standing armed forces in the world and situated in a geopolitically sensitive region, India consistently allocates a significant share of its annual budget to defence. The expenditure covers a broad range of components including salaries, pensions, capital outlay for equipment and modernization, and maintenance costs. In the Union Budget 2024-25, the defence allocation stood at around ₹6.2 lakh crore, accounting for approximately 13% of the total budget and about 2% of the country's GDP. A large portion of India's defence spending is directed towards revenue expenditure, primarily on salaries and pensions for the personnel in the Army, Navy, and Air Force. The capital outlay, though relatively smaller, is crucial for modernizing the armed forces with advanced weaponry, technology upgrades, and indigenous defence production under the "Atmanirbhar Bharat" (self-reliant India) initiative. India has been making increasing efforts to reduce dependency on imports by boosting domestic defence manufacturing, involving both public and private sector participation, and promoting Make in India policies in defence procurement. The trend of defence expenditure in India over the years shows a multifaceted pattern when examined through three key aspects: the absolute rise in spending, the revenue-capital composition, and its proportion relative to GDP.

India does not release formal defence white papers or comprehensive national security strategy documents. Instead, a general outline of its defence policy is found in the Ministry of Defence's annual reports and individual doctrines of the Army, Navy, and Air Force. In reality, India's military spending is largely shaped by its immediate security challenges. Foremost among these is the ongoing insurgency in Kashmir and the longstanding tensions with Pakistan. Despite India's significantly larger defence budget compared to Pakistan's, the unresolved nature of the Kashmir conflict and concerns over Pakistani involvement in incidents like the 2008 Mumbai attacks ensure that the region remains central to Indian defence planning. The 1999 Kargil War underscored the need for modernization, pushing India toward developing advanced aircraft and network-centric systems. However, with both nations being nuclear-armed, India views full-scale war as impractical, opting instead to develop rapid-response strategies, such as the 2004 'Cold Start' doctrine aimed at quick, targeted operations. While some voices advocate redirecting defence spending toward development needs, public opinion in India generally supports a strong military, with widespread concern over threats from Pakistan, Islamic terrorism, and China (Perlo-Freeman et al, 2010).

Beyond Pakistan, internal and external security concerns further justify India's growing defence budget. The Maoist insurgency, often referred to as the Naxalite movement, has emerged as the most lethal internal conflict since 2009, fueled by socio-economic grievances among marginalized communities. Externally, China is increasingly seen as India's primary strategic competitor. The long-standing border disputes, particularly over Arunachal Pradesh, combined with China's rapid military modernization, have led to growing unease in Indian defence circles. India is also wary of China's expanding influence in the Indian Ocean through its investments in ports across neighboring countries — a pattern India fears could evolve into strategic military outposts. Although both nations continue to strengthen economic ties and downplay open hostility, these underlying tensions, coupled with domestic instability and global strategic ambitions, have driven India to maintain a robust and modern military posture, even amid criticism regarding the country's persistent levels of poverty (Perlo-Freeman et al, 2010).

LITERATURE REVIEW

Theoretical Foundations and Global Perspectives on Military Expenditure in India

The relationship between military expenditure and economic growth has long attracted scholarly debate, yielding diverse theoretical perspectives and empirical findings. Early modeling efforts, such as those by Ward and Mahajan (1984), focused specifically on India, highlighting how defence spending is driven by perceived external threats, fiscal constraints, and acceleration effects. Their simulation-based analysis for the period 1952–1979 revealed a dynamic interplay where rising military outlays contributed to inflation and fiscal deficits, creating a self-limiting cycle in defence budgeting.

Broader theoretical developments have since challenged and expanded upon such models. Dunne, Smith, and Willenbockel (2005) critically evaluated the Feder–Ram model, commonly used in defence-growth studies, arguing that it lacks theoretical coherence with contemporary growth literature. They proposed the adoption of more comprehensive frameworks such as the Augmented Solow and Barro-type models, which allow for richer macroeconomic interactions and institutional heterogeneity.

In an effort to incorporate complexity, Aizenman and Glick (2006) introduced non-linear dynamics into the discussion. They contended that the economic consequences of military expenditure depend heavily on a country's threat perception and governance quality. Their findings suggest that in nations like India—where persistent border tensions and regional rivalries are prevalent—defence spending can, under certain conditions, act as a growth catalyst.

Extending the analysis to a global scale, several studies have situated India's defence profile within a broader geopolitical context. For example, research by Perlo-Freeman, Ismail, and Solmirano (2010) and Stålenheim et al. (2008) placed

India among the world's leading military spenders, noting that this trend is closely linked to its rising economic capacity and regional strategic ambitions. These studies highlight that India's defence trajectory mirrors a wider movement among emerging economies pursuing military modernization.

Berthelemy, Herrera, and Sen (1995) offered a more integrated theoretical framework by embedding military expenditure within an endogenous growth model. Their work emphasized that defence spending can have both productive and disruptive effects, with outcomes shaped by national institutions, development priorities, and security needs. The analysis stressed the importance of weighing welfare and security dimensions simultaneously when evaluating long-term impacts.

A global comparative lens is further provided by Sköns et al. (1999) and Sandler and George (2016), who examined how international military dynamics—ranging from China's strategic assertiveness to the evolving role of NATO and the U.S.—shape India's defence calculus. Such external factors often reinforce domestic imperatives for sustained investment in military capabilities.

These trends are supported by findings from Perlo-Freeman et al. (2013), who observed a shift in global military expenditure, with stagnation or decline in Western defence budgets contrasted by significant increases in Asia. India's rising defence allocation thus reflects both its regional security aspirations and its emergence as a pivotal actor in the evolving global security architecture.

The theoretical debate on military expenditure also splits between two contrasting schools of thought. One draws from Keynesian economics, asserting that defence spending can stimulate demand, promote industrial development, and generate employment (Benoit, 1973). The other critiques military outlays as carrying substantial opportunity costs, diverting resources from vital social sectors such as health, education, and infrastructure (Ball, 1983; Ismail, 2017). In the Indian scenario, this trade-off is particularly salient. Nair (2009), for instance, argued that increased defence budgets often come at the expense of social development funding, thus intensifying the "guns versus butter" dilemma.

More recent discourse, however, suggests a shift toward balancing these competing priorities. Scholars like Sköns and colleagues have called for a broader conception of security that encompasses developmental and peace-building objectives alongside conventional military spending. This view aligns with India's contemporary policy orientation, which promotes the indigenization of defence production, dual-use technology development, and strategic partnerships that seek to harmonize national security with economic development.

Military Expenditure in India and Developing Economies

The relationship between military expenditure and economic development in developing countries, particularly in India, has been widely debated in the literature. One central concern is the development-defence trade-off, where scarce resources allocated to defence potentially undermine social and economic investments.

Early contributions by Deger and Sen (1983, 1995) emphasize that military spending in low- and middle-income countries tends to divert funds away from critical development needs, such as health and education. While there may be limited technological spillovers, they argue that these are insufficient to justify the high opportunity costs, particularly in the Indian context. Their critique of the "military Keynesianism" hypothesis highlights the limited multiplier effects of defence spending in such economies.

Empirical studies further affirm these concerns. Hou (2010), in a country-specific analysis, establishes a significant negative correlation between defence expenditure and economic growth in India and other developing nations. He attributes much of this to regional security dynamics, particularly the persistent arms competition between India and Pakistan. His application of the Richardson arms race model underscores the "security dilemma" wherein defence build-ups by one state provoke reciprocal increases by the other, fueling an ongoing spiral.

The India-Pakistan defence dynamic has also been examined through causal and strategic lenses. Amir-ud-Din, Sajjad, and Aziz (2020) identify an asymmetric causality in military budgets, where Pakistani defence spending is heavily influenced by Indian expenditure, while India's military outlays appear to be more globally and strategically driven. Complementing this, Mansoob Murshed and Mamoon (2010) explore the triadic interaction between bilateral trade, military spending, and democracy, concluding that diminished trade and higher defence spending exacerbate conflict. Their findings support the argument for strengthening economic interdependence and democratic institutions as a means to reduce regional tensions.

Reinforcing the bilateral causality narrative, Shah et al. (2015) find mutual influences between Indian and Pakistani military budgets. Their analysis also notes that both defence and civilian government spending have significant impacts on India's GDP, revealing a complex interlinkage between public finance structures and economic performance.

Beyond the India-Pakistan context, broader geopolitical considerations also shape India's defence policy. Studies by Srinivas (2006) and Öcal (2003) explore India-China-Pakistan strategic relations, suggesting that military spending is driven not only by economic growth but also by geopolitical rivalry. Öcal's nonlinear model indicates asymmetric responses, where Indian defence moves carry more weight in shaping Pakistan's policy than the reverse—a conclusion echoed by Hou (2010).

Meanwhile, Perlo-Freeman et al. (2010) and Stålenheim et al. (2008) highlight that military expenditure in developing countries often correlates with increased resource availability. Although India's spending is not directly tied to resource booms, its robust economic growth has enabled sustained modernization of its military apparatus without major reallocations from other sectors.

Despite concerns about economic trade-offs, several studies suggest a more nuanced view of the military-growth nexus in India. Mukhopadhyay, Sinha, and Sengupta (2018), using SIPRI data and Johansen co-integration tests, identify a long-term equilibrium relationship between defence spending and economic growth in India. Unlike China, where such a link was absent, India's military investments were found to spur technological and industrial development, especially in sectors like steel and manufacturing.

Similarly, Patra (2018) reports a positive association between military expenditure and GDP per capita in South Asia, with India benefiting more than its neighbors. This finding suggests that under appropriate strategies, defence spending can contribute to economic productivity and structural transformation.

However, this optimistic outlook is not universally shared. Datta (2019) contends that the multiplier effects of defence spending are overshadowed by a crowding-out effect, where public investment in employment-generating and welfare sectors suffers. This misallocation may deepen socio-economic disparities in the long run. Along the same lines, Ismail (2017) highlights the high opportunity cost of military outlays. While acknowledging some short-term growth benefits, the study concludes that reallocating resources to non-military areas—such as education, health, or infrastructure—would likely yield greater and more inclusive economic gains.

Empirical Evidence on India's Military Expenditure

Empirical studies analyzing India's military spending reflect a complex interplay between defence needs, economic performance, and fiscal priorities. Several econometric investigations have attempted to unravel this relationship using diverse methodological approaches.

One stream of research investigates the causal linkage between military expenditure and economic growth. Abdel-Khalek, Mazloum, and El Zeiny (2020), employing a Hendry General-to-Specific (GTS) model over the period 1980–2016, found no evidence of causality between military spending and GDP. Nonetheless, they emphasized India's evolving defence strategy, particularly the push toward indigenization and private sector engagement through liberalized FDI policies. A related analysis by Khalid and Mustapha (2014), using the ARDL bounds testing approach, revealed a short-run association between military spending and GDP, but no long-term correlation. Their Granger causality tests suggested a unidirectional influence running from GDP to military expenditure, reinforcing the notion that economic capacity tends to shape defence outlays rather than the other way around.

Contrastingly, Raju and Ahmed (2019), through cointegration and causality frameworks, identified a positive long-term correlation between defence spending and GDP in India, though short-run effects were negligible. Their analysis, which also included Pakistan and China, suggested that defence investments may yield economic returns over time, especially when linked with broader strategic goals. However, a divergent perspective emerges in UR (2022), which posits a negative long-run relationship, implying that rising GDP might reduce the relative necessity for high defence expenditure, especially in cases where military budgets are politically, rather than economically, motivated.

Historical insights provided by Ward et al. (1991) further contextualize India's defence trajectory. Their study noted a consistent rise in military expenditure amidst post-liberalization reforms and regional instability. They also flagged significant opportunity costs, particularly the diversion of resources from social sectors like health and education.

This budgetary tension between defence and developmental priorities is further examined by Jana et al. (2018), who explored the dynamic relationship among military spending, education expenditure, and GDP. Their findings pointed to long-run causality from both military and educational spending to economic growth, though in the short run, only defence expenditure exhibited a significant causal influence. Such results highlight the delicate trade-offs policymakers face in allocating limited fiscal resources between national security and human capital development. Reinforcing these patterns, both Raju and Ahmed (2019) and UR (2022) reported persistent underinvestment in social sectors, suggesting a structural prioritization of defence amidst fiscal constraints.

In terms of forecasting future expenditure trends, recent studies have employed time-series modeling. Sharma and Phulli (2020), using the Box-Jenkins ARIMA method, projected a nearly 37% increase in India's defence budget by 2024, based on data from 1960–2019. Their findings raised concerns about the long-term fiscal sustainability of such growth. Complementing this, Zhu (2024) offered a detailed analysis of India's defence allocations from FY 2013–14 to FY 2022–23, employing both ARIMA and grey prediction models. His work underscored the rising share of defence within GDP and its per capita cost, despite mounting fiscal pressures.

From a public finance perspective, Behera and Nayak (2021) provided a critical assessment of India's defence resource allocation. They highlighted the challenges posed by stagnant tax revenues and competing budgetary demands, particularly in manpower-intensive sectors of the military. Their study advocated for a more efficient reallocation of defence spending, suggesting that reforms in personnel management could significantly enhance financial sustainability.

Policies and Implications of Military Expenditure in India

India's defence spending has undergone a notable transformation in recent years, driven by policy shifts aimed at modernizing the defence sector and enhancing its linkages with broader economic objectives. As Abdel-Khalek et al. (2020) and Jana et al. (2018) observe, recent policy initiatives such as the liberalization of Foreign Direct Investment (FDI) in defence, a push for domestic manufacturing under the "Make in India" campaign, and the integration of defence research with civilian technological sectors have repositioned military expenditure as a strategic investment rather than a mere fiscal liability. These developments reflect a paradigm shift, where defence is increasingly viewed as a catalyst for technological advancement and industrial growth.

However, the extent to which military spending contributes to wider economic development remains contested. While the defence sector may offer technological spillovers, Deger and Sen (1983) caution that such benefits are often overstated. Similarly, Hou (2010) questions whether the defence-led technological evolution in India effectively permeates into the civilian economy or results in tangible gains in productivity.

Chakraborty (2018) situates India's defence expenditure within the broader national development framework, stressing the importance of efficiency and governance in defence planning. The study warns that unchecked increases in military spending—particularly under the pretext of external threats—can detract from long-term growth if issues like corruption and bureaucratic inefficiencies persist. This reinforces Ball's (1983) earlier argument regarding the opportunity cost of defence budgets in developing countries, where military outlays can crowd out essential social investments, especially in education and health.

Empirical findings further complicate the relationship between defence spending and economic growth in the Indian context. For example, Jalil, Abbasi, and Bibi (2016) identify a non-linear, U-shaped relationship, where military expenditure initially supports growth but becomes counterproductive beyond a certain threshold. This suggests diminishing returns to defence investment over time and underscores the importance of maintaining a balanced defence budget.

Exploring the interplay between military, social, and economic allocations, Bhattacharyya (2018) uses ARDL and ECM techniques to examine India, China, and Bangladesh. The study finds no long-run causal link between military spending, GDP, and social sector expenditures in India, implying a disconnect between economic growth and allocations to health and education in the presence of substantial defence budgets.

The relationship between internal security concerns and defence spending adds another layer of complexity. Das (2019) identifies a co-integrating relationship between terrorism and military expenditure in India, suggesting that increased security threats spur defence spending. However, the study also highlights that such responses do not necessarily translate into higher foreign investment, indicating potential trade-offs between national security and investor confidence.

Looking beyond India, Budhathoki et al. (2024) provide regional context through a panel ARDL analysis of South Asia. They find that while military spending may marginally support long-term growth, its short-run impact is negative, particularly in the absence of strategies to curb unemployment and bolster capital formation. These insights suggest that military expenditure alone cannot drive sustainable development without complementary economic reforms.

Governance quality emerges as another crucial factor. Gupta, De Mello, and Sharan (2001) empirically link higher levels of corruption with increased military expenditure, particularly in countries where defence procurement lacks transparency. In India, where defence deals often face scrutiny, this finding has significant implications for public accountability and fiscal efficiency.

The distributional consequences of defence spending also warrant attention. Raza, Shahbaz, and Paramati (2017), although focused on Pakistan, uncover a positive association between military expenditure and income inequality—raising relevant concerns for India, given regional similarities and structural parallels.

Finally, Guo, Jiang, and Yu (2013) examine India's defence spending from 1970 to 2009, uncovering a long-term relationship between military expenditure, budget deficits, and income redistribution. Their findings suggest that while military spending may offer short-term redistributive benefits, it can aggravate fiscal pressures over time.

The relationship between military expenditure and economic growth in India is complex, non-linear, and shaped by a range of strategic, economic, and institutional factors. While several studies highlight potential positive effects—such as employment generation, technological advancement, and industrial growth—these benefits often come with significant trade-offs, including fiscal strain, income inequality, and underinvestment in essential social sectors. The academic literature reveals divergent findings: some studies find neutral or negative impacts, whereas others identify long-term complementarities, especially when defence spending is linked to domestic manufacturing and R&D. India's geopolitical context—particularly its rivalry with China and Pakistan—has historically influenced defence allocations, although recent policy shifts toward self-reliance and civil-military integration may alter the developmental implications of such spending. Importantly, the effectiveness of military expenditure is contingent upon factors like fiscal space, institutional quality, governance transparency, trade openness, and regional threat perceptions. Therefore, a strategic balance between defence and development is imperative. Policymakers must ensure that military spending is both efficient and aligned with national security and socioeconomic objectives. Future research should explore more disaggregated and sector-specific models that incorporate non-military security indicators and assess the broader developmental role of defence expenditure in India.

OBJECTIVES, MATHDOLOGY AND DATA SOURE

Objectives

The major objectives of the present study are as follows.

a) To analyze the long-term trends in India's defence expenditure by examining the composition of revenue and capital components from 1970 to 2024.
b) To evaluate the relationship between total defence expenditure and Gross Domestic Product (GDP) at current prices, highlighting changes in the percentage share of defence in GDP over time.

Methodology

To find the impact of GDP on defence expenditure in India we have used the following regression model (Eq.1) which has been estimated using time series econometrics of cointegration and error correction mechanism (ECM)

$$\ln DEFEXP_t = \alpha + \beta \ln GDP_t + u_t \qquad (1)$$

$\ln DEFEXP_t$ = log of defence expenditure (Rs. Crore) at t-th period
$\ln GDP_t$ = log of GDP (Rs. Crore) at t-th period

Since cointegration has become possible, we proceed to estimate the error correction mechanism (ECM). The cointegrating equation gives long run relationship between two variables, but does not shed any light on short run dynamics. ECM combines short run and long run dynamics.

The ECM model is given by Eq. (2)

$$\Delta \ln DEFEXP_t = \varphi + \gamma \Delta \ln GDP_t + \lambda \hat{\varepsilon}_{t-1} + w_t \qquad (2)$$

Where, $\hat{\varepsilon}_{t-1} = \ln DEFEXP_t - \widehat{lnDEFEXP}_{t-1}$ is one period lagged value of the error term from the cointegrating regression. When $\hat{\varepsilon}_{t-1}$ is non-zero, there is disequilibrium in the short run. However, equilibrium will be restored in the long run if and only if the coefficient of $\hat{\varepsilon}_{t-1}$ ie. λ is negative.

Data Source

The present study is based on secondary data for India. The data has been collected from different sources like *Handbook of Statistics on the Indian Economy* published by Reserve Bank of India.

FINDINGS OF THE STUDY

Defence Expenditure in India

In the initial years following Independence, India's defence sector was heavily reliant on the United Kingdom for equipment and technological support. This dependency was shaped by historical ties and the limited domestic capability at the time. As India began diversifying its sources of defence procurement, there was a need for continuity and administrative expertise to manage these existing relationships, particularly with UK-based firms. The Industrial Policy Resolution of April 1956 further entrenched the role of the public sector in defence and heavy industries, contrasting sharply with countries like the United States, where such industries were dominated by private enterprises. This structural difference made it difficult for India to establish robust defence trade relations with the US. Despite potential openings during President Kennedy's administration, opportunities for closer India–US ties were not effectively utilized. A more proactive approach might have mitigated Washington's strategic tilt toward Pakistan, but as a developing economy, India ultimately bore the brunt of this missed alignment (Bhagwati, 2019)..

The 1962 border conflict with China marked a turning point in India's defence posture, exposing vulnerabilities in its military preparedness. Prime Minister Nehru's urgent appeals to President Kennedy for advanced fighter aircraft, bombers, and logistical support reflected the gravity of the crisis. Though the Chinese declared a unilateral ceasefire shortly after, the episode underscored the necessity for stronger defence capabilities. Subsequently, under Prime Minister Rajiv Gandhi in the 1980s, India witnessed a sharp increase in defence spending, surpassing 3% of GDP consistently, peaking at 3.95% in 1987–88—the highest in independent India's history up to 2019. This increase was driven by significant arms acquisitions, including French Mirage fighters and upgraded Soviet MiGs, as well as domestic initiatives reflecting a more assertive defence stance. Actions such as Operation Brasstacks and the deployment of the Indian Peace Keeping Force (IPKF) in Sri Lanka demonstrated India's willingness to project power beyond its borders, even at considerable financial and strategic costs (Bhagwati, 2019).

Figure 1 presents India's defence expenditure from 1970–71 to 2024–25, classified into Revenue Account, Capital Account, and Total Defence Expenditure (in ₹ crore). In the early decades (1970s and 1980s), the defence budget remained relatively modest, with the total expenditure growing gradually from ₹1200 crore in 1970–71 to ₹14,416 crore in 1989–90. The Revenue Account, which includes salaries, maintenance, and operational costs, consistently formed the bulk of the expenditure. Capital spending, although smaller, began rising steadily — from 148 crore in 1970–71 to ₹4222 crore in 1989–90 — reflecting increasing focus on equipment acquisition and modernization.

The 1990s and early 2000s witnessed a sharp escalation in defence spending, coinciding with the liberalization of the Indian economy and increasing regional security challenges. Total defence expenditure surged from ₹15,426 crore in 1990–91 to ₹60,066 crore by 2003–04. Notably, capital expenditure saw significant jumps during this period — nearly quadrupling from ₹4552 crore to ₹16,863 crore — reflecting enhanced investment in military hardware and infrastructure. The jump in 1999–2000 (₹47,071 crore) is particularly prominent, likely due to the aftermath of the Kargil War and its implications for national defence preparedness.

From 2004–05 onward, the growth in defence spending became even more pronounced, particularly in the capital component, which crossed ₹1 lakh crore by 2019–20 and stood at ₹1.72 lakh crore in 2024–25. Total expenditure grew almost tenfold from ₹75,856 crore in 2004–05 to over ₹4.54 lakh crore in 2024–25. The increasing capital outlays reflect India's continued military modernization, procurement of advanced systems, and indigenous defence production under initiatives like 'Make in India'. The fiscal trajectory underscores the country's strategic shift toward strengthening long-term defence capabilities while sustaining operational readiness through substantial revenue allocations.

Figure 1. Defence expenditure (Rs. Crore) in India during 1970-71 to 2024-25

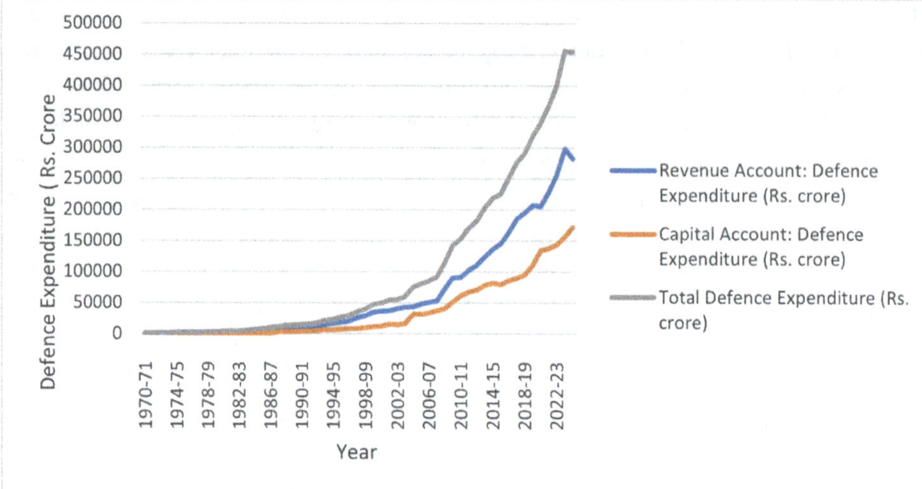

Reserve Bank of India (2025).

Share of Defence Expenditure in Revenue Account, Capital Account and Total Expenditure

Table 1 illustrates the changing share of defence expenditure in India's total government spending across revenue, capital, and overall expenditure categories over six decades (1970–71 to 2024–25). In the 1970s, defence occupied a prominent place in the national budget, accounting for 30.16% of revenue expenditure and 4.76% of capital expenditure, with a total share of 19.49%. This reflects the early post-independence emphasis on maintaining a robust defence structure in a geopolitically tense environment, particularly following the wars of 1965 and 1971. Defence was a significant component of public spending at the time, especially within the revenue account, indicating a focus on operations, personnel, and basic logistics.

In the 1980s and 1990s, a shift in expenditure pattern is evident. While the share of defence in the revenue account steadily declined — from 21.37% in the 1980s to 13.82% in the 1990s — its capital share increased sharply, reaching 18.64% in the 1990s. This points to a transition from routine defence spending toward infrastructure and asset creation, including procurement of advanced weapon systems, especially post the 1999 Kargil conflict. However, the total share of defence in overall expenditure also declined gradually, from 16.36% in the 1980s to 14.85% in the 1990s, indicating rising competition from other government priorities like social and economic development.

From 2000 onward, the trend continued with a further drop in revenue share to just 7.46% by 2020–25, while capital expenditure's share peaked at 36.88% in 2010–20, before moderating slightly to 21.22% in 2020–25. The overall share of defence in total government expenditure declined significantly to 9.69% in the most recent period. This suggests that although India is modernizing and enhancing its military capabilities through capital investment, the relative priority of defence in the national budget is declining, likely due to increased spending on welfare, health, education, and infrastructure. The data reflects a long-term structural rebalancing of public expenditure, with defence remaining important but no longer dominating the fiscal landscape.

Table 1. Percentage share of defence expenditure in revenue account, capital account and total expenditure

	Share of defence expenditure in Revenue Account	Share of defence expenditure in Capital Account	Share of defence expenditure in total expenditure
1970-71 to 1979-80	30.16	4.76	19.49
1980-71 to 1989-90	21.37	7.76	16.36
1990-91 to 1999-2000	13.82	18.64	14.85
2000-01 to 2009-10	11.07	33.67	14.19
2010-11 to 2019-20	9.29	36.88	12.78
2020-21 to 2024-25	7.46	21.22	9.69

Source: Authors' calculation based on Reserve Bank of India (2025)

Share of Defence Expenditure in GDP

Figure 2 shows the percentage share of India's defence expenditure in GDP from 1970–71 to 2024–25, highlighting a clear long-term declining trend. During the 1970s and 1980s, defence spending as a share of GDP generally ranged between 2.5% to over 3%, peaking during 1986–88 at around 3.31%, a period marked by heightened regional tensions and military modernization. However, from the 1990s onward, the share began a gradual decline, dropping to around 2.2–2.4% by the late 1990s and early 2000s. This downward shift reflects India's changing fiscal priorities, structural economic reforms, and growing GDP base. After 2010, the fall became more pronounced, with defence expenditure falling below 2% of GDP, reaching 1.61% in 2019–20 and further down to 1.38% by 2024–25. Despite increases in absolute defence spending, the share in GDP has shrunk, indicating that defence has not kept pace with overall economic growth, potentially raising concerns about the adequacy of defence allocations in the context of evolving security challenges.

Figure 2. Percentage share of defence expenditure in GDP in India during 1970-71 to 2022-23 (Government of India)

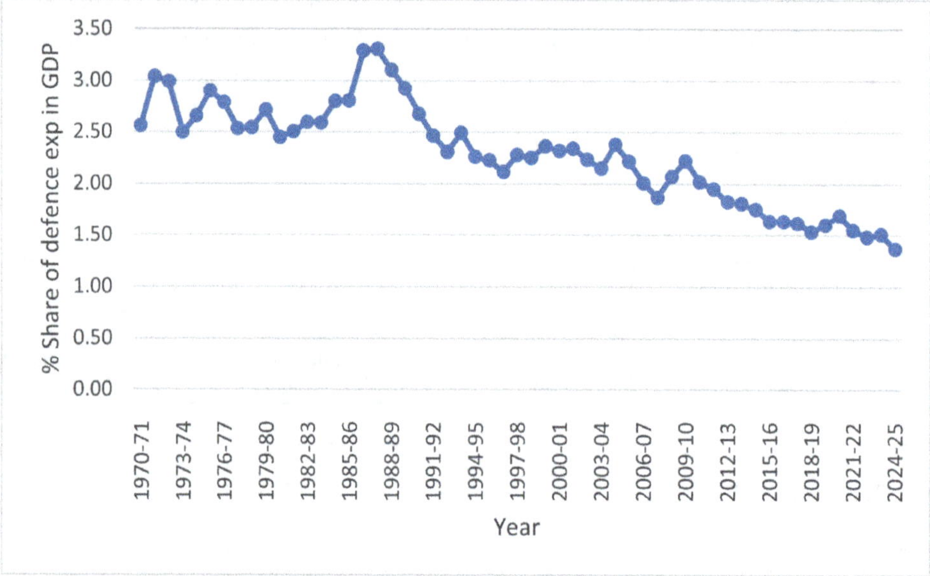

Source: Authors' calculation based on Reserve Bank of India (2025)

Union Budget 2025

The Union Budget 2025 of India underscores India's strategic push toward self-reliance in defence and national security, with a substantial allocation of ₹6.81 lakh crore (approximately US$78.57 billion), reflecting a 9.5% rise over the previous year. This includes a capital budget of ₹1.8 lakh crore (around US$20.76 billion), signifying focused investments in the modernization of the armed forces through the procurement of indigenous light combat aircraft, helicopters, drones, and next-generation weapon systems. Approximately 75% of the capital outlay is expected to support the domestic defence industry, aligning with the Atmanirbhar Bharat initiative. The total modernization budget of ₹2.66 lakh crore includes capital and relevant revenue expenditures, with notable increases in allocations for aircraft, aero-engines, and equipment for the Indian Coast Guard to enhance maritime surveillance. The budget also emphasizes the adoption of advanced technologies such as AI, cybersecurity, and surveillance systems, along with improved border infrastructure and personnel welfare. Research and development receive a dedicated boost with ₹26,817 crore (US$3.09 billion), including a 13% rise in capital R&D spending and significant funding set aside for industry and startups under initiatives like ADITI. Defence exports reached ₹21,083 crore in FY24 and are projected to exceed ₹25,000 crore in FY25, supporting the government's long-term vision of achieving US$35 billion in annual defence production and US$6 billion in exports by FY28 (Khatter 2025).

Self-Reliance in Defence Production

India's journey toward self-reliance in defence production has evolved through distinct phases shaped by historical, strategic, and industrial factors. Initially guided by the ideals of self-sufficiency, the post-Independence period saw state-led industrialisation as the cornerstone of defence manufacturing. Policies like the Industrial Policy Resolutions of 1948 and 1956 placed critical defence sectors under public sector control. The early efforts focused on establishing ordnance factories, developing basic R&D infrastructure like DRDO, and expanding public-sector undertakings like HAL and Bharat Electronics. Though India aimed for in-house production of military equipment, limitations in industrial capacity and technological expertise restricted the ambition of full self-sufficiency. Recognising this, analysts like K. Subrahmanyam proposed a more realistic framework of self-reliance—emphasising equipping the armed forces through both domestic and foreign sources, while ensuring operational autonomy. Consequently, India adopted a policy of licensing and co-production, particularly with the Soviet Union, which enhanced military strength but did little to boost indigenous technological capabilities (Behera, 2013).

In recent decades, the focus has shifted toward deeper self-reliance through increased participation of the private sector and structural reforms in procurement. The liberalisation of the defence industry in 2001 and the introduction of offset policies, as well as procurement categories like 'Make' and 'Buy and Make (Indian)', have been pivotal. These initiatives aim to support indigenous design and development by offering incentives and shared development costs, particularly to private enterprises. The establishment of offset obligations for foreign suppliers and the encouragement of joint ventures have opened new avenues for capability building within Indian industry. Despite initial institutional hurdles, these reforms represent a major departure from the earlier public sector-dominated model, signalling a more inclusive and innovation-driven approach to defence manufacturing. With over a hundred projects under the 'Make' category and policy support for startups and private players, India is steadily moving toward becoming a self-reliant defence producer, aligning with the broader vision of Atmanirbhar Bharat (Behera, 2013).

India's civil-military drone sector is undergoing a significant shift toward becoming a research- and innovation-driven industry. While policy reforms since 2021 have spurred the growth of small drones and their commercial use, further progress now depends on targeted technological reforms. This includes launching dedicated UAV development initiatives, designating a nodal ministry with R&D capabilities, and creating an ecosystem with testing sites, trial-based standards, and clear certification guidelines. Establishing an indigenous design certification policy and applying uniform Indigenous Content (IC) evaluation across ministries will promote local innovation. Additionally, restructuring funding programs under DST, MeitY, and MoD to better support UAV-focused startups and academic research is essential to achieving India's vision of becoming a global drone hub by 2030 (Narang, 2024).

To enhance competitiveness in India's defence sector, particularly in the public domain, systemic reforms in research and development (R&D) are crucial. The current R&D ecosystem is heavily bureaucratized, limiting collaboration with private players and international original equipment manufacturers (OEMs). For meaningful transformation, public research institutes must actively pursue global partnerships to co-develop advanced technologies. Forming consortiums involving OEMs, venture capitalists, and marketing firms can help these institutions gain access to both domestic and international defence and industrial markets. This model would facilitate joint R&D activities, especially through offset agreements, thereby spreading the financial and technological risks. Ultimately, this approach would strengthen India's indigenous defence capabilities by fostering innovation, lowering development costs, and making the system more agile and globally competitive (Singh, 2014).

A robust framework for product development and commercialization must also be established, featuring a layered architecture involving specialized integrators and financing mechanisms. Key components include systems integrators for assembling and validating prototypes, a lead systems integrator tasked with managing production, and a core systems integrator responsible for aligning military and commercial needs. A dedicated innovation support agency should handle technology transfer, international marketing, patenting, and investor relations. Financing this architecture requires an autonomous financial commission and possibly a dedicated technology development bank to support high-risk ventures. In the long term, the creation of specialized research hubs and incentives for private investment can lead to a globally recognized and self-reliant defence manufacturing ecosystem. These reforms, however, demand strong political will, de-bureaucratization, and continuity in legislative oversight to sustain momentum and ensure results over a 5–15-year horizon (Singh, 2014).

India's defence sector has undergone significant structural and strategic reforms in alignment with the vision of Aatmanirbhar Bharat. The restructured National Security Council Secretariat (NSCS) has been given an expanded role, with institutionalized responsibilities in areas such as maritime and economic security, climate-related threats, and technological innovation. Strengthened coordination between NSCS and

NITI Aayog is expected to harmonize national security goals with developmental priorities. One of the landmark reforms has been the establishment of the Chief of Defence Staff (CDS) and the Department of Military Affairs (DMA), aiming to enhance integration among the armed forces and improve joint operational planning. Specialized agencies like the Defence Cyber Agency, Defence Space Agency, and Special Operations Division have been created under the CDS to tackle emerging non-traditional security threats. Additionally, efforts to enhance jointness in theatre commands and rationalize resource allocation across the services reflect a forward-looking strategy aimed at operational efficiency (Doval, 2022).

Since 2014, India has introduced wide-ranging reforms to promote domestic defence production and reduce reliance on imports. These include simplified procurement procedures, increased foreign direct investment (FDI) limits (from 49% to 74% under the automatic route), and the promotion of public-private partnerships and start-ups in the defence sector. Key indigenous projects such as the INS Vikrant (IAC-1), Light Combat Aircraft (LCA), Arjun tanks, and BrahMos-integrated Su-30 MKI represent milestones in India’s path to self-reliance. Fiscal reforms, like reduced GST on MRO services, have further incentivized local manufacturing. The government’s push for $5 billion in defence exports by 2025, supported by active diplomatic promotion and defence exhibitions, highlights India's ambition to emerge as a global defence manufacturing hub. The implementation of a positive indigenization list and a negative import list signals a shift in procurement strategy, compelling stakeholders to prioritize indigenous capabilities. This transformation is essential not only to reduce long-term costs of foreign systems but also to ensure sustainable and autonomous defence preparedness (Doval, 2022).

Comparison of India with Other Countries in Defence Spending

The 2024 global military expenditure landscape, as reported by the Stockholm International Peace Research Institute, highlights significant disparities in both absolute spending and its share of national GDP. The United States remains by far the largest military spender, allocating US$ 997 billion, which constitutes 37% of global military expenditure and 3.4% of its GDP. China, though far behind in absolute terms with US$ 314 billion, ranks second and contributes 12% to global spending, yet it spends only 1.7% of its GDP, indicating a restrained defence allocation relative to its economic size. Russia, with US$ 149 billion and 7.1% of GDP, has the third-highest budget, reflecting the military intensity of its ongoing conflict in Ukraine.

Among other major spenders, India ranks fifth, with a military budget of US$ 86.1 billion, accounting for 2.3% of its GDP and 3.2% of global defence spending, showcasing its growing strategic importance and modernization goals. European nations such as Germany, France, and the United Kingdom maintain relatively moderate spending in absolute terms but collectively contribute to a significant share of NATO's overall military capability. Notably, Ukraine, though ranked eighth, spends a staggering 34% of its GDP on defence due to its ongoing war, underlining the extraordinary economic burden of prolonged conflict. Saudi Arabia and Israel also allocate very high percentages of their GDPs — 7.3% and 8.8% respectively — underscoring their prioritization of military strength in a volatile regional environment.

The bottom half of the top fifteen spenders in Table 2 includes countries like Japan, South Korea, Poland, Italy, and Australia, all of which maintain significant defence budgets but within a more modest percentage of their GDPs, typically between 1.4% and 2.6%, except for Poland, which stands out with 4.2%. This suggests that while these nations invest in military modernization and readiness, their spending is relatively balanced with broader fiscal considerations. Overall, the 2024 data reflect both geopolitical tensions and regional security imperatives, with countries like Ukraine, Russia, Israel, and Saudi Arabia spending heavily relative to their economies, while major powers like China and Japan maintain strong capabilities with relatively restrained defence-to-GDP ratios.

Table 2. Countries with the highest military spending worldwide in 2024

Rank	Country	Defence spending (US$ bn)	Percentage share of defence spending in GDP of the Country	Percentage share of global defence spending of the country
1	United States	997.0	3.4	37.0
2	China	314.0	1.7	12.0
3	Russia	149.0	7.1	5.5
4	Germany	88.5	1.9	3.3
5	India	86.1	2.3	3.2
6	United Kingdom	81.8	2.3	3.0
7	Saudi Arabia	80.3	7.3	3.0
8	Ukraine	64.7	34.0	2.4
9	France	64.7	2.1	2.4
10	Japan	55.3	1.4	2.0
11	South Korea	47.6	2.6	1.8
12	Israel	46.5	8.8	1.7
13	Poland	38.0	4.2	1.4
14	Italy	38.0	1.6	1.4
15	Australia	33.8	1.9	1.2

Stockholm International Peace Research Institute. (2025, April)

Components of Defence Expenditure

Most analyses of India's military expenditure focus primarily on the budget allocated to the defence services, which covers both current and capital expenses of the army, navy, and air force, along with research and development. In the fiscal year 2010–11, this portion amounted to ₹1,473 billion (approximately $32.2 billion). However, SIPRI's assessment of India's total military spending takes a broader view by also incorporating the 'defence civil estimates' and spending on paramilitary forces. The 'defence civil estimates' encompass expenditures by the Ministry of Defence's central administration and military pensions, which totaled 284 billion (about $6.2 billion) in the same fiscal year. Additionally, spending on paramilitary forces—playing a key role in internal security operations such as counterinsurgency against Naxalite groups—has surged since 2001, reaching 153 billion ($3.3 billion) by 2010–11.

Some components of defence expenditure as have been pointed out by PRS Legislative Research (2025) are discussed below.

Army Expenditure

The Indian Army, being the largest of the three services in terms of personnel, allocates a substantial portion of its budget to revenue expenditure—primarily for salaries, pensions, and operational costs. In 2025-26, about 80% of its budget is expected to go toward such expenses. The Standing Committee on Defence has repeatedly noted the Army's slow pace in modernising its equipment, with only 15% of current holdings considered "new generation." Despite plans for over 500 modernisation schemes over the next 15 years, budget allocations remain a limiting factor. Additionally, delays in acquiring essential gear for troops in high-altitude zones have raised operational readiness concerns.

Navy Expenditure

The Indian Navy plays a dual role in addressing both traditional threats from hostile nations and non-traditional challenges like piracy. Its capital spending has grown significantly since 2020-21, with ongoing construction of 65 ships and submarines. However, key projects like the submarine acquisition under Project-75 have faced significant delays, some spanning several years. The Navy also struggles with shortages in aircraft and reconnaissance helicopters. The Standing Committee has emphasized the need for timely procurement to bolster India's maritime dominance, especially in the Indian Ocean Region.

Air Force Expenditure

The Air Force consistently receives the highest share of the modernisation budget among the three services. However, its capital allocation is still considered insufficient, especially given the urgent need to replace its ageing fleet. India's indigenous Light Combat Aircraft (LCA) project, launched in 1983, has seen prolonged delays, with the first aircraft entering service only in 2016. Currently, the Air Force operates 31 fighter squadrons against the sanctioned strength of 42, with more reductions expected as older aircraft are phased out. The Standing Committee has urged that delays in indigenous manufacturing be addressed, and that over-the-counter purchases of advanced aircraft be considered if necessary.

Key Issues in Defence Expenditure in India

Here is a concise paragraph on each key issue related to India's defence expenditure (PRS Legislative Research, 2025).

Heavy Dependence on Arms Imports Despite Rising Indigenous Efforts: India has long maintained its position as the world's largest importer of arms, accounting for 10% of global arms imports between 2013 and 2023, as per SIPRI. While there have been efforts to reduce reliance on foreign suppliers—reflected in only six of the 271 capital acquisition contracts being signed with overseas vendors in 2023-24 and early 2024-25—a significant portion of defence modernisation still depends on imports. In 2023-24, 28% of modernisation spending was directed toward foreign procurement. Committees such as the Standing Committee on Defence have highlighted the strategic risks of such dependence, especially during emergencies when foreign suppliers may not deliver critical hardware.

Lengthy Procurement Process and Need for Faster Acquisition: The procurement of defence equipment in India remains a time-consuming process, with acquisition timelines ranging from 19 to 26 months. Such delays can result in outdated technologies being inducted into service, thereby weakening national defence readiness. The Defence Acquisition Procedure (DAP), 2020, was introduced to enhance domestic content and streamline processes, but the long procurement cycle continues to be a concern. The Ministry has been advised to explore ways to expedite these processes, especially given changing geopolitical scenarios that may disrupt traditional supply chains.

Growth in Indigenous Production Overshadowed by Quality Issues: India's domestic defence production has grown steadily at about 8% annually since 2016-17, reaching ₹1.27 lakh crore in 2023-24. However, this growth has been marred by concerns regarding product quality, particularly from the erstwhile Ordnance Factory Board. Audits by the Comptroller and Auditor General (CAG) have reported several instances of accidents involving domestically produced small arms due to defects in materials and non-adherence to specifications. High overhead costs and failed R&D efforts further led the armed forces to rely on imports to fill capability gaps during 2016-2019.

Rise in Defence Exports, But Global Share Remains Small: India's defence exports have seen significant growth—rising from ₹1,522 crore in 2016-17 to ₹21,083 crore in 2023-24—driven mainly by the private sector. Items exported include missiles, radars, and armoured vehicles to over 85 countries. Despite this progress, India's share in global arms exports remains negligible at just 0.2% during 2016-2023. The government has set an ambitious export target of ₹35,000 crore by 2025. To meet this, Defence Public Sector Undertakings (DPSUs) need to ramp up innovation and compete effectively in terms of pricing and technology in global markets.

Decline in Budget Allocation for Research and Delays in DRDO Projects:The share of the defence budget allocated to research and development (R&D) has dropped from 4.7% in 2014-15 to 3.9% in 2025-26 (estimated), even as the Defence Research and Development Organisation (DRDO) shoulders the responsibility for indigenous innovation in key defence technologies. Audit reports show widespread delays in DRDO projects—119 out of 178 studied projects exceeded their timelines, often without meeting core objectives. This has led to cost overruns and limited capabilities for the armed forces. Strengthening DRDO's internal review mechanisms and investing more in R&D is essential to build self-reliant and modern defence capabilities.

Relation between Defence Expenditure and GDP of India: Econometric Relation

We first check the unit root test for defence expenditure (DEFEXP) and GDP to check the stationarity. The Dickey-Fuller test shows that there is unit root for both the series. We then check the unit root test for first difference of both the series to check for the stationarity. The Dickey-Fuller test shows that there is no unit root for both the series, meaning the first difference of both the series is stationary. As both the defence expenditure and GDP are stationary at first difference i.e. integrated of order (1) as given in Table 3, we run the OLS regression of defence expenditure on GDP and find the significant impact of GDP on defence expenditure.

To check whether there is cointegrating relationship between defence expenditure and GDP, we generate the residual series (RESID01) from the previous OLS regression and check the stationarity. To know if these pairs of variables are cointegrated, we verify that the residuals are cointegrated. We find from the Dickey-Fuller test that the residual series has no unit root i.e. the series is stationary at the level.

This shows that the co integration between the variables is valid. The cointegration reflects the presence of a long-run equilibrium the variables.

Table 3. Results of augmented Dickey-Fuller test for the variables considered in the analysis

	t-Statistic	**MacKinnon (1996) one-sided p-values.**
Null Hypothesis: *lnDEFEXP* has a unit root	-2.047	0.2662
Null Hypothesis: *D(lnDEFEXP)* has a unit root	-6.13218	0.000
Null Hypothesis: *lnGDP* has a unit root	-1.165	0.6883
Null Hypothesis: *D(lnGDP)* has a unit root	-3.61223	0.0000.

On the basis of the estimated results for the relation between *lnDEFEXP* and *lnGDP* given in Eq.(1), we may write the estimated cointegrating relationship as

$$lnDEFEXP = -2.41^{*} + 0.901^{*}\ lnGDP$$

Sig = (0.00) (0.00)
Adj R-squared = 0.9968

The above equation provides the long run relationship between defence expenditure and GDP of India . The estimated coefficients are significant at 1% level of significance (denoted by *). The slope coefficient (0.901) represents long run elasticity of defence expenditure to change in GDP. The value of elasticity has been found to be 0.901 indicating thereby that GDP influences defence expenditure by 12.9%. The result reveal that 99 percent variation in defence expenditure have been explained by GDP.

As the above cointegrating relationship has been validated by the ADF unit root test for residuals, we look into the results of estimated ECM of Eq. 2, which may be summarized as follows.

$$D(lnDEFEXP) = 0.079 + 0.254D(lnGDP) - 0.181(\text{res})_{t-1}$$

Sig = (0.018) (0.330) (0.053)
Adj R-squared = 0.0373

Here the value of lambda is negative and significant. This means if there is any short-term disturbance, long run stable relationship will be restored.

CONCLUSION

The study reveals that India's defence expenditure trajectory has been shaped by a complex interplay of historical legacies, strategic compulsions, fiscal constraints, and institutional reforms. From early dependence on the UK and public sector-led industrialisation under the 1956 Industrial Policy to the diversification of procurement sources and post-Kargil modernisation push, India's defence strategy has evolved to meet both conventional and emerging security threats. The expenditure patterns indicate a transition from revenue-heavy budgets focused on salaries and maintenance, toward increasing capital outlays directed at force modernization and indigenous production. However, while absolute defence spending has grown substantially, its share in both total government expenditure and GDP has steadily declined, reflecting a structural rebalancing of fiscal priorities toward welfare and infrastructure needs. This shift underscores the challenge of sustaining military preparedness while addressing developmental demands in a growing economy.

Furthermore, the econometric analysis confirms a long-term equilibrium relationship between GDP and defence spending, suggesting that economic growth remains a key determinant of military expenditure. Yet, India's defence sector faces several persistent issues: a high dependence on imports, inefficiencies in procurement, R&D delays, and concerns over the quality of domestic production. While reforms under the Atmanirbhar Bharat initiative—such as increased private participation, technological innovation, and support for start-ups—signal a promising shift toward self-reliance, significant hurdles remain. The establishment of institutional mechanisms like the CDS and integrated theatre commands further strengthens India's defence posture. Going forward, sustaining these reforms, increasing R&D investments, and enhancing export competitiveness will be crucial for India to secure its strategic autonomy and emerge as a global player in defence manufacturing.

REFERENCES

Abbas, S., & Wizarat, S. (2018). Military expenditure and external debt in South Asia: A panel data analysis. *Peace Economics, Peace. Science & Public Policy, 24*(3).

Abdel-Khalek, G., Mazloum, M. G., & El Zeiny, M. R. M. (2020). Military expenditure and economic growth: The case of India. *Review of Economics and Political Science, 5*(2), 116–135. DOI: 10.1108/REPS-03-2019-0025

Aizenman, J., & Glick, R. (2006). Military expenditure, threats, and growth. *The Journal of International Trade & Economic Development, 15*(2), 129–155. DOI: 10.1080/09638190600689095

Amir-ud-Din, R., Sajjad, F. W., & Aziz, S. (2020). Revisiting arms race between India and Pakistan: A case of asymmetric causal relationship of military expenditures. *Defence and Peace Economics, 31*(6), 721–741. DOI: 10.1080/10242694.2019.1624334

Azam, M., Khan, F., Zaman, K., & Rasli, A. M. (2016). Military expenditures and unemployment nexus for selected South Asian countries. *Social Indicators Research, 127*(3), 1103–1117. DOI: 10.1007/s11205-015-0993-7

Ball, N. (1983). Military Expenditure, Economic Growth, and Socio-economic Development in the Third World. *Iberoamericana–Nordic Journal of Latin American and Caribbean Studies, 12*(1-2).

Ball, N. (1983). Military expenditure and socio-economic development. *International Social Science Journal, 35*(95), 411–429.

Behera, L. K. (2013). *Indian defence industry: Issues of self-reliance* (IDSA Monograph Series No. 21). Institute for Defence Studies and Analyses.

Behera, L. K., & Nayak, P. M. (2021). India's Defence Expenditure: A Trend Analysis. *Strategic Analysis, 45*(5), 395–410. DOI: 10.1080/09700161.2021.1965343

Berthelemy, J. C., Herrera, R., & Sen, S. (1995). Military expenditure and economic development: An endogenous growth perspective. *Economics of Planning, 28*(2), 205–233. DOI: 10.1007/BF01263638

Bhagwati, J. (2019). *The Promise of India: How Prime Ministers Nehru to Modi Shaped the Nation (1947–2019)*. Penguin Random House India Private Limited.

Bhattacharyya, R. (2018). Relationship Between Military Expenditure, Economic Growth, and Social Expenditure in India, China, and Bangladesh. In *Handbook of Research on Military Expenditure on Economic and Political Resources* (pp. 285–306). IGI Global.

Budhathoki, P. B., Dahal, A. K., & Bhattarai, G. (2024). Does the military expenditure hurt the economic growth? *Journal of Business and Management Review, 5*(3), 189–204.

Chakraborty, S. (2018). The Impact of Military Spending on Economic Development: A Study of the Indian Economy. In *Handbook of Research on Military Expenditure on Economic and Political Resources* (pp. 182–191). IGI Global. DOI: 10.4018/978-1-5225-4778-5.ch010

Das, K. (2019). Terrorism, Military Expenditure, and Foreign Capital Inflow: An Empirical Study for India. In *The Impact of Global Terrorism on Economic and Political Development* (pp. 279–291). Emerald Publishing.

Datta, K. (2019). Military expenditure and economic growth relationship revisited in some South Asian countries: with special reference to India. In *National Security: Breakthroughs in Research and Practice* (pp. 810–835). IGI Global. DOI: 10.4018/978-1-5225-7912-0.ch041

Deger, S., & Sen, S. (1983). Military expenditure, spin-off and economic development. *Journal of Development Economics, 13*(1-2), 67–83. DOI: 10.1016/0304-3878(83)90050-0

Deger, S., & Sen, S. (1995). Military expenditure and developing countries. In Hartley, K., & Sandler, T. (Eds.), *Handbook of Defence Economics* (Vol. 1, pp. 275–307). Elsevier.

Doval, A. (2022). Tackling adversaries through strong and effective national security policies. In BlueKraft Digital Foundation (Ed.), *Modi@20: Dreams meet delivery* (pp. [insert page numbers]). Rupa Publications.

Dunne, J. P., Smith, R. P., & Willenbockel, D. (2005). Models of military expenditure and growth: A critical review. *Defence and Peace Economics, 16*(6), 449–461. DOI: 10.1080/10242690500167791

Guo, Z., Jiang, Y., & Yu, H. (2013). Defence expenditure, budget deficits, and income distribution in India (1970–2009). In *Cooperation for a Peaceful and Sustainable World Part 2* (pp. 25–37). Emerald Group Publishing Limited. DOI: 10.1108/S1572-8323(2013)00020.2006

Gupta, D., & Sriram, K. (2018). Impact of security expenditures in military alliances on violence from non-state actors: Evidence from India. *World Development, 107*, 338–357. DOI: 10.1016/j.worlddev.2018.03.004

Gupta, S., De Mello, L., & Sharan, R. (2001). Corruption and military spending. *European Journal of Political Economy*, *17*(4), 749–777. DOI: 10.1016/S0176-2680(01)00054-4

Hou, N. (2010). *Arms race, military expenditure and economic growth in India* (Doctoral dissertation, University of Birmingham).

Ismail, S. (2017). Military expenditure and economic growth in South Asian countries: Empirical evidences. *International Journal of Economics and Financial Issues*, *7*(3), 318–325.

Jalil, A., Abbasi, H. K. N., & Bibi, N. (2016). Military expenditures and economic growth: Allowing structural breaks in time series analysis in the case of India and Pakistan. *Quality & Quantity*, *50*(4), 1487–1505. DOI: 10.1007/s11135-015-0217-x

Jana, S. K., Karmakar, A. K., & Maiti, A. (2018). Military Expenditure in India: Trends and Its Relation With GDP and Education Expenditure. In *Handbook of Research on Military Expenditure on Economic and Political Resources* (pp. 367–381). IGI Global.

Khalid, M. A., & Mustapha, A. B. (2014). Long-run relationships and causality tests between military expenditure and economic growth in India. *The Economics and Finance Letters*, *1*(6), 49–58. DOI: 10.18488/journal.29/2014.1.4/29.4.49.58

Khatter, P. (2025). *Union Budget: 2025–26, government continues modernization efforts and enhancement of indigenisation in defence sector*. Ernst & Young LLP.

Kumar, G. (2017). Countries military expenditures: Definitions and determinants. *Economic Affairs*, *62*(4), 647–654. DOI: 10.5958/0976-4666.2017.00078.X

Mansoob Murshed, S., & Mamoon, D. (2010). Not loving thy neighbour as thyself: Trade, democracy and military expenditure explanations underlying India—Pakistan rivalry. *Journal of Peace Research*, *47*(4), 463–476. DOI: 10.1177/0022343310364577

Markowski, S., Chand, S., & Wylie, R. (2017). Economic growth and demand for military expenditure in the Indo-Pacific Asia region. *Defence and Peace Economics*, *28*(4), 473–490. DOI: 10.1080/10242694.2016.1274059

Mukhopadhyay, D., & Das, D. (2018). FDI inflows and military expenditure: A study across the emerging market economies. In *Handbook of Research on Military Expenditure on Economic and Political Resources* (pp. 211–225). IGI Global. DOI: 10.4018/978-1-5225-4778-5.ch012

Mukhopadhyay, P., Sinha, M., & Sengupta, P. P. (2018). Public Expenditure on Defence and Economic Development: A Comparative Study on India and China. In *Handbook of Research on Military Expenditure on Economic and Political Resources* (pp. 170–181). IGI Global.

Nair, P. (2009). An Evaluation of India's Defence Expenditure. *Economic and Political Weekly*, 40–46.

Narang, R. K. (2024, Sep). *Military–civil technology fusion (MCTF) for making India Atmanirbhar: Global drone hub @2030* (MP-IDSA Monograph Series No. 87). Manohar Parrikar Institute for Defence Studies and Analyses.

Öcal, N. (2003). Are the military expenditures of India and Pakistan external determinants for each other: An empirical investigation. *Defence and Peace Economics*, *14*(2), 141–149. DOI: 10.1080/10242690302917

Patra, S. (2018). Trend and Impact of Military Expenditure on Economic Growth in South Asia. In *Handbook of Research on Military Expenditure on Economic and Political Resources* (pp. 253–269). IGI Global. DOI: 10.4018/978-1-5225-4778-5.ch014

Perlo-Freeman, S., Ismail, O., & Solmirano, C. (2010). Military expenditure. In *SIPRI Yearbook 2009* (pp. 179–211). Stockholm International Peace Research Institute.

Perlo-Freeman, S., Solmirano, C., & Wilandh, H. (2013). Global developments in military expenditure. *SIPRI Yearbook*, *2013*, 127–134.

Pieroni, L. (2009). Military expenditure and economic growth. *Defence and Peace Economics*, *20*(4), 327–339. DOI: 10.1080/10242690701589876

Pradhan, R. P., Arvin, M. B., Norman, N. R., & Bhinder, H. K. (2013). Military expenditure and economic growth: Using causality, cointegration and missing variables. *International Journal of Computational Economics and Econometrics*, *3*(3-4), 164–186. DOI: 10.1504/IJCEE.2013.058496

PRS Legislative Research. (2025). *Demand for Grants 2025-26 Analysis: Defence*. https://prsindia.org

Raju, M. H., & Ahmed, Z. (2019). Effect of military expenditure on economic growth: Evidences from India Pakistan and China using cointegration and causality analysis. *Asian Journal of German and European Studies*, *4*(1), 3. DOI: 10.1186/s40856-019-0040-6

Raza, S. A., Shahbaz, M., & Paramati, S. R. (2017). Dynamics of military expenditure and income inequality in Pakistan. *Social Indicators Research, 131*(3), 1035–1055. DOI: 10.1007/s11205-016-1284-7

Reserve Bank of India. (2025). Major heads of expenditure of the central government. Government of India. https://rbi.org.in/scripts/PublicationsView.aspx?id=21190

Sandler, T., & George, J. (2016). Military expenditure trends for 1960–2014 and what they reveal. *Global Policy*, *7*(2), 174–184. DOI: 10.1111/1758-5899.12328

Sasidhar, M. (2024). Balancing Defence and Diplomacy: A Deep Strategic Analysis of India's Military Expenditure and Its Impact on Global Peace *SSRN* 5240582.

Shah, S. A., He, C., Makhijani, H. B., & Shah, M. (2015). Arms race, economic growth, and government expenditure: Empirical investigation for India and Pakistan. *Journal of Economics and Sustainable Development*, *6*(6), 23–30.

Sharma, D., & Phulli, K. (2020). Forecasting and Analyzing the Military Expenditure of India Using Box-Jenkins ARIMA Model. *arXiv preprint arXiv:2011.06060.*

Singh, R. P. (2014). Building advanced defence technology capacity. In Debroy, B., Tellis, A. J., & Trevor, R. (Eds.), *Getting India back on track: An action agenda for reform* (pp. 281–294). Carnegie Endowment for International Peace. DOI: 10.2307/j.ctt1n2ttcb.21

Sköns, E., Allebeck, A. C., Loose-Weintraub, E., & Stålenheim, P. (1999). Military expenditure. *SIPRI Yearbook*, 269–350.

Srinivas, V. N. (2006). Trends in Defence Expenditure: India, China and Pakistan. *Air Power Journal*, *3*(1), 63–82.

Stålenheim, P., Perdomo, C., & Sköns, E. (2008). Military expenditure. *SIPRI Yearbook*, 175–206.

Stockholm International Peace Research Institute. (2025, Apr). *Trends in military expenditure 2024* [PDF]. https://www.sipri.org

UR, R. (2022). Military Expenditure and Economic Growth: Evidence from India and Pakistan. *Research Journal of Humanities and Social Sciences*, *13*(1), 12–16.

Ward, M. D., Davis, D., Penubarti, M., Rajmaira, S., & Cochran, M. (1991). Country survey I–military spending in India. *Defence and Peace Economics*, *3*(1), 41–63. DOI: 10.1080/10430719108404714

Ward, M. D., & Mahajan, A. K. (1984). Defence expenditures, security threats, and governmental deficits: A case study of India, 1952–1979. *The Journal of Conflict Resolution*, *28*(3), 382–419. DOI: 10.1177/0022002784028003002

Zhu, Z. (2024, Dec). Analysis and Forecasting of India's Defence Expenditure. In *2024 9th International Conference on Modern Management, Education and Social Sciences (MMET 2024)* (pp. 835–843). Atlantis Press.

Chapter 4

Defense Expenditures and Economic Growth of Countries of the World: Determinants and Channels of Interrelations

Nika Chitadze
https://orcid.org/0000-0003-2806-6426
International Black Sea University, Tbilisi, Georgia

ABSTRACT

This study is devoted to assessing the relationship between the dynamics of defense spending in countries worldwide and their economic growth. This problem is becoming increasingly relevant as geopolitical conflicts in the modern world intensify. Within the framework of this chapter of the book, global defense spending and key channels of influence of defense spending on the development of individual national economies are assessed, the main structural and dynamic changes in defense spending in the context of an unstable geopolitical situation are shown, and aspects of increasing defense spending in the context of the economic problems that developed countries are currently facing are demonstrated.

INTRODUCTION

The relationship between defense spending and economic growth in various countries has traditionally been the subject of close study, but first of all, it is necessary to mention the breakthrough works in this area that appeared about twenty years ago. Empirical studies of economic growth in the early 1990s led to the erroneous

DOI: 10.4018/979-8-3373-3456-1.ch004

assumption that scientific and technological progress is constant over time and uniform across countries, although this hypothesis was later refuted (Aziz, 2017). More recent studies indicate that the intensity of defense spending can have both positive and negative effects on the dynamics of gross domestic product (GDP). In the least developed countries, as noted in some studies, a highly positive relationship is found between defense spending and the dynamics of economic growth, while, for example, inward foreign investment (FDI) does not significantly affect economic growth. In addition, some evidence has emerged in the literature in recent years on the existence of a positive relationship between democratization and a decrease in defense spending, based on an assessment of various channels of interaction that link defense spending with the development of democratic political institutions. The absence of a single, coherent, and consistent theory of economic growth makes it difficult to establish clear relationships between defense spending and GDP dynamics, as well as to integrate defense spending into such a unified structure (if it existed). This is surprising since defense spending has always been an important item of total spending (i.e., dependent on GDP), despite the decline in its share in developed countries compared to, for example, socially significant sectors. The goal of our study is to analyze the changes that have historically been observed in the relationship between defense spending and economic growth, as well as the main determinants of these relationships in the context of modern geopolitical conflicts and the unstable state of the world economy.

Modern Unpredictable World

The modern world has become explosive and unpredictable. Global changes are underway, such as those that have occurred several times over the past century after the First and Second World Wars and the collapse of the Soviet Union. The nature of military confrontation is also changing. For example, local wars and armed conflicts during the so-called Cold War or the Iron Curtain were not accompanied by such intense confrontation and rhetoric between the world's leading, especially nuclear, states as we are now observing. Russia's invasion of Ukraine was followed by economic sanctions from the West, the likes of which history does not remember. The global security system created in the second half of the twentieth century has effectively collapsed. The global security architecture was based on fundamental arms control agreements and treaties: the Nuclear Test Ban Treaty (1963), the Nuclear Non-Proliferation Treaty (1968), the Anti-Ballistic Missile Treaty (1972), the Strategic Arms Limitation Treaty (1979), the Intermediate-Range Nuclear Forces Treaty (1987), the Conventional Armed Forces in Europe Treaty (1990), the Strategic Arms Reduction Treaty (1991), the Strategic Arms Reduction Treaty (2001) (signed, but not yet in force, although other additional agreements were concluded - 1993), the Strategic Offensive Potential Treaty on Reduction (2002), Strategic Offensive Arms Reduction Treaty - 3 (2010) (Cavatorta & sMITH 2017). Of the above-mentioned agreements, only the treaties on nuclear weapons testing and proliferation remain in force. However, given Russia's recent statement, the practice of nuclear weapons testing may resume. By the decision of the Russian President, Russia suspended the Strategic Offensive Arms Reduction Treaty - 3 (Cooper, 2022). There is no dialogue between Russia and the West. Diplomatic relations are at zero. In this situation, the suspension of another arms control treaty by Russia further aggravates the geopolitical background.

The Situation in the World, Factors, and Trends in the Growth of Military Spending

Analysis of the trends in wars in recent years shows that military confrontation requires the full, total mobilization of resources from the states participating in the conflict, the readiness of the economy for war, and a large number of military-technical and mobilization resources. In new wars, ultimately, success will go to the side that has more resources and greater resilience in the face of challenges. For example, we can cite the 44-day confrontation between Azerbaijan and Armenia in 2020. The results of the war were influenced not only by military art, the intervention of the international community, or other factors but also by the difference in resources. This includes both human resources and the quantity of weapons and equipment, the qualitative difference, and the stocks of ammunition. Russia's unprovoked war in Ukraine also shows the same trend. Enormous resources are being spent on both sides. Ukraine's resilience and success are largely determined by the international community's unity against Russian aggression and the provision of colossal assistance to Ukraine. In 2022-2024, Ukraine received at least more than $200 billion in assistance (Dorn et al., 2024). The Russian government most likely did not expect to find such large-scale support for Ukraine.

What is the Impact of Military Spending on Economic Development?

There is no unambiguous answer to this question. However, to illustrate the direct connection between military spending and economic development, economists cite several examples.

As some experts argue, it increased military spending in the 1930s that pulled the US economy out of the Great Depression.

The same can be said about fascist Germany. According to experts, it was the increased military spending and the military-industrial complex that became the main locomotive of the German economy at that time. In part, experts link the growing military spending to the economic achievements of the United States before the spread of Covid. As economic commentators note, the increase in military spending also made a certain contribution to the 2.9% growth of the US economy in 2017 (D'Agostino et al., 2019). As indicated in the analysis of the US Department of Commerce, the effect of military spending on overall economic growth exceeded 0.31 percentage points (D'Agostino et al., 2019).

New jobs, the development of infrastructure, and modern technologies - according to experts, all this is directly related to military spending. However, it is necessary to maintain a certain balance and properly distribute financial resources, otherwise, we will end up with what happened to the Soviet Union. They say that it was the growing armaments and increasing military spending that caused the economic collapse of the Soviet Union.

World War II as an Example of the Successful Attraction of Internal Financial Resources

The experience of World War II shows that spending significant funds relative to the size of one's GDP is a feasible task. In desperate times, Germany and Japan spent more than 70% of their GDP on the war (Chitadze, 2011). Great Britain and the USA were not far behind, maintaining expenditures at the level of half of the gross domestic product. How exactly did these countries manage to achieve this?

Realizing the vulnerability of their position and the need to make quick decisions, economists in Western countries were already thinking about ways to attract a colossal amount of funds to finance defense at the beginning of the war. And, of course, they were interested in the possible macroeconomic consequences of these or those options.

The two most effective options are a certain combination of government bonds and tax increases. Other options, such as emission, do not work so well: these solutions are short-term and create critical imbalances in the country's economy, which will inevitably "come back to haunt them" sooner or later.

Option 1: Government Bonds

British economist John M. Keynes argued in his 1940 essay "How to Pay for the War" that the best solution to finance a war was to strongly encourage households, especially high-income households, to save and buy government bonds (Alptekin, 2012).

For Keynes, the advantage of such a strategy was the ability to spread the burden of paying back the cost of the bonds with interest over 20-40 years. The population had the option of long-term investment with a guarantee from the state, and the state received the funds it needed here and now. However, Keynes believed that Britain would not be able to finance the war by borrowing alone, and therefore the optimal strategy was a certain combination of war bonds and taxes (Kollias & Paleologou, 2019).

It is not known for sure whether Franklin D. Roosevelt read this essay, but it was during World War II that the United States had a similar structure for financing the war. About 40% of the war expenses were paid for by taxes, and the rest by borrowing and emissions (Malizard, 2015).

Historical Background. Series E bond is the name of the US Treasury Department government bonds issued from 1941 to 1945. Roosevelt himself bought the first bond to popularize this type of investment. Overall, the government managed to effectively use this instrument: during 7 issues of the war loan (War Loan Drives), 85 million Americans bought bonds for $185.7 billion (Saeed, 2023). Borrowing from citizens helped the United States finance more than a quarter of budget expenditures during the war (Saeed, 2023).

This is fairly typical of the history of U.S. war financing. Except for the Korean War, most wars have been financed primarily through borrowing:

Option 2: Taxes

If government bonds fail to raise enough money, the next best option is to increase taxes. However, there are a few caveats: the tax must be on luxury consumption, the rate must be progressive, and the increase must be gradual and non-aggressive, otherwise the policy risks discouraging citizens from working and saving.

So, the theory emphasizes the significant role of borrowing in maintaining stable war financing.

Defense Budget Planning. Military, also known as defense budget planning, its formation is an important component of the military policy of any state. The parameters of the military spending of states are used to assess how militarized a country, region, or the world is. The trend of increasing military spending continues. It is worth noting that in 2024, the total military spending of all countries amounted to a record - 2.46 trillion US dollars (CNBC, 2025). The structure of military spending of any state, the study of the dynamics of its changes, maintaining spending at a stable level, or decreasing or increasing, allows specialists to draw many conclusions. When studying the structure of spending, attention is paid to what components the emphasis is placed on developing, whether surplus stocks are accumulated, etc. Military spending - these are the financial expenditures of the state to prepare the defense forces for military operations, as well as to fully provide them, both in peacetime and during military operations. In general, the following factors influence the trend of expenditure growth: inflation, price increases for armaments; tense geopolitical situations; the nature of recent wars and conflicts; and bets on modern weapons and high technologies. The state's military spending should allow: to ensure the equipment of the defense forces with modern weapons, equipment, equipment, and adequate supplies of ammunition; to create a military-material base for the defense forces; to develop the local military industry; to develop modern military technologies; to create a base for the socio-economic support of military personnel. The growth of military spending directly depends, on the one hand, on the geopolitical situation, the threats and risks facing the state, and on the other hand, on the economic development of the state.

Analysis of the military spending of any country, the dynamics of changes, growth or decrease, and budget priorities allows us to assess the following: are the threats facing this particular country increasing or decreasing? Of course, this will be a view of these authorities and not assessments seen from the outside. Analysis of military spending priorities also allows for different conclusions. In military spending, it is seen whether the emphasis is on the social problems of the army and military in a particular country, or the combat component, ground component, aviation, defensive armament, or vice versa, offensive. The analysis also shows that the deficit in existing stocks is being filled, surplus stocks are being created, the standard armament is being replenished, or any component is being strengthened, even in comparison with neighboring countries.

The United States remains the world's largest military spender. In 2003, the US defense budget was \$368 billion, and in 2024 it will be \$968 billion, although it is worth noting that the Trump administration, which was re-elected as US president in 2024, plans to reduce the defense budget by 8% annually (SCTO, 2025).

Defense Spending to Increase in 2023-2024

Global defense spending reaches record high - Almost half of it is spent by the United States and China.

In 2023, global military spending increased by 6.8% to a record \$2.443 trillion, or 2.3% of global GDP, (Stockholm International Peace Research Institute - SIPRI, 2024). This was the largest increase since 2009 and the highest level of global defense spending ever recorded.

"The increase in global military spending in 2023 can be attributed primarily to the ongoing war in Ukraine and the escalation of geopolitical tensions in Asia, Oceania, and the Middle East. This trend is observed in all five geographic regions, with the strongest growth in Europe, Asia Oceania, and the Middle East.

The top 5 countries that spent the most on defense in 2023 remained the same as in 2022.

1. USA — $916 billion, or 3.4% of national GDP. In 2022 — $877 billion, or 3.5% of GDP.
2. China — $296 billion, or 1.7% of GDP. In 2022 — $292 billion, or the same 1.7% of GDP.
3. Russia — $109 billion, or 5.9% of GDP. In 2022 — $86.4 billion, or 4.1% of GDP.
4. India — $83.6 billion, or 2.4% of GDP. In 2022 — $81.4 billion, or also 2.4% of GDP.
5. Saudi Arabia — $75.8 billion, or 7.1% of GDP. In 2022 — $75 billion, or 7.4% of GDP (SIPRI, 2023).

The United States and China together accounted for almost half of global defense spending in 2023, at 37% and 12% of the global total, respectively (SIPRI, 2023). The United States spends three times more than China; Washington's priority area is research, development, test, and evaluation (RDT&E), where it spent 9.4% more than in 2022. "This is consistent with the [U.S.] decision to shift its focus from counter-insurgency operations and asymmetric warfare to developing new weapons systems that could be used in potential conflict with adversaries with advanced military capabilities" (SIPRI, 2023).

Beijing's spending increased by 6% compared to 2022. China accounts for half of all military spending in Asia and Oceania (Chitadze, 2024). Experts note that China is provoking other countries in the region to also spend more on defense — they perceive China's growing military power as a reason to strengthen its military potential. Beijing has been increasing its spending continuously for the past 29 years, but the pace has slowed over the past 10 years, which is due to the slowing growth of the Chinese economy.

Russia's military spending in 2023 increased by 24% compared to 2022 and by 57% compared to 2014 (Chitadze, 2024). However, these figures are "highly uncertain" due to the growing opacity of the Russian financial system. In addition to the state budget, funds for the military come from such extra-budgetary sources as enterprises, individuals, and organizations - and although these contributions are much smaller than the official budget, the estimates may be underestimated.

"Russia's military spending growth in 2023 was largely driven by Russia's economic performance, which exceeded expectations despite a significant drop in the country's oil and gas revenues" (SIPRI, 2023). Based on the Russian state budget for 2024-2026, it can be predicted that Moscow will continue to increase its military spending in the coming years. India's spending increased by 4.2% in 2023 compared to 2022. This is primarily due to the growth of operational costs and investments in personnel - in 2023, they accounted for almost 80% of the total military budget (SIPRI, 2023). It can be said that this is in line with the government's priority - to improve the operational readiness of its troops amid tensions with China and Pakistan. About 20% of the budget is spent on military purchases - three-quarters of these funds were spent on the acquisition of domestically produced equipment (SIPRI, 2023). This indicates that India's goal is to become a self-sufficient country in the development and production of weapons.

Saudi Arabia spent 4.3% more on defense in 2023 than in 2022 (SIPRI, 2023). It should be noted that the kingdom is the world's largest exporter of crude oil, and its military spending was partly financed by the fact that global oil prices and demand for this resource from outside Russia rose.

How many nuclear missiles do different countries have?

The top ten in defense spending also includes four more European countries and Japan.

6. The United Kingdom - $74.9 billion, or 2.3% of GDP. In 2022 - $68.5 billion, or 2.2% of GDP.
7. Germany - $66.8 billion, or 1.5% of GDP. In 2022 - $55.8 billion, or 1.4% of GDP.
8. Ukraine — $64.8 billion, or 37% of GDP. In 2022 — $44 billion, or 34% of GDP.
9. France — $61.3 billion, or 2.1% of GDP. In 2022 — $53.6 billion, or 1.9% of GDP.
10. Japan — $50.2 billion, or 1.2% of GDP. In 2022 — $46 billion, or 1.1% of GDP (SIPRI, 2023).

In total, the top ten accounted for 74% of global spending, or $1.799 trillion. The combined spending of 31 NATO members (the 32nd member, Sweden, joined the alliance in 2024) amounted to $1.341 trillion, or 55% of global spending; 68% of this investment is accounted for by the United States (SIPRI, 2023). Israel, which occupies 15th place, against the backdrop of the outbreak of the war with Hamas, Israel invested 24% more in defense in 2023 than in 2022, bringing its spending in this area to $27.5 billion; after Saudi Arabia, Israel is the second largest country in military spending in the Middle East (SIPRI, 2023).

With regard to 2024, Global defence spending as mentioned above increased to USD 2. 46 trillion. Much of this growth was driven by countries in Asia, Europe, the Middle East, and North Africa in response to rising threat perceptions (CNBC, 2025).

Top 15 Countries by Military Expenditures in 2024 in Billion USD.

USA-968
China- 235
Russia-145

Germany – 86
UK – 81
India- 74
Saudi Arabia – 72
France – 64
Japan – 52

S. Korea – 44

Australia – 36
Italy – 35
Israel- 34
Poland – 28
Ukraine -28 (CNBC, 2025)

Global Arms Exports in 2024 and for the Period 2021-2024

After considering the issue of global defense spending, Let's consider the rating of the twenty largest arms-exporting countries based on the results of 2024.

The rankings were distributed as follows:

1. USA – $42,329 billion (37.92%)
2. Russia – $13.75 billion (12.32%)
3. France – $7,698 billion (6.90%)
4. South Korea – $5,691 billion (5.10%)
5. Italy – $5,690 billion (5.10%)
6. Germany – $5,424 billion (4.86%)
7. Sweden – $4,254 billion (3.81%)
8. Israel – $4,163 billion (3.73%)
9. Norway – $3,293 billion (2.95%)
10. China – $3,216 billion (2.88%)
11. Spain – 3,152 billion dollars
12. Great Britain – $2.552 billion
13. Turkey – $2.536 billion
14. Netherlands – $2.183 billion
15. Australia – $1.107 billion
16. Switzerland – $757 million
17. Poland – $620 million
18. Canada – $454 million
19. India – $430 million

20. Brazil – $410 million (CSTO, 2025).

The presented rating takes into account only commercial contracts for the supply of weapons and military equipment to foreign customers; it does not include gratuitous military assistance that was and continues to be provided to Ukraine by the countries of the Western coalition. In 2024, the volume of world exports/imports of conventional arms (according to the UN Register classification) amounted to $111.615 billion, which is the highest result since the end of the Cold War era (CSTO, 2025).

All calculations are made in "current" US dollars, that is, at the dollar exchange rate at the time of concluding a particular contract in the prices of the corresponding year.

For comparison: in 2021, the volume of world exports of Arms amounted to $82.942 billion, in 2022 - $106.185 billion, and in 2023 - $96.889 billion (CSTO, 2025).

The sharp increase in world arms exports/imports is associated with several factors, including the situation around Ukraine. Having gotten rid of outdated weapons systems as part of military aid to Kyiv, the countries of the Western democratic community began large-scale purchases of modern and more expensive types of weapons. At the same time, the main beneficiary and benefiter in this situation was the United States of America, which practically monopolized the arms market of NATO member countries.

For comparison: in 2022, the global volume of exports/imports of conventional weapons (according to the classification of the UN Register) increased by 28% compared to 2021 (SCTO, 2025). This is a colossal one-time increase on an annual basis. It is explained, among other things, by the long period of escalation of the situation around Ukraine and the aggressive policy of Russia in the last three years before the invasion of Ukraine, as well as short-term contracts concluded after the start of military interventions. In 2023, the global volume of arms exports/imports increased by 16.8% compared to 2021 (although it decreased by 8.75% compared to 2022). This "rebound" was purely technical due to the fact that in 2022-2023 (SIPRI, 2023) deliveries were made under short-term contracts, while contracts with longer execution periods, concluded, among other things, based on the development of the situation around Ukraine, were still in the implementation stage.

In 2026 and beyond, to replace the equipment transferred to the Armed Forces of Ukraine, a number of countries of the Western coalition will carry out large purchases of more expensive weapons requiring a longer production cycle.

In general, over the past 4 years (2021-2024), the global volume of arms exports amounted to $ 397.631 billion (CSTO, 2025). The United States ranks first in terms of actual arms export volume in 2024. The volume of identified US military exports in 2024 was $42.329 billion, or 37.92% of the world's total military exports. 2024 was the third year in a row when the annual volume of US arms exports exceeded $40 billion (CSTO, 2025).

Along with reaching maximum volumes of export deliveries of expensive F-35 fighters, the record figures for the United States in 2022-2024 are largely associated, among other things, with the start of large-scale deliveries of modern American military equipment to allied countries to replace the outdated weapons they transferred as military aid to Kyiv. Almost all of Washington's allies are purchasing American fighters. For comparison: in 2021, the volume of identified American military exports amounted to $ 27.641 billion (33.33% of the world market), in 2022 - $ 42.619 billion (40.14% - this is the highest result for the United States in the last 4 years), in 2023 - $ 40.672 billion (41.98%), in 2024 - $ 42.329 billion (37.92%). In general, over the last 4-year period, the United States exported weapons worth $153.261 billion (38.54% of the world market) (CSTO, 2025).

Russia ranks second by the end of 2024 with arms exports estimated at $13.75 billion (12.32% of the world's total exports of military products) (CSTO, 2025).

It should be noted that due to the implementation of the Second World War, the Russian state defense order has increased many times over. Many export-oriented enterprises of the Russian defense industry have been partially re-profiled, primarily to fulfill the state defense order. A sharp increase in the production of military products to meet the needs of the Russian Armed Forces and at the same time maintain an acceptable level of export deliveries were achieved by switching the Russian defense (in reality, aggressive) industry to a "war footing". Thus, at present, the Russian defense industry is able to fulfill both the state defense order and export contracts. Due to Washington's tough and principled position regarding countries importing Russian weapons, the level of transparency of the data provided by the Russian Federation and JSC Rosoboronexport has certainly dropped sharply - to maintain the confidentiality of deliveries, so as not to "expose" importers of Russian weapons to possible secondary sanctions of the United States and the European Union.

With the start of military aggression against Ukraine, Russian official structures stopped publishing data on the implementation of export contracts for the supply of weapons and military equipment.

In general, it should be noted that due to Moscow's aggressive policy, the imposed Western sanctions affected the volume of Russian arms exports and forced the Russian Federation and foreign customers to seek alternative payment options for the supplied weapons and military equipment, to refuse to advertise both the types of weapons supplied and the customer countries, as well as specific volumes of deliveries. For Russia, the assessment of arms exports under identified contracts gradually lost its relevance after the adoption of the US Countering America's Adversaries Through Sanctions Act (CAATSA) in 2017. Since then, the transparency of the data provided regarding new contracts concluded for the export of Russian weapons and military equipment has been steadily declining every year, which automatically worsened Russia's performance in the world rankings of leading Western analytical centers monitoring the global arms market, including the Stockholm International Peace Research Institute (SIPRI), whose ratings regarding the Russian Federation are no longer verified. At the moment, due to the almost complete closure of relevant statistics, only an expert assessment can be given for Russia's indicators, in particular, based on the fact that, according to official data, the portfolio of Russian arms export orders as of the beginning of 2021 amounted to $ 55 billion (Chitadze, 2024). At the end of 2024, Alexander Mikheev, Director General of JSC Rosoboronexport, reported that the order portfolio of the company he heads had reached a record high of $57 billion and provides for the supply of Russian military products to 44 countries around the world (CSTO, 2025).

Taking into account several other entities, in addition to JSC Rosoboronexport, involved in military-technical cooperation between Russia and foreign countries, which have the right to independently supply spare parts to foreign customers, provide maintenance services, etc., the final portfolio of orders for the supply of Russian military equipment can be estimated at $60 billion (CSTO, 2025).

The increase in the order portfolio as a whole suggests that the volume of contracts concluded in the period under review was somewhat larger (but not significantly) than the actual volume of Russian arms exports.

In the foreseeable future, the main buyers of Russian weapons will primarily be the countries of the Global South.

France took third place by the end of 2024 - $7.698 billion, or 6.90% of global supplies (VPK, 2025).

For comparison: in 2021, the volume of identified French military exports amounted to $11.248 billion (13.56% of the world market), in 2022 - $12.143 billion (11.44%), in 2023 - $5.732 billion (5.92%). In general, over the last 4-year period, France exported weapons worth $36.821 billion (9.26% of the world market) and also ranks third (VPK, 2025).

French military exports have increased significantly in recent years. In 2021, France's share reached its maximum value over a 4-year period and amounted to 13.56% (VPK, 2025).

South Korea is in fourth place by the end of 2024 - $ 5.691 billion, or 5.10% of total global supplies (VPK, 2025), which slightly exceeded the result of Italy. Seoul took such a high position in the ranking for the first time by the end of the year.

For comparison: in 2021, the volume of identified military exports of South Korea amounted to $ 1.043 billion (1.26% of the world market), in 2022 - $ 695.4 million (0.65%), in 2023 - $ 1.844 billion (1.90%). In general, over the past 4-year period, South Korea exported weapons worth $ 9.274 billion (2.33% of the world market) and ranks only 10th (VPK, 2025). Italy ranks fifth in 2024 with $5.690 billion, or 5.10% of global supplies (SIPRI, 2025).

For comparison: in 2021, the volume of identified military exports from Italy amounted to $5.252 billion (6.33% of the world market), in 2022 - $6.817 billion (6.42%), in 2023 - $5.971 billion (6.16%). In general, over the past 4-year period, Italy exported weapons worth $23.732 billion (5.97% of the world market) and ranks 4th in the ranking (SIPRI, 2025).

The following places in the top ten in terms of arms exports by the end of 2024 are occupied by: Germany - $5.424 billion (4.86%), Sweden - $4.254 billion (3.81%, for the first time it took such a high position in the ranking by the end of the year), Israel - $4.163 billion (3.73%), Norway - $3.293 billion (2.95%, for the first time it took such a high position in the ranking by the end of the year), China - $3.216 billion (2.88%) (SIPRI, 2025). The second ten exporting countries by the end of 2024 are as follows: Spain - $3.152 billion (11th place), Great Britain - $2.552 billion (12th place), Turkey - $2.536 billion (13th place), the Netherlands - $2.183 billion (14th place), Australia - $1.107 billion (15th place), Switzerland - $757 million (16th place), Poland - $620 million (17th place), Canada - $454 million (18th place), India - $430 million (19th place) and Brazil - $410 million (20th place) (SIPRI, 2025).

By the end of 2024, 41 countries that have exported arms are included.

Taking into account the 4 years (2021-2024), the rating of exporting countries ranked 1st through 10th will look like this:

1. USA - $153.261 billion (38.54%);
2. Russia - about $56 billion (14.08%);
3. France - $36.821 billion (9.26%);
4. Italy $23.732 billion (5.97%);
5. Germany - $16.783 billion (4.22%);
6. Israel - $15.890 billion (4.00%);
7. Spain – $14.734 billion (3.71%);
8. China – $14.718 billion (3.70%);
9. Great Britain – $11.187 billion (2.81%);
10. South Korea – $9.274 billion (2.33%) (SIPRI, 2025).

In general, based on the results of military exports over the past 4 years (2021-2024), the second ten countries in terms of arms export value are as follows:

Turkey - $ 7.829 billion (11th place), Sweden - $ 7.052 billion (12th place), Norway - $ 5.958 billion (13th place), the Netherlands - $ 4.680 billion (14th place), Australia - $ 3.928 billion (15th place), Switzerland - $ 2.435 billion (16th place), Canada - $ 2.368 billion (17th place), Ukraine - $ 1.543 billion (18th place), Poland - $ 1.257 billion (19th place) and Brazil - $ 1.138 billion (20th place) (SIPRI, 2025).

The English-language version of the National Defense magazine is presented at major arms exhibitions, providing advertising and information support for military-technical cooperation.

For the period 2021-2024, the rating includes 58 countries that carried out arms exports (or re-exports) during this period.

Countries with long maritime borders are actively purchasing modern diesel-electric submarines. The structure of identified global supplies by main categories of weapons in 2021-2024.

In general, the total volume of global conventional arms exports (according to the UN Register classification) in 2021-2024. is estimated at $397.631 billion, including $82.942 billion in 2021, $106.185 billion in 2022, $96.889 billion in 2023, and $111.615 billion in 2024 (SIPRI, 2025).

In terms of value, export sales volumes for the period 2021-2024 were distributed as follows:

1. Aircraft equipment - $131.623 billion (33.1% of sales of all categories of weapons and military equipment);
2. Helicopter equipment - $52.241 billion (13.14%);
3. Naval equipment - $46.918 billion (11.80%);
4. Air defense equipment - $39.660 billion (9.22%);
5. Armored vehicles - $34.846 billion (8.76%);
6. Missile and artillery weapons - $14.966 billion (3.76%);
7. Unmanned aerial vehicles - $12.602 billion (3.17%) (SIPRI, 2025).

All other types of weapons and military equipment, including estimated (not identified by main types of weapons and military equipment) deliveries accounted for $64.775 billion (16.29%) (SIPRI, 2025).

Demand for unmanned aerial vehicles is growing at a record pace.

Criteria for the Forecast of Exports by Main Categories of Weapons in 2025-2028

As for the forecast related to arms exports, which is related to the next 3-4 years, Of course, the closest to reality forecast is the data for 2026. Nevertheless, even for the current year, the real figure will be further adjusted.

The number of contracts concluded with a deadline in 2026-2028 will be even more significant. That is, the specified rating gives an idea of the volume of exports by types of weapons and military equipment for the existing current portfolio of orders in terms of both its total volume and the fulfillment of contractual obligations and intentions by year.

Due to the difficult economic situation in many countries and the aggravation of the military-political situation in the world, a number of already concluded contracts may be further adjusted both in terms of the amount of equipment supplied and in terms of execution. Several contracts may be radically revised up to their complete cancellation, but the predicted number of completely canceled contracts will be small in the total volume of concluded agreements.

Poland offers a wide range of weapons and military equipment for ground forces on the world arms market. In 2024, arms exports brought the Polish military-industrial complex $ 620 million.

General assessment of the situation on the world market of weapons and military equipment in 2025-2028. by individual categories of weapons

By value parameter, the volume of export sales for the period 2025-2028 was distributed as follows:

1. Aircraft equipment - $175.022 billion (30.62%);
2. Air defense equipment - $76.460 billion (13.38%);
3. Armored vehicles - $76.217 billion (13.34%);
4. Naval equipment - $65.899 billion (11.53%);
5. Helicopter equipment - $62.729 billion (10.97%);
6. Missile and artillery weapons - $34.370 billion (6.01%);
7. Unmanned aerial vehicles - $15.279 billion (2.67%) (Report Linker, 2025).

All other types of weapons and military equipment account for $65.552 billion (11.47%) (Report Linker, 2025).

In percentage terms (comparing the period 2025-2028 with the period 2021-2024), there will be significant changes in the ranking by value of deliveries for individual categories of weapons and military equipment.

The most significant change concerns the category "Armored vehicles", which will move from fifth to third place in the ranking (and will only slightly give up second place). This is largely due to the current situation around Ukraine, which has caused a very sharp increase in orders and deliveries of military equipment in this particular market segment (during the Second World War, armored vehicles demonstrated their importance and indispensability in the modern theater of military operations). In percentage terms, the share of armored vehicles will increase from 8.76% to 13.34% (an increase of +4.58%) (Report Linker, 2025).

The second significant change concerns the category "Air Defense Equipment", which will rise from fourth to second place in the ranking. In percentage terms, the share of air defense assets will increase from 9.22% to 13.38% (+4.16%) (Report Linker, 2025). A very significant increase in the percentage share of this category is also due to the situation around Ukraine.

The third significant change concerns the category "Helicopter Equipment", which will fall in the ranking from second to fifth place. This indicates an oversaturation of the global military helicopter market. In percentage terms, the share of helicopter equipment will decrease from 13.14% to 10.97% (-2.17%) (Report Linker, 2025). The category "Naval equipment" will drop one position in the ranking (from third to fourth place). In percentage terms, the share of naval equipment will decrease very slightly (from 11.80% to 11.53%) (Report Linker, 2025).

The following categories will retain their positions in the ranking: "Aviation equipment" (first place), "Missile and artillery weapons" (sixth place), and "Unmanned aerial vehicles" (seventh place). At the same time, the share of "Aviation equipment" in percentage terms will decrease from 33.10% to 30.62% (-2.48%, a very significant decrease), the share of the "Missile and artillery weapons" (RAW) category in percentage terms will increase from 3.76% to 6.01% (Report Linker, 2025). For the RAW category, even though it will retain sixth place, the growth in percentage terms will be very significant (+2.25%), which, like for the "Armored vehicles" and "Air defense equipment" categories, is primarily due to the situation around Ukraine (Report Linker, 2025). That is, in the next four years, a significant increase in demand is expected, primarily in the categories of "Armored vehicles", "Air defense equipment" and RAV.

The market growth in terms of the value of deliveries will also be in the category of "Unmanned aerial vehicles" (UAVs), although in percentage terms the share of this category will decrease by 0.5%. The growth of "physical" volumes of UAV deliveries (from $ 12.602 billion to $ 15.279 billion) is also associated with the implementation of the SVO, where drones of all types have proven their indispensability in the modern theater of operations (Report Linker, 2025).

Air defense equipment is the most in-demand segment of weapons worldwide today.

The situation around Ukraine will lead to a significant increase in the global arms trade in the near term.

In 2022-2024, Ukraine became the world's largest recipient of major conventional weapons systems as part of Western military aid to Kyiv.

Since the weapons were provided to the Ukrainian defenders mainly as part of gratuitous deliveries, we are talking about the world's largest recipient of weapons, and not an importer of weapons and military equipment. According to the UN Register, the category of major conventional weapons systems includes military aircraft (all types), military helicopters (all types), UAVs (all types), various types of armored vehicles (tanks, armored combat vehicles, infantry fighting vehicles, armored personnel carriers, MRAP armored vehicles, armored cars), ground forces weapons (MLRS, towed guns, self-propelled artillery units, field artillery guns, mortars of all calibers, ATGMs/ATGMs), short-range, short-, medium- and long-range air defense systems, MANPADS, ZAU, naval equipment. It is fair to say that the supply of used, obsolete weapons to Ukraine initiated a large-scale rearmament program, primarily in Eastern European countries. This affected Western European countries to a lesser extent, although large-scale rearmament has begun there as well.

The EU countries intend to continue supporting Ukraine with weapons and ammunition as part of the gratuitous military aid. The US Department of Defense also organized a large-scale supply of used equipment from stock to the Ukrainian Armed Forces and, during the NVO, concluded multi-billion dollar contracts with leading enterprises of the American military-industrial complex to replace them with more advanced weapons.

It should also be noted that a number of countries are solving their rearmament problems at the expense of Germany, which has implemented a "round-robin exchange" scheme for old armored vehicles supplied to the Ukrainian Armed Forces by donor countries for more modern models. Germany is implementing a similar scheme with the Czech Republic, Slovakia, Greece, and a number of other countries.

The volume of military aid to Ukraine for major weapons systems has already exceeded $100 billion (US Department of Defense, 2025).

The large-scale pumping of weapons into Ukraine will lead to a significant increase in global exports/imports of military equipment in the near term (over the next four years).

Western countries, as noted above, supply weapons to Ukraine as part of gratuitous military aid. However, there are exceptions. Thus, Poland has concluded a large commercial contract with Kyiv for the supply of self-propelled howitzers "Crab", and a commercial contract has been concluded with Slovakia for the supply of self-propelled howitzers "Zuzana-2". At the moment, a sufficient number of commercial contracts for the supply of weapons to Ukraine have already accumulated.

The situation around Ukraine will cause an annual growth of the global arms trade in the near term (over a three- to four-year horizon) at a level of about 15-20% (due to the volume of military aid provided to Ukraine in the period from February 2022 to December 2024) (Macharashvili, 2025). This is a colossal, virtually instantaneous growth in the value of the global arms market, the main beneficiaries of which will be Western countries. In general, for Ukraine's donor countries, the value of additional arms purchases by them for import only to replenish existing arsenals will amount to up to $97 billion (this concerns compensation for arms supplies to Kyiv in the period 2022-2024) (Macharashvili, 2025). In reality, this value will be even higher, since the above calculation is made "at a minimum". It can be reasonably increased to $100 billion, given that European countries are increasing their defense budgets and they need not only to replenish their weapons arsenals but also a serious quantitative and qualitative increase in military potential.

Statistics confirm the "heating up" of the arms market in the near term, the trigger for which was the situation around Ukraine.

According to forecasts, in 2025, if the initially announced delivery schedules are met, the volume of global arms exports/imports could amount to about $120 billion (Chitadze, 2024).

In the next two years (according to the current order portfolio), sales are projected to be as follows: $126.6 billion in 2026 and $145.7 billion in 2027 (Macharashvili, 2025).

In 2028, if the global economy overcomes the consequences of the global economic crisis and avoids possible new shocks that are not even predicted yet, the volume of global arms exports may reach $179 billion, and it should be emphasized once again that this estimate was made as of December 2024 (Macharashvili, 2025). Due to new contracts concluded in 2025-2028 with a deadline of up to the end of 2028, this figure may increase even more.

Defense Spending and Economic Growth of Countries: Determinants and Channels of Relationships

As already noted, Global defense spending has reached a historic high. Almost half of it is accounted for by the United States and China. As already noted, according to the review of defense spending by countries of the world for 2023, compared to 2022, they have generally increased by 6.8% (Repnikov, 2024). The United States is in first place, Russia is in third, and Ukraine is in eighth.

ASSESSMENTS OF THE CHANNELS OF IMPACT OF DEFENCE SPENDING ON ECONOMIC GROWTH

Since 1966, the authoritative Stockholm International Peace Research Institute (SIPRI) has been conducting analytical accounting of defense spending, assessing its drivers and consequences, the relationship between spending and debt, spending and corruption, and also considering a number of aspects of the political economy of defense spending. The SIPRI database currently includes data for 1949-2022 for 174 countries, and provides information not only on the absolute values of defense spending but also on their share in GDP, the structure of total government spending, as well as defense spending per capita (SIPRI, 2024). The most common indicators of defense spending in economic analysis are absolute values of spending denominated in dollars, as well as defense spending as a share of a country's GDP (the so-called "military" or "defense" burden, which characterizes what part of a country's total output is directed to its defense-related activities). The indicator of defense spending as a share of GDP is good for cross-country or international comparisons. At the same time, certain difficulties arise associated with calculating the impact of defense spending on a country's economic growth. In one of the studies conducted by A.-K. Bran, these problems are analyzed based on econometric approaches, with special attention to the investment channel (Bran, 2023). Based on data for 1960-2014 for a large and balanced group of countries, a close relationship is established between economic growth, investment, and defense spending (Repnikov, 2024). In parallel, there is a growing scientific literature analyzing the relationship between defense spending and economic growth, adding new categories and purposes of such spending (in addition to the purchase and production of weapons and military equipment, this may include spending on training, physical infrastructure, and wages for those employed in the defense industry complex (DIC). These types of spending have different effects on economic growth. Even though half a century ago, many studies confirmed the positive impact of an increase in the share of defense spending in GDP on its dynamics, these results were often refuted later.

The negative relationship between the dynamics of defense spending and economic growth was especially clearly traced in studies after the end of the Cold War. This is natural due to the fact that only during periods of active military action do countries tend to increase defense spending and transfer the economy to a "war footing". In this regard, it would be more interesting to consider not just the relationship between defense spending and economic growth, but through the category of fixed capital (investments), and in recent years several remarkable studies have appeared devoted to the relationship between investment, defense spending and economic growth. Moreover, some special studies covered the analysis of changes in countries' defense budgets under the influence of unemployment and financial pressure, or the distribution of the burden of defense spending among the European Union (EU) member states. Meanwhile, it is important to assess the consequences of different types of defense spending both for economic growth and for a country's participation in international trade in arms and military equipment (AME). Some scholars link the problem of defense spending both to the cost of AME imports in peacetime and to the number of neighboring countries suffering from conflicts. The cost of AME imports is positively related to defense spending, but this cost is not determined by economic growth, since there is a time lag (which can reach years) between placing an order for an AME purchase and its actual delivery. It is also necessary to take into account that the world AME market and countries' defense spending are areas that experience periodic shocks from modern geopolitical conflicts, so the need for defense spending should be assessed based on a set of strategic factors. Changing over time, the growth of defense spending may hurt the economy at some stage but may have a positive effect in the future as the country's economy reconfigures and adapts (Becker, 2021). In general, the ambiguity of the impact of defense spending on economic growth is reflected in the fact that it can promote employment growth and technology transfer to civilian industries. On the other hand, it can slow down economic growth by crowding out investment from other sectors of the economy (Chitadze, 2024).

In general, various specifications of growth models have emerged, where defense spending is an endogenous variable. In particular, economic growth, if it is higher, can provide additional opportunities for increasing defense spending. In turn, if we consider neighboring countries (such as EU countries bordering Ukraine), regional tensions can lead to countries resorting to increasing defense spending as a preventive measure.

STRUCTURAL AND DYNAMIC CHANGES IN DEFENSE EXPENDITURES DUE TO MODERN GEOPOLITICAL CONFLICTS

As already noted, in 2022, the defense expenditures of countries around the world have been growing for eight years in a row, which was mainly due to the beginning of Russia's military aggression against Ukraine, which caused an increase in defense spending in many regions of the world, but mainly in Europe and some Asian countries (mainly India, China and Japan) (Repnikov, 2024). In specialized sources, military assistance to Ukraine in 2022 is estimated at $ 30 billion, of which the United States accounted for two-thirds of the donation (Chitadze, 2024). There is significant heterogeneity in the level of defense burden between regions of the world since the regions themselves are significantly heterogeneous. Global defense spending itself began to grow even during the pandemic, and in 2021-2022 it grew by 3.7%, reaching $2.24 trillion in 2022, which was mainly due to the Russia-Ukraine crisis (SIPRI, 2024). However, the global defense burden was stable and did not exceed 2.2% of global GDP, since global GDP grew in parallel with the growth of defense spending (SIPRI, 2024). The figure of 2.2% is the highest since the end of the Cold War, but the same level was observed in 2014, 2018, 2021. Geographically, defense spending was distributed among the Americas (42%), Asia and Oceania (26%), Europe (22%), the Middle East (8.3%) and Africa (1.8%) (Repnikov, 2024). In terms of countries, however, defense spending is highly concentrated, with the United States, China, and Russia accounting for 56% of global defense spending (and the 15 largest countries accounting for 82%) (Repnikov, 2024). The United States spent $877 billion on defense in 2022, or 39% of total global defense spending, including 2.3% of the country's defense spending on aid to Ukraine (this is the largest amount of aid to one country since the end of the Cold War) (Repnikov, 2024). For the United States, the question that is popular in studies on defense spending and links it to the country's debt remains relevant. In the United States, defense spending is one of the factors behind the country's growing public debt (from 95% to 120% of GDP in 2013-2021) (Repnikov, 2024). China's defense spending in 2022 amounted to $292 billion (Repnikov, 2024), but the growth in spending in 2022 was the second largest (excluding 2021) since 1995. The country's defense burden remained at 1.6% and has been generally stable over the past decade (Repnikov, 2024). China's defense spending has been growing in parallel with GDP growth over the past 20 years, especially during the period of intensive economic growth in the 1990s and 2000s, when the defense budget increased sharply (by 122% in 1993-2002; by 152% in 2003-2012; by only 63% in 2013-2022). At the same time, the share of defense spending in total government spending decreased from 13% to 4.8% in 1989-2022 (Repnikov, 2024). The overall increase in defense spending is due to the strengthening of the defense industry base, the modernization of the army, and the introduction of the latest military technologies, including artificial intelligence. At the same time, it is a generally recognized fact that China's official defense budget does not take into account all defense spending; a certain degree of transparency of these expenditures and their disaggregation, data on them are published infrequently, irregularly, and without much detail. To provide a detailed assessment of defense expenditure, SIPRI changed its earlier methodology in 2021, which now includes six components (in China, five of them are not included in the official defense budget). Information on defense expenditure is available for 4 (out of 6) components, and for the remaining two, SIPRI estimates that it will account for 8.7% of total defense expenditure in 2022 (which is why SIPRI's figure differs from China's official budget) (SIPRI, 2023). For Russia, one of the remarkable estimates of defense expenditure was developed by J. Cooper back in 1998, and it divides these expenditures into two large groups - the official defense budget (estimated at 70-80% of total expenditure) and additional items ("other military expenditure") (Cooper, 2022), which may include, for example, services health care and education, housing and communal services for the military. In any case, there has been a significant increase in defense spending in 2011-2020, with a 50% increase in 2011-2016. After a decline in 2017, defense spending has resumed growth since 2018. In 2022, Russia's defense spending increased by 9.2% compared to the previous year, reaching $86 billion (Cooper, 2022), which was mainly due to the start of military aggression against Ukraine. Prioritizing defense (in reality, offensive) spending has become the basis of the Kremlin's budget policy, and this trend is likely to continue in the coming years. If we consider the situation in a regional context, then in 2022, defense spending increased in four out of five continents (except Africa, where spending fell in countries with the largest defense industries in the region - Algeria and Nigeria). In America, where the US and Canada account for 94% of the region's defense spending, it grew by 0.3% in 2022. In Asia, the growth in spending was

2.7% (while in countries where a decrease was observed, experts attribute it to the economic crisis). In Europe, defense spending grew significantly, by 13%, with, for example, 36% in Finland and 11% in Poland (spending grew the most in countries bordering Russia or Ukraine) (SIPRI, 2023). At the same time, in many countries, spending was dictated by both security considerations and the need to achieve the target indicator of NATO member states' spending in relation to GDP (some modern studies are devoted to the distribution of the burden of such spending among member states). In the Middle East, defense spending increased by 3.2% (including 16% in Saudi Arabia, due to its involvement in the conflict in Yemen) (SIPRI, 2023). It is noteworthy that many Middle Eastern countries are characterized by a high share of defense spending in the economy, amounting to 4 to 7% of GDP (D. Lopes da Silva explains this by political reasons, and Y. Töngür, S. Xu and A. Elveren - by the specifics of autocratic regimes) (Lopes da Silva, 2023; Töngür, 2015). In turn, the increase in military spending, as noted by M. Hauenstein, M. Smith M., and M. Suva, is explained by the high level of perception of a potential threat (in the run-up to the NWO, many countries actively increased defense spending) (Hauenstein, 2021). At the same time, comparing the dynamics of defense spending over several years is ambiguous, since different inflation rates indicate different differentiation in the dynamics of defense spending. Moreover, inflation in developed countries has reached its highest level since the 1970s. High inflation in some European countries led to a significant gap between defense spending expressed in current and constant prices (for example, in Lithuania and Estonia this gap exceeded 20 percentage points) (Repnikov, 2024). An important component of military spending in developed countries in 2022 was aid to Ukraine, which obviously varies across countries, but is the largest aid ever provided to one country in one year. SIPRI estimates that in 2022, the amount of financial military aid to Ukraine amounted to $30 billion, provided by at least 25 countries, and the largest donors were the United Kingdom, Germany, and the United States (SIPRI, 2023). Overall, defense spending reached its highest level ever in 2022, but it was concentrated in 15 countries, which accounted for 82% of global spending (SIPRI, 2023).

ECONOMIC CONTEXT OF INCREASING DEFENSE SPENDING

An important aspect of increasing defense spending by a country is the interconnection of this issue with ensuring stable economic development, namely, with the formation of sufficient budget space. This is especially relevant for European countries, where the tax burden and public debt are high, and a new tax increase or the issuance of new debt obligations is associated with high socio-economic risks. The literature indicates that after the end of the Cold War, European countries were concerned with building a "welfare" society, and if they had directed one percent of non-military spending to defense purposes, they could easily have achieved the target of 2% of GDP (Repnikov, 2024). Therefore, as a result, Europe today faces a dilemma when, on the one hand, it needs to increase defense spending, and on the other, transform the economy and increase its competitiveness (taking into account the sustainable development goals). Since the end of the Cold War, European countries have reduced their defense potential and have become more dependent on the United States, whose share in NATO's total defense spending increased from 61% to 70% in 1990-2022 (Trebesch, 2023). One study indicates that the total military aid to Ukraine from the United States is comparable to that of all European countries and the EU as a whole. 40% of the top 100 manufacturers of weapons and military equipment are located in the United States (in all European countries this figure is only 26%) (Reuters, 2023). These 5 American companies produce weapons and military equipment in volumes three times greater than European defense companies. In recent decades, most European countries have accumulated so-called "peace dividends" (i.e. funds diverted from defense spending to address the most important tasks of socio-economic development) for 1.8 trillion euros, saving on defense spending and directing them to the development of other areas (Reuters, 2023). It is interesting that if we consider the threshold indicator of defense spending by NATO countries agreed upon in 2006 (2% of GDP), then at the end of the Cold War it exceeded 4% for NATO countries, but today only a few developed countries have reached the threshold of 2% (Repnikov, 2024). In turn, Russia, according to foreign estimates, plans to spend 6% of GDP on defense in 2025-2026 (Repnikov, 2023). On the other hand, in 1991-2023, there was an almost twofold increase in the defense budgets of countries, for example, in Great Britain, Germany, and France, the increase over this period was 600 billion euros, but the relative share of defense spending in GDP has hardly changed (Repnikov, 2024). An important problem of increasing defense spending for European countries is the financial aspect. Growing threats and geopolitical tensions require an increase in defense spending today since investment processes in the defense industry are long-term and decisions are already being made on the Military equipment that will be deployed in a decade. It should also be taken into account that the European military-industrial complex will invest in innovation and expand capacity if consistently high defense spending is ensured over a long period. Increased investment will lead to increased costs for the maintenance of military equipment, and this will put additional pressure on defense spending. At the same time, many European countries are characterized by high public debt, which has been growing rapidly due to virtually zero interest rates in recent years. The rise in interest rates in recent years has led to a sharp increase in interest payments, and the lion's share of budget revenues is already going to these payments (in 7 European countries, interest payments already exceed defense spending, and in

Italy, public debt payments are 2.7 times higher than defense spending). The rising cost of debt servicing is the result of a high debt burden, exceeding 100% of GDP in the largest European economies. The share of interest payments on public debt in total government expenditure varies from 1.1% in Lithuania to 7.2% in Italy, 8.1% in the UK, and 9.2% in Hungary (Dorn et al., 2024). High debt servicing costs are squeezing budget space, but the interest burden will worsen. In the case of long-term bonds, if the debt is not repaid, an extension occurs under new conditions (that is, in the current situation, at higher interest rates). This will seriously affect defense spending, which for the first time since the Cold War fell sharply after the global crisis of 2008. As for Russia, the aggressor country, the army modernization program in recent years has been supported by rapid growth in defense spending. According to SIPRI, Russia spends less than the scale of its activities in the defense industry suggests. Before the military intervention in Ukraine, defense spending peaked in 2016, reaching 5.5% of GDP (compared to 3.9% in 2019) (Wezeman, 2020). Russia has consistently been among the top five defense spenders in the world. However, defense spending cannot be used as an indicator of military power or potential. The latter is characterized by production volume, which, in addition to financing, depends on a range of qualitative factors. In addition, defense spending data do not measure the country's stocks of weapons military equipment, and other related assets. These factors explain that the army may be stronger than current defense spending levels indicate. It is also important to consider that, given the lower prices for weapons and military equipment in Russia (as well as for other goods/services) compared to developed countries, Russian defense spending has corresponding purchasing power. In addition, in the decade preceding the pandemic, Russia spent 40% of its defense spending on weapons and military equipment purchases, which is more than other developed countries (Repnikov, 2024). In general, assessments of Russia's military potential cannot be made solely based on defense spending; additional research into the military-industrial complex is needed.

Ukraine's Financial System During the War

The war of attrition has led to an increase in defense budget spending to a level unprecedented in the history of Ukraine. However, even with Western assistance, these funds are still not enough to reach the level of Russian military spending. Therefore, in order to further increase support for the Defense Forces, it is worth assessing Ukraine's financial solvency, taking into account the experience of other countries in the 20th century.

On October 31, 2024, Yuriy Gorodnichenko, a professor at the University of California (Berkeley), a researcher in monetary and fiscal policy, and a member of the editorial board of Vox Ukraine, gave an online lecture on the topic of Ukraine's financial stability during the war.

The topic of Ukrainian finances during the war is extremely voluminous. Therefore, Yuriy Gorodnichenko focused his lecture on the question of how Ukraine can finance the war of attrition. How much money do we have available, where can we get additional resources, and what is the role of the financial system in the current conditions? The incomparability of military spending is the key challenge in the war of attrition.

The main problem of finance and war has been the same for more than a decade: the defense spending of Ukraine and Russia has been and remains incomparable. In 2013, Ukraine spent 30 times less on the army than the Russian Federation (Voxukraine, 2025). After the outbreak of the war in Donbas and the annexation of Crimea, although this difference gradually decreased, the funding remained an order of magnitude less.

Even from February 24 until now, parity has not been achieved, and the gap between Ukrainian and Russian defense spending in 2023 and 2024 amounted to $100 billion (Voxukraine, 2025). The problem remains in the 2025 budget because we cannot avoid 1) military spending, 2) social security spending, and 3) servicing the national debt.

Fortunately, the support of allies has helped, is helping, and will help to reduce this gap next year. However, even the amount of our resources and aid is still $20-30 billion less than Russia's military spending (Voxukraine, 2025).

Domestic political turmoil in Western countries means that covering this gap will always be questionable and will be accompanied by difficulties. We have seen this from the delay in aid from the United States this year.

Therefore, to keep up with the enemy, the state must attract as many funds as possible that form the Ukrainian GDP.

Therefore, the main question is: what volume of funds can the financial system of Ukraine direct to defense needs through debt instruments?

To answer this question, let us review the main markers of the solvency of the financial system:

- the state of the stock market;
- private debt market;
- deposits;
- health of the banking system;
- access to external markets;
- savings;
- assets (buildings, ports, roads, etc.)
- reserves.

Let's start with what is currently unavailable to Ukraine.

Gaps in the Ukrainian Financial Market

Stock Market and Private Debt Market

We do not have a stock market – We saw a peak period of capitalization in 2007, but, as it turned out after the recession of 2008, this growth was artificial. And therefore there is simply nothing to redirect financial flows for defense.

A similar story is with institutional investors such as pension funds and the mortgage market. In pre-war times, their ratio to GDP did not exceed 2-3% - incredibly far from the goal of covering the deficit of 20-30% of GDP, which we noted at the beginning (Voxukraine, 2025).

Deposits and the Health of the Banking System

Looking at the volume of deposits in the Ukrainian economy, it seems that things look good - their pre-war level was about 25% of GDP (Voxukraine, 2025):

This is already a significant resource that could be tried to mobilize by redirecting it to the state, for example, if these deposits were used to increase investment in war bonds.

However, two key problems arise here. The first is that with the current budget deficit, this resource may last for a year or two. That is, we are not talking about a long-term solution.

The second problem is the health of the national banking system, or rather its poor condition. Since the Great Recession of 2008-2009 and the events of 2014, the volume of non-performing loans in Ukraine has grown significantly (about 50%, - editor's note), which limits banks' ability to finance any projects (Voxukraine, 2025).

Access to External Markets

Under normal circumstances, access to external markets enables private businesses to attract more funds abroad, which will have a certain level of return: each hryvnia invested can become an additional 1, 2, or 3 hryvnias - this is the so-called “multiplier effect”. Ultimately, this can increase both the filling of the treasury and the amount of funds that can be invested in military bonds (Voxukraine, 2025).

However, Ukraine is currently in a state of actual default: although the government has not formally declared it, the state is unable to service its existing debts independently, which is a blow to the Ukrainian credit rating. The state's low credit rating causes mistrust on the part of foreign investors, effectively cutting off Ukrainian private business from external financial markets. As a result, loans to the private sector cannot become a source of ability to finance the war.

The above options demonstrate the gaps in the financial system in the ability to finance the budget deficit and the Defense Forces. So what tools are promising?

Potential sources of deficit financing

Savings

Of course, not all the money in the country is on deposit in banks. Some are kept "under the mattresses" of citizens in foreign currency or hryvnia. According to official statistics, in October 2024, citizens saved UAH 1,325.7 billion. However, the total amount of savings may be higher, and this should be kept in mind (Voxukraine, 2025).

Assets

We are talking about the privatization of buildings, ports, roads, minerals, land, and other assets owned by the state.

In 2023, $4 billion was collected in this way, half of which came from the privatization of the Ukraine Hotel. Given the size of the deficit, it may seem that this is not such a promising direction. However, compared to most countries in the world, Ukraine has a large portfolio of state-owned enterprises. At the central government level, there were 3,293 in 2021 with a total shareholder value of $32.8 billion (Voxukraine, 2025).

Of course, this resource should be considered primarily in the context of raising funds for reconstruction needs, since the privatization process is time-consuming. In addition, we need an estimate of how much national wealth will remain after the end of hostilities.

Reserves

Currently, the National Bank of Ukraine has about UAH 39 billion in reserves. This is approximately the amount of assistance from Western partners for one year - this is how much this reserve will last if we suddenly find ourselves cut off from Western support.

Possible Ways to Mobilize Resources. So, what can we do with the available resources? Let's turn to historical experience: what share of the government debt do different financial market participants hold and how exactly did we mobilize resources through the financial system before?

Today, the domestic debt is UAH 1 trillion 600 billion, with the largest creditors being banks and the NBU, holding 46% and 42% of the debt, respectively (Voxukraine, 2025). Is this the ceiling on banks' ability to finance the Defense Forces?

There is still room for action. In particular, net claims on central government bodies amount to UAH 856 billion - these are investments in government bonds, which were mentioned above.

There are two more possible sources of war financing. The first is claims on the National Bank of Ukraine for UAH 773 billion (Voxukraine, 2025). These are mainly deposit certificates, i.e. short-term "deposits" that banks place with the NBU, receiving interest for this. In this way, the NBU "ties up" excess liquidity in the banking system, curbing inflation.

If the state finds a way to redirect these assets, for example, to military bonds, these funds can be used to finance the Defense Forces.

The second possible resource is more than UAH 1 trillion in loans that currently feed the economy. However, redirecting these funds to the army should be done with caution: the civilian sector also requires significant lending to maintain economic activity.

So, although the banking system has a certain potential, it cannot fully cover the budget deficit in the long term.

Finally, non-residents (1%), territorial communities (0%) and, most importantly, legal entities and individuals (2% and 8% of the debt, respectively) were not mentioned in the financing of domestic debt (Voxukraine, 2025). These agents hardly finance military expenditures through the purchase of domestic debt, so the state should concentrate on involving them more in financing the budget deficit

Options for Further Action: How to Find More Funds?

Taking into account the weaknesses and strengths of the financial capacity, potential resources that have not yet been attracted, and possible options for continuing the war, the following combination of measures can help maintain the pace of its financing:

Seigniorage (printing money) - this mechanism should not be used, because it can lead to significant inflation. Ukraine has already had a negative experience: in 2022, printing money caused inflation at the level of 25% (Voxukraine, 2025).

Control over interest rates - will help maintain stability in the financial market and provide access to credit.

Democratization of the purchase of government bonds (for example, "end") - an example is the US practice in 1941-1945, when the state attracted $ 186 billion through retail bonds, to which 86 million Americans contributed (Voxukraine, 2025).

Despite the different scales in Ukraine, even if every second Ukrainian invests in bonds, this will provide a significant resource for partially covering the deficit.

Increase in taxes - increase in indirect taxes (VAT), focus on introducing a progressive tax scale (for example, the highest marginal tax rates for personal income in the USA during the VAT reached 90%), luxury taxes (of course, at the same time there should be an increase in the efficiency of tax administration and budget spending) (Voxukraine, 2025).

Maintaining funding for the Defense Forces in such a long war of attrition is a truly non-trivial task, the way to solve this is regulatory creativity and the use of all possible levers to avoid overheating of the economy and high inflation, as well as balancing the fiscal position.

CONCLUSION

Overall, our study has shown that the current demand for defense spending is largely associated with geopolitical challenges and budget constraints, while there is a risk of weak benefits from increasing defense spending since there is no clear evidence that increasing defense spending will stimulate economic growth and investment. In addition, the heterogeneity of countries in terms of socio-economic development and foreign policy interests leads to significant differences in the defense burden for individual national economies, which is likely to grow. In a number of developed countries, the lack of interest in increasing the defense burden and absolute values of military spending is due to the need to maintain the competitiveness of the economy in the context of intensifying geopolitical competition. At the same time, the current dynamics of defense spending in different countries of the world actualizes an important research question regarding the determinants of these expenses, as well as the sources of these expenses for the implementation of predictable financing, since the corresponding changes in the tax system have significant socio-economic consequences for countries increasing defense spending.

REFERENCES

Alptekin, A., & Levine, P. (2012). Military Expenditure and Economic Growth: A Meta analysis. *European Journal of Political Economy*, *28*(4), 636–650. DOI: 10.1016/j.ejpoleco.2012.07.002

Aziz, N., & Asadullah, M. N. (2017). Military Spending, Armed Conflict, and Economic Growth in Developing Countries in the Post-Cold War Era. *Journal of Economic Studies (Glasgow, Scotland)*, *44*(1), 47–68. DOI: 10.1108/JES-01-2015-0021

Becker, J. (2021). Rusty Guns and Buttery Soldiers: Unemployment and the Domestic Origins of Defense Spending. *European Political Science Review*, *13*(3), 307–330. DOI: 10.1017/S1755773921000102

Bran, A. C. (2023). Does Military Spending Spur Economic Growth? An Empirical Approach. *Proceedings of the International Conference on Business Excellence*, Vol. 17(1), pp. 178-187. DOI: 10.2478/picbe-2023-0020

Cavatorta, E., & Smith, R. P. (2017). Factor Models in Panels with Cross-sectional Dependence: An Application to the Extended SIPRI Military Expenditure Data. *Defence and Peace Economics*, *28*(4), 437–456. DOI: 10.1080/10242694.2016.1261428

Chitadze, N. (2011). *Geopolitics*. Universal.

Chitadze, N. (2024). *World Politics*. International Black Sea University.

CNBC. (2025). *Global military spending hits $2.46 trillion in 2024: IISS Report*. CNBC. https://www.cnbctv18.com/world/global-military-spending-hits-2-46-trillion-dollars-in-2024-us-india-russia-ukraine-defence-budget-19571050.htm

Cooper, J. (1998). The Military Expenditure of the USSR and the Russian Federation, 1987–97. *SIPRI Yearbook*, *1999*, 243–259.

Cooper, J. (2022). *Implementation of the Russian Federal Budget During January-July 2022 and Spending on the Military*. SIPRI Background Paper. DOI: 10.55163/STMI3484

D'Agostino, G., Dunne, J. P., & Pieroni, L. (2019). Military Expenditure, Endogeneity, and Economic Growth. *Defence and Peace Economics*, *30*(5), 509–524. DOI: 10.1080/10242694.2017.1422314

Dorn, F., Potrafke, N., & Schlepper, M. (2024). European Defence Spending in 2024 and Beyond: How to Provide Security in an Economically Challenging Environment. EconPol POLICY REPORT. *CESifo Research Network*, 35 p.

Hauenstein, M., Smith, M., & Souva, M. (2021). Democracy, External Threat and Military Spending. *Research & Politics*, *8*(4), 1–13. DOI: 10.1177/20531680211049660

Kollias, C., & Paleologou, S. (2019). Military Spending, Economic Growth and Investment: A Disaggregated Analysis by Income Group. *Empirical Economics*, *56*(3), 935–958. DOI: 10.1007/s00181-017-1379-2

Linker, R. (2025). *Weapon Market Outlook 2024 – 2028*. Report Linker. https://www.reportlinker.com/clp/global/663365

Lopes da Silva, D. (2023). Political Accountability and Military Spending. *Defence and Peace Economics*, *34*(5), 563–580. DOI: 10.1080/10242694.2022.2129128

Macharashvili, N. (2025). *Can Europe Defend Itself and Ukraine without U.S. Support?* Gfsis.org. https://gfsis.org/en/can-europe-defend-itself-and-ukraine-without-u-s-support/

Malizard, J. (2015). Does Military Expenditure Crowd Out Private Investment: A Disaggregate Perspective for the Case of France. *Economic Modelling*, *46*(C), 44–52. DOI: 10.1016/j.econmod.2014.10.049

Repnikov, A. (2024). *Defense Expenditures and Economic Growth of Countries of the World: Determinants and Channels of Interrelations*. Ideas. file:///D:/nchitadze/Downloads/48-58+Article+Repnikova%20(3).pdf

Reuters (2023). *Russia Plans Huge Defense Spending Hike in 2024 as War Drags*. Bloomberg. https://www.reuters.com/business/aerospace-defense/russia-plans-hugedefence-spending-hike-2024-bloomberg-2023-09-22/ (дата обращения: 16.03.2024).

Saeed, L. (2023). The Impact of Military Expenditures on Economic Growth: A New Instrumental Variables Approach. *Defence and Peace Economics*. DOI: 10.1080/10242694.2023.2259651

SIPRI. (2024). *Sources and methods*. SIPRI. https://www.sipri.org/databases/milex/sources-andmethods

SIPRI. (2025). Unprecedented rise in global military expenditure as European and Middle East spending surges. https://www.sipri.org/media/press-release/2025/unprecedented-rise-global-military-expenditure-european-and-middle-east-spending-surges

Stockholm International Peace Research Institute. (2023). *SIPRI Military Expenditure Database*. SIPRI. https://www.sipri.org/databases/milex

Töngür, Ü., Hsu, S., & Elveren, A. Y. (2015). Military Expenditures and Political Regimes: Evidence from Global Data, 1963-2000. *Economic Modelling*, *44*, 68–79. DOI: 10.1016/j.econmod.2014.10.004

Trebesch, C. (2023). The Ukraine support tracker: which countries help Ukraine and how? *KIEL Working Paper,* No. 2218, 75 p.

US Department of Defense. (2025). *Ukraine Events Timeline*. US Department of Defense. https://www.defense.gov/Spotlights/Support-for-Ukraine/Timeline/

VPK. (2025). *Global arms exports in 2024 and for the period 2021-2024*. TimeWeb. https://odkb-csto.org/analytics/?ELEMENT_ID=24011#loaded

Wezeman, S. T. (2020). *Russia's Military Spending: Frequently Asked Questions*. SIPRI. https://www.sipri.org/commentary/topical-backgrounder/2020/russias-militaryspending-frequently-asked-questions (дата обращения: 12.02.2024).

ADDITIONAL READING

Ball, D., Béraud-Sudreau, L., Huxley, T., & Mohan, C. (2021). Asia's New Geopolitics: Military Power and Regional Order. *Adelphi Series*, *59*, 478–480.

Bayraktar-Saglam, B., & Yetkiner, H. 2012. A Romanian Contribution to the Empirics of Economic Growth. *Working Papers in Economics*, No. 12/01. Izmir University of Economics, Department of Economics, Izmir, 41 p.

Droff J., Malizard J. 2019. Qui porte le fardeau? Les coûts de la production de défense dans l'Union européenne. *Revue francaise d'economie*, Vol. XXXIV (3), pp. 83–121.

Dunne, J. P., Smith, R., & Willenbockel, D. (2005). Models of Military Expenditure and Growth: A Critical Review. *Defence and Peace Economics*, *16*(6), 449–461. DOI: 10.1080/10242690500167791

Dunne, J. P., & Tian, N. (2016). Military Expenditure and Economic Growth 1960–2014. *Economics of Peace and Security Journal*, *11*(2), 50–56. DOI: 10.15355/epsj.11.2.50

Hegre, H., Bernhard, M., & Teorell, J. (2020). Civil Society and the Democratic Peace. *The Journal of Conflict Resolution*, *64*(1), 32–62. DOI: 10.1177/0022002719850620

Mankiw, N. G., Romer, D., & Weil, D. N. (1992). A Contribution to the Empirics of Economic Growth. Quarterly Journal of Economics, Vol. 107, pp. 407- 437. 21. NATO (2024). URL: http:// www.nato.int/cps/en/natohq/topics_49198.htm

Norrlof, C., & Wohlforth, W. C. (2019). Is the US Grand Strategy Self-Defeating? Deep Engagement, Military Spending, and Sovereign Debt. *Conflict Management and Peace Science*, *36*(3), 227–247. DOI: 10.1177/0738894216674953

Pacific Y.K.T., Shan L.J., Ramadhan A.A. (2017). Military Expenditure, Export, FDI and Economic Performance in Cameroon. Global Business Review, Vol. 18.3 (2), p. 577-589. DOI: . 24.DOI: 10.1177/0972150917692065

Phillips, B. J. (2015). Civil War, Spillover and Neighbors' Military Spending. *Conflict Management and Peace Science*, *32*(4), 425–442. DOI: 10.1177/0738894214530853

Sandler, T., & Shimizu, H. (2014). NATO Burden Sharing 1999-2010: An Altered Alliance. *Foreign Policy Analysis*, *10*(1), 43–60. DOI: 10.1111/j.1743-8594.2012.00192.x

Tian, N., Lopes da Silva, D., Liang, X., Scarazzato, L., & Assis, A. (2023). Developments in Military Expenditure and the Effects of the War in Ukraine. *Defence and Peace Economics*, *34*(5), 547–562. DOI: 10.1080/10242694.2023.2221877

Tian, N., & Su, F. 2021. A New Estimate of China's Military Expenditure. SIPRI, Stockholm, p. 26

Yesilyurt, F., & Yesilyurt, M. E. (2019). Meta-analysis, Military Expenditures and Growth. *Journal of Peace Research*, *56*(3), 352–363. DOI: 10.1177/0022343318808841

Yetkiner, I. H. 2012. Defense Spending and Economic Growth: A Theoretical Manifestation for Empirical Studies. Working Papers in Economics, No. 12/02. Izmir University of Economics, Department of Economics, Izmir, 25 p. b

Chapter 5

No Butter Without Guns: Security, Sovereignty, and Strategic Accumulation in the South China Sea

Tin Maung Htwe
https://orcid.org/0009-0002-3002-169X
Chiang Mai University, Thailand

ABSTRACT

This paper reinterprets military expenditure in the South China Sea not as a deviation from economic rationality, but as a historically consistent strategy of statecraft. Challenging the conventional "guns versus butter" dichotomy, it contends that militarization is embedded within the political economy of development. Defense spending becomes a dual-purpose asset: projecting power while stimulating industrial capacity and reinforcing state authority in contested maritime zones. Building on the concepts of the security-growth nexus and Military Keynesianism, the paper argues that defense expenditure functions as strategic rent-seeking in a fragmented order marked by legal ambiguity and institutional fragility. In the absence of enforceable regimes, military infrastructure substitutes for law, and presence replaces treaty-based legitimacy. Through an analysis of military spending and its geopolitical implications, this study examines how China, the United States, ASEAN, and claimant states convert defense budgets into tools of strategic accumulation.

INTRODUCTION

The South China Sea, as defined by the International Hydrographic Bureau, extends in a southwest-to-northeast direction. Its southern boundary is marked by

DOI: 10.4018/979-8-3373-3456-1.ch005

3 degrees south latitude, situated between South Sumatra and Kalimantan (Karimata Straits), while its northern boundary is the Taiwan Strait, stretching from the northern tip of Taiwan to the Fujian coast of China (Rosenberg, 2002).

Figure 1. China claims a big backyard in the South China Sea (wwww.southchinasea.org)

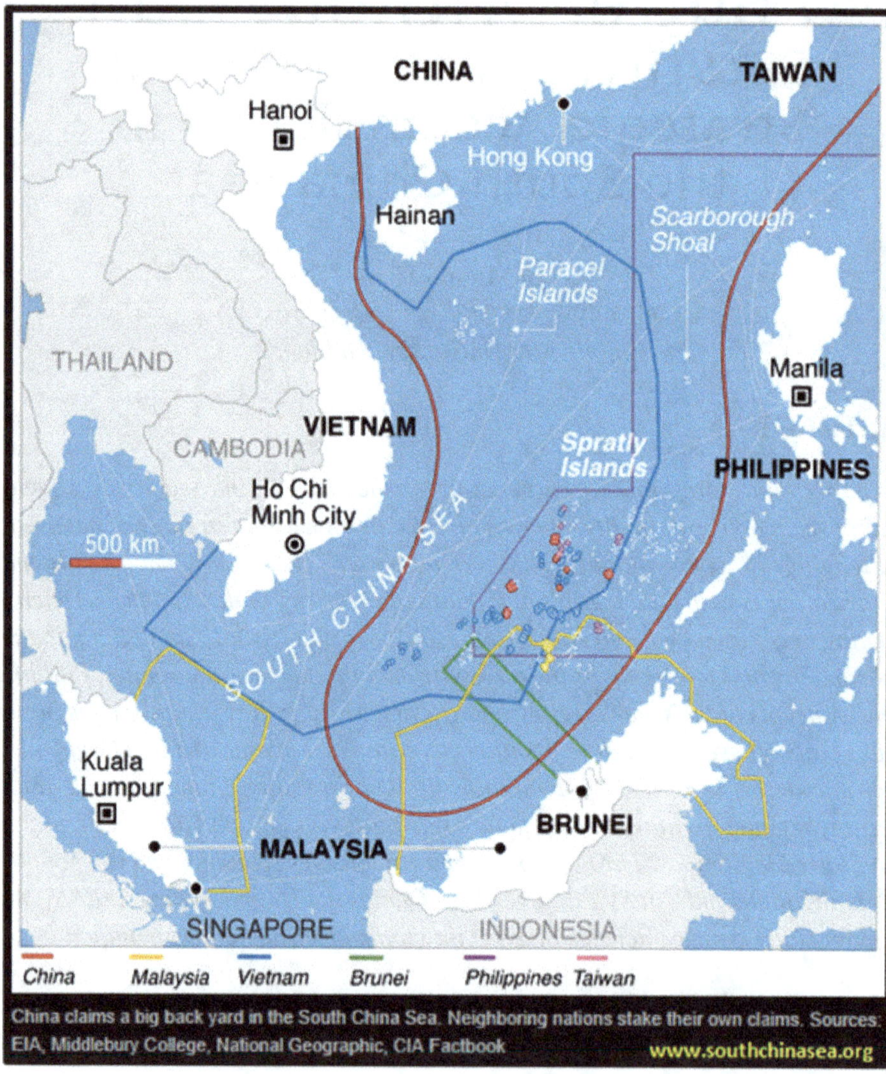

China claims a big back yard in the South China Sea. Neighboring nations stake their own claims. Sources: EIA, Middlebury College, National Geographic, CIA Factbook www.southchinasea.org

In the South China Sea, military expenditure has undergone a structural transformation as from a conventional tool of deterrence to a rational instrument of coercive appropriation. Situated within a fragmented maritime domain marked by overlapping claims and institutional fragility, defense spending now operates less as a residual security measure and more as an economic input—a strategic allocation of national capital to secure access, extract rents, and project authority in the absence of enforceable norms (Green & Anderson, 2024). Where legal frameworks lack the capacity to adjudicate disputes or enforce territorial integrity, coercive force becomes not only politically expedient but economically rational as a substitute for law, and a mechanism for wealth acquisition.

Despite a modest decline in fossil fuels' share, global energy use hit a record 620 exajoules in 2023, with CO_2 emissions surpassing 40 gigatonnes—driven largely by China and India's expanding demand. This mirrors a deeper pattern seen in the South China Sea, where economic growth and energy security are tightly bound to military investment (Harvey, 2024). Military Spending becomes the logic of strategic accumulation persists that states prioritize national power over global sustainability. The failure to decouple growth from emissions reflects not a lack of solutions, but a deficit in political will and institutional coherence. In this setting, military capital yields returns not through conflict avoidance but through territorial consolidation, strategic deterrence, and resource control. As conflict economics posits, when the expected payoff from appropriation exceeds that of peaceful production, rational actors reallocate fiscal and technological resources to defense (Short, 2025). The result is a political economy in which military spending assumes the form of investment that is generating access to vital sea lanes, hydrocarbons, and contested fisheries through displays of force, fortified installations, and platform-based deterrence.

For smaller ASEAN states, however, the calculus is constrained by fiscal capacity and strategic dependency. The Philippines and Vietnam must trade off developmental needs for defense investment, often relying on external financing to fund frigates, surveillance platforms, and coastal defense systems (Marimuthu, Khan, & Bangash, 2021). This adaptation of military Keynesianism under peripheral constraints reflects not a dysfunction, but a localized variant of the security-growth nexus. Deterrence becomes a precondition for economic agency in a hostile strategic environment (Dunne, 2013). This dynamic raises a critical question: in a volatile, legally ambiguous maritime order, is military expenditure a drain on developmental capacity, or a prerequisite for economic participation? The stakes are not abstract. The U.S. Energy Information Administration (2013) estimates that the South China Sea holds up to 11 billion barrels of oil and 190 trillion cubic feet of natural gas. In such a landscape, access is not granted by multilateral treaties but secured by airstrips, surveillance platforms, and coastal missile systems. Force, in this context, functions not as overhead but as productive capital—an input into a system of coercive rent-seeking and territorial entrenchment.

Figure 2. South China Sea oil and neutral gas proved and probable reserves

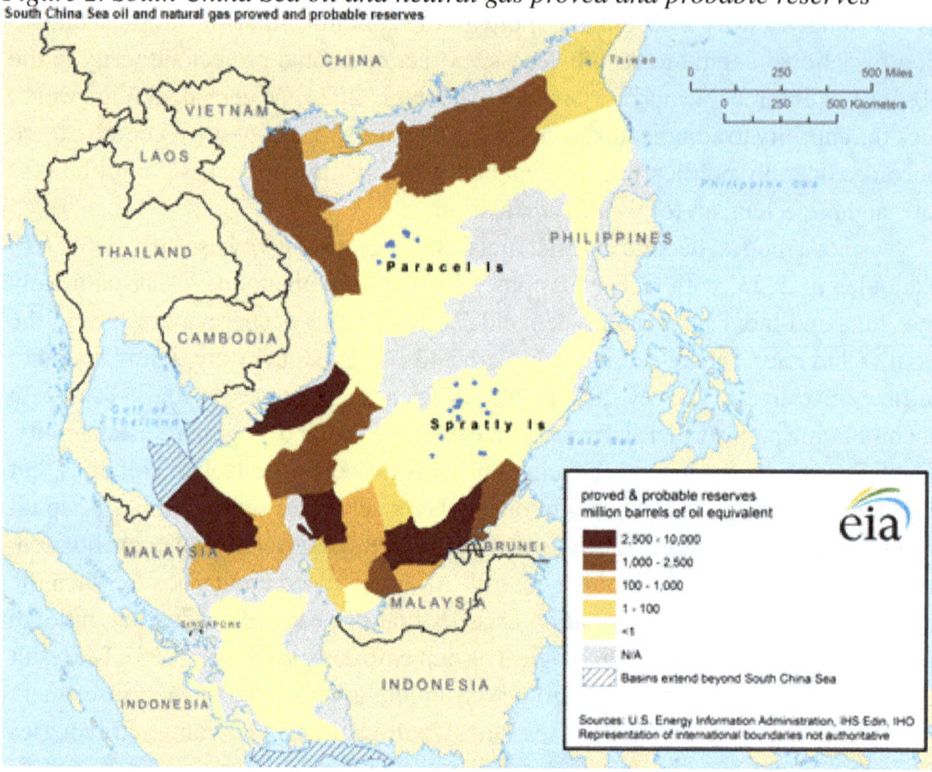

Based on the Statistical Review of World Energy 2024, the South China Sea remains a vital zone for hydrocarbon production and reserves. Malaysia leads among claimants with 3 billion barrels of oil and 75 trillion cubic feet (tcf) of gas reserves, producing 1.79 EJ of oil and 1.66 EJ of gas in 2023. China, though holding smaller reserves in the area (1 billion barrels of oil, 5 tcf of gas), reported significantly higher national output, with portions sourced from Hainan and reclaimed islands. Brunei, with 1.4 billion barrels and 13.8 tcf in reserves, remains heavily reliant on offshore fields. Vietnam and Indonesia also contribute substantially, particularly from disputed zones like the Natuna block. The Philippines and Taiwan are smaller producers, with the former dependent on the declining Malampaya field. By 2024, the region collectively held 7 billion barrels of oil and 150.3 tcf of gas, producing around 2.17 million barrels of oil and 3.24 tcf of gas annually (Energy Institute, KPMG, & Kearney, 2024). These figures highlight the strategic importance of energy access in shaping the South China Sea's contested maritime dynamics.

According to the World Bank (2017), unresolved maritime tensions jeopardize over $3.4 trillion in annual trade flows. A significant share of global trade—estimated between $3.4 trillion and $5.3 trillion annually—flows through the South China Sea, underscoring its critical role in the global economy. In 2016, over 64% of China's maritime trade, nearly 42% of Japan's, and about 55% of India's trade transited this vital waterway (Turker, 2023). These figures highlight the region's centrality not only to regional powers but to global supply chain stability. Marked by clashes between China, the Philippines, and Vietnam, Rising tensions in the South China Sea highlight a return to geopolitics where power, not interdependence, secures trade (Invezz, 2024). As a key artery linking major economies, disruptions here threaten global supply chains. Military force is increasingly used to safeguard economic interests. Moreover, A Taiwan blockade could cost the global economy up to $2.7 trillion (Vision of Humanity, 2024), showing that globalization rests not on harmony, but on the balance of coercive power. Therefore, the economics of security extend far beyond defense budgets, deeply embedded in the material flows and supply chain vulnerabilities of regional and global economies.

The logic of conflict provides explanatory power for this transformation. When institutions fail to protect property rights or resolve disputes, rational actors shift resources toward appropriation. Conflict, far from being a departure from economic rationality, becomes a mechanism of resource acquisition in the absence of legal enforcement. This study challenges the classic guns-versus-butter dichotomy in anarcy areas (Powell, 1993) by reframing military spending through the lenses of Military Keynesianism and the security-growth nexus. My study argues that in Southeast Asia's maritime arena, production and appropriation coexist as rival strategies of capital formation. Here, defense budgets function not as fiscal waste but as strategic investment but generating coercive leverage, geopolitical stability and long-term access to contested economic spaces.

Grounded in the logic of military Keynesianism and the security-growth nexus. The first component involves an econometric assessment of military expenditures and strategic outcomes among South China Sea claimant states during 2024–2025 and capturing patterns of capital allocation to trace how states operationalize defense investments as instruments of geoeconomic positioning. Rather than treating military capacity as a sunk cost for deterrence, the analysis reveals a structural shift. Coercive assets are increasingly mobilized as productive capital in the competitive pursuit of maritime influence and economic rent.

LITRATURE REVIEW

The security-growth nexus does not merely describe a correlation between force and prosperity (Schmidt, 2004). It constitutes a fundamental allocation problem that rational agents, whether states or individuals distribute limited resources between productive activity and coercive appropriation (Roberts, 2011). In strategic environments where law is weak and property rights insecure, security functions simultaneously as enabler and competitor to economic growth (Stern & Öjendal, 2010). Security is not merely the absence of conflict but encompasses broader aspects such as political stability, economic growth, and social inclusion (Mavrotas, 2011). The modern state, as the institutional monopolist of violence, manages this trade-off by allocating capital toward coercive infrastructure to both suppress internal appropriation and pursue external control (Bardhan, 2004). States leverage their centrality in global economic networks through two key mechanisms: the panopticon effect, using strategic surveillance for informational advantage, and the chokepoint effect, restricting access to critical nodes to exert pressure (Farrell & Newman, 2019). These dynamics turn interdependence into a tool of coercive power. The result is a recursive dynamic in which security stabilizes production (Shafer, 1994), while surplus from economic growth reinforces coercive capability.

This interdependence has deep theoretical roots. Hobbes (1651) framed the prepolitical state as one in which violence precluded production. In such a world, the fear of appropriation renders trade impossible. While globalization has the potential to foster economic growth and cultural exchange, it also exacerbates inequalities and can undermine local traditions and economies. (Cohen, 2006). Adam Smith (1776) mentioned without coercively enforced property rights, specialization and capital accumulation cannot take place. Institutionalized coercion is not a departure from economic rationality but rather its precondition, essential for the establishment and maintenance of market systems and growth (Rueschemeyer & Evans, 1985). Modern development theory builds on this foundation. Challenging the assumption that defense spending is inherently distortive, Emile Benoit (1973) argued that in low-capacity states, military expenditure could serve as an engine of modernization, generating spillovers in infrastructure, technology, and organizational competence. In such contexts, coercive capital functions as a public good through enabling the conditions for later productive growth (Hartley & Sandler, 1990). Yet this logic is conditional. As Ron Smith (1980) noted, the marginal utility of defense spending is contingent on structural parameters. In capital-rich economies, excessive defense outlays may divert investment from more efficient uses. But in fragile or capital-scarce environments, it may be rational for states to frontload military investment in order to reduce disorder or project capacity outward (Kindleberger, 1988). Thus, military expenditure is best assessed not in absolute normative terms, but within its institutional and geopolitical context.

From a macroeconomic perspective, Acocella (1992) reconceptualized defense spending as a fiscal variable whose effects depend on the degree of institutional coordination. In some systems, it acts as Keynesian stimulus, stabilizing demand and industrial capacity. In others, it reinforces fiscal rigidity and structural imbalance (Vicarelli, 1984). The old "guns-versus-butter" trade-off becomes (Reiter, 2017), in this view, a question of context-dependent productivity that not all coercion is wasteful, but not all is wealth-enhancing either in South China Sea (Tan, 2015). Military expenditures can influence social services and economic performance (Chan & Mintz, 1992). However, over the long term, the growth effects of defense spending are generally neutral or negative. Especially where coercive power becomes parasitic rather than developmental (Becker & Dunne, 2023). Deger and Sen (1995) observed similar dynamics in developing states, where military spending often reduces domestic savings and undercuts investments in human capital. In these cases, coercive accumulation undermines its own productive base.

Yet global political economy frameworks offer a countervailing perspective. Kindleberger (1970) argues that global economic stability depends on the leadership of a hegemon capable of supplying essential public goods such as security, open markets, and financial stability. He emphasizes that the interplay of military force and economic strength is crucial, as only a dominant power can underwrite the rules and institutions necessary to sustain an open and orderly international system. Gilpin (1988) argue that military hegemony acts as a global public good, securing trade routes and suppressing predatory appropriation. The hegemon, as the monopolist of violence on a planetary scale, enforces a liberal order that enables decentralized production (Miller, 2018: Cohn & Hira, 2020). Dependency is not merely a consequence of global inequality, but a deliberate, structured mechanism through which hierarchical power relations are maintained and reproduced over time. (Winnebeck, Sutter, Hermann, Antweiler, & Conermann, 2023). Thus, even coercive asymmetry may serve a developmental function and so long as it is systemically stabilizing.

Conflict economics sharpens this insight. Hirshleifer (1987) formalized the trade-off between production and appropriation. In his model, where enforcement is weak, appropriation can become the dominant strategy. Rational actors reallocate from labor and capital investment to coercive extraction. In environments of institutional fragility, military investment becomes not a policy error, but an equilibrium response. Effective policy responses must integrate both security and development priorities rather than treating them in isolation Carment, Prest, & Samy, 2009). Wallerstein (1984) advances the core tenets of **World-Systems Theory. He mentions that** state behavior of military spending is structurally conditioned by a state's position within this system. This provides a structural explanation for defense spending in weakly institutionalized regions. In regions like the South China Sea, where legal ambiguity and institutional weakness persist, defense expenditures are not irrational anomalies but strategic tools for rent capture and positional advantage in a competitive global economy (Green, 2016). It is not an aberration, but a mechanism for capturing rents in a competitive and legally ambiguous order.

Military Keynesianism offers a distinct lens, especially relevant during periods of geopolitical tension or economic stagnation (Cypher, 2007). It frames defense spending not only as a security imperative but as a stimulus tool—injecting demand, sustaining industries, and legitimizing state intervention in the economy under the guise of national defense (Stubbs, 2017). Defense spending operates as counter-cyclical stimulus through preserving industrial capacity and creating technological spillovers (Elveren, 2025). China's Military-Civil Fusion (MCF) strategy exemplifies this synthesis. AI, aerospace, and cybersecurity sectors are simultaneously civilian and coercive (Kania & Laskai, 2021). Here, defense budgets are not just strategic allocations but they are tools of state-led industrial policy (Matthews, 2019). Besley and Persson (2011) have added institutional nuance. They argue that the growth effects of security spending hinge on fiscal capacity and state competence. Where rule-enforcing institutions are strong, military investment can enhance predictability and crowd-in investment. Where institutions are weak, defense budgets risk morphing into rents and predation, undermining the very stability they aim to secure.

The South China Sea today operates as a laboratory for these competing logics. China's militarized island bases, patrol vessels, and surveillance systems are not merely defensive tools (Erickson, 2024). They are mechanisms of economic control. They secure maritime rents and project power in ways that resemble infrastructural coercion (Tabelli, 2024). Chinese public opinion on military expenditure, revealing a complex interplay between national pride and domestic priorities. While there is general support for a strong military, the research finds that citizens' approval diminishes when defense spending is weighed against social welfare needs (Xiao, Sadler, & Quek, 2021) For smaller ASEAN states like the Philippines and Vietnam, arms procurement and defense diplomacy represent strategic hedging under conditions of fragmented sovereignty (Zha, 2025). Viewed through this lens, military spending in the South China Sea is not overhead, but strategic capital. It shifts the frontier between production and appropriation, shaping who has access to trade, energy, and legitimacy. In this contested maritime order, coercive investment becomes not just rational but often necessary.

REGIONAL MILITARIZATION AS STRATEGIC ECONOMIC BEHAVIOR

In the contested political economy of the South China Sea, military expenditure has ceased to function merely as a deterrent against external aggression. It has instead evolved into a rational economic behavior. A calculated deployment of coercive capital by states navigating institutional scarcity and intensifying strategic rivalry, where military assets serve not only security aims but also geoeconomic ambitions (Mia, Tao, & Anderson, 2024). The largest rise in nearly four decades, Global military spending surged by 9.4%. It is reflecting the return of great power rivalry and weakening liberal norms. Driven by conflicts in Ukraine and Gaza, and U.S.-China tensions, countries like Japan, the Philippines, and Germany are expanding defense budgets as security is increasingly defined by power, not institutions (Lendon, 2025). Within this fragmented regional order, militarization is not a sunk cost but a forward-looking investment. It is a mechanism through which states capture rents, assert control over maritime resources, and convert ambiguous sovereignty into material leverage (Kuzemko et al., 2025).

This shift reflects a fundamental tenet of conflict economics. Where enforcement institutions are weak and legal authority ambiguous, coercion becomes a substitute for rules and a pathway to value acquisition (Schwartz, 2023). Defense spending, in this logic, becomes productive, not by stimulating aggregate demand alone, but by securing access to resources that are otherwise inaccessible through market exchange or diplomatic settlement (Kim, 2022). In a maritime order defined less by norms than by power, militarization emerges as a form of strategic accumulation of rational, targeted, and economically generative (Van Veeren, Stevens, & Senu, 2024).

Empirical data corroborate this shift. The 2025 SIPRI Fact Sheet reports that China's defense budget reached $314 billion in 2024, extending a three-decade streak of uninterrupted growth and consolidating its rank as the world's second-largest military spender. Concurrently, Southeast Asian states collectively allocated $54.9 billion to defense in 2024, representing a 7.5% annual increase. Among these, the Philippines raised its military budget by 19%; Singapore retained the region's highest per capita defense outlay; and Vietnam continued to expand its opaque but deliberate posture. These figures do not merely reflect rising security concerns (Liang et al., 2025). They represent the emergence of military spending as a mode of geoeconomic positioning, where coercive capacity functions not only to deter adversaries but to secure rents, shape market access, and reinforce claims over maritime territory.

CHINA'S STRATEGIC ACCUMULATION THROUGH DEFENSE-DRIVEN GEOECONOMICS

Nowhere is this logic more evident than in China's sustained military buildup and maritime assertiveness. With the world's second-largest defense budget, China is the dominant military power in the South China Sea, with a defense budget of $314 billion in 2024, projected to rise to $334 billion in 2025 (Fleck, 2025). China's interests in the region are largely driven by its territorial claims over almost the entire South China Sea, an area rich in natural resources like oil, gas, and fisheries (Duman, 2024). To assert these claims, China has militarized several islands and reefs, constructing artificial islands with advanced infrastructure, including airstrips, radar systems, and missile defense systems (Oztuna, 2024). China has institutionalized military modernization as both a geostrategic imperative and a vehicle for economic statecraft. Through systematic reallocations from civilian sectors to the People's Liberation Army Navy (PLAN), Beijing has operationalized the South China Sea as a dual-use space: a geopolitical buffer and an economic frontier. Now China commands the world's largest fleet by number of hulls in the world (Cole, 2024).

Since 2013, China has reclaimed over 3,200 acres of land in the Spratly Islands, effectively burying more than 4,600 acres of coral reef in the process (Asia Maritime Transparency Initiative, 2024). This activity represents not merely ecological transformation but capital investment on a strategic frontier. Airstrips, hardened outposts, radar facilities, and naval harbors form the physical architecture of coercive control, converting legally ambiguous maritime features into de facto extensions of sovereign territory. These assets secure access to an estimated \$3.4 trillion in annual maritime trade and vast reserves of hydrocarbons and fisheries—rendering military force a productive input in regional economic flows.

China's militarization is not reactive. It is part of a long-term program of defense-driven geoeconomic accumulation. In March 2025, Beijing announced a defense allocation of RMB 1.78 trillion (\$246.5 billion), a 7.2% nominal increase from the previous year. This continues a trend of consistent single-digit annual growth. Yet official figures likely underestimate the true scale (ChinaPower Project, 2025). Hidden expenditures (military R&D, cyber capabilities, paramilitary forces like the China Coast Guard and the People's Armed Forces Maritime Militia, and dual-use infrastructure) drive actual defense spending far beyond official figures (Williams, 2025), revealing a broader, more opaque investment in coercive capacity. Rather than diverting resources from development, China's defense outlays reinforce it through Military-Civil Fusion (MCF). This doctrine blurs the line between national defense and industrial modernization, fusing security policy with technological innovation. Investments in AI, aerospace, quantum communications, and cyber infrastructure yield both strategic advantage and civilian applications (Nan, 2025). It can use as the dual-use innovation ecosystem. Here, military expenditure becomes not a distortion, but a productive factor: a capital input that sustains both coercive reach and economic competitiveness.

China's platform investments exemplify this synergy. The Fujian aircraft carrier, the Type 076 amphibious assault ship, and the J-35A stealth fighter are not simply instruments of deterrence—they are vehicles of power projectionthat extend control far beyond the South China Sea (Li, 2024). The launch of the Type 076 ship Sichuan in December 2024, equipped with electromagnetic catapults and a full-length flight deck, signals a doctrinal shift toward multi-domain warfare and far-seas operations (Xinhua, 2024). These platforms serve geoeconomic objectives by reinforcing China's ability to regulate chokepoints, secure SLOCs, and establish strategic infrastructure-as-dominance in the maritime commons (Sultana & Cohen,

2025). Such developments expose the conceptual weakness of liberal assumptions about defense as fiscal overhead. In Beijing's political economy, military capital is neither idle nor extractive. It is an asset class deployed to reshape regional order, consolidate sovereign claims, and extend access to valuable resources. Through MCF, coercion and innovation are no longer competing imperatives. They are fused into a feedback loop of strategic accumulation.

In the South China Sea, guns and growth are not antithetical. They are fused in a grand strategy of maritime dominance. Possessing the world's largest navy by number of vessels, China now wields maritime force as a form of coercive capital. Military spending secures strategic advantage, enables regional signaling, and underwrites both domestic legitimacy and international leverage.

THE GEOECONOMICS OF U.S. DEFENSE SPENDING IN A FRAGMENTING INDO-PACIFIC ORDER

The United States, with a military expenditure of $997 billion in 2024, is a key player in the South China Sea, despite not having territorial claims in the region. The U.S. military strategy in the South China Sea primarily revolves around ensuring freedom of navigation and countering China's expansive territorial claims (SCSPI, 2025). The U.S. Navy conducts regular Freedom of Navigation Operations (FONOPs) to challenge China's excessive claims and maintain open access to international waters. In addition, the U.S. plays a critical role in regional security through alliances and partnerships, particularly with countries like the Philippines, Japan, and South Korea (International Crisis Group, 2024). The U.S. military's substantial presence in the region, including its aircraft carriers, submarines, and fighter jets, helps maintain a balance of power and supports its broader geopolitical interests, particularly in countering China's influence (GSDN, 2025). The United States accounted for nearly 40% of global military expenditure. This colossal outlay is not simply a response to rising geopolitical threats; it reflects the structural logic of military Keynesianism, wherein defense spending serves not only as a guarantor of national security but as a pillar of industrial policy, technological innovation, and hegemonic maintenance. The FY 2025 budget request of $849.8 billion is framed by the Pentagon as part of a "decisive decade" as a deliberate investment in strategic deterrence, supply chain resilience, and alliance stabilization during a period of accelerating global fragmentation (U.S. Department of Defense, 2024).

Where China embeds military expenditure into the machinery of geoeconomic statecraft, the U.S. approach reflects the persistence of military primacy as a structural asset of the liberal international order. Yet this model carries macroeconomic trade-offs. With $881 billion spent on debt servicing in 2024 alone, fiscal capacity is increasingly contested terrain—reviving classic debates about the long-term viability of defense-led growth (Peter G. Peterson Foundation, 2025). Nevertheless, the U.S. commitment of $143.2 billion to RDT&E and $167.5 billion for procurement sustains its edge at the frontier of military-industrial development, reinforcing its status as both a coercive superpower and a technological leader.

This coercion-innovation synthesis is evident in current investment priorities. Those hypersonic weapons, space platforms, and AI-enabled warfare represent the fusion of security imperatives and economic dynamism. In this model, military expenditure is not a drain on productive output, but a stimulus for strategic sectors with spillover potential through embedding defense into the very fabric of national competitiveness. Despite global overstretch, the U.S. intensified its military posture in the South China Sea in 2024, albeit with a recalibrated focus. While direct provocations like Freedom of Navigation Operations (FONOPs) and Taiwan Strait transits declined, alliance-based deployments and joint exercises proliferated (Singh, 2025). According to the South China Sea Strategic Situation Probing Initiative (SCSPI), even as U.S. forces were dispersed by simultaneous crises in Europe and the Middle East, strategic cooperation with allies such as the Philippines expanded. Channelled through arms sales exceeding $17 billion, 40 annual joint exercises, and maritime domain awareness initiatives, U.S. defense assistance now functions as a vector of geoeconomic influence, stabilizing local regimes while reinforcing U.S.-led order (U.S. Department of Defense, 2024).

This posture reflects a shift from direct confrontation to coalition-enabled deterrence. It recognizes that in a multipolar context, influence must be distributed, embedded, and infrastructural rather than solely kinetic. Yet even this strategy has limitations. As SCSPI reports, U.S. platform deployment and sortie frequency plateaued in 2024 (Liu & Liang, 2025). The operational bottleneck reflects the reality of finite resources in a world of rising demands. Coercive power, while abundant, faces diminishing marginal returns when spread across multiple theaters. Moreover, intensified activity in contested zones risks strategic miscalculation. Incidents like the USS Connecticut submarine collision and the F-35C crash underscore how coercive competition can undermine both regional stability and the economic utility of maritime commons. Nevertheless, the U.S. continues to invest in strategic prepositioning as a hedge against overstretch. Slated for completion by 2026, The proposed 33,000-square-meter logistics hub at Subic Bay and Clark is emblematic of a deeper transformation in U.S. Indo-Pacific posture. It marks a shift from temporary rotational presence to semi-permanent logistical entrenchment, reinforcing the latticework of coalition-based deterrence (Lariosa, 2025). This transition aligns with trends identified in the 2025 Deloitte Outlook, which notes the convergence of geopolitical insecurity, technological acceleration, and defense-industrial growth as key drivers of military modernization globally. The South China Sea is a microcosm of this convergence: unmanned systems, AI logistics, and advanced air mobility (AAM) platforms signal the materialization of a coercion-development feedback loop, where security spending shapes not only deterrence but also industrial trajectories and regional hierarchies. Unlike peripheral or semi-peripheral states constrained by austerity, the U.S. retains the institutional elasticity to sustain high defense outlays without immediate developmental crowding-out (Berckman et al., 2024). Yet even this fiscal resilience is bounded. The costs of maintaining high-intensity coercive strategies under multipolar constraints increasingly pressure strategic planners to optimize force projection through partnerships and capacity-sharing arrangements. These second-order strategies aim to preserve influence without provoking escalation or exhausting capital.

In this context, military expenditure must be understood not simply as an indicator of dominance, but as a calibrated tool of strategic capital. Shaping balance-of-power dynamics, enabling economic flows, and managing global volatility, The U.S. model illustrates how coercive force operates as productive investment in a fragmented world order embedded in alliance infrastructures and dual-use innovation. It is not the expenditure itself, but the institutional robustness and spatial design of its application that determines its efficacy. Thus, in the South China Sea, U.S. defense spending reveals a structural asymmetry. While China invests in coercive control through militarized territory, the United States embeds coercive influence through logistics, alliances, and technological leverage. Each strategy reflects a different mode of strategic accumulation that one focused on entrenchment, the other on extensibility. Both are rational responses to institutional vacuum and economic rivalry. And both, in their own way, reaffirm the logic at the heart of the security-growth nexus. In a world of contested sovereignty, guns and growth are not in opposition but are fused in the struggle to shape the regional order.

EU, JAPAN, TAIWAN, INDIA, AND SOUTH KOREA IN THE EVOLVING SOUTH CHINA SEA SECURITY ORDER

While the South China Sea remains the core axis of Sino-American maritime rivalry, the region's security architecture is increasingly shaped by secondary and adjacent powers whose differentiated strategies reflect a broader diffusion of coercive capital across the Indo-Pacific (Htwe, 2025). The European Union, Japan, Taiwan, India, and South Korea are embedding military modernization, strategic deterrence, and defense-industrial policy into their regional postures, underscoring the deep interlinkages between security investment and geoeconomic positioning (Kirchner, 2024: Steindl, 2024).

In a maritime system defined by legal ambiguity and institutional weakness, military spending functions not simply as protection, but as productive input as a way to secure trade corridors, signal sovereign resolve, and build bargaining capacity (Bueger, 2015). Despite variance in proximity and doctrine, These actors have engaged in the strategic accumulation of deterrence capital. Japan and Taiwan pursue direct kinetic capacity to offset strategic asymmetries (Zhang, 2025), while the EU and South Korea prioritize institutional scaffolding and capacity-building (Honrada, Ranjbar, & Mukan, 2023: Kim, 2024). Each reflects a variant of military Keynesianism, tailored to fiscal structure, alliance orientation, and geopolitical exposure.

The European Union plays a non-kinetic but strategic role, leveraging defense spending as institutional capital to reinforce international norms and maritime order. Lacking a unified military projection platform, the EU emphasizes regulatory sovereignty through mechanisms such as the 2025 Defense Strategy and the €800 billion ReArm Europe initiative, aimed at achieving strategic autonomy and maintaining influence in global security governance (European Parliament, 2025). Japan represents a high-capability model of coercive accumulation. Facing unresolved maritime disputes and expanding Chinese naval presence, Tokyo approved a record ¥8.7 trillion ($55 billion) defense budget in 2025, marking its thirteenth consecutive annual increase (Arthur, 2025). From standoff missiles to MQ-9B Sea Guardians, Japan's strategy blends technological revitalization with coalition-enabled deterrence, reinforcing alignment with U.S., Australian, and Southeast Asian partners (Kamisuna, 2025). Japan avoids Freedom of Navigation Operations FONOPs. However, Japan participates actively in joint naval exercises, reinforcing an interoperable deterrence framework (Furuya, 2023).

Taiwan operates within severe structural constraints but employs military spending as sovereignty capital—transforming fiscal allocations into asymmetric resilience. Taiwan, with a defense budget of $16.5 billion in 2024 and in 2025 NT$2 trillion (US$60.73 billion) for defense spending has significant strategic interests in the South China Sea, particularly regarding its claims over the Pratas Islands and its broader security concerns with China. In the South China Sea, Taiwan has invested in asymmetric defense capabilities, including submarines, anti-ship missiles, and advanced fighter jets, to ensure it can defend its maritime claims. With defense outlays exceeding 10% of GDP in 2025, Taipei's strategy of "resolute defense and multilayered deterrence" includes indigenous submarine production, light frigates, missile systems, and UAV integration (Liu & Teng, 2025). Taiwan's defense posture is shaped by its ongoing conflict with China, which views Taiwan as a breakaway province. Taiwan's military spending is focused on strengthening its naval and air defense capabilities to deter Chinese aggression and maintain its sovereignty (Rathi, 2025).

While traditionally focused on North Korea, South Korea has broadened its strategic aperture to engage the Indo-Pacific balance. With a 2025 defense budget of $45.6 billion (GlobalData, 2025), Seoul is going to invest in both indigenous platforms (e.g., KF-21 fighter, K239 MLRS) and multilateral security frameworks (Godard, 2024). Although its direct presence in the South China Sea is limited, Seoul's 2022 Indo-Pacific Strategy signals a conceptual shift from peninsular defense to maritime influence. Through trilateral cooperation with the U.S. and Japan and forums such as Partners in the Blue Pacific (Yu, 2025), South Korea supports a non-confrontational variant of military Keynesianism.

India's strategic posture in the South China Sea reflects a hybrid logic: part energy-security rationalism, part strategic hedging. With $86.1 billion in defense spending in 2024 and a 9.53% projected increase, India is among the top global military spenders and ranks 5th in global military spending (India Sentinels, 2025). However, with nearly half allocated to personnel costs, its coercive investment is constrained by structural fiscal pressures. Nevertheless, India has rebalanced toward maritime force, raising its naval share from 14% to 19%, commissioning its first indigenous aircraft carrier (INS Vikrant), and expanding procurement of Rafale fighters, BrahMos missiles, and MQ-9B drones (Shivam, 2025). India has significant economic stakes in the region, particularly in the form of energy exploration rights in contested areas of the South China Sea (U.S. Navy. 2025: India Today, 2025). These moves are geoeconomically motivated: 55% of Indian oil imports transit the South China Sea, and India's ONGC Vidcsh holds exploration rights in contested Vietnamese waters (Ha & Tien, 2024).

SOUTHEAST ASIA'S DEFENSE MODERNIZATION AND THE POLITICAL ECONOMY OF DETERRENCE

In Southeast Asia, military spending is no longer merely a reactive measure to external threat, nor solely a projection of national sovereignty. It has become a calculated expression of coercive capital within a volatile regional order where institutional guarantees are thin, and security functions as both an enabler and constraint on economic growth. Most ASEAN states have seen a sustained increase in absolute defense expenditures over the past decade. Yet, as a percentage of GDP, this growth has remained modest or stabilized, suggesting that economic expansion—rather than classical arms racing—is the fiscal engine behind rising budgets (Modern Diplomacy, 2025).

However, the current phase of militarization signals a deeper shift. ASEAN regional military expenditures rose from $34 billion to $47.8 billion in Between 2013 and 2023. 2024 saw defense spending reach $54.9 billion, a 7.5% year-on-year increase (Liang et al., 2025). This is less about inflationary drift and more about strategic recalibration. It is a transition from internal security postures to externally oriented deterrence frameworks. In a fragmented security environment marked by great power rivalry and institutional weakness, defense budgets have become instruments of developmental risk management as the insurance mechanisms against geopolitical volatility and tools of regional bargaining power.

Responses vary across ASEAN, but the underlying logic is shared. Indonesia retains a conservative approach, focusing its $11 billion defense budget on internal stability and modest naval upgrades. In contrast, smaller but geopolitically exposed states like the Philippines, Vietnam, and Indonesia itself are investing in next-generation fighters, submarines, and missile systems—not merely as deterrents, but as productive inputs into strategic autonomy (Hossain, 2025). These investments reflect the core of the security-growth nexus: that coercive force, rationally deployed, generates both political insulation and economic opportunity.

The Philippines: Alliance-Based Militarization and Strategic Dependency

For the Philippines, militarization is not pursued in isolation but as a function of externalized coercive capacity. The Philippines, with a military expenditure of $5.6 billion in 2024 (Liang et al., 2025), faces significant security challenges due to its territorial disputes in the South China Sea, particularly with China over the Spratly Islands and Scarborough Shoal. The Philippines has increasingly turned to military modernization to safeguard its claims, including acquiring new naval assets such as Jose Rizal-class frigates and surveillance platforms. With a 19% increase in its 2024 defense budget and deepening institutional ties through the Enhanced Defense Cooperation Agreement (EDCA) with the United States, Manila has opted to import security as a substitute for capacity. Anchored in base access agreements, joint exercises, and arms transfers (International Institute for Strategic Studies [IISS], 2024). This model represents a form of externally financed Military Keynesianism, wherein coercive deterrence is bundled with infrastructure, training and strategic legitimacy.

The Philippines is acquiring new patrol vessels, Jose Rizal-class frigates, and potentially submarines (Bisht, 2025). Investments in the Philippine Coast Guard (PCG) signal Manila's attempt to stabilize its maritime domain through both hardware and partnerships (Lariosa, 2024). Strategic basing infrastructure at Subic Bay (Naval Station Nabasan) and Oyster Bay is being upgraded with U.S. support (Zona Militar, 2025), reinforcing Manila's embeddedness within Indo-Pacific defense architectures coordinated by Japan, Australia, and the United States (U.S. Department of State, 2025). This approach reflects the outsourcing of coercion as strategic efficiency. Rather than bearing the full burden of indigenous buildup, the Philippines leverages alliance frameworks to stabilize contested fishing grounds, secure hydrocarbon deposits, and underwrite regional alignment.

Vietnam: Silent Deterrence and Sovereignty Assertion

Vietnam, in contrast, pursues a more autonomous and opaque strategy of silent deterrence. Locked in longstanding territorial disputes with China over the Paracel and Spratly Islands, Hanoi continues to invest in coercive infrastructure and maritime resilience (Linh, 2024). Vietnam has a robust defense strategy focused on protecting its sovereignty over the Paracel and Spratly Islands, where it faces ongoing territorial disputes with China. With a defense budget of $10 billion in 2024 (Liang et al., 2025), Vietnam is increasingly investing in its maritime defense capabilities to counter China's assertiveness. The country has made significant investments in naval modernization, including the acquisition of Kilo-class submarines, offshore patrol vessels, and frigates. With an 8% increase in its 2025 defense budget, Vietnam now ranks among Southeast Asia's top military spenders (VietnamPlus, 2025). Its strategy prioritizes naval modernization, including Kilo-class submarines, new frigates, and six offshore patrol vessels (Singh, 2023).

Vietnam's defense spending functions as capital accumulation under asymmetry—mobilizing coercive assets to deter encroachment while avoiding overt provocation. Since June 2024, Vietnam has reclaimed approximately 641 acres in the Spratly Islands, mirroring earlier Chinese activities and signaling its intent to convert legal ambiguity into de facto control (Strangio, 2025) New harbors and airstrips have enabled extended deployments across the 49 to 51 outposts it occupies on 27 maritime features, reinforcing its claim not just through diplomacy but through coercive permanence (AMTI, 2025).

Centered on advanced fighter jets and maritime strike platforms, Vietnam's quiet military buildup reflects a calibrated response to growing tensions in the South China Sea (Al Jazeera, 2025). In contrast to the Philippines' overt alignment with external powers, Hanoi has charted a more restrained course, avoiding formal alliances while steadily reinforcing its defense capabilities (Førrisdahl, 2024). This "sovereignty-through-endurance" strategy speaks to Vietnam's long view as deterrence built slowly, deliberately, and on its own terms. It is the logic of autonomous coercive capital through projecting just enough strength to matter, but never enough to tip the balance into confrontation (Wu & Velasco, 2024).

Indonesia: Maritime Sovereignty and Defense Keynesianism

Indonesia's defense trajectory represents a paradigmatic shift from internal stabilization to externally oriented deterrence, reflecting the recalibration of military strategy under intensifying geopolitical pressure in the South China Sea. Under President-elect Prabowo Subianto, Jakarta has launched an expansive military modernization campaign—structured around the logic of defense Keynesianism, wherein defense spending serves dual roles as a tool of geostrategic assertion and domestic industrial policy (Sari, 2025). At the core of this transformation is a long-term procurement framework backed by US$125 billion in defense loans over 25 years (Guild, 2024). This funding is not merely budgetary. It is a sovereign investment strategy that aligns military capital formation with both national security and industrial upgrading. Within this framework, Indonesia's defense sector becomes a node of coercive-industrial integration, mobilizing fiscal resources to stimulate domestic production while expanding operational reach (Malufti, 2025).

In the aerospace domain, the phased acquisition of 42 Rafale fighter jets from France (US$8.1 billion) and negotiations for 24 F-15EX Eagle II jets from the United States signify a decisive pivot toward high-end kinetic capacity (Dangwal, 2024; Dhanya, 2025). These platforms embed Indonesia within coalition-based deterrence architectures, signaling a commitment to interoperability and technological convergence with Western defense ecosystems. Equally consequential is Indonesia's maritime buildup. The April 2024 agreement with France's Naval Group to co-produce Scorpène-class submarines (US$2 billion) and the projected deployment of 35 coastal surveillance stationsand eight underwater detection systems by 2044 signal Jakarta's intent to transform maritime deterrence into a productive asset class (Guild, 2024). These investments directly reinforce territorial claims and secure maritime resource flows—notably around the Natuna Islands, where Chinese incursions have repeatedly tested Indonesia's domain awareness.

Indonesia's strategic posture is not reducible to hardware alone. The proposal to establish a fourth military branch dedicated to cyber operations underscores a multidimensional doctrine of deterrence. The formation of a Cyber Force, tasked with both infrastructure protection and offensive digital capabilities, represents the integration of informational coercion into national defense planning (Oktafian, 2024). This shift reflects the broader evolution of defense logic from kinetic dominance to hybrid strategic accumulation in digital and physical domains. Indonesia's military modernization is neither excess nor overreach. It is a rational allocation of capital within a maritime economy shaped by legal ambiguity and competitive appropriation.

Singapore: Next-Gen Security Architecture in a Small State

Singapore continues to leverage strategic foresight and high-tech defense modernization to offset its geographic and demographic limitations, reaffirming its role as a per capita heavyweight in regional security investment. For FY2025, its defense budget is projected to grow by 12.4%, reaching S$23.4 billion (US$17.4 billion)—solidifying its position among the world's highest military spenders per capita (Arthur, 2025). With a consistent defense allocation of around 3% of GDP, Singapore's posture is not reactive, but proactively developmental through deploying coercive capital not only for deterrence but for economic resilience and technological autonomy.

At the heart of this strategy is a deliberate pursuit of qualitative military superiority. Aligned with the security-growth nexus, where small states substitute scale with sophistication. The acquisition of 12 F-35B STOVLaircraft and 8 F-35A variants constitutes a major leap in airpower projection, multi-domain situational awareness, and regional deterrence. These fifth-generation platforms are not merely tools of aerial dominance but embedded components in a networked force architecture capable of asserting operational superiority over vital maritime corridors (Army Recognition, 2025). Simultaneously, Singapore has prioritized cyber-capable deterrence. In 2025, the Singapore Armed Forces (SAF)launched two new institutional nodes: the Defence Cyber Command (DCCOM) and the SAF C4 and Digitalisation Command (SAFC4DC). While DCCOM consolidates military cybersecurity into a coherent strategic asset, SAFC4DC focuses on integrating AI, cloud systems, and real-time communications into battle management (Brian, 2025). These initiatives reflect the core logic of military Keynesianism in a digital era that defense spending not only secures sovereignty but catalyzes innovation ecosystems and public-private interoperability.

The maritime dimension further anchors Singapore's security-industrial strategy. With the acquisition of two additional Type 218SG Invincible-class submarines, Singapore expands its submarine fleet to six. These stealth platforms, optimized for shallow-water endurance and intelligence operations, reinforce Singapore's ability to monitor and shape flows through the Malacca Strait and southern South China Sea—arteries vital to global trade and regional security (Cheng, 2025). Submarine investment here represents not just hard power, but a form of coercive infrastructure: embedding deterrence into geography through invisible presence and strategic ambiguity. Singapore's model affirms the principle that in a contested regional order, military expenditure is not overhead. It is strategic capital: securing market access, policy autonomy, and technological edge under conditions of growing maritime volatility.

Malaysia: Strategic Ambiguity, Dual-Use Deterrence, and Developmental Restraint

Malaysia's defense strategy in the South China Sea is driven by its strategic location and maritime claims, particularly over the Luconia Shoals and parts of the Spratly Islands. With a defense budget of $4.8 billion in 2024, Malaysia has focused on a dual-use strategy, balancing limited but effective defense investments with regional cooperation (Liang et al., 2025). Malaysia's maritime defense strategy represents a calibrated synthesis of limited coercive capacity, technological integration, and strategic ambiguity—a model well-suited to the security dilemmas of a semi-peripheral state operating within a contested yet institutionally weak regional order. Anchored by its two Scorpène-class submarines, KD Tunku Abdul Rahman and KD Tun Razak, Malaysia's deterrence posture emphasizes undersea situational awareness and control over vital maritime corridors. While no immediate expansion of the submarine fleet has been pursued, the commitment to capability maintenance and incremental upgrading reflects a doctrine of selective deterrence rather than escalation (Tyebjee, 2025). Concurrently, Malaysia is advancing a dual-use strategy by embedding cyber defense and digital infrastructure within its broader defense framework. Under Budget 2024, the allocation of RM20 million for a national AI frameworksignals an institutional shift toward the technologization of national security (Sangfor Technologies, 2025). These investments serve a dual function: enhancing cyber-resilience while stimulating the indigenous defense-industrial base, illustrating how even modest military economies increasingly treat defense spending as productive capitalwithin the logic of military Keynesianism.

Geopolitically, Malaysia adheres to an "equidistance doctrine," deepening trade and infrastructure ties with China, while sustaining quiet security cooperation with the United States. As ASEAN Chair in 2025, Kuala Lumpur has emphasized the imperatives of regional autonomy and multilateral conflict management, positioning itself as both mediator and stakeholder in the evolving maritime order. This strategic posture is manifest in Malaysia's assertions over the Luconia Shoals, where sovereignty is defended not through overt militarization but through normative reaffirmation (Strangio, 2024; Eldessouki & Al Midfa, 2024). Malaysia thus embodies a developmentally restrained form of militarization: avoiding arms races while still embedding defense within technological development, industrial uplift, and strategic hedging (Kuik, 2024). Its behavior aligns with the broader ASEAN logic of institutional hedging, wherein semi-peripheral actors resist binary alignment by treating defense expenditure as a multifunctional instrument.

Brunei, Thailand in the South China Sea Security Complex

Brunei's defense strategy adheres to a minimalist doctrine of situational sovereignty. Despite holding legal claims in the South China Sea, the monarchy has eschewed overt militarization in favor of multilateral diplomacy. Nonetheless, in 2024 Brunei increased its military budget by 31.6%, reaching BND 796.3 million (USD 440 million)—a substantial rise that reflects strategic anxiety even within traditionally neutral actors (Arthur, 2024). The bulk of this increase is directed toward ISTAR capabilities (Intelligence, Surveillance, Target Acquisition, and Reconnaissance), signaling a desire to assert domain awareness without disrupting regional equilibrium. Brunei's approach exemplifies a soft form of coercive capital: investing in strategic knowledge infrastructure to monitor contested waters without provoking escalation. In a region where military visibility often translates into de facto control, Brunei's model seeks to preserve flexibility while minimizing reputational risk and geopolitical entanglement.

While Thailand is not a direct claimant in the South China Sea, its defense strategy is shaped by the region's maritime securitization and escalating great power rivalry. Thailand maintains a strategic adjacency to contested chokepoints and vital trade routes, giving it a vested interest in freedom of navigation and regional order stability. As one of Asia's longest-standing U.S. security partners, Thailand continues to procure high-end defense equipment from the United States while benefiting from military training, logistics assistance, and interoperability programs (International Trade Administration, 2024).

Therefore, ASEAN posture reflects the logic of coercive alignment without territorial entanglement. While not driven by maritime claims, its defense spending reflects an effort to preserve alliance capital, ensure strategic relevance, and hedge against regional instability—particularly as great power militarization in adjacent waters threatens to disrupt established trade flows and diplomatic equilibrium.

DISCUSSION: THE LOGIC OF SECURITY-GROWTH IN THE SOUTH CHINA SEA

Throughout history, great powers have risen or declined not simply on the battlefield, but in the shadow of a deeper contest—the balance between military ambition and economic sustainability. In the contested waters of the South China Sea, we are witnessing not a peripheral skirmish but a strategic arena in which the age-old dilemma of "guns versus butter" is being reconfigured. Traditional economic theory often frames defense outlays as fiscal distortions as diversions from productive sectors (Schoeni, 2016). In the absence of robust institutional enforcement, militarization emerges as a rational adaptation. Defense spending is recalibrated as a form of "sovereignty insurance (Lobo-Guerrero, 2012)," enabling exclusionary control, signaling resolve, and securing long-term resource appropriation. Here, military spending does not represent a distortion of development, but rather its strategic recalibration. It can seem as an instrument deployed by states seeking to navigate the intricate intersection of national growth, sovereign assertion, and geoeconomic positioning in an increasingly contested regional order.

China exemplifies this trajectory. The Military-Civil Fusion doctrine does not simply modernize the People's Liberation Army. It could integrate defense R&D into the broader structure of industrial policy through driving innovation in artificial intelligence, aerospace, and cyber capabilities. The artificial islands across the Spratlys are emblematic of a broader pattern—military installations that double as platforms for sovereign assertion and economic extraction. This is strategic accumulation in action, wherein coercive infrastructure underwrites not only security but technological and economic ascendancy. It echoes historical patterns where rising powers fused economic dynamism with military capability to alter regional balances.

Yet China is not alone. Confronting the rise of a near-peer competitor, The United States has responded by reengineering its regional presence. Its Indo-Pacific strategy has moved beyond hub-and-spoke alliances toward what might be called a latticework of embedded deterrence—alliances fortified by joint exercises, base access, and industrial co-development (Li, 2023). The U.S. has responded with its "latticework model" of Indo-Pacific deterrence through integrating military aid, logistics cooperation, and digital interoperability to embed itself within regional security ecosystems (Parameswaran, 2024). In doing so, the U.S. is not merely projecting power but underwriting the defense economies of its partners. It is a return, in many ways, to a Cold War logic: security as a public good, financed through military Keynesianism and legitimized through institutional leadership (Sakwa, 2025). What makes this region particularly instructive is the extent to which militarization has become both a response to systemic disorder and a driver of national development strategies.

In an environment marked by legal ambiguity and institutional fragility, multilateral mechanisms such as UNCLOS and ASEAN's normative frameworks have proven inadequate in restraining assertive behavior. Confronted with these systemic shortcomings, states have turned, often quite rationally, to the deployment of coercive capital, using military assets not merely for defense, but as instruments of influence, enforcement, and strategic advantage (Gannon, 2021). Naval expansion, surveillance infrastructure, and forward-deployed assets are not merely security instruments. They are levers of resource capture and geopolitical assertion. Defense expenditure, in this view, functions less as a cost and more as an investment in strategic rent-seeking.

Therefore, militarization in Southeast Asia does not manifest as arms races or sudden strategic shocks. Rather, it unfolds as incremental, fiscally bounded, and technologically embedded accumulation. This reflects a conflict equilibrium in which states pursue selective deterrence, dual-use technological investment, and strategic alignmentwithin budgetary limits. Defense budgets, in this context, are not wasteful. They are productive allocations of coercive capital, deployed as both shield and currency to shield sovereignty while purchasing alliance credibility and strategic attention. For smaller states as ASEAN, hedging becomes the rational strategy. Avoiding exclusive alignment while drawing resources from competing poles. But such flexibility carries its own burdens to manage the risk of entrapment, coercive diplomacy, and strategic irrelevance in moments of crisis (Jones & Jenne, 2022). Rather than committing to either China or the U.S., ASEAN states pursue flexible alignments. Trading with Beijing while deepening security ties with Washington, Tokyo, and Canberra. Platforms like ADMM-Plus and IMET allow for capacity-building without formal entanglements. However, this posture could come with risks. Strategic ambiguity can erode credibility, provoke coercion, or weaken alliance commitments in the long term. Vietnam, the Philippines, and indonisia are adopting their own forms of defense-industrial symbiosis. For Vietnam, sovereignty-through-endurance reflects a deliberate strategy to invest in military modernization without overt dependency on great powers. The Philippines, bolstered by U.S. assistance, treats defense budgets as both national signaling and economic stimulus, embedding procurement into governance reform and infrastructure development. Indonisia emphasis on domestic arms production speaks to a broader ambition toward strategic autonomy through industrial resilience. As the strategic environment becomes increasingly polarized by external actors through the Quad, EU naval deployments, and other Western coalitions, ASEAN's vision of regional autonomy is eroded. The region risks becoming a proxy theater of great-power deterrence, where security dilemmas proliferate and maritime governance is increasingly securitized.

These patterns reflect a structural shift. In the absence of enforceable law, power projection becomes the de facto arbiter of order. Ports, airstrips, and digital grids are increasingly calibrated for dual-use. Infrastructure development becomes synonymous with strategic positioning. Indeed, the South China Sea is not merely a contested maritime zone. iIt is a stage upon which the political economy of power is being rewritten. Here, coercion substitutes for law, presence for paper, and defense budgets for treaties. And this is not irrational. It conforms to a deeper historical pattern observed in earlier maritime struggles, where access to trade routes, resource frontiers, and strategic waterways was determined not by principles but by force in the grammar of legitimacy (Kraska, 2011).

In sum, the security-growth nexus as it plays out in the South China Sea affirms an enduring truth: that military power, if wisely deployed and economically underpinned, can become a vector of national development. But it also carries a warning. The overextension of military commitments without corresponding economic adaptability often presages decline. Whether today's powers are sowing the seeds of strategic resilience or imperial overreach remains to be seen. What is certain is that the balance of guns and growth, coercion and capital, continues to shape not only regional dynamics but the future of global order. Therefore, defense spending in the South China Sea reflects a deeper structural reality: development and militarization are not mutually exclusive. In fragmented orders, coercion becomes a mode of governance, infrastructure, and diplomacy. Military expenditure is embedded within the political economy of regional contestation. It can seem not as distortion, but as a rational response to institutional failure and strategic asymmetry. far from being antithetical, guns and growth are increasingly fused in the pursuit of influence, access, and survival in a contested Indo-Pacific.

CONCLUSION

This chapter has argued that military spending in the South China Sea is not a distortion of economic logic but a rational strategy of accumulation within a conflict economy. In an environment defined by legal ambiguity, institutional fragility, and geopolitical competition, coercive force substitutes for formal governance. Defense expenditure becomes a productive input—allocating capital toward deterrence, territorial consolidation, and strategic rent-seeking.

China's Military-Civil Fusion exemplifies the integration of military spending with industrial upgrading, transforming coercive capacity into dual-use infrastructure and technological innovation. The Philippines' alliance-dependent militarization, while enhancing short-term deterrence, illustrates the structural limits of externally financed security under asymmetric conditions. Across Southeast Asia, the region's 7.5% annual increase in defense budgets reflects not escalation, but calibrated adaptation to a system where power, not law, adjudicates access.

Reframing the "guns versus butter" dichotomy, the chapter situates defense spending within the security-growth nexus. Military Keynesianism—particularly in semi-peripheral states—emerges as both stimulus and strategy, supporting domestic legitimacy, industrial capacity, and geopolitical leverage. Coercive capital, in this context, functions as a developmental tool in a region where sovereignty is enforced through presence rather than principle. The South China Sea reveals a broader shift from rules-based development to power-based order. Militarization here is not a failure of economics, but its evolution in a contested regional system. As states navigate a fragmented Indo-Pacific, understanding defense spending as coercive capital is central to decoding both regional dynamics and the transformation of global maritime governance.

REFERENCES

Acocella, N. (1992). The multinational firm and the theory of industrial organization. In Del Monte, A. (Ed.), *Recent developments in the theory of industrial organization* (pp. 232–251)., DOI: 10.1007/978-1-349-11771-0_10

Al Jazeera. (2025). *US approves sale of 20 F-16 fighter jets worth $5.58bn to Philippines.* AlJazeera. https://www.aljazeera.com/news/2025/4/2/us-approves-sale-of-20-f-16-fighter-jets-worth-5-58bn-to-philippines

Army Recognition. (2025). *Singapore confirms the purchase of eight more F-35A fighter jets to complement earlier F-35B acquisition.* Global Defense News Army Recognition Group. https://armyrecognition.com/news/aerospace-news/2025/singapore-confirms-the-purchase-of-eight-more-f-35a-fighter-jets-to-complement-earlier-f-35b-acquisition

Arthur, G. (2024). *Brunei defense budget surges by 32%, with focus on intel, targeting*. Defense News. https://www.defensenews.com/global/asia-pacific/2024/03/07/brunei-defense-budget-surges-by-32-with-focus-on-intel-targeting/

Arthur, G. (2025). *Japan passes record defense budget, while still playing catch-up.* Defense News. https://www.defensenews.com/global/asia-pacific/2025/01/16/japans-passes-record-defense-budget-while-still-playing-catch-up/

Arthur, G. (2025). *Singapore raises defense budget, readies new military acquisitions.* Defense News. https://www.defensenews.com/global/asia-pacific/2025/03/07/singapore-raises-defense-budget-readies-new-military-acquisitions/

Asia Maritime Transparency Initiative. (2024). *Chinese power projection.* Center for Strategic and International Studies. https://amti.csis.org/chinese-power-projection/

Asia Maritime Transparency Initiative. (2025). *Vietnam Island Tracker.* Center for Strategic and International Studies. https://amti.csis.org/island-tracker/vietnam/

Bardhan, P. (2004). *Scarcity, conflicts, and cooperation: Essays in the political and institutional economics of development.* MIT Press. https://www.amazon.com/Scarcity-Conflicts-Cooperation-Institutional-Development/dp/0262524295

Becker, J., & Dunne, J. P. (2023). Military spending composition and economic growth. *Defence and Peace Economics, 34*(3), 259–271. DOI: 10.1080/10242694.2021.2003530

Beckley, M., Gvosdev, N., Fiddler, C., Vaughn, S., Park, J., & Matsuda, T. (2025). *Strengthening US alliances in the Indo-Pacific*. Foreign Policy Research Institute. https://www.fpri.org/article/2025/03/strengthening-us-alliances-in-the-indo-pacific/

Benoit, E. (1978). Growth and defense in developing countries. *Economic Development and Cultural Change*, *26*(2), 271–280. https://www.journals.uchicago.edu/doi/abs/10.1086/451015. DOI: 10.1086/451015

Berckman, L., Chavali, A., Hardin, K., Sloane, M., & Dronamraju, T. (2024). *2025 aerospace and defense industry outlook*. Deloitte Insights. https://www2.deloitte.com/us/en/insights/industry/aerospace-defense/aerospace-and-defense-industry-outlook.html

Besley, T., & Persson, T. (2011). *Pillars of prosperity: The political economics of development clusters*. Princeton University Press., https://www.degruyter.com/document/doi/10.1515/9781400840526/html

Bisht, I. S. (2025). *Fincantieri, TKMS join forces to offer submarine to Philippine Navy*. The Defense Post. https://thedefensepost.com/2025/04/18/fincantieri-tkms-submarines-philippines/

Brian. (2025). *Singapore strengthens cyber defence with new SAF commands*. CyberCover.sg. https://cybercover.sg/2025/singapore-strengthens-cyber-defence-with-new-saf-commands/

Bueger, C. (2015). What is maritime security? *Marine Policy*, *53*, 159–164. DOI: 10.1016/j.marpol.2014.12.005

Carment, D., Prest, S., & Samy, Y. (2009). *Security, development and the fragile state: Bridging the gap between theory and policy*. Routledge. https://www.taylorfrancis.com/books/mono/10.4324/9780203873977/security-development-fragile-state-david-carment-stewart-prest-yiagadeesen-samy

Chan, S., & Mintz, A. (Eds.). (1992). *Defense, welfare and growth: Perspectives and evidence*. Routledge. DOI: 10.4324/9780203203590

Cheng, I. (2025). Mindef signs contract to acquire two more Invincible-class submarines. *The Straits Times*. https://www.straitstimes.com/singapore/mindef-signs-contract-to-acquire-two-more-invincible-class-submarines

ChinaPower Project. (2025). *How much does China spend on its military?* Center for Strategic and International Studies. https://chinapower.csis.org/military-spending

Cohen, D. (2006). *Globalization and its enemies*. MIT press. DOI: 10.7551/mitpress/3311.001.0001

Cohn, T. H., & Hira, A. (2020). *Global political economy: Theory and practice*. Routledge. DOI: 10.4324/9781003056881

Cole, B. D. (2024). *The evolution of China's naval strategy.* The National Bureau of Asian Research – Strategic Space. https://strategicspace.nbr.org/the-evolution-of-chinas-naval-strategy/

Cypher, J. M. (2007). From military Keynesianism to global-neoliberal militarism. *Monthly Review (New York, N.Y.)*, *59*(2), 37–50. https://search.proquest.com/openview/d68c9a0da01fd2c21277facab55146dd/1.pdf?pq-origsite=gscholar&cbl=48155. DOI: 10.14452/MR-059-02-2007-06_4

Dangwal, A. (2024). Cash-strapped Indonesia OKs third & final batch of Rafale fighters after struggling to buy Mirage-2000s. *EurAsian Times*. https://www.eurasiantimes.com/cash-strapped-indonesia-oks-third-final-batch-of-rafale-fighters/

Defence Security Asia. (2025). Regional skies on fire: Rafale, F-35B, Gripen E/F and F-15EX to ignite Southeast Asia's arms race. *Defence Security Asia*. https://defencesecurityasia.com/en/regional-skies-on-fire-rafale-f-35b-gripen-e-f-and-f-15ex-to-ignite-southeast-asias-arms-race/

Deger, S., & Sen, S. (1995). Military expenditure and developing countries. In Hartley, K., & Sandler, T. (Eds.), *Handbook of defense economics* (Vol. 1, pp. 275–307). Elsevier., https://www.sciencedirect.com/science/article/pii/S1574001305800134 DOI: 10.1016/S1574-0013(05)80013-4

Dhanya, D. (2025). *Indonesia set to acquire F-15EX fighter jets: Here's what you need to know*. Tempo.co. https://en.tempo.co/read/1998518/indonesia-set-to-acquire-f-15ex-fighter-jets-heres-what-you-need-to-know

Duman, N. (2024). *Understanding China's pursuit of power in the South China Sea* (Doctoral dissertation, San Francisco State University). https://scholarworks.calstate.edu/downloads/nc580w80b

Dunne, J. P. (2013). Military Keynesianism: An assessment. In Jain, L. C. (Ed.), *Cooperation for a Peaceful and Sustainable World: Part 2* (pp. 117–129). Emerald Group Publishing Limited., DOI: 10.1108/S1572-8323(2013)00020.2011

Eldessouki, A., & Al Midfa, N. (2024, Sep 16). Malaysia's strategic hedging toward China and the United States. *TRENDS Research & Advisory*. https://trendsresearch.org/insight/malaysias-strategic-hedging-toward-china-and-the-united-states/

Elveren, A. Y. (2025). *Heterodox economics of military spending*. Taylor & Francis. https://books.google.com/books?hl=en&lr=&id=FU1NEQAAQBAJ&oi=fnd&pg=PP1

Energy Institute. KPMG, & Kearney. (2024). *Statistical Review of World Energy 2024 (73rd ed.)*. Energy Institute. https://assets.kpmg.com/content/dam/kpmg/az/pdf/2024/Statistical-Review-of-World-Energy.pdf

Erickson, A. S. (2024). Essence of distinction: The ends, ways, and means of China's military maritime quest. *Frontiers in Political Science, 6*, 1448241. https://www.frontiersin.org/journals/political-science/articles/10.3389/fpos.2024.1448241/full. DOI: 10.3389/fpos.2024.1448241

European Parliament. (2025). *Defence: How the EU is boosting its security*. European Parliament. https://www.europarl.europa.eu/topics/en/article/20190612STO54310/defence-how-the-eu-is-boosting-its-security

Farrell, H., & Newman, A. L. (2019). Weaponized interdependence: How global economic networks shape state coercion. *International Security, 44*(1), 42–79. DOI: 10.1162/isec_a_00351

Førrisdahl, M. B. (2024). *Cooperation and struggle: A comparative analysis of Vietnam and the Philippines in the South China Sea disputes* (Master's thesis, Norwegian University of Science and Technology). https://ntnuopen.ntnu.no/ntnu-xmlui/handle/11250/3141959

Furuya, K. (2023). The Japan Coast Guard's role in realizing a Free and Open Indo-Pacific. *Pacific Forum*. https://pacforum.org/publications/pacnet-4-the-japan-coast-guards-role-in-realizing-a-free-and-open-indo-pacific/

Gannon, J. A. (2021). *Use Their Force: Interstate Security Alignments and the Distribution of Military Capabilities*. University of California.

Gilpin, R. (1988). The theory of hegemonic war. *The Journal of Interdisciplinary History, 18*(4), 591–613. https://www.jstor.org/stable/204816. DOI: 10.2307/204816

GlobalData. (2025, May 25). South Korea spent $222 billion on defence from 2021–2025. Asia Pacific Defence Reporter. https://asiapacificdefencereporter.com/south-korea-spent-222-billion-on-defence-from-2021-2025/

Godard, G. (2024). *South Korea as the New International Defence Industrial Powerhouse: Implications for Europe(Briefing Paper No. 2/2024)*. European Institute for Asian Studies. https://eias.org/wp-content/uploads/2024/07/South-Korea-as-the-New-International-Defence-Industrial-Powerhouse-Implications-For-Europe.pdf

Green, D. J. (2016). *The third option for the South China Sea: The political economy of regional conflict and cooperation*. Springer. https://books.google.com/books?hl=en&lr=&id=tMs6DQAAQBAJ&oi=fnd&pg=PR5

Green, D. R., & Anderson, J. H. (2024). *Confronting China: US defense policy in an era of great power competition*. Bloomsbury Publishing. https://www.torrossa.com/it/resources/an/5868699

GSDN. (2025). *Increased U.S. military presence in the Indo-Pacific: Global implications*. Global Strategic & Defense News. https://gsdn.live/increased-u-s-military-presence-in-the-indo-pacific-global-implications/

Guild, J. (2024). *Indonesia's Scorpene submarine deal with France, explained*. The Diplomat. https://thediplomat.com/2024/04/indonesias-scorpene-submarine-deal-with-france-explained/

Ha, D. T., & Tien, T. N. (2024). Vietnam - India oil and gas cooperation: From "Strategic Partnership" to "Comprehensive Strategic Partnership". *International Journal of Religion*, *5*(7), 212–225. DOI: 10.61707/mk4k8805

Hartley, K., & Sandler, T. (Eds.). (1990). *The economics of defence spending: An international survey*. Routledge.

Harvey, D. (2017). The 'new' imperialism: Accumulation by dispossession. In Resnick, S., & Wolff, R. (Eds.), *Karl Marx* (pp. 213–237). Routledge., DOI: 10.4324/9781315251196-10

Harvey, R. (2024). *Fossil fuel use, emissions hit records in 2023, report says*. Reuters. https://www.reuters.com/business/environment/fossil-fuel-use-emissions-hit-records-2023-report-says-2024-06-19/

Hirshleifer, J. (1987). *Economic behaviour in adversity*. University of Chicago Press.

Hobbes, T. (1651). *Leviathan: Or the matter, forme, & power of a common-wealth ecclesiastical and civil*. Project Gutenberg. https://www.gutenberg.org/files/3207/3207-h/3207-h.htm

Honrada, G. J., Ranjbar, D., & Mukan, S. (2023). Regional democratization: A comparative analysis of EU and US efforts in Central Asia and Southeast Asia. *Journal of International Students*, *19*(2), 277–306. https://e-journal.uum.edu.my/index.php/jis/article/view/16476

Hoong, L. W. (2024). Malaysia will strengthen territorial defence while keeping diplomatic channels open in South China Sea. *The Straits Times*. https://www.straitstimes.com/asia/se-asia/malaysia-will-strengthen-territorial-defence-while-keeping-diplomatic-channels-open

Hossain, M. S. (2025). Surging arms stockpile in Southeast Asia: Preparation for war? Modern Diplomacy. https://moderndiplomacy.eu/2025/02/22/surging-arms-stockpile-in-southeast-asia-preparation-for-war/

Htwe, T. M. (2025). China's strategic influence and rivalries in Southeast Asia: BRIC and China's geopolitical strategy. In Sabir, A. R., & Fatima, A. M. (Eds.), *Changing the global political economy: BRICS countries and alternative relations strategies* (pp. 119–146). IGI Global., https://www.igi-global.com/chapter/chinas-strategic-influence-and-rivalries-in-southeast-asia/365241

India Today. (2025, Mar 25). *Despite US forces being stretched thin, South China Sea activity grows: Report.* India Today. https://www.indiatoday.in/world/story/despite-us-forces-being-stretched-thin-south-china-sea-activity-grows-report-glbs-2698939-2025-03-25

International Crisis Group. (2024). *Asia in flux and US-China military competition.* Crisi Group. https://www.crisisgroup.org/asia/north-east-asia/china-united-states/asia-flux-and-us-china-military-competition

International Institute for Strategic Studies. (2024). Asia-Pacific regional security assessment 2024: Key developments and trends. IISS. https://www.iiss.org/publications/strategic-dossiers/asia-pacific-regional-security-assessment-2024/

International Trade Administration. (2024, Jan 8). Thailand - Defense and Security. U.S. Department of Commerce. https://www.trade.gov/country-commercial-guides/thailand-defense-and-security

Invezz. (2024, Oct 11). Rising tensions in South China Sea threaten global trade routes. https://invezz.com/news/2024/10/11/rising-tensions-in-south-china-sea-threaten-global-trade-routes/

Jones, D. M., & Jenne, N. (2022). Hedging and grand strategy in Southeast Asian foreign policy. *International Relations of the Asia-Pacific*, *22*(2), 205–235. DOI: 10.1093/irap/lcab003

Kamisuna, T. (2025, Apr 14). Japan's maritime cooperation in Southeast Asia. International Institute for Strategic Studies. https://www.iiss.org/online-analysis/online-analysis/2025/04/japans-maritime-cooperation-in-southeast-asia/

Kania, E. B., & Laskai, L. (2021). Myths and realities of China's military-civil fusion strategy. Center for a New American Security. https://s3.us-east-1.amazonaws.com/files.cnas.org/documents/Myths-and-Realities-of-China's-Military-Civil-Fusion-Strategy_FINAL-min.pdf

Kim, D. J. (2022). *Compound containment: A reigning power's military-economic countermeasures against a challenging power*. University of Michigan Press., https://library.oapen.org/handle/20.500.12657/53689 DOI: 10.3998/mpub.11622137

Kim, S. K. (2024). Challenges to the capacity-building of Maritime Domain Awareness (MDA) in East Asia: What is at stake? *Ocean Development and International Law, 55*(3), 395–416. DOI: 10.1080/00908320.2024.2405501

Kindleberger, C. P. (1970). *Power and money.* Springer. https://books.google.com/books?hl=en&lr=&id=6DiuCwAAQBAJ&oi=fnd&pg=PA3

Kindleberger, C. P. (1988). *International capital movements.* Cambridge University Press.

Kirchner, E. (2024). Geo-economic and geopolitical developments in EU–Asia security relations. *Asia Europe Journal, 22*(3), 333–349. DOI: 10.1007/s10308-024-00706-z

Kraska, J. (2011). *Maritime Power and the Law of the Sea: Expeditionary Operations in World Politics.* Oxford University Press. DOI: 10.1093/acprof:oso/9780199773381.001.0001

Kuik, C.-C. (2024, Jul 8). Tilting toward Beijing? Malaysia's relations with China after Li Qiang's visit. Carnegie Endowment for International Peace. https://carnegieendowment.org/posts/2024/07/malaysias-relations-with-china-after-li-qiangs-visit?lang=en

Kuzemko, C., Blondeel, M., Bradshaw, M., Bridge, G., Faigen, E., & Fletcher, L. (2025). Rethinking energy geopolitics: Towards a geopolitical economy of global energy transformation. *Geopolitics, 30*(2), 531–565. DOI: 10.1080/14650045.2024.2351075

Lariosa, A.-M. (2025, May 23). Philippine Navy to open new bases in Subic Bay, Mindanao. Naval News. https://www.navalnews.com/naval-news/2025/05/philippine-navy-to-open-new-bases-in-subic-bay-mindanao/

Lendon, B. (2025, Apr 30). World's military spending rises at highest rate in nearly four decades, report says. CNN. https://edition.cnn.com/2025/04/30/world/world-military-spending-report-sipri-intl-hnk-ml

Li, C. P. (2023). An analysis of the US Indo-Pacific strategy in US-China competition. *American Journal of Chinese Studies, 30*(1), 43–59. https://www.jstor.org/stable/45474900

Liang, X., Tian, N., Lopes da Silva, D., Scarazzato, L., Karim, Z. A., & Guiberteau Ricard, J. (2025, Apr). *Trends in world military expenditure, 2024*. Stockholm International Peace Research Institute. DOI: 10.55163/AVEC8366

Linh, N. T. (2024). Vietnam and the South China Sea. In Nguyen, T. H. (Ed.), *Security dynamics in the South China Sea* (pp. 198–218). Routledge., https://www.taylorfrancis.com/chapters/edit/10.4324/9781032657493-15/vietnam-south-china-sea-thanh-hai-nguyen-thi-linh

Liu, X. (2025, Mar 5). China plans 7.2% defense budget rise, marking 10th consecutive year of single-digit growth. *Global Times*. https://www.globaltimes.cn/page/202503/1329511.shtml

Lobo-Guerrero, L. (2012). *Insuring war: Sovereignty, security and risk*. Routledge. DOI: 10.4324/9780203122075

Malufti, F. (2025, Apr 30). *Indonesian Navy seeks SOSUS-like systems to detect foreign submarines*. Naval News. https://www.navalnews.com/naval-news/2025/04/indonesian-navy-seeks-sosus-like-systems-to-detect-foreign-submarines/

Marimuthu, M., Khan, H., & Bangash, R. (2021). Is the fiscal deficit of ASEAN alarming? Evidence from fiscal deficit consequences and contribution towards sustainable economic growth. *Sustainability (Basel)*, *13*(18), 10045. DOI: 10.3390/su131810045

Matthews, R. (Ed.). (2019). *The political economy of defence*. Cambridge University Press., https://books.google.com/books?hl=en&lr=&id=lLOQDwAAQBAJ&oi=fnd&pg=PR10 DOI: 10.1017/9781108348058

Mavrotas, G. (2011). Security and development: Delving deeper into the nexus. In Mavrotas, G. (Ed.), *Security and development* (pp. 1–17). Edward Elgar Publishing., DOI: 10.4337/9781781007037.00006

Mia, M. R., Tao, J. L., & Anderson, C. D. (2024). The South China Sea dispute and regional response. Quest Journal of Management and Social Sciences, 6(1), 74–86. https://nepjol.info/index.php/qjmss/article/view/67377

Miller, R. C. (2018). *International political economy: Contrasting world views*. Routledge.

Modern Diplomacy. (2025, Feb 22). *Surging arms stockpile in Southeast Asia: Preparation for war?* Modern Diplomacy. https://moderndiplomacy.eu/2025/02/22/surging-arms-stockpile-in-southeast-asia-preparation-for-war/

Nan, H. (2025, May 7). *China's military-civil fusion: A challenge to the US military-industrial complex?* ThinkChina. https://www.thinkchina.sg/technology/chinas-military-civil-fusion-challenge-us-military-industrial-complex

Nikolov, B. (2025, Apr 21). *Philippines receives India's game-changing BrahMos missile system.* Bulgarian Military. https://bulgarianmilitary.com/2025/04/21/philippines-receives-indias-game-changing-brahmos-missile-system/

Oktafian, I. (2024, Sep 23). *Indonesia to launch cyber force as fourth branch of military.* Jakarta Globe. https://jakartaglobe.id/news/indonesia-to-launch-cyber-force-as-fourth-branch-of-military

Oztuna, A. (2024). *Assessing the Chinese naval infrastructure changes in the South China Sea using geospatial intelligence* (Master's thesis). Johns Hopkins University. https://jscholarship.library.jhu.edu/items/ffda3520-ef96-4dab-afd5-2ee3f712d41e

Parameswaran, P. (2024). Southeast Asia and US–China competition: Realities, responses, and regional futures. In Khoo, N. K. S., Nicklin, G., & Tan, A. C. (Eds.), *Indo-Pacific security: US–China rivalry and regional states' responses* (pp. 115–129). World Scientific., https://books.google.com/books?hl=en&lr=&id=3_L3EAAAQBAJ&oi=fnd&pg=PA115 DOI: 10.1142/9781800614857_0008

Peter, G. Peterson Foundation. (2025, May 5). The United States spends more on defense than the next 9 countries combined. https://www.pgpf.org/article/the-united-states-spends-more-on-defense-than-the-next-9-countries-combined

Powell, R. (1993). Guns, butter, and anarchy. *The American Political Science Review, 87*(1), 115–132. DOI: 10.2307/2938960

Raska, M. (2024). Reimagining defense innovation: Defense AI in Singapore. In Borchert, H., Schütz, T., & Verbovszky, J. (Eds.), *The very long game* (pp. 22–27). Springer., DOI: 10.1007/978-3-031-58649-1_25

Rathi, R. (2025, Apr 17). *Island Defence: Assessing Taiwan's Military Capabilities.* Modern Diplomacy. https://moderndiplomacy.eu/2025/04/17/island-defence-assessing-taiwans-military-capabilities/

Reiter, D. (Ed.). (2017). *The sword's other edge: Trade-offs in the pursuit of military effectiveness.* Cambridge University Press. DOI: 10.1017/9781108241786

Roberts, B. (2011). Exploitation, appropriation, and subsumption. *Rethinking Marxism, 23*(3), 341–351. DOI: 10.1080/08935696.2011.583005

Rosenberg, D. (2002). The rise of China: Implications for security flashpoints and resource politics in the South China Sea. In Dent, C. M. (Ed.), *The rise of China in Asia: Security implications* (pp. 229–261). Routledge.

Rueschemeyer, D., & Evans, P. B. (1985). The state and economic transformation: Toward an analysis of the conditions underlying effective intervention. In Evans, P. B., Rueschemeyer, D., & Skocpol, T. (Eds.), *Bringing the state back* (pp. 44–77). Cambridge University Press., DOI: 10.1017/CBO9780511628283.004

Sakwa, R. (2025). *The Culture of the Second Cold War.* Anthem Press. DOI: 10.2307/jj.24751871

Sangfor Technologies. (2025, Mar 7). *Cybersecurity in Malaysia: AI investments on the rise.* Sangfor. https://www.sangfor.com/blog/cybersecurity/cybersecurity-malaysia-ai-investments-rise

Sari, M. I. (2025, Apr 5). *Indonesia's defence strategy is in urgent need of a refresh.* East Asia Forum. https://eastasiaforum.org/2025/04/05/indonesias-defence-strategy-is-in-urgent-need-of-a-refresh/

Schmidt, J. D. (2004). *Rethinking the nexus between development theory and IR: From old divisions to new encounters*(Working Paper No. 107). Research Center on Development and International Relations, Aalborg University. https://vbn.aau.dk/files/33748899/DIR_wp_107.pdf

Schoeni, D. E. (2016). Defense offsets and public policy: Beyond economic efficiency. *The Air Force Law Review, 76*, 95–135. https://heinonline.org/hol-cgi-bin/get_pdf.cgi?handle=hein.journals/airfor76&section=4

Schwartz, R. A. (2023). *Undermining the state from within.* Cambridge University Press. DOI: 10.1017/9781009219907

Shafer, D. M. (1994). *Winners and losers: How sectors shape the developmental prospects of states.* Cornell University Press.

Shivam. (2025, Apr 29). *Top Military Spenders of 2024–25: India's Position in the Global Military Expenditure Race.* Adda247. https://currentaffairs.adda247.com/top-military-spenders-of-2024-25-indias-position-in-the-global-military-expenditure-race/

Short, J. R. (2025). *Hedging and Conflict in the South China Sea.* Taylor & Francis., DOI: 10.4324/9781003537298

Singh, R. (2023, May 12). *Vietnam's purchase of Kilo-class submarines and military modernization*. CESCUBE. https://www.cescube.com/vp-vietnam-s-purchase-of-kilo-class-submarines-and-military-modernization

Singh, S. (2025, Mar 25). *Despite US forces being stretched thin, South China Sea activity grows: Report.* India Today. https://www.indiatoday.in/world/story/despite-us-forces-being-stretched-thin-south-china-sea-activity-grows-report-glbs-2698939-2025-03-25

Smith, A. (1776). *An inquiry into the nature and causes of the wealth of nations.* W. Strahan and T. Cadell. https://www.britannica.com/topic/the-Wealth-of-Nations

Smith, R. P. (1980). The demand for military expenditure. *Economic Journal (London), 90*(360), 811–820. DOI: 10.2307/2231744

South China Sea Strategic Situation Probing Initiative. (2025). *An incomplete report on U.S. military activities in the South China Sea in 2024.* https://www.scspi.org/en/yjbg/incomplete-report-us-military-activities-south-china-sea-2024

Steindl, U. M. (2024). Geopolitical instability and escalating conflicts: The impact on East Asian defence innovation systems. *Vienna Journal of East Asian Studies, 15*(1), 159–186. DOI: 10.30965/25217038-01501008

Strangio, S. (2024, Oct 17). *Malaysia's Anwar again says oil and gas exploration will continue.* The Diplomat. https://thediplomat.com/2024/10/malaysias-anwar-again-says-oil-and-gas-exploration-will-continue/

Strangio, S. (2025, Mar 25). *Vietnam island building in South China Sea continuing at 'breakneck pace'.* The Diplomat. https://thediplomat.com/2025/03/vietnam-island-building-in-south-china-sea-continuing-at-breakneck-pace/

Stubbs, R. (2017). *Rethinking Asia's economic miracle: The political economy of war, prosperity and crisis* (2nd ed.). Macmillan International Higher Education., https://link.springer.com/content/pdf/10.1057/978-1-137-55726-1.pdf

Tabelli, V. (2024). Trade and diplomacy through interconnectivity: The Belt and Road Initiative and its mitigating role in the South China Sea (Master's thesis). Charles University. https://dspace.cuni.cz/bitstream/handle/20.500.11956/197719/120483394.pdf?sequence=1

Tan, W. K. D. (2015). Fueled by wealth, funneled by politics: The dominance of domestic drivers of arms procurement in Southeast Asia (Doctoral dissertation, Naval Postgraduate School, Monterey, CA). https://calhoun.nps.edu/bitstream/handle/10945/47882/15Dec_Tan_Wah%20Kheng%20Dean.pdf?sequence=1

Turillazzi, A. (2024). Navigating risk: China's aircraft carrier strategy. *SAIS Europe Journal of Global Affairs,* 27. https://www.saisjournal.eu/article/99-Aina-Turillazzi-Navigating-Risk.cfm

Turker, H. (2023, Aug 24). Maritime chessboard: The geopolitical dynamics of the South China Sea. *Geopolitical Monitor.* https://www.geopoliticalmonitor.com/maritime-chessboard-the-geopolitical-dynamics-of-the-south-china-sea/

Tyebjee, F. F. (2025, Mar 10). Malaysia's unseen, silent underwater warriors. *The Vibes*. https://www.thevibes.com/articles/lifestyle/105719/malaysias-unseen-silent-underwater-warriors

U.S. Department of Defense. (2024, Mar 11). Department of Defense releases the President's Fiscal Year 2025 defense budget [Press release]. https://www.defense.gov/News/Releases/Release/Article/3718698/department-of-defense-releases-the-presidents-fiscal-year-2025-defense-budget/

U.S. Department of Defense. (2025, Mar). Vision statement for a prosperous and secure Southeast Asia. https://www.defense.gov/News/Releases/Release/Article/3973788/us-department-of-defense-vision-statement-for-a-prosperous-and-secure-southeast/

U.S. Department of State. (2025, Jan 20). U.S. security cooperation with the Philippines. Bureau of Political-Military Affairs. https://www.state.gov/u-s-security-cooperation-with-the-philippines/

U.S. Energy Information Administration. (2013). *Contested areas of South China Sea likely have few conventional oil and gas resources*. Eia. https://www.eia.gov/todayinenergy/detail.php?id=10651

U.S. Navy. (2025). *NIWC Pacific enhances India's maritime security capabilities*. America's Navy. https://www.navy.mil/Press-Office/News-Stories/display-news/Article/4196056/niwc-pacific-enhances-indias-maritime-security-capabilities/

Van Veeren, E., Stevens, C., & Senu, A. (2024). Secrecy games, power, and resistance in global politics. *Review of International Studies*, 1–18. https://www.cambridge.org/core/journals/review-of-international-studies/article/secrecy-games-power-and-resistance-in-global-politics/A9F2834F169D66304FD5F39722CFAA0C. DOI: 10.1017/S0260210524000275

Vicarelli, F. (1984). *Keynes: The instability of capitalism*. Palgrave Macmillan., DOI: 10.9783/9781512819892

VietnamPlus. (2025). *Vietnam eyes 8% growth in 2025 through strategic reforms.* Vietnam Plus. https://en.vietnamplus.vn/vietnam-eyes-8-growth-in-2025-through-strategic-reforms-post319053.vnp

Vision of Humanity. (2024, May 19). *Navigating tensions, conflict and prosperity in the South China Sea.* Vision of Humanity. https://www.visionofhumanity.org/navigating-tensions-conflict-and-prosperity-in-the-south-china-sea/

Wallerstein, I. (1984). *The politics of the world-economy: The states, the movements and the civilizations.* Cambridge University Press., https://books.google.com/books?hl=en&lr=&id=tXmk4Izf4RUC&oi=fnd&pg=PP9

Williams, L. (2025, Mar 5). China's defense budget: The real figures behind the world's second-largest military. *The Rio Times.* https://www.riotimesonline.com/chinas-defense-budget-the-real-figures-behind-the-worlds-second-largest-military/

Winnebeck, J., Sutter, O., Hermann, A., Antweiler, C., & Conermann, S. (2023). The analytical concept of asymmetrical dependency. *Journal of Global Slavery*, *8*(1), 1–59. https://brill.com/view/journals/jgs/8/1/article-p1_1.xml. DOI: 10.1163/2405836X-00801002

World Bank. (2017). *Global economic prospects: A fragile recovery* (June 2017). World Bank Group. https://openknowledge.worldbank.org/bitstream/handle/10986/26800/9781464810244.pdf

Wu, X., & Velasco, J. C. (2024). Navigating the Indo-Pacific: Vietnam's hedging strategies amid the geopolitical rivalry between China and the United States. *Asian Perspective*, *48*(1), 95–118. DOI: 10.1353/apr.2024.a919883

Xiao, H., Sadler, M., & Quek, K. (2021). Guns and butter in China: How Chinese citizens respond to military spending. *The China Quarterly*, *245*, 248–261. DOI: 10.1017/S0305741020000260

Xinhua News Agency. (2024, Dec 27). China launches new-generation amphibious assault ship. Xinhuanet. http://www.news.cn/english/2023-12/27/c_1212345678.htm

Yu, J. (2025, May 23). *The Evolving Role of U.S. Forces in Korea and Its Implications for the ROK-U.S. Alliance.* RealClearDefense. https://www.realcleardefense.com/articles/2025/05/23/the_evolving_role_of_us_forces_in_korea_1112227.html

Zha, W. (2025). Hedging without strategy. *Contemporary Southeast Asia*, *47*(1), 33–66. https://www.jstor.org/stable/27378715?casa_token=7nYaWBFQ0vIAAAAA:LI8Ezs62squC1nGfNdqI66StviFeQNZLDy406Al2Mftp7ypYC5fH4hd7jQFpybQieSV5WWT1rcZitomSkR3Hp1DSNTZiAzOCEm6noAB_RjYchA06Z-afpA. DOI: 10.1355/CS47-1b

Zhang, M. (2025). China–Japan–South Korea trilateral cooperation: Institution building and power politics. Springer Nature. https://books.google.com/books?hl=en&lr=&id=YsE7EQAAQBAJ&oi=fnd&pg=PR5

Zona Militar. (2025, May 21). *The U.S. will upgrade the facilities of a key base for the deployment of the Philippine Navy in the South China Sea.* Zona Militar. https://www.zona-militar.com/en/2025/05/21/the-u-s-will-upgrade-the-facilities-of-a-key-base-for-the-deployment-of-the-philippine-navy-in-the-south-china-sea/

Chapter 6
Guns and Growth:
Unveiling the Real Effect of Military and Public Expenditures

Mikail Pehlivan
https://orcid.org/0000-0002-7273-333X
Trakya University, Merkez, Turkey

Umut Akduğan
https://orcid.org/0000-0001-8659-541X
Trakya University, Merkez, Turkey

ABSTRACT

This study explores the relationship between military expenditure and economic growth in 10 MENA countries using a country-specific time-series approach. Employing advanced empirical techniques—namely the Bootstrap Fourier-Kruse Unit Root Test and Bootstrap Fourier-Shin cointegration analysis—it accounts for structural breaks and data nonlinearity. The findings reveal a heterogeneous and context-dependent relationship: while countries such as Algeria, Egypt, Israel, Morocco, and Oman exhibit a positive association between military expenditure and growth, others like Saudi Arabia and Tunisia show limited or no significant impact. These results challenge assumptions of panel-based analyses and underscore the importance of methodological rigor and contextual nuance. The study concludes military expenditure can act as either a catalyst or a constraint for growth, depending on national conditions. Policy recommendations stress defense efficiency, fiscal balance, diversification, and regional stability for sustainable development in MENA.

DOI: 10.4018/979-8-3373-3456-1.ch006

INTRODUCTION

Military expenditure (milexp) is a major element that can affect a nation's economic well-being and stability, particularly in developing and transitioning countries (Constantinescu 2023; Tran 2024). Milexp is primarily intended to safeguard national security and protect against both domestic and international threats. However, such spending can redirect government funds away from more economically beneficial areas, such as public services, infrastructure development, or tax reductions—resources that might otherwise enhance social welfare (Dunne and Uye 2010). At the same time, military investment has the potential to boost innovation-driven industries, generate employment, and open up new export markets (Heo 2010). In developing and transitional nations, a substantial share of national budgets is often allocated to milexp—either in response to ongoing conflict, as a preventive measure against internal unrest, or to serve political agendas. Once a country expands its milexp, particularly during times of war, internal political and economic pressures can push for the continuation of elevated military budgets (Collier 2006).

The current body of empirical research presents mixed and inconclusive findings on the subject. A major challenge in drawing firm conclusions lies in the variation across studies in terms of the countries analyzed—often grouped by geography or level of development—as well as differences in timeframes and research methods. Early investigations, which primarily focused on the period shortly after the Cold War and were constrained by limited data availability, tended to analyze more technologically advanced developing nations with stable economic growth (growth hereafter). These studies generally reported a positive link between milexp and growth (Benoit 1973, 1978). In contrast, later research that spans both the Cold War and substantial post-Cold War years tends to find negative effects, particularly when including nations with less robust economies (Chang et al. 2011; Dunne and Tian 2013). Further complicating the overall assessment is the fact that roughly half of the available studies are case-specific, with about 63% of those concentrating on just five countries—Greece, India, Pakistan, Turkey, and the United States (Dunne and Tian 2013).

Building on the existing body of research, which presents diverse conclusions regarding the relationship between milexp and growth, this study aims to offer new insights through the application of a novel empirical approach. To achieve this, the following paragraphs present the hypotheses developed and tested in this paper, along with its main objective and original contribution.

H1: Military expenditure reduces economic growth – defence burden.

H2: The effect of military expenditure on economic growth is positive.

The first hypothesis concerns crowding-out effects, which argue that there is a trade-off between productive government spending (such as investment in infrastructure or education) and unproductive spending (such as milexp). The second hypothesis focuses on supply-side spillovers and aggregate demand effects, suggesting that milexp can generate positive economic outcomes through technological innovations or increased demand in the economy. Last but not least, in addition to testing these hypotheses, an important objective is to compare the sign and magnitude of the coefficients for milexp and public expenditure (pubexp - non-military public expenditures) to understand the effect of milexp on growth within the context of pubexp. Building on the hypotheses, this study focuses on 10 MENA countries (namely Algeria, Bahrain, Egypt, Israel, Jordan, Kuwait, Morocco, Oman, Saudi Arabia and Tunusia) to examine the impact of both milexp and pubexp on growth.

In addition to these objectives, the originality of the paper stems from two key aspects: (i) Methodology and (ii) the Discussion and Conclusion sections on policy implications. (ia) Most studies have used panel data sets to investigate the relationship between milexp, pubexp and growth. A common critique of these studies is the use of panel data and panel selection, particularly the potential heterogeneity among countries in the panel and cross-sectional dependence. This issue can be addressed with estimation methods designed for heterogeneous panels with cross-sectional dependence. However, this does not make heterogeneous panel data analyses with different country characteristics more robust than time-series analyses with larger numbers of observations. (ib) This study estimates long-term output elasticities for 10 MENA countries. Conducting these analyses separately on a country-specific basis offers an advantage over panel data analyses, as time-series techniques yield more accurate results. These elasticity estimates reflect long-term demand for milexp and pubexp in the growth process, providing valuable tools for policy purposes. (ic) The empirical analysis employs a novel technique based on Fourier transforms that account for structural breaks and nonlinearity in the series. As stated, global milexp reached its highest point in the late 1980s, coinciding with improving East-West relations, before decreasing by approximately one-third over the following decade with the conclusion of the Cold War. However, in 1999, this downward trend shifted, and by 2001, a period of significant growth in military spending began, especially in the United States. This surge was largely driven by the enormous costs associated with the "global war on terror", primarily the wars in Afghanistan and Iraq (Sköns et al. 2004). Based on this idea, it seems likely that MENA countries have experienced at least one such change in the past. Therefore, overlooking the presence of structural breaks and nonlinearity in time-series analysis can lead to inaccurate conclusions and forecasting mistakes. (iia) Another distinctive feature of this paper is its assessment of the milexp-growth relationship, based on the findings from the empirical analysis presented in the Discussion section.

To set the scene, the next section provides a brief review of the literature on the relationship between milexp and growth. This is followed by sections introducing the model, data, and methodology. The findings are then presented, followed by a discussion. The final section concludes the paper with a summary of the main findings and policy recommendations.

GUNS AND GROWTH

The literature on milexp's impact on growth generally falls into three categories: supply-side effects, demand-side influences, and national security implications (Dunne et al. 2005). The supply-side view, based on neoclassical theory, suggests that higher milexp can improve administrative efficiency, infrastructure, and technology, benefiting the broader economy (Dunne and Nikolaidou 2001; Dunne et al. 2001). It may also enhance human capital, as military training can improve worker productivity once individuals return to the civilian workforce (Dunne et al. 2005). Most neoclassical studies find a positive link between milexp and growth.

The demand-side approach, based on Keynesian theory, focuses on how government spending affects overall economic activity (Dunne et al. 2001; Dunne et al. 2005). It highlights the Keynesian multiplier effect, which suggests that increased milexp can boost aggregate demand and utilize idle resources if the economy has unused capacity. Some underconsumption theories argue that milexp stimulates demand (Dunne et al. 2005). However, milexp can also harm the economy by reducing private investment, causing inflation, and diverting funds from essential sectors like infrastructure, healthcare, and education, thus slowing growth (Dunne et al. 2001). Additionally, maintaining high milexp often requires higher taxes, increased debt, or money printing, which can further harm economic performance (Ward and Davis 1992).

The security-focused perspective emphasizes the importance of national defense in protecting people and property from internal and external threats. A stable, secure environment is crucial for market efficiency, as instability can deter investment and innovation (Dunne et al. 2005). Higher defense spending can boost investor confidence by enhancing security (Maizels and Nissanke 1987). This is especially true for nations emerging from conflict, where increased milexp has been linked to higher foreign direct investment and tourism (Aziz and Khalid 2019; Khalid et al. 2020). Economic theory has long recognized the role of public security in development, with Adam Smith highlighting the government's duty to protect citizens and ensure justice (Smith 1776). While milexp can reduce growth barriers caused by insecurity, spending without clear security goals can encourage rent-seeking behavior. Excessive military buildup may also trigger arms races or tensions, leading to conflict and economic harm (Dunne et al. 2005).

In this sense, the existing literature on this topic can be categorized into four main perspectives: The first group argues that milexp contributes positively to growth (Benoit 1973, 1978; Kaldor 1976; Frederiksen and Looney 1983; Looney and Frederiksen 1986; Murdoch et al. 1997; Ando 2009; Halicioglu 2003, 2004; Yildirim et al. 2005; Brooks and Wohlforth 2008; Atesoglu 2009; Ikenberry 2011; Alptekin and Levine 2012; Brooks et al. 2013; Drezner 2013; Maass et al. 2014; Heo and Ye 2016; Desli et al. 2017; Ortiz et al. 2019). The second group holds the opposite view, suggesting that milexp negatively impacts growth (Rothschild 1973; Smith 1977, 1980a, 1980b; Lim 1983; Deger and Smith 1983; Cappelen et al. 1984; Faini et al. 1984; Deger and Smith 1985; Deger 1986; Cowan and Foray 1995; Roux 1996; Knight et al. 1996; Antonakis 1997; Heo 1998; Batchelor et al. 2000; Dunne et al. 2001; Chang et al. 2011; Dunne and Tian 2013, 2016; Shahbaz et al. 2013; d'Agostino et al. 2016; 2019; Churchill and Yew 2018; Sempere 2018; Desli and Gkoulgkoutsika 2021). A third school of thought asserts that the direction of causality flows from growth toward milexp (Joerding 1986; Kollias et al. 2004; Ali and Abdellatif 2015; Ma et al. 2015). Lastly, some studies find no causal relationship between milexp and growth at all (Biswas and Ram 1986; Landau 1986; Alexander 1990; Mintz and Huang 1990; Chowdhury 1991; Kusi 1994; Dunne and Mohammed 1995; Heo 2000, 2010; Dakurah et al. 2001; Dritsakis 2004; Pradhan 2010; Dunne and Nikolaidou 2012; Kollias and Paleologou 2013; Dunne and Tian 2015; Cevik and Ricco 2018; Yesilyurt and Yesilyurt 2019; Dunne and Smith 2020).

The divergent conclusions in the empirical literature may arise from the fact that many of the theoretical impacts discussed earlier are dependent on the specific political, economic, and security conditions in each context. As a result, the outcomes of such analyses can differ based on factors like the level of resource utilization, the methods of financing milexp, the externalities associated with defense spending, and how effectively milexp addresses security threats (Dunne et al. 2005). Furthermore, existing empirical studies often overlook the different timeframes within which these effects might unfold. For example, supply-side impacts may take longer to manifest compared to demand-side effects, due to the nature of the processes involved. Similarly, positive security effects may only become visible in the medium to long term, as sustained efforts are needed to ensure a stable security environment and foster investor confidence (Fatehi-Sedeh and Safizadeh 1989). This study adopts a comprehensive approach by examining the link between milexp and growth over various time periods, while accounting for country-specific time series characteristics, including nonlinearity and structural breaks, to isolate and unravel the impact of multiple, opposing factors.

MODEL AND DATA

In this section of the paper, the variables, data sources, and model specifications are explained. The paper focuses on the potential change between milexp and pubexp in terms of growth in the countries under investigation. The general form of the model to be used in examining the relationship between these variables has been constructed as follows:

$$GDP = f(milexp, pubexp) \quad (1)$$

Where milexp is the military expenditure (current US Dollar), pubexp is the general government expenditure without military expenditure (current US Dollar) and GDP is the gross domestic product (current US Dollar) as a measure of economic growth. The series of the milexp, pubexp and the GDP are obtained from "World Development Indicators".

This study focuses on the long-term relationships between the variables in Eq. (1). In this context, the model specifications for examining the long-term relationship between the variables are as follows:

$$ln\,GDP_t = \gamma_0 + \gamma_1 trend + \gamma_2 ln\,milexp_t + \gamma_3 ln\,pubexp_t + u_t \quad (2)$$

where $t = 1, \ldots, T$ represents the time period, u_t is white noise stochastic disturbance term, assumed to be normally distributed. In order to have consistent empirical results, and considering the possibility of heteroscedasticity in data, all variables are transformed into natural logarithmic forms. Eq. (2) includes the logarithm of GDP (lnGDP) as the dependent variable, and the logarithms of milexp (lnmilexp) and pubexp (lnpubexp) as independent variables. The long-term relationships between these variables will be investigated for each country based on Eq. (2). In the case of identifying a cointegration relationship, the next step will involve estimating the long-term coefficients. Here, γ_2 represents the long-term elasticity of GDP with respect to milexp, while γ_3 indicates the long-term elasticity of GDP with respect to pubexp. The signs and absolute values of these coefficients, which represent the elasticities, will allow us to draw inferences regarding the impact of the substitution between milexp and pubexp on growth.

In testing the hypotheses and identifying the relationships between the variables, data from selected 10 MENA countries were utilized. These countries, along with the sample period for each, are presented in Table 1.

Table 1. Countries and period

Countries	Period		Countries	Period
Algeria	1960-2023		Kuwait	1970-2023
Bahrain	1980-2023		Morocco	1960-2023
Egypt	1960-2023		Oman	1971-2023
Israel	1970-2023		Saudi Arabia	1968-2023
Jordan	1976-2023		Tunusia	1965-2023

For each country, annual data for the sample periods have been converted to quarterly frequency. To achieve this, the sum-match quadratic method has been employed, following the studies of Sbia et al. (2014) and Shahbaz et al. (2017, 2018, 2023). This approach automatically accounts for seasonal fluctuations in raw data while transforming low-frequency data into high-frequency data, by minimizing point-to-point variations (Cheng et al. 2012; Shahbaz et al. 2018). The quadratic match-sum method is favored over other interpolation techniques because of its straightforward operating process (Shahbaz et al. 2018). In this framework, the empirical methodology for investigating the cointegration relationship between the variables and determining the long-term coefficients will be explained in the following section.

METHODOLOGY

This section will begin by providing a detailed overview of the conventional linear unit root test and the non-linear unit root test method using the Fourier transform, both of which are employed in this research. Next, theoretical information on the Fourier-based cointegration test, used to analyze the long-term relationship between the variables, will be presented.

Fourier Unit Root Tests

A substantial amount of empirical research has explored how structural changes (or breaks) in time series affect unit root processes, from multiple angles. Traditional unit root tests—such as the Dickey-Fuller types like DF-GLS or ADF-GLS—are widely regarded as weak because they do not consider the presence of structural breaks. This limitation has drawn criticism, as these tests often fail to reject the null hypothesis of a unit root when breaks are present, leading to biased outcomes. For instance, a time series might actually be stationary despite a break, but these standard tests may misleadingly suggest otherwise (Cheung and Chinn 1997). Moreover, evidence suggests that as the number of breaks increases, these tests become even less reliable at rejecting the null hypothesis (Silvapulle 1996).

To address this shortcoming, Perron (1989) introduced a unit root test that incorporates a structural break, either pre-specified or integrated into the ADF framework. Later, Zivot and Andrews (1992) and Perron (1997) proposed determining breakpoints "endogenously" from the data to avoid subjectivity in break selection (Glynn et al. 2007). Perron's method uses dummy variables, assuming abrupt structural changes. However, Leybourne et al. (1998) criticized this assumption, arguing that economic shifts typically occur gradually. In response, Leybourne et al. (1998) and Harvey and Mills (2002) developed unit root tests that allow for smooth, gradual structural breaks. Still, these methods are limited in the number of breaks they can detect.

In contrast, unit root tests using Fourier transforms offer a major advantage—they can model an unlimited number of smooth structural breaks without requiring prior knowledge of their form or location. Notable examples include the Fourier-KPSS test (Becker et al. 2006) and the Fourier-ADF test (Christopoulos and León-Ledesma 2010). While these tests accommodate smooth breaks, they do not address nonlinear dynamics. For time series with nonlinear patterns, nonlinear unit root tests generally yield more accurate results. Some Fourier-based tests handle both nonlinearity and smooth breaks, such as the Fourier-KSS (Christopoulos and León-Ledesma 2010), the Fourier-Sollis (Ranjbar et al. 2018), and the Fourier-Kruse (Güriş 2019).

In this study, alongside the conventional ADF test, the more advanced Fourier-Kruse (F-Kruse) unit root test is employed to examine the stationarity characteristics of the series.

Bootstrap Fourier-Kruse Unit Root Test

F-Kruse unit root test is based on the ESTAR. The following is the formula for the ESTAR process (Kruse 2011):

$$\Delta y_t = \alpha y_{t-1} + \varphi y_{t-1}\left(1 - exp\left\{-\gamma (y_{t-1} - c)^2\right\}\right) + \varepsilon_t \tag{3}$$

Where $\varepsilon_t \sim iid(0, \sigma^2)$ and γ is smoothness parameter. The ESTAR model transforms into a linear AR(1) model when the smoothness parameter γ gets closer to zero. Kapetanios et al. (2003) show the case where the ESTAR model transforms into a random walk process under the constraint $\alpha = 0$ when $\gamma = 0$ as follows:

$$\Delta y_t = \varphi y_{t-1}\left(1 - exp\left\{-\gamma (y_{t-1} - c)^2\right\}\right) + \varepsilon_t \tag{4}$$

In Eq. (4), the random walk model is obtained under the constraint $\varphi = 0$. This indicates that there is no way to directly test the unit root hypothesis. Because in order to test $H_0{:}\gamma = 0$ and *vice versa*, φ must be defined. A common method for avoiding unnecessary parameter presence under the null hypothesis is to approximate the smooth transition function with a Taylor approximation. On the other hand, for the application of the first order Taylor expansion, an auxiliary regression is needed as follows:

$$\Delta y_t = \beta_1 y_{t-1}^3 + \beta_2 y_{t-1}^2 + \sum_{i=1}^{p} \rho_i \Delta y_{t-i} + u_t \tag{5}$$

In Eq. (5), u_t is a noise term depends on ε_t and φ. At the same time u_t is the residual of the Taylor expansion. The null hypothesis ($H_0{:}\beta_1 = \beta_2 = 0$), which indicates that the series has a unit root, is tested against the alternative hypothesis ($H_1{:}\beta_1 < 0, \beta_2 \neq 0$), which suggests that the series is stationary and follows an ESTAR process. The test statistic proposed by Kruse (2011) is as follows:

$$\tau = t_{\beta_2=0}^2 + 1\left(\hat{\beta}_1 < 0\right) t_{\beta_1=0}^2 \tag{6}$$

Güriş (2019) extended the unit root test of Kruse (2011) by incorporating Fourier functions, using the test procedure proposed by Christopoulos and Le n-Ledesma (2010). The test procedure developed by Güriş (2019) by incorporating Fourier functions into the nonlinear unit root test model is particularly significant, as it simultaneously addresses both smooth structural breaks and nonlinearity. The application of the unit root test in Güriş (2019) consists of three main stages. In the first stage, the nonlinear deterministic component is defined as follows:

$$y_t = \alpha_0 + \alpha_1 sin\left(\frac{2\pi k^* t}{T}\right) + \alpha_2 cos\left(\frac{2\pi k^* t}{T}\right) + v_t \tag{7}$$

Here, k^* represents the frequency of the model. This frequency value is obtained by estimating the model for $k = 1, 2, ..., 5$ using OLS, and identifying the value that yields least of the sum of the squares residuals. The error term for the model that yields least of the sum of the squares residuals is obtained by Eq. (8). In the second stage of the test, the test statistic for the error term obtained from the first stage is calculated with the model in Eq. (9).

$$v_t = y_t - \alpha_0 - \alpha_1 sin\left(\frac{2\pi k^* t}{T}\right) - \alpha_2 cos\left(\frac{2\pi k^* t}{T}\right) \tag{8}$$

$$\Delta v_t = \delta_1 v_{t-1}^3 + \delta_2 v_{t-1}^2 + \sum_{j=1}^{p} \rho_j \Delta v_{t-j} + \varepsilon_t \tag{9}$$

In this test, the null hypothesis $H_0{:}\delta_1 = \delta_2 = 0$ expresses the presence of a unit root in the series and is tested against the alternative hypothesis $H_1{:}\delta_1 = \delta_2 \neq 0$. If the null hypothesis of a unit root is rejected, the significance of the Fourier terms is then assessed using an F-test. If the Fourier terms are found to be significant, it is concluded that the variable is stationary around a deterministic function. In the decision-making phase, the critical values calculated by Becker et al. (2006) are used (Güriş 2019).

However, in the present study, the test statistics obtained are compared not with the critical values from Güriş (2019), but with those computed using the bootstrap procedure for each test. In this way, the study investigates the stationarity processes of the series using the Bootstrap Fourier-Kruse nonlinear unit root test. Due to the bootstrap's strong performance with finite samples in stationary processes, its use with nonstationary series has recently gained increasing popularity.

Bootstrap procedure provides the opportunity to account for factors such as sample size, initial condition characteristics, and the distribution of errors. Therefore, it may exhibit stronger finite sample properties compared to procedures that rely on asymptotic approaches, which do not take such factors into account. The steps of the bootstrap procedure can be outlined as follows (Palm et al. 2006):

(i) First, the residuals of the unit root test regression are obtained. Fit an AR(p) model to $\hat{u}_t$, where $\hat{u}_t = \Delta y_t$ if there is only a constant term as the deterministic component, and $\hat{u}_t = \Delta y_t - n^{-1}\sum_{t=1}^{n}\Delta y_t$ if there is both a constant term and a linear time trend as the deterministic component.

$$\hat{\varepsilon}_t = \hat{u}_t - \sum_{j=1}^{p}\hat{\phi}_j\hat{u}_{t-j},\ t = 1 + p, \ldots, n \tag{10}$$

(ii) With the help of Eq. (11), an i.i.d. sample ε_t^* is created by randomly drawing from the residuals.

$$\hat{\varepsilon}_t - (n - p)^{-1}\sum_{t=1+p}^{n}\hat{\varepsilon}_t \tag{11}$$

(iii) Bootstrap errors are obtained by successive iterations of Eq. (12).

$$u_t^* = \sum_{j=1}^{p}\hat{\phi}_j u_{t-j}^* + \varepsilon_t^* \tag{12}$$

(iv) The bootstrap sample y_t^* of the time series used in the unit root test is obtained by Eq. (13) and Eq. (14). If there are no deterministic components or only a constant term, Eq. (13) should be used. However, if both a constant term and a linear trend are present, Eq. (14) should be applied.

$$y_t^* = y_{t-1}^* + u_t^* \tag{13}$$

$$y_t^* = n^{-1}\sum_{t=1}^{n}\Delta y_t + y_{t-1}^* + u_t^* \tag{14}$$

(v) The coefficient and test statistics of the unit root test are calculated using the bootstrap sample for the previously specified deterministic specification.

(vi) Steps (ii) to (v) are repeated *N* times to obtain the bootstrap distributions, test statistics and critical values, where *N* denotes the number of bootstrap iterations.

Bootstrap Fourier-Shin Cointegration Test

In this study, the first Fourier-based cointegration test in the literature, which primarily relies on residuals and follows a two-stage approach, is used. Ignoring structural changes in time series can affect the stationarity process of the series and lead to biased results in cointegration tests. Therefore, Tsong et al. (2016) propose the Fourier-Shin cointegration test, an extension of the cointegration test developed by Shin (1994), which incorporates trigonometric terms to examine the long-term relationship between variables. This test, which takes into account multiple structural breaks through the Fourier function, is not affected by the number, location, or form of structural breaks that may arise in long-term relationships. In Tsong et al. (2016), the cointegration relationship is addressed using the following regression model:

$$y_t = d_t + x_t'\beta + \eta_t \tag{15}$$

Here, for t = 1,2, …, T, $\eta_t = \gamma_t + v_{1t}$, $\gamma_0 = 0$, $\gamma_t = \gamma_{t-1} + u_t$ $\left[u_t \sim (0, \sigma^2)\right]$ and $x_t = x_{t-1} + v_{2t}$ are defined. d_t represents the deterministic component and is defined as follows:

$$d_t = \sum_{i=0}^{m}\delta_i t^i + f_t \tag{16}$$

For $m = 0$, a model with a constant is obtained, and for $m = 1$, a model with both a constant and a trend is derived. In Eq. (16), f_t represents the Fourier function, which is defined as follows:

$$f_t = \alpha_k sin\left(\frac{2\pi kt}{T}\right) + \beta_k cos\left(\frac{2\pi kt}{T}\right) \tag{17}$$

Finally, the regression equation used to test the presence of cointegration takes the following form:

$$y_t = \sum_{i=0}^{m} \delta_i t^i + \alpha_k sin\left(\frac{2\pi kt}{T}\right) + \beta_k cos\left(\frac{2\pi kt}{T}\right) + x_t'\beta + v_{1t} \quad (18)$$

Here, the variables y_t and x_t must be first-order stationary [$y_t \sim I(1)$; $x_t \sim I(1)$]. Thus, the null hypothesis indicating the presence of cointegration is $H_0 : \sigma_u^2 = 0$, and it is tested against the alternative hypothesis $H_1 : \sigma_u^2 > 0$, which indicates the absence of a cointegrating relationship. The Shin-type cointegration test statistic The Shin-type cointegration test statistic $\left(CI_f^m\right)$ is calculated as follows:

$$CI_f^m = T^{-2} \widehat{\omega}_1^{-2} \sum_{t=1}^{T} S_t^2 \quad (19)$$

Here is $S_t = \sum_{t=1}^{T} v_{1t}$ the partial sum of the residuals from Eq. (18) and $\widehat{\omega}_1^2$ is the steady estimator for the long-term variance v_{1t}. Asymptotic critical values for the CI_f^m test statistic are demonstrated in Tsong et al. (2016). However, in this study, the test statistics calculated will not be compared with the critical values obtained from Tsong et al. (2016), but with the critical values derived using the bootstrap procedure. This approach allows for the analysis of the cointegration process through the Bootstrap Fourier-Shin cointegration test. The aforementioned bootstrap procedure has been explained in detail in the previous section.

FINDINGS

The integration order of the variables is determined, before examining the long-term relationship between them. Since the variables need to be integrated at first order in order to perform the cointegration tests. In this context, the ADF unit root tests, which are widely used in the literature, were initially applied to determine the stationarity characteristics of the series. The results of applied unit root tests are presented in Table 2.

Table 2. The results of unit root tests

Countries	Variables	ADF		Bootstrap F-Kruse	
		Level	First Differences	Test Statistic	Bootstrap p-value
		Test Statistic	Test Statistic		
Algeria	lnGDP	-1.974	-3.236**	29.27	0.5648
	lnmilexp	-1.556	-4.124*	14.36	0.1896
	lnpubexp	-1.556	-3.965**	16.87	0.4869
Bahrain	lnGDP	-1.626	-6.458*	32.69	0.7856
	lnmilexp	-2.032	-4.426*	45.12	0.1236
	lnpubexp	-1.764	-3.923**	17.86	0.4569
Egypt	lnGDP	-0.356	-3.459**	32.45	0.3547
	lnmilexp	-2.563	-3.052***	27.24	0.6541
	lnpubexp	-1.263	-5.871*	24.65	0.7540
Israel	lnGDP	-2.263	-3.124***	18.63	0.2306
	lnmilexp	-3.632	-4.458*	26.84	0.4695
	lnpubexp	0.523	-3.763**	23.02	0.4815
Jordan	lnGDP	-0.746	-2.947**	42.15	0.8523
	lnmilexp	-2.852	-4.798*	22.62	0.2365
	lnpubexp	-1.652	-3.102**	24.11	0.5691
Kuwait	lnGDP	-1.556	-2.874**	26.41	0.7852
	lnmilexp	-1.178	-3.169***	34.14	0.6324
	lnpubexp	-1.456	-3.747**	26.58	0.2148
Morocco	lnGDP	-1.225	-5.765*	24.98	0.3624
	lnmilexp	-0.456	-3.848**	30.36	0.6582
	lnpubexp	-1.637	-3.646**	28.15	0.5472
Oman	lnGDP	-0.258	-2.992**	19.41	0.4641
	lnmilexp	-2.964	-2.726***	20.64	0.2310
	lnpubexp	-2.267	-3.125**	17.06	0.1262
Saudi Arabia	lnGDP	-1.614	-3.536**	42.69	0.4136
	lnmilexp	-1.774	-3.026**	48.65	0.6035
	lnpubexp	-1.364	-3.226***	39.41	0.7402
Tunusia	lnGDP	-1.145	-3.156**	27.69	0.2369
	lnmilexp	-2.128	-3.853**	39.02	0.2536
	lnpubexp	-1.964	-3.903**	27.51	0.3456

In the Bootstrap F-Kruse test, the null hypothesis (H_0) suggests that the series has a unit root. The symbols *, **, and *** indicate that the null hypothesis is rejected at the 1, 5, and 10% significance levels, respectively.

Upon examining the ADF unit root test results, it is observed that the level values of the variables *lnGDP*, *lnmilexp*, and *lnpubexp* exhibit unit roots in all countries; however, they become stationary after first differencing. In other words, the series are integrated of order one (I(1)) across all countries examined.

As mentioned previously, there is a growing consensus that conventional unit root tests give biased results due to the tendency to fail to reject the unit root hypothesis because they do not allow for structural breaks. Therefore, when there are multiple structural breaks or smooth breaks in the series, the results of conventional unit root tests can be misleading. For this reason, this paper examines the stochastic properties of the series using the Fourier based unit root tests, which accounts for multiple smooth or sharp breaks. According to the results of the Fourier Kruse unit root test, the null hypothesis stating that the level values of the variables *lnGDP*, *lnmilexp*, and *lnpubexp* contain a unit root cannot be rejected for any of the countries examined. Therefore, the level values of all series are non-stationary.

In unit root tests based on Fourier functions, while determining the stationarity order of variables that are non-stationary at their level values, the results of the ADF unit root test applied to the differenced series will be taken into account. This is because the use of Fourier unit root tests is not recommended for differenced series. The reason for this is that structural changes are sought in the deterministic components (such as constant and trend), and when the series is differenced, these deterministic components are eliminated.

Considering the unit root test results in Table 2, the long-term relationship among the *lnGDP*, *lnmilexp* and *lnpubexp* variables, which are first-order stationary for all countries, can be examined. In this context, the Fourier-Shin cointegration test developed by Tsong et al. (2016) was applied for each of the aforementioned countries using the model in Eq. (20).

$$lnGDP_t = \beta_0 + \beta_1 t + \alpha_1 sin\left(\frac{2\pi kt}{T}\right) + \alpha_2 cos\left(\frac{2\pi kt}{T}\right) + \beta_2 lnmilexp_t + \beta_3 lnpubexp_t + u_t \quad (20)$$

Bootstrap Fourier-Shin cointegration test results are reported in Table 3. Based on these results, the null hypothesis, which suggests the existence of a cointegration relationship among the variables in Eq. (20), cannot be rejected for all the countries included in the cointegration analysis, except for Bahrain, Jordan and Kuwait. However, in all models, the null hypothesis that the coefficients of the Fourier terms are insignificant is rejected according to the F-test results. Therefore, the coefficients of the Fourier terms are statistically significant, allowing the use of the Fourier-Shin cointegration test results. Considering the potential presence of an unknown number of smooth structural breaks, it has been identified that a long-term relationship exists between the dependent variable *lnGDP* and the independent variables *lnmilexp* and *lnpubexp*.

Table 3. The results of Bootstrap Fourier-Shin cointegration test

Countries	Frequency (k)	Bootstrap Fourier-Shin Test Statistic	Bootstraped p-value	Bootstrap F-Test Statistic	Bootstraped p-value
Algeria	2	0.02127	0.91030	154.600*	0.0000
Bahrain	1	0.28220**	0.01300	-	-
Egypt	2	0.02963	0.68940	182.202*	0.0000
Israel	1	0.03617	0.11380	138.369*	0.0000
Jordan	1	0.13458**	0.01820	-	-
Kuwait	2	0.11095*	0.00540	-	-
Morocco	2	0.02821	0.49560	166.307*	0.0000
Oman	2	0.12317	0.31350	187.228*	0.0000
Saudi Arabia	1	0.06034	0.28740	186.470*	0.0000
Tunusia	1	0.07148	0.70280	245.215*	0.0000

***,** and *** denote the rejection of the null hypothesis at the 1, 5 and 10%, respectively.**

Since a long-term relationship exists between the variables in the cointegration analysis for all the countries, the long-term coefficients representing the elasticities for each country have been estimated at this stage. In this context, the long-term parameters in Eq. (20) were estimated using the Dynamic OLS (DOLS) method, and the results are presented in Table 4. Upon examining the long-term coefficients, it is observed that for each country with a determined cointegration relationship, at least one of the coefficients of the independent variables is statistically significant. When looking at each variable individually:

- In Algeria and Morocco, the long-run coefficients of *lnmilexp* and *lnpubexp* are statistically significant, with the coefficient of *lnpubexp* larger than *lnmilexp*. Thus, in these countries, the long-run elasticity of economic growth with respect to non-military public expenditures is greater than that of military expenditures.
- In Egypt, Israel, and Oman, both *lnmilexp* and *lnpubexp* are statistically significant, but the coefficient of *lnmilexp* is larger than *lnpubexp*. Hence, in these countries, the long-run elasticity of economic growth with respect to military expenditures exceeds that of non-military public expenditures.
- In Saudi Arabia, the long-run coefficient of *lnmilexp* is insignificant, while *lnpubexp* is significant. The long-run elasticity of economic growth with respect to non-military public expenditures is high, with a 1% increase in non-military public expenditure leading to a 6.83% increase in economic growth.
- In Tunisia, both *lnmilexp* and *lnpubexp* are statistically insignificant.

Table 4. The estimated long-term coefficients

Countries	Variables	Coefficient	t-statistic
Algeria	lnmilexp	0.24082*	6.753
	lnpubexp	0.71075*	31.734
Egypt	lnmilexp	0.39985*	21.595
	lnpubexp	0.33628*	16.590
Israel	lnmilexp	0.52444*	17.443
	lnpubexp	0.46488*	17.202
Morocco	lnmilexp	0.29517*	7.627
	lnpubexp	0.32028*	5.640
Oman	lnmilexp	17.5800*	3.616
	lnpubexp	5.42337*	6.800
Saudi Arabia	lnmilexp	0.69478	0.297
	lnpubexp	6.83348**	2.338
Tunusia	lnmilexp	-18.23666	-0.948
	lnpubexp	18.37460	0.620

*** and ** denote the statistically significance of the coefficients at the 1 and 5% significance level, respectively.**

DISCUSSION

In theory, economic theory should precede empirical analysis, but many economic models do not specifically account for milexp as a distinct economic activity. As a result, there is considerable variation in the theoretical approaches used in empirical studies (Dunne and Coulomb 2008). The neoclassical perspective treats the state as a rational decision-maker, weighing the opportunity costs and security benefits of milexp to maximize national interests. Within this framework, milexp is viewed as a public good, and its economic impact is determined by its opportunity cost—the trade-off between milexp and other types of spending. Early economic growth models, which assumed that technological progress occurred independently of economic factors, have since been expanded to consider the effects of changes in education and technology, leading to endogenous growth (d'Agostino et al. 2012).

Beginning in the late 1970s, this field has attracted considerable academic attention. The prevailing perspective, however, suggests that any potential benefits are likely counterbalanced by accompanying drawbacks. In general terms, while some argue that defense spending can stimulate growth through enhanced security and positive spillovers on the supply side, others point out the downside–namely, the reallocation of funds and resources away from civilian sectors of the economy. Since the end of the Cold War, global milexp has been rising rapidly. According to data from the Stockholm International Peace Research Institute (SIPRI), worldwide military spending reached $1.98 trillion in 2020, reflecting a real-term increase of 2.6% compared to 2019 and a growth of over 9.3% from 2011. In 2019, seven out of the top 10 countries with the highest military spending relative to their gross domestic product (GDP) were located in the MENA region[1]. MENA countries increased their milexp by 113% from 1990 to 2020, more than doubling their spending. In comparison, regions like sub-Saharan Africa and Latin America experienced more modest growth, with military spending rising by 72% and 54%, respectively, during the same period (Silva et al. 2020).

Empirical studies have produced mixed results, and there is no consensus regarding the net effect of milexp on growth, complicating efforts to accurately assess its impact. This paper acknowledges the existing ambiguity in the literature concerning the milexp-growth nexus. However, it is important to emphasize that the analysis presented here is country-specific. Consequently, the economic costs and benefits of milexp are framed within two hypotheses, with the objective of unveiling the real impact of milexp on economic growth: Military expenditure reduces economic growth – defence burden (H1); the effect of military expenditure on economic growth is positive (H2).

In Algeria and Morocco, the results favor H1, suggesting that milexp has a smaller impact on growth compared pubexp. In contrast, Egypt, Israel, and Oman show a stronger alignment with H2, where milexp appears to positively influence growth. Saudi Arabia's results reinforce H1, as pubexp plays a more significant role in driving growth, while Tunisia's findings indicate that neither milexp nor pubexp has a notable effect on growth. These variations underscore the need for country-specific analyses when assessing the role of milexp in economic development.

A general deduction might be drawn that milexp tends to have a positive impact on growth; however, this inference should be made with caution. The evidence from Saudi Arabia and Tunisia presents an important caveat, as the relationship between milexp and growth in these countries appears to be either statistically insignificant or less pronounced, suggesting that the effect of milexp may be context-dependent and not uniformly positive across all cases. Nonetheless, the findings appear to align with the line of research suggesting a positive association between milexp and growth, as reflected in the works of Benoit (1973, 1978), Kaldor (1976), Frederiksen and Looney (1983), Looney and Frederiksen (1986), Murdoch et al. (1997), Ando (2009), Halıcıoğlu (2003, 2004), Yıldırım et al. (2005), Brooks and Wohlforth (2008), Ateşoğlu (2009), Ikenberry (2011), Alptekin and Levine (2012), Brooks et al. (2013), Drezner (2013), Maass et al. (2014), Heo and Ye (2016), Desli et al. (2017), and Ortiz et al. (2019), particularly for Algeria, Egypt, Israel, Morocco, and Oman. In contrast, the results for Saudi Arabia and Tunisia are more consistent with studies that emphasize a statistically insignificant relationship between milexp and growth, including those by Biswas and Ram (1986), Landau (1986), Alexander (1990), Mintz and Huang (1990), Chowdhury (1991), Kusi (1994), Dunne and Mohammed (1995), Heo (2000, 2010), Dakurah et al. (2001), Dritsakis (2004), Pradhan (2010), Dunne and Nikolaidou (2012), Kollias and Paleologou (2013), Dunne and Tian (2015), Cevik and Ricco (2018), Yeşilyurt and Yeşilyurt (2019), and Dunne and Smith (2020).

The heightened risk of turmoil and conflict may lead to an increase in milexp. Collier and Hoeffler (2002) examine the potential impact of both external and internal conflicts on milexp, concluding that internal conflict is a significant driver of elevated milexp. Additionally, it is important to acknowledge that some countries engage in military research and development (R&D), which is often argued to produce positive externalities for the civilian sector. However, the extent and effectiveness of technological spillovers from military R&D to civilian applications remain subjects of considerable debate (Smith 2009).

In conclusion, from a security-oriented perspective, national defense plays a critical role in safeguarding both citizens and economic assets from internal and external threats. A stable and secure environment is fundamental to market efficiency, as instability tends to deter investment and stifle innovation. This perspective is consistent with a foundational principle in economic theory: that the state holds the primary responsibility for ensuring the protection of its citizens and the maintenance of justice.

CONCLUSION

This study makes a substantial contribution to the literature on the relationship between military expenditure and economic growth by employing a novel empirical methodology — Bootstrap Fourier-Kruse Unit Root Test and Bootstrap Fourier-Shin cointegration analysis — which accounts for structural breaks and nonlinearity in time-series data. By focusing on a country-specific approach, this study examines the impact of military and public expenditure (without military expenditure) on economic growth across 10 MENA countries. The results reveal a complex and context-dependent relationship between military spending and economic performance. Specifically, while countries such as Algeria, Egypt, Israel, Morocco and Oman exhibit a positive relationship between military expenditure and growth, other nations like Saudi Arabia provide support for the crowding-out hypothesis, wherein military expenditure appears to have a lesser effect on growth compared to other forms of public spending. Tunisia's case further highlights that neither military nor public expenditure significantly influences growth, underlining the heterogeneous nature of the effects across different national contexts. These findings challenge the generalizations often drawn from panel data analyses and emphasize the importance of using advanced techniques, such as the Bootstrap Fourier-Kruse and Shin approach, to capture the full dynamics of military expenditure's impact on economic growth. Ultimately, this study underscores that military spending can act as both a potential driver of economic growth and a fiscal burden, contingent upon the broader political, economic, and security conditions within each country. As such, strategic prioritization and prudent allocation of government spending are essential to ensure sustainable economic development in the MENA region. Building on the findings and insights derived from the empirical analysis, the following section outlines key policy recommendations aimed at optimizing military expenditure for sustainable economic growth, while considering the unique economic and security dynamics of each country in the MENA region:

(i) Enhanced Military Expenditure Efficiency: For countries in the MENA region where military expenditure shows a positive effect on growth, it is important to focus on improving the efficiency of defense spending. This can be achieved by investing in military research and development (R&D) that leads to technological advancements with civilian applications. Efforts should be made to ensure that military R&D generates positive spillovers, benefiting both the defense and civilian sectors. Moreover, transparency in defense spending and the adoption of efficient procurement practices can help maximize the economic returns from military investments.
(ii) Monitor and Mitigate Risks of Over-Militarization: Excessive reliance on military spending in some countries can exacerbate economic instability. For countries like Saudi Arabia and Tunisia, which exhibit either weak or no positive relationship between military expenditure and growth, it is vital to monitor the levels of military spending relative to other critical sectors. Notably, seven of the countries with the highest military burdens in the world in 2019 were located in the MENA region—Algeria (6.0%), Israel (5.3%), Jordan (4.7%), Kuwait (5.6%), Lebanon (4.2%), Saudi Arabia (8.0%), and Oman, with the highest rate globally at 8.8% of GDP—underscoring the urgency of this issue. Governments should aim to reduce the risks associated with over-militarization by focusing on security objectives that do not disproportionately drain national resources. Additionally, fostering international cooperation and security agreements could help reduce the need for excessive military spending, allowing resources to be redirected to more productive uses.
(iii) Long-Term Structural Reforms and Diversification: As military expenditure is often tied to broader security concerns and geopolitical dynamics, MENA

countries should prioritize long-term structural reforms that promote economic diversification. Relying too heavily on military expenditure without broader economic development can limit the region's resilience in the face of global shifts. Policymakers should aim to diversify the economy away from oil and military-focused industries by investing in sectors like technology, renewable energy, and manufacturing. These investments will help create a more balanced and sustainable economic growth model.

(iv) Promote Regional Stability for Economic Growth: From a security-oriented perspective, fostering regional stability is crucial for unlocking the economic potential of military expenditure. For countries emerging from conflict or facing internal unrest, it is important to link military spending with efforts to promote political stability, peacebuilding, and conflict resolution. Stability fosters investor confidence, encourages foreign direct investment, and helps stimulate economic growth. Hence, governments should not only focus on defense but also on diplomatic efforts to resolve conflicts and reduce tensions in the region.

REFERENCES

Alexander, W. R. (1990). The impact of defence spending on economic growth: A multi-sectoral approach to defence spending and economic growth with evidence from developed economies". *Defence and Peace Economics*, *2*(1), 39–55. DOI: 10.1080/10430719008404677

Ali, H. E., & Abdellatif, O. A. (2015). Military expenditures and natural resources: Evidence from rentier states in the Middle East and North Africa". *Defence and Peace Economics*, *26*(1), 5–13. DOI: 10.1080/10242694.2013.848574

Alptekin, A., & Levine, P. (2012). Military expenditure and economic growth: A meta-analysis. *European Journal of Political Economy*, *28*(4), 636–650. DOI: 10.1016/j.ejpoleco.2012.07.002

Ando, S. (2009). The impact of defence expenditure on economic growth: Panel data analysis based on feder model". *International Journal of Economic Policy Studies*, *4*(1), 141–154. DOI: 10.1007/BF03405719

Antonakis, N. (1997). Military expenditure and economic growth in Greece, 1960-90. *Journal of Peace Research*, *34*(1), 89–100. DOI: 10.1177/0022343397034001007

Atesoglu, H. S. (2009). Defense spending and aggregate output in the United States. *Defence and Peace Economics*, *20*(1), 21–26. DOI: 10.1080/10242690701775533

Aziz, N., & Khalid, U. (2019). Armed conflict, military expenses and FDI inflow to developing countries. *Defence and Peace Economics*, *30*(2), 238–251. DOI: 10.1080/10242694.2017.1388066

Batchelor, P., Dunne, J. P., & Saal, D. S. (2000). Military spending and economic growth in South Africa. *Defence and Peace Economics*, *11*(4), 553–571. DOI: 10.1080/10430710008404966

Becker, R., Enders, W., & Lee, J. (2006). A stationarity test in the presence of an unknown number of smooth breaks. *Journal of Time Series Analysis*, *27*(3), 381–409. DOI: 10.1111/j.1467-9892.2006.00478.x

Benoit, E. (1973). Defense and Economic Growth in Developing Countries. US: Boston: Health and Co., Lexington Books.

Benoit, E. (1978). Growth and defense in developing countries". *Economic Development and Cultural Change*, *26*(2), 271–280. DOI: 10.1086/451015

Biswas, B., & Ram, R. (1986). Military expenditures and economic growth in less developed countries: An augmented model and further evidence". *Economic Development and Cultural Change*, *34*(2), 361–372. DOI: 10.1086/451533

Brooks, S. G., Ikenberry, J. G., & Wohlforth, W. C. (2013). Don't come home, America: The case against retrenchment". *International Security*, *37*(3), 7–51. DOI: 10.1162/ISEC_a_00107

Brooks, S. G., & Wohlforth, W. C. (2008). *World out of Balance: International Relations and the Challenge of American Primacy*. Princeton University Press.

Cappelen, Å., Gleditsch, N. P., & Bjerkholt, O. (1984). Military spending and economic growth in the OECD countries". *Journal of Peace Research*, *21*(4), 361–373. DOI: 10.1177/002234338402100404

Cevik, S., & Ricco, J. (2018). No buck for the bang: Revisiting the military-growth nexus. *Empirica*, *45*(4), 639–653. DOI: 10.1007/s10663-017-9380-8

Chang, H.-C., Huang, B.-N., & Yang, C. W. (2011). Military expenditure and economic growth across different groups: A dynamic panel Granger-causality approach. *Economic Modelling*, *28*(6), 2416–2423. DOI: 10.1016/j.econmod.2011.06.001

Cheng, M., Chung, L., Tam, C., Yuen, R., Chan, S., & Yu, I. (2012). *"Tracking the Hong Kong Economy"*. Occasional Paper, 3, 1-30.

Cheung, Y.-W., & Chinn, M. (1997). Further investigation of the uncertain unit root in GNP. *Journal of Business & Economic Statistics*, *15*(1), 68–73. DOI: 10.1080/07350015.1997.10524688

Chowdhury, A. R. (1991). A causal analysis of defense spending and economic growth. *The Journal of Conflict Resolution*, *35*(1), 80–97. DOI: 10.1177/0022002791035001005

Christopoulos, D., & León-Ledesma, M. (2010). Smooth breaks and non-linear mean reversion: Post-Bretton Woods real exchange rates. *Journal of International Money and Finance*, *29*(6), 1076–1093. DOI: 10.1016/j.jimonfin.2010.02.003

Churchill, S. A., & Yew, S. L. (2018). The effect of military expenditure on growth: An empirical synthesis. *Empirical Economics*, *55*(3), 1357–1387. DOI: 10.1007/s00181-017-1300-z

Collier, P. (2006). War and military spending in developing countries and their consequences for development. *The Economics of Peace & Security Journal*, *1*(1), 10–13. DOI: 10.15355/epsj.1.1.10

Collier, P., & Hoeffler, A. (2002). *Military Expenditure — Threats, Aid, and Arms Races*. Policy Research Working Paper Series 2927. The World Bank.

Constantinescu, M. (2023). Measuring economic resilience for the CEE and Black Sea countries in the framework of comprehensive defence. *Security and Defence Quarterly*, *44*(4), 55–83.

Cowan, R., & Foray, D. (1995). Quandaries in the economics of dual technologies and spillovers from military to civilian research and development. *Research Policy*, *24*(6), 851–868. DOI: 10.1016/0048-7333(94)00802-7

d'Agostini, G., Dunne, J. P., & Pieroni, L. (2012). Corruption, military spending and growth". *Defence and Peace Economics*, *23*(2), 591–604. DOI: 10.1080/10242694.2012.663579

d'Agostino, G., Dunne, J. P., & Pieroni, L. (2016). Government spending, corruption and economic growth". *World Development*, *84*, 190–205. DOI: 10.1016/j.worlddev.2016.03.011

d'Agostino, G., Dunne, J. P., & Pieroni, L. (2019). Military expenditure, endogeneity and economic growth. *Defence and Peace Economics*, *30*(5), 509–524. DOI: 10.1080/10242694.2017.1422314

Dakurah, A. H., Davies, S. P., & Sampath, R. K. (2001). Defense spending and economic growth in developing countries: A causality analysis". *Journal of Policy Modeling*, *23*(6), 651–658. DOI: 10.1016/S0161-8938(01)00079-5

Deger, S. (1986). Economic development and defense expenditure". *Economic Development and Cultural Change*, *35*(1), 179–196. DOI: 10.1086/451577

Deger, S., & Smith, R. (1983). Military expenditure and growth in less developed countries. *The Journal of Conflict Resolution*, *27*(2), 335–353. DOI: 10.1177/0022002783027002006

Deger, S., & Smith, R. (1985). Military expenditure and development: The economic linkages. *IDS Bulletin*, *16*(4), 49–54. DOI: 10.1111/j.1759-5436.1985.mp16004010.x

Desli, E., & Gkoulgkoutsika, A. (2021). Military spending and economic growth: A panel data investigation". *Economic Change and Restructuring*, *54*(3), 781–806. DOI: 10.1007/s10644-020-09267-8

Desli, E., Gkoulgkoutsika, A., & Katrakilidis, C. (2017). Investigating the dynamic interaction between military spending and economic growth. *Review of Development Economics*, *21*(3), 511–526. DOI: 10.1111/rode.12268

Drezner, D. W. (2013). Military primacy doesn't pay (nearly as much as you think)". *International Security*, *38*(1), 52–79. DOI: 10.1162/ISEC_a_00124

Dritsakis, N. (2004). Defense spending and economic growth: An empirical investigation for Greece and Turkey". *Journal of Policy Modeling*, *26*(2), 249–264. DOI: 10.1016/j.jpolmod.2004.03.011

Dunne, J., & Uye, M. (2010). Military Spending and Development. In Tan, A. (Ed.), *The Global Arms Trade: A Handbook* (pp. 293–305). Routledge.

Dunne, J. P., & Mohammed, N. A. (1995). Military spending in sub-saharan africa: Some evidence for 1967-85. *Journal of Peace Research*, *32*(3), 331–343. DOI: 10.1177/0022343395032003006

Dunne, J. P., & Nikolaidou, E. (2012). Defence spending and economic growth in the EU15". *Defence and Peace Economics*, *23*(6), 537–548. DOI: 10.1080/10242694.2012.663575

Dunne, J. P., & Smith, R. P. (2020). Military expenditure, investment and growth". *Defence and Peace Economics*, *31*(6), 601–614. DOI: 10.1080/10242694.2019.1636182

Dunne, J. P., Smith, R. P., & Willenbockel, D. (2005). Models of military expenditure and growth: A critical review. *Defence and Peace Economics*, *16*(6), 449–461. DOI: 10.1080/10242690500167791

Dunne, J. P., & Tian, N. (2015). Military expenditure, economic growth and heterogeneity". *Defence and Peace Economics*, *26*(1), 15–31. DOI: 10.1080/10242694.2013.848575

Dunne, J. P., & Tian, N. (2016). Military expenditure and economic growth, 1960–2014. *The Economics of Peace and Security Journal*, *11*(2), 50–56. DOI: 10.15355/epsj.11.2.50

Dunne, P., & Coulomb, F. (2008). Peace, War and International Security: Economic Theories. In Fontanel, J., & Chatterji, M. (Eds.), *War, Peace and Security* (pp. 13–36). Emerald Group Publishing Limited. DOI: 10.1016/S1572-8323(08)06002-5

Dunne, P., & Nikolaidou, E. (2001). Military expenditure and economic growth: A demand and supply model for Greece, 1960-96. *Defence and Peace Economics*, *12*(1), 47–67. DOI: 10.1080/10430710108404976

Dunne, P., Nikolaidou, E., & Vougas, D. (2001). Defence spending and economic growth: A causal analysis for Greece and Turkey. *Defence and Peace Economics*, *12*(1), 5–26. DOI: 10.1080/10430710108404974

Dunne, P., & Tian, N. (2013). Military expenditure and economic growth: A survey. *The Economics of Peace and Security Journal*, *8*(1), 5–11. DOI: 10.15355/epsj.8.1.5

Faini, R., Annez, P., & Taylor, L. (1984). Defense spending, economic structure, and growth: Evidence among countries and over time". *Economic Development and Cultural Change*, *32*(3), 487–498. DOI: 10.1086/451402

Fatehi-Sedeh, K., & Safizadeh, M. H. (1989). The association between political instability and flow of foreign direct investment. *Management International Review*, 4–13.

Frederiksen, P. C., & Looney, R. E. (1983). Defense expenditures and economic growth in development countries: Some further empirical evidence". *Armed Forces and Society*, *9*(4), 633–645. DOI: 10.1177/0095327X8300900406

Glynn, J., Perera, N., & Verma, R. (2007). Unit root tests and structural breaks: A survey with applications. *Journal of Quantitative Methods for Economics and Business Administration*, *3*(1), 63–79.

Güriş, B. (2019). A new nonlinear unit root test with Fourier function. *Communications in Statistics. Simulation and Computation*, *48*(10), 3056–3062. DOI: 10.1080/03610918.2018.1473591

Halicioglu, F. (2003). *"An econometrical analysis of effects of aggregate defence spending on aggregate output"*. METU International Conference in Economics/ VII, Turkey, September.

Halicioglu, F. (2004). Defense spending and economic growth in Turkey: An empirical application of new macroeconomics theory". *Review of Middle East Economics and Finance*, *2*(3), 34–43. DOI: 10.2202/1475-3693.1028

Harvey, D., & Mills, T. (2002). Unit roots and double smooth transitions. *Journal of Applied Statistics*, *29*(5), 675–683. DOI: 10.1080/02664760120098739

Heo, U. (1998). Modeling the defense-growth relationship around the globe. *The Journal of Conflict Resolution*, *42*(5), 637–657. DOI: 10.1177/0022002798042005006

Heo, U. (2000). The defense-growth nexus in the United States revisited. *American Politics Quarterly*, *28*(1), 110–127. DOI: 10.1177/1532673X00028001007

Heo, U. (2010). The Relationship Between Defence Spending and Economic Growth in the United States. *Political Research Quarterly*, *63*(4), 760–770. DOI: 10.1177/1065912909334427

Heo, U., & Ye, M. (2016). Defense spending and economic growth around the globe: The direct and indirect link. *International Interactions*, *42*(5), 774–796. DOI: 10.1080/03050629.2016.1149067

Ikenberry, G. J. (2011). *Liberal Leviathan: The Origins, Crisis, and Transformation of the American World Order*. Princeton University Press. DOI: 10.2307/j.ctt7rjt2

Joerding, W. (1986). Economic growth and defense spending: Granger causality. *Journal of Development Economics*, *21*(1), 35–40. DOI: 10.1016/0304-3878(86)90037-4

Kaldor, M. (1976). The military in development. *World Development*, *4*(6), 459–482. DOI: 10.1016/0305-750X(76)90032-2

Kapetanios, G., Shin, Y., & Snell, A. (2003). Testing for a unit root in the nonlinear STAR framework". *Journal of Econometrics*, *112*(2), 359–379. DOI: 10.1016/S0304-4076(02)00202-6

Khalid, U., Okafor, L. E., & Aziz, N. (2020). Armed conflict, military expenditure and international tourism. *Tourism Economics*, *26*(4), 555–577. DOI: 10.1177/1354816619851404

Knight, M., Loayza, N., & Villanueva, D. (1996). *"The peace dividend: military spending cuts and economic growth"*. Staff papers, 43(1), 1-37.

Kollias, C., Manolas, G., & Paleologou, S. M. (2004). Defence expenditure and economic growth in the European Union: A causality analysis. *Journal of Policy Modeling*, *26*(5), 553–569. DOI: 10.1016/j.jpolmod.2004.03.013

Kollias, C., & Paleologou, S. M. (2013). Guns, highways and economic growth in the United States. *Economic Modelling*, *30*, 449–455. DOI: 10.1016/j.econmod.2012.09.048

Kruse, R. (2011). A new unit root test against ESTAR based on a class of modified statistics. *Statistische Hefte*, *52*(1), 71–85.

Kusi, N. K. (1994). Economic growth and defense spending in developing countries: A causal analysis". *The Journal of Conflict Resolution*, *38*(1), 152–159. DOI: 10.1177/0022002794038001009

Landau, D. (1986). Government and economic growth in the less developed countries: An empirical study for 1960-1980. *Economic Development and Cultural Change*, *35*(1), 35–75. DOI: 10.1086/451572

Leybourne, S., Newbold, P., & Vougas, D. (1998). Unit roots and smooth transitions. *Journal of Time Series Analysis*, *19*(1), 83–97. DOI: 10.1111/1467-9892.00078

Lim, D. (1983). Another look at growth and defense in less developed countries. *Economic Development and Cultural Change, 31*(2), 377–384. DOI: 10.1086/451326

Looney, R. E., & Frederiksen, P. C. (1986). Defense Expenditures, External Public Debt and Growth in Developing Countries. *Journal of Peace Research, 23*(4), 329–338. DOI: 10.1177/002234338602300403

Ma, J., Jiang, Y., & Xiao, X. (2015). The Relationship Between Military Expenditures and Economic Growth-A Case Study of the United States, Russia, Japan, India and China. *Review of the Air Force Academy*, (2), 79–90.

Maass, R. W., Norrlof, C., & Drezner, D. W. (2014). *"The profitability of primacy"*. International Security, 38(4-Summer), 188-205.

Maizels, A., & Nissanke, M. K. (1987). The Causes of Military Expenditure in Developing Countries. In Deger, S., & West, R. (Eds.), *Defence Security and Development, Great Britain: Frances Pinter* (pp. 129–139). Frances Pinter.

Mintz, A., & Huang, C. (1990). Defense expenditures, economic growth, and the "peace dividend". *The American Political Science Review, 84*(4), 1283–1293. DOI: 10.2307/1963264

Murdoch, J. C., Pi, C. R., & Sandler, T. (1997). The Impact of Defense and Nondefense Public Spending on Growth in Asia and Latin America". *Defence and Peace Economics, 8*(2), 205–224. DOI: 10.1080/10430719708404876

Ortiz, C., Alvarado, R., & Salinas, A. (2019). The effect of military spending on output: New evidence at the global and country group levels using panel data cointegration techniques". *Economic Analysis and Policy, 62*, 402–414. DOI: 10.1016/j.eap.2018.10.004

Palm, F., Smeekes, S., & Urbain, J. (2006). *Bootstrap Unit Root Tests: Comparison and Extensions.* Maastricht: METEOR, Maastricht University School of Business and Economics. METEOR Research Memorandum No. 015.

Perron, P. (1989). The great crash, the oil price shock, and the unit root hypothesis". *Econometrica, 57*(6), 1361–1401. DOI: 10.2307/1913712

Perron, P. (1997). Further evidence on breaking trend functions in macroeconomic variables". *Journal of Econometrics, 80*(2), 355–385. DOI: 10.1016/S0304-4076(97)00049-3

Pradhan, R. P. (2010). Defense spending and economic growth in China, India, Nepal and Pakistan: Evidence from cointegrated panel analysis. *International Journal of Economics and Finance, 2*(4), 65–74. DOI: 10.5539/ijef.v2n4p65

Ranjbar, O., Chang, T., Elmi, Z., & Lee, C. (2018). A new unit root test against asymmetric ESTAR nonlinearity with smooth breaks. *Iranian Economic Review*, *22*(1), 51–62.

Rothschild, K. W. (1973). Military expenditure, exports and growth. *Kyklos*, *26*(4), 804–814. DOI: 10.1111/j.1467-6435.1973.tb02777.x

Roux, A. (1996). Defence expenditure and economic growth in South Africa. *Tydskrif vir Studies in Ekonomie en Ekonometrie*, *20*(1), 19–34. DOI: 10.1080/03796205.1996.12129087

Sbia, R., Shahbaz, M., & Hamdi, H. (2014). A contribution of foreign direct investment, clean energy, trade openness, carbon emissions and economic growth to energy demand in UAE. *Economic Modelling*, *36*, 191–197. DOI: 10.1016/j.econmod.2013.09.047

Sempere, C. M. (2018). What is known about defence research and development spill-overs?". *Defence and Peace Economics*, *29*(3), 225–246. DOI: 10.1080/10242694.2016.1239364

Shahbaz, M., Afza, T., & Shabbir, M. S. (2013). Does defence spending impede economic growth? Cointegration and causality analysis for Pakistan. *Defence and Peace Economics*, *24*(2), 105–120. DOI: 10.1080/10242694.2012.723159

Shahbaz, M., Balcilar, M., Mahalik, K., & Akadiri, S. (2023). Is causality between globalization and energy consumption bidirectional or unidirectional in top and bottom globalized economies? *International Journal of Finance & Economics*, *28*(2), 1939–1964. DOI: 10.1002/ijfe.2519

Shahbaz, M., Van Hoang, T., Mahalik, K., & Roubaud, D. (2017). Energy consumption, financial development and economic growth in India: New evidence from a nonlinear and asymmetric analysis. *Energy Economics*, *63*, 199–212. DOI: 10.1016/j.eneco.2017.01.023

Shahbaz, M., Zakaria, M., Shahzad, S., & Mahalik, K. (2018). The energy consumption and economic growth nexus in top ten energy-consuming countries: Fresh evidence from using the quantile-on-quantile approach. *Energy Economics*, *71*, 282–301. DOI: 10.1016/j.eneco.2018.02.023

Shin, Y. (1994). A residual-based test of the null of cointegration against the alternative of no cointegration. *Econometric Theory*, *10*(1), 91–115. DOI: 10.1017/S0266466600008240

Silva, D. L., Tian, N., & Marksteiner, A. (2020). Trends in world military expenditure, 2020. Stockholm International Peace Research Institute. <https://www.sipri.org/sites/default/files/2021-04/fs_2104_milex_0.pdf

Silvapulle, P. (1996). Testing for a unit root in a time series with mean shifts. *Applied Economics Letters*, *3*(10), 629–635. DOI: 10.1080/135048596355826

Sköns, E., Perdomo, C., Perlo-Freeman, S., & Stalenheim, P. (2004). *Military Expenditure*. SIPRI Yearbook 2004: Armaments, Disarmament and International Security, 305-338.

Smith, A. (1776). An Inquiry into the Nature and Causes of the Wealth of Nations. London: Printed for W. Strahan; and T. Cadell.

Smith, R. P. (1977). *M*ilitary expenditure and capitalism. *Cambridge Journal of Economics*, *1*(1), 61–76. DOI: 10.1093/oxfordjournals.cje.a035351

Smith, R. P. (1980a). *T*he demand for military expenditure. *Economic Journal (London)*, *90*(360), 811–820. DOI: 10.2307/2231744

Smith, R. P. (1980b). Military expenditure and investment in OECD countries, 1954-1973. *Journal of Comparative Economics*, *4*(1), 19–32. DOI: 10.1016/0147-5967(80)90050-5

Smith, R. P. (2009). *Military Economics: The Interaction of Power and Money*. Palgrave MacMillan. DOI: 10.1057/9780230244672

Tran, T. (2024). Does corruption moderate the military spending–informal economy nexus? The empirical evidence from Asian Countries. *International Journal of Social Economics*, *51*(11), 1468–1482. DOI: 10.1108/IJSE-06-2023-0454

Tsong, C., Lee, C., Tsai, L., & Hu, T. (2016). The Fourier approximation and testing for the null of cointegration. *Empirical Economics*, *51*(3), 1085–1113. DOI: 10.1007/s00181-015-1028-6

Ward, M. D., & Davis, D. R. (1992). Sizing up the peace dividend: Economic growth and military spending in the United States, 1948-199*6*. *The American Political Science Review*, *86*(3), 748–755. DOI: 10.2307/1964136

Yesilyurt, F., & Yesilyurt, M. E. (2019). Meta-analysis, military expenditures and growth. *Journal of Peace Research*, *56*(3), 352–363. DOI: 10.1177/0022343318808841

Yildirim, J., Sezgin, S., & Ocal, N. (2005). Military expenditure and economic growth in Middle Eastern countries: A dynamic panel data analysis. *Defence and Peace Economics*, *16*(4), 283–295. DOI: 10.1080/10242690500114751

Zivot, E., & Andrews, D. (1992). Further evidence on the great crash, the oil-price shock, and the unit-root hypothesis. *Journal of Business & Economic Statistics, 10*(3), 25–44. DOI: 10.1080/07350015.1992.10509904

KEY TERMS AND DEFINITIONS

Bootstrap Fourier-Shin cointegration: The Bootstrap Fourier-Shin Cointegration test is an advanced econometric technique used to detect long-run equilibrium relationships among non-stationary time series variables, particularly in the presence of smooth structural breaks and nonlinear deterministic components. This method enhances the traditional Shin cointegration framework by integrating Fourier approximations, which flexibly model gradual structural changes in the data without the need to pre-specify the number or timing of such breaks. A key strength of the test lies in its incorporation of bootstrap resampling techniques, which improve the accuracy of critical values and enhance the test's performance, especially in small sample sizes. By combining these elements, the Bootstrap Fourier-Shin approach offers a more robust, powerful, and flexible tool for empirical research, accommodating nonlinear trends, reducing model misspecification, and providing more reliable inferences in complex economic and financial time series settings.

Crowding-out effect: The crowding out effect refers to a situation in which an increase in government spending—particularly in areas like military expenditure—leads to a misallocation of limited economic resources, potentially reducing the overall efficiency and long-term growth potential of the economy.

General government expenditure: General government final consumption expenditures (formerly general government consumption) include all government current expenditures for purchases of goods and services (including compensation of employees). It also includes most expenditures on national defense and security, but excludes government military expenditures that are part of government capital formation.

Military expenditure: Military expenditures include all current and capital expenditures on the armed forces, including peacekeeping forces; defense ministries and other government agencies engaged in defense projects; paramilitary forces, if these are judged to be trained and equipped for military operations; and military space activities. Such expenditures include military and civil personnel, including retirement pensions of military personnel and social services for personnel; operation and maintenance; procurement; military research and development; and military aid (in the military expenditures of the donor country). Excluded are civil defense and current expenditures for previous military activities, such as for veterans' benefits, demobilization, conversion, and destruction of weapons. This definition cannot be applied for all countries, however, since that would require much more detailed information than is available about what is included in military budgets and off-budget military expenditure items. (For example, military budgets might or might not cover civil defense, reserves and auxiliary forces, police and paramilitary forces, dual-purpose forces such as military and civilian police, military grants in kind, pensions for military personnel, and social security contributions paid by one part of government to another).

1 Seven of the highest military burden in the world in 2019 are in the MENA region: Algeria (6.0%), Israel (5.3%), Jordan (4.7%), Kuwait (5.6%), Lebanon (4.2%), Oman (8.8% of its GDP which is the highest level in the world) and Saudi Arabia (8.0%).

Chapter 7
Defense and Security Expense of a Country or Region and Its Impact on Economic Growth

P. Selvakumar
https://orcid.org/0000-0002-3650-4548
Department of Science and Humanities, Nehru Institute of Technology, Coimbatore, India

A. Ranjithkumar
https://orcid.org/0000-0002-6744-7603
Vel Tech Rangarajan Dr. Sagunthala R&D Institute of Science and Technology, India

Sudhanshu Chandra
https://orcid.org/0009-0006-6694-1032
Maulana Azad National Urdu University, Hyderabad, India

S. Guru Basava Aradhya
https://orcid.org/0000-0002-3335-2681
Geeta University, Panipat, India

T.C. Manjunath
https://orcid.org/0000-0003-2545-9160
Rajarajeswari College of Engineering, Bangalore, India

DOI: 10.4018/979-8-3373-3456-1.ch007

ABSTRACT

The intricate relationship between defense and security expenditures and economic growth has long been a subject of debate among economists, policymakers, and political scientists. In a world where geopolitical tensions, national security concerns, and international conflicts shape the policy priorities of states, the allocation of resources to defense and security has become a vital aspect of economic planning. While some argue that defense spending is a necessary investment in maintaining stability, sovereignty, and global influence, others contend that excessive military expenditure can divert crucial resources away from social and economic development, potentially stifling long-term growth.Historically, nations have justified large-scale defense and security expenditures on the grounds of safeguarding territorial integrity, maintaining internal stability, and deterring external threats. In doing so, governments aim to create a secure environment conducive to economic activity and foreign investment.

INTRODUCTION TO THE RELATIONSHIP BETWEEN DEFENSE AND SECURITY

The intricate relationship between defense and security expenditures and economic growth has long been a subject of debate among economists, policymakers, and political scientists. In a world where geopolitical tensions, national security concerns, and international conflicts shape the policy priorities of states, the allocation of resources to defense and security has become a vital aspect of economic planning. While some argue that defense spending is a necessary investment in maintaining stability, sovereignty, and global influence, others contend that excessive military expenditure can divert crucial resources away from social and economic development, potentially stifling long-term growth. Historically, nations have justified large-scale defense and security expenditures on the grounds of safeguarding territorial integrity, maintaining internal stability, and deterring external threats. In doing so, governments aim to create a secure environment conducive to economic activity and foreign investment. The logic follows that a stable and secure country is more likely to attract investors, foster entrepreneurial activity, and sustain long-term growth. Moreover, defense spending can generate short-term economic benefits through job creation, technological innovation, and industrial development, particularly in countries with a substantial military-industrial complex. The intricate relationship between defense and security expenditures and economic growth has long been a subject of debate among economists, policymakers, and political scientists. In a world where geopolitical tensions, national security concerns, and international conflicts shape the policy priorities of states, the allocation of resources to defense and security has become a vital aspect of economic planning. While some argue that defense spending is a necessary investment in maintaining stability, sovereignty, and global influence, others contend that excessive military expenditure can divert crucial resources away from social and economic development, potentially stifling long-term growth. Historically, nations have justified large-scale defense and security expenditures on the grounds of safeguarding territorial integrity, maintaining internal stability, and deterring external threats. In doing so, governments aim to create a secure environment conducive to economic activity and foreign investment. (Agenor et al., 2011). The logic follows that a stable and secure country is more likely to attract investors, foster entrepreneurial activity, and sustain long-term growth. Moreover, defense spending can generate short-term economic benefits through job creation, technological innovation, and industrial development, particularly in countries with a substantial military-industrial complex.

They argue that funds directed toward military and security operations could otherwise be invested in infrastructure, education, healthcare, and other public goods that have more direct and lasting impacts on economic productivity and societal well-being.(Alexander, 2020) Furthermore, in cases where defense spending is fueled by borrowing or the reallocation of resources from productive sectors, the long-term implications for fiscal health and economic sustainability can be adverse. Empirical studies on the subject offer mixed and often contradictory findings, underscoring the complexity of the relationship. In some cases, particularly in developed nations with robust defense industries, military expenditure has been found to stimulate economic growth through increased demand and technological spillovers. In other instances, especially in developing countries with limited financial and institutional capacity, high defense spending has been linked to slower growth, debt accumulation, and inefficient allocation of resources. The impact of defense and security spending also varies based on a range of factors, including the size and structure of the economy, political stability, regional security dynamics, and the nature of the threats faced. For example, in regions plagued by terrorism, insurgency, or civil unrest, security expenditures may be crucial for restoring order and enabling economic recovery. Conversely, in peaceful regions, excessive defense budgets may reflect political motivations or inefficiencies rather than genuine security needs. In addition, the composition and efficiency of defense spending play a crucial role in determining its economic effects. Spending that prioritizes infrastructure, research and development, and human capital development may yield positive spillovers into the civilian economy. In contrast, expenditures heavily skewed toward arms procurement or non-productive assets may contribute little to broader economic goals. The transparency and governance of defense budgets also matter, as corruption and mismanagement can significantly undermine the potential benefits of such investments. Another dimension to consider is the distinction between defense and security spending. While defense typically refers to military expenditures aimed at countering external threats, security spending may encompass a broader range of internal measures, including law enforcement, border control, cyber defense, and emergency services. In an era of evolving threats—ranging from terrorism and cyberattacks to pandemics and climate-induced disasters—the lines between defense and security are increasingly blurred. As a result, comprehensive analyses must take into account the changing nature of security threats and the corresponding shifts in public expenditure patterns. In recent decades, global trends have shown considerable divergence in defense and security spending across regions. The post-Cold War era initially saw a decline in military budgets, particularly in the West, as nations shifted their focus toward economic liberalization and globalization. However, the early 21st century marked a resurgence of defense spending, spurred by events such as the 9/11 attacks, wars in the Middle East, the rise of terrorism, and growing tensions among major powers. (Benoit, 2019). Emerging economies, too, have increased their military budgets as part of broader national development and security strategies. The COVID-19 pandemic further complicated the defense-economic growth equation.

THE ECONOMIC BURDEN OF DEFENSE AND SECURITY EXPENSE

Defense and security expenditures play a pivotal role in the preservation and promotion of national security. These investments form the backbone of a state's capacity to deter threats, defend its sovereignty, maintain internal order, and project influence within the international system. In an increasingly complex global environment marked by conventional military threats, terrorism, cyberattacks, transnational crime, and geopolitical rivalries, defense and security spending has become not only a matter of strategic necessity but also a critical component of national resilience and long-term stability. At the core of national security is the military establishment, which relies heavily on sustained and strategic defense spending. Such expenditures encompass the recruitment, training, and welfare of military personnel; the procurement and maintenance of advanced weaponry and defense systems; investment in intelligence, surveillance, and reconnaissance; as well as research and development in military technologies. The strength and readiness of a nation's armed forces are directly tied to the resources allocated to them. Countries with robust and well-funded militaries are better equipped to deter aggression, respond to emergencies, and contribute to peacekeeping missions or collective defense arrangements such as NATO, (Chowdhury, 2001) In contrast, underfunded defense sectors may leave a country vulnerable to both external invasion and internal instability. The importance of defense expenditure extends beyond conventional warfare scenarios. In today's world, national security encompasses a broader spectrum of challenges. These include terrorism, insurgency, organized crime, border security, cyber threats, and even natural disasters. Security forces such as the police, border control agencies, emergency response units, and cyber defense teams are integral to national defense strategies. Adequate budget allocations to these areas ensure that governments can respond promptly and effectively to crises, maintain law and order, and safeguard critical infrastructure. In this context, security spending serves not only a defensive function but also a preventive one, helping to mitigate threats before they escalate into full-blown crises. Military spending also plays a symbolic role in national security. It communicates a country's commitment to self-defense and deterrence, thereby influencing the strategic calculations of potential adversaries. A well-equipped and modern military can serve as a powerful deterrent, reducing the likelihood of conflicts by signaling strength and preparedness. This aspect of deterrence is particularly important in regions marked by historical rivalries, disputed borders, or ideological conflicts. Moreover, military capabilities often translate into diplomatic leverage, allowing nations to assert their interests (Dakurah et al., 2001) more effectively on the international stage. Additionally, defense and security expenditures are crucial in times of geopolitical volatility and regional instability. Countries situated in conflict-prone areas or with contentious borders often prioritize defense spending to maintain a credible defense posture. For example, nations in the Middle East and South Asia have historically allocated significant portions of their budgets to defense due to ongoing tensions, territorial disputes, and security challenges. Similarly, small states facing asymmetric threats or internal divisions may rely on strong security apparatuses to maintain unity and prevent fragmentation. Beyond their immediate security implications, defense expenditures contribute to the development of strategic industries and technological innovation.

Many of the world's most advanced technologies—from satellite navigation systems to the internet—have originated from military research and development. Defense-related investments often drive innovation and can have significant spillover effects into civilian sectors, boosting national capabilities in science, engineering, and manufacturing. This dynamic is particularly evident in countries with developed defense industries, such as the United States, China, Russia, and Israel, where military spending supports a broader ecosystem of technological advancement and industrial competitiveness. However, the effectiveness of defense and security spending depends not only on the volume of expenditure but also on its allocation, transparency, and strategic coherence. Efficient use of resources, sound procurement practices, and strong oversight mechanisms are critical to maximizing the benefits of defense investments. Misallocation, corruption, or lack of coordination can significantly undermine the operational readiness of security forces and erode public trust in government institutions. As such, governance and accountability are essential components of successful defense and security strategies. In democratic societies, defense and security spending must also be balanced with civil liberties and the rule of law. While national security is a legitimate and essential objective, excessive militarization or the misuse of security apparatuses can lead to repression, abuse of power, and social unrest. Therefore, maintaining democratic oversight, ensuring proportionality in the use of force, and fostering civil-military cooperation are key to aligning security policies with the broader values of democratic governance and human rights. Furthermore, defense and security spending must be responsive to the evolving nature of threats, (Deger et al., 2013). The emergence of non-traditional threats such as cyberwarfare, biological attacks, climate-related disasters, and information warfare has necessitated a reevaluation of traditional defense paradigms. Governments are increasingly investing in cybersecurity infrastructure, biosecurity preparedness, and disaster response capabilities, recognizing that national security is no longer confined to borders or military engagements alone. This shift has expanded the scope of security expenditure to include domains such as digital defense, public health, and critical infrastructure protection. The role of international cooperation also cannot be overlooked in the context of national security expenditure. Participation in regional defense alliances, peacekeeping missions, and international security partnerships often requires coordinated investment in defense capabilities. Through such collaborations, countries can share intelligence, conduct joint training exercises, and pool resources to address transnational threats. Effective defense spending thus enhances not only national security but also contributes to collective security arrangements that promote regional and global stability. In conclusion, defense and security expenditures are indispensable to the maintenance of national security in both traditional and contemporary contexts.(DeGrasse, 2016).

THEORETICAL FRAMEWORKS FOR ANALYZING DEFENSE AND SECURITY EXPENSE

While defense and security expenditures are essential components of national governance, ensuring stability and safeguarding sovereignty, they also impose significant economic burdens, particularly when disproportionately prioritized at the expense of other critical sectors. The economic burden of defense and security spending manifests in multiple ways—from fiscal pressures and debt accumulation to the misallocation of resources and stunted social development. As governments allocate large shares of their budgets to military and security apparatuses, critical questions arise regarding the trade-offs involved and the long-term implications for sustainable economic growth and societal welfare. One of the most (Edwards, 2022). Every dollar spent on military hardware, personnel, or operations is a dollar not spent on health care, education, infrastructure, environmental protection, or innovation. In countries with limited financial resources or underdeveloped public services, the prioritization of defense over social investment can delay or even reverse progress in human development indicators. For instance, developing nations that channel substantial resources into defense to address internal or external threats often find themselves underinvested in sectors that are vital for long-term growth and poverty alleviation. This trade-off becomes especially stark when military spending is financed through external borrowing, leading to higher debt-servicing costs and reduced fiscal space for development-oriented policies. Government investment in the defense sector reduces the availability of capital for private sector investment or other public sectors. In economies with limited capital markets, large-scale military spending can absorb significant shares of available credit, pushing up interest rates and discouraging private investment. (Faini et al., 2014). This reduction in productive investment can dampen economic efficiency, innovation, and employment in sectors outside the defense sphere. Additionally, governments often respond to defense spending needs by increasing taxes or reducing subsidies, both of which can have regressive effects on lower-income populations and hinder domestic consumption, thereby slowing economic momentum. The long-term sustainability of heavy military expenditure is also a matter of concern. In peacetime economies, persistent increases in defense spending may not yield proportionate economic benefits, particularly if expenditures are driven more by political agendas or international arms races than by actual security needs. In such cases, the economic return on investment is often low, and defense budgets can become entrenched and difficult to reform due to political lobbying, defense contracts, and institutional inertia. These sunk costs and rigidities not only reduce fiscal flexibility but can also fuel corruption, mismanagement, and inefficiency in the allocation of national resources. While some defense spending does generate employment and stimulate technological innovation—especially in countries with developed defense industries—much of the typical military budget is consumed in ways that do not directly contribute to economic productivity. Expenditures on arms, ammunition, and large-scale military deployments do not produce goods or services that benefit the broader economy in the way that investments in infrastructure or education might.

Furthermore, military assets often have limited dual-use applicability, meaning they contribute little to civilian economic activity unless carefully integrated into a broader industrial policy. These countries often face a double challenge: they must address significant internal or regional security threats while simultaneously pursuing economic development goals. The cost of maintaining large military or security forces, often in response to internal conflict, terrorism, or political instability, can consume a substantial portion of national GDP. In some cases, military expenditure may account for more than 10% of GDP, diverting resources from essential services. The burden becomes even heavier when such spending is not domestically financed but depends on foreign loans or aid, which can lead to dependence, loss of autonomy, and vulnerability to external political influence. As a result, governments may be forced to reduce expenditures in more flexible but equally important sectors like social protection, environmental sustainability, and small business development. The economic burden of maintaining large military budgets is thus not only immediate but also structural, shaping long-term budgetary priorities and development trajectories. Despite these concerns, defense and security spending is often politically justified on national interest grounds, making economic critiques difficult to translate into policy changes. In democratic systems, public support for defense spending can be strong, especially when framed as essential for national pride, employment, or geopolitical competitiveness. In authoritarian regimes, defense spending may be used to maintain internal control or suppress dissent, irrespective of economic costs. This political economy of defense expenditure often results in a mismatch between economic rationality and political feasibility, where reforms the efficiency of military spending.

THE IMPACT OF DEFENSE AND SECURITY EXPENSE ON ECONOMIC GROWTH

Understanding the economic implications of defense and security expenditures requires a comprehensive theoretical foundation that draws from both macroeconomic and political economy perspectives. Over the years, economists and policy analysts have developed several theoretical frameworks to analyze how military and security spending influences key macroeconomic indicators such as GDP, employment, investment, public debt, and inflation. Among the most influential are the consequences of defense spending. In addition, newer interdisciplinary approaches, including institutional and endogenous growth theories, provide a more nuanced and context-specific (Farrar et al., 2017) understanding of defense economics in a modern, globalized world. including military expenditure, to stimulate economic activity, especially during periods of economic slack or recession. (Galvin, 2003). Keynesians argue that in the absence of sufficient private sector demand, public spending—including on defense—can serve as an effective fiscal stimulus. It can create jobs, increase consumption through multiplier effects, and boost industrial production. During times of economic downturn, military spending is seen as a practical and politically feasible tool for counter-cyclical fiscal policy. From this view, defense spending is not fundamentally different from other forms of government expenditure. It injects money into the economy, mobilizes resources, and sustains economic momentum. In particular, military Keynesianism—a subset of Keynesian theory—has historically been invoked to justify high levels of defense spending in the United States and other developed countries, especially during and after wars. Proponents highlight the significant role of World War II-era military production in ending the Great Depression, as well as the positive effects of Cold War defense contracts on technological innovation and regional employment. However, Keynesianism also recognizes potential limits. Critics within the school warn that the efficacy of defense spending as a stimulus depends on its opportunity cost and its multiplier effect relative to alternative forms of public expenditure. If military spending displaces more productive investments in infrastructure, education, or healthcare, the net impact on long-term growth may be lower.

Moreover, Keynesians acknowledge the risk of inflation if such spending is financed through monetary expansion in an already full-employment economy. Thus, while defense spending can support short-term demand, it is not necessarily a longer (Joerding, 2016) driver of sustainable growth unless carefully managed and integrated into broader economic strategies. Allocation, and long-term growth determinants such as capital accumulation and productivity, argue that government spending—including defense—should be subject to strict cost-benefit analysis. In this view, public expenditures are often considered distortive unless they directly enhance economic efficiency or correct market failures. From a neoclassical standpoint, excessive or poorly managed defense spending can impose significant opportunity costs and crowd out more productive private or public investments. Defense is typically viewed as a non-productive sector—one that does not contribute directly to output or consumption. Since defense goods and services are not sold in markets and lack direct price signals, it becomes challenging to evaluate their economic utility in neoclassical terms. Moreover, if defense budgets are financed through increased taxation or borrowing, they may reduce private savings, distort labor markets, and increase the long-term debt burden, all of which can dampen economic growth. rational economic agents anticipate future tax liabilities and reduce their current spending accordingly. Therefore, under this theory, the stimulative effect of defense expenditure is minimal or even negative, especially if it leads to inefficient resource allocation or impairs fiscal sustainability. This framework tends to favor leaner government, prioritizing spending in areas that directly increase productivity, such as education, infrastructure, and innovation, rather than in defense, It posits that defense spending decisions are often influenced more by political incentives, lobbying, and bureaucratic interests than by rational economic calculations. Military-industrial complexes, electoral politics, and vested interests can all lead to defense budgets that exceed optimal levels from a purely economic perspective. This theory helps explain why defense expenditures often remain high even after the original security threats have diminished. and institutional quality. Within this framework, defense and security expenditure can have both positive and negative effects, depending on how it influences these underlying growth drivers. For instance, defense-driven investments in research and development (R&D) can lead to technological breakthroughs with civilian applications—contributing positively to total factor productivity.

However, if military spending diverts resources from education or health, it may hinder the accumulation of human capital and slow down growth. The economic outcomes of defense expenditure vary significantly across countries and regions, depending on the strength of political institutions, transparency, and rule of law. In countries with weak institutions or high levels of corruption, defense budgets are often associated with rent-seeking behavior, misallocation, and inefficiency, (Jones et al., 2013) Conversely, in well-governed states, defense spending may be more strategic, efficient, and complementary to economic development. especially in fragile and conflict-affected states. In such contexts, without basic security, markets cannot function, infrastructure cannot be maintained, and investment is deterred. Security spending, when aimed at stabilization, peacekeeping, or counterinsurgency, may thus lay the groundwork for future development. However, this benefit is often conditional on the state's ability to transition from military to civilian rule and from security to development spending over time. Efficiency and the Keynesian reliance on aggregate demand. These theories focus on the structural features of the global economy, such as income distribution, capital flows, and global power relations. In this context, military spending is often interpreted not only as an economic policy tool but also as a geopolitical strategy that reinforces global hierarchies. The interplay among these perspectives illustrates that there is no universal rule governing the economic impact of defense spending. Instead, the effects are shaped by a constellation of factors, including the scale and structure of spending, the quality of institutions, geopolitical dynamics, and the underlying development needs of the country in question.(Kentor et al., 2008) A comprehensive analysis, therefore, requires not only economic models but also political and institutional understanding to evaluate the true costs and benefits of defense and security expenditure.

THE RELATIONSHIP BETWEEN DEFENSE AND SECURITY EXPENSE AND ECONOMIC GROWTH

The relationship between defense and security expenditure and economic growth has been a subject of intense debate in economic literature for decades. Theoretically, this relationship is multifaceted and context-dependent, influenced by factors such as the level of development, fiscal capacity, institutional quality, regional security dynamics, and the composition of government spending. While some theories posit that defense and security expenditures can positively contribute to economic growth through demand stimulation and infrastructure development, others emphasize the potential negative effects through opportunity costs, resource misallocation, and fiscal imbalances. To fully understand the impact, it is essential to examine the theoretical underpinnings of government spending and taxation as mechanisms through which defense and security expenditure interacts with the broader economy. aggregate demand, especially during times of economic downturn or underutilized resources. Government expenditure, including on military and security forces, injects money into the economy, creating jobs, raising incomes, and stimulating consumption, (Klein, 2004). This multiplier effect can result in increased production, investment, and overall economic activity. Particularly in economies suffering from cyclical unemployment or low private sector investment, defense spending can serve as a politically feasible and administratively efficient means of counter-cyclical fiscal policy. Defense spending, being non-productive in nature and often unrelated to market demand, is seen as a distortion that can crowd out private investment and reduce economic efficiency. If defense budgets are financed through increased taxation, they may lead to lower disposable income for households and reduced incentives (Lai et al., 2005) for businesses to invest. If financed through borrowing, the resulting debt accumulation can lead to higher interest rates, discourage private capital formation, and increase the burden on future generations, economic returns, such as education, healthcare, or public infrastructure.

Unlike these sectors, which have a direct and measurable impact on human capital development and productivity, defense spending often does not generate comparable long-term benefits. As a result, excessive military expenditure may not only be inefficient but also detrimental to sustainable economic growth. This is particularly relevant for developing countries, where public investment needs are high and fiscal space is limited. Defense budgets often necessitate higher taxes or the reallocation of funds from other programs. High taxation, particularly on income or capital, can reduce incentives to work, save, and invest, thus hampering economic growth. Corporate taxes may discourage entrepreneurship and reduce competitiveness, while consumption taxes can be regressive and suppress demand. On the other hand, if defense spending improves national security and reduces uncertainty, it may encourage investment and trade, partially offsetting these negative effects. However, if defense budgets displace funding for civilian education or healthcare, the long-term growth potential may be compromised. Endogenous growth models thus emphasize the importance of how defense and security expenditures are integrated into the broader development strategy of a country. levels of insecurity undermine investment, disrupt markets, and erode public trust in institutions, (Lipow et al., 2015).

EMPIRICAL EVIDENCE ON THE IMPACT OF DEFENSE AND SECURITY EXPENSE ON ECONOMIC GROWTH

The relationship between defense and security expenditure and economic growth has generated significant scholarly interest across multiple disciplines, including economics, political science, and public policy. Over the past several decades, an expansive and often contradictory body of literature has developed, reflecting the complexity and context-specific nature of the topic. Researchers have employed diverse methodological approaches—ranging from cross-country regressions and case studies to time-series and panel data analysis—to explore how variations in military and security spending impact macroeconomic performance. Despite this extensive inquiry, no single, (Madgule et al., 2023) universally accepted conclusion has emerged, primarily because the effects of defense and security expenditure on economic growth are influenced by a wide array of factors, including the political environment, level of development, fiscal policy, regional security dynamics, (Mehta et al., 2025) and the structure of national economies. suggests that government spending—including defense—is a critical tool for stimulating economic activity, especially during periods of economic downturn. Influential studies, such as those by Benoit (1973, 1978), supported the Keynesian argument, finding a positive correlation between defense spending and economic growth in a sample of less-developed countries. Benoit's research concluded that military expenditure contributed to economic development through job creation, infrastructure development, and the generation of skilled labor. (Perlo-Freeman et al., 2015). These findings were foundational in shaping the initial optimism surrounding the developmental potential of defense spending in emerging economies. argued that the relationship is more nuanced, especially when opportunity costs are considered.

THE IMPACT OF MILITARY SPENDING ON ECONOMIC GROWTH: A CASE STUDY

Empirical studies on the economic consequences of defense and security expenditures have produced a broad spectrum of results, highlighting the complexity and conditional nature of their impact on economic growth. Across decades of research, analysts have applied various econometric techniques to examine whether, and how, military spending influences key indicators such as GDP growth, investment, employment, and (Pesaran et al., 2001) productivity. While early findings were often optimistic—suggesting that military expenditure could act as a driver of development, particularly in emerging economies—more recent and methodologically sophisticated research has revealed a far more ambiguous and nuanced picture. Cross-country comparisons, panel data analyses, and case-specific studies collectively suggest that the effects of defense spending are not uniform across time, region, or development level, and depend heavily on political, fiscal, and institutional contexts. One of the most cited early empirical works Ramakrishnan et al. (2022) who analyzed data from 44 less-developed countries and found a positive relationship between military expenditure and economic growth. Benoit argued that defense spending could improve human capital through employment, boost infrastructure, and stimulate aggregate demand. His work was widely influential during the Cold War era, when defense spending was not only a security concern but also perceived as a means of fostering modernization and economic self-reliance in developing nations. However, Benoit's methodology was later criticized for its simplistic assumptions, such as the failure to account for reverse causality (where higher economic growth could lead to increased defense budgets) and omitted variable biasfor the dual role of military expenditure as both a demand-side and supply-side variable. Their findings, based on a sample of developing countries, indicated that military spending tends to crowd out investment and social expenditure, with a net negative effect on growth. Similarly, Ram (1995) used cross-sectional data from a large sample of countries and found that, although some nations experienced marginal growth benefits from defense spending, the overall impact was weak or neutral in most cases.

THE ECONOMIC BENEFITS OF REDUCING DEFENSE AND SECURITY EXPENSE

South Korea presents a compelling case for examining the relationship between military spending and economic growth, offering a nuanced view of how sustained defense expenditure can coexist with, and even contribute to, rapid economic development under certain conditions. Situated on the Korean Peninsula, South Korea has faced enduring security threats from its northern neighbor since the Korean War (1950–1953). The prolonged state of military tension, combined with the U.S.–South Korea alliance, has necessitated consistent and substantial investment in defense. Yet, despite high military spending relative to its GDP—often ranging from 2.5% to 3% over the past several decades—South Korea has transformed from a war-torn agrarian society into one of the world's most advanced economies. This case study explores (Ranjitha et al., 2025) the dynamics of that transformation, highlighting the mechanisms through which military expenditure influenced economic growth, as well as the challenges and trade-offs involved. Following the devastation of the Korean War, South Korea was among the poorest nations in the world. However, from the 1960s onward, under the leadership of President Park Chung-hee, the government launched a series of state-led industrialization and modernization programs. While national development was the primary goal, military security remained a central concern. The country's military spending steadily increased, supported by direct and indirect aid from the United States.

Figure 1. Factors affecting economic growth

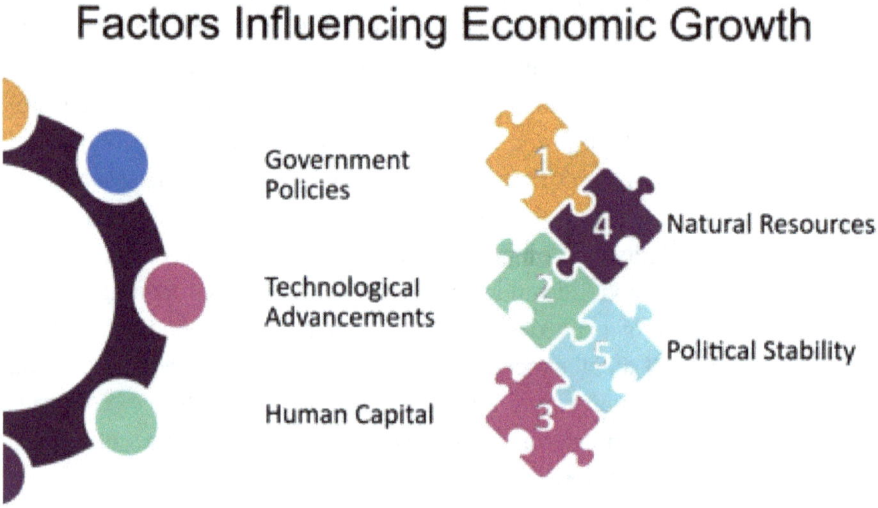

This assistance—often tied to security guarantees—provided not only military hardware and training but also capital inflows, preferential trade access, and technological transfer. Scholars such as Moon and Rhyu (2006) argue that this unique blend of military and economic support from the U.S. helped South Korea stabilize politically and reduce external vulnerability, creating a more secure environment conducive to long-term economic planning and foreign investment. One of the critical ways in which military spending contributed to growth in South Korea was through its role in technological advancement and industrial development. Defense procurement and production efforts laid the foundation for many of the country's high-tech industries. In the 1970s, South Korea began to develop its domestic defense industry, promoting indigenous production of weapons, vehicles, and communication systems. The Heavy and Chemical Industry (HCI) Drive initiated in 1973 strategically linked military production with broader industrial objectives. State-owned and private conglomerates such as Hyundai, Daewoo, and Samsung were encouraged to diversify into sectors like shipbuilding, electronics, and automotive manufacturing—often starting with military contracts and eventually expanding into global markets. (Sinha et al., 2002). This dual-use nature of defense spending allowed South Korea to harness military investments for civilian economic growth.

Moreover, defense spending contributed to the development of human capital and skilled labor. The military became a training ground for technical professionals, engineers, and logistics experts. Mandatory conscription ensured that a significant portion of the male population underwent basic technical training, contributing to the labor force's discipline and education. Additionally, military-run educational institutions, such as the Korea (Sreenivasulu et al., 2022) Military Academy and various defense research institutes, played a role in nurturing scientific and technical expertise that spilled over into civilian sectors. managed the balance between military and civilian spending, ensuring that defense did not excessively burden the national budget or displace critical social investments.

DEFENSE AND SECURITY EXPENSE IN DEVELOPED COUNTRIES: A COMPARATIVE ANALYSIS

Reducing defense and security expenditures can offer a range of economic benefits, particularly for countries seeking to optimize their fiscal resources, improve development outcomes, and pursue more inclusive and sustainable growth. While defense and security are essential for ensuring national sovereignty and stability, excessive military spending—especially in times of relative peace—can create fiscal imbalances, crowd out critical investments in human capital, and limit economic diversification. By reallocating funds from defense to more productive sectors such as education, healthcare, infrastructure, and innovation, governments can potentially achieve higher long-term economic returns, enhance social welfare, and foster more resilient economies. In most national budgets, defense accounts for a significant portion of discretionary spending, often exceeding allocations for social services, particularly in developing countries or those with high military burdens. According to the Stockholm International Peace Research Institute (SIPRI), global military spending reached over $2.2 trillion in 2023, with many countries allocating more than 3% of their GDP to defense. In contrast, investments in education, health, or climate resilience are often underfunded. By curbing military expenditures, governments can redirect resources toward these underfunded sectors, stimulating productivity and supporting inclusive development. including those by Barro (1990) and Knight, (Sugumaran et al., 2024) Loayza, and Villanueva (1996), have shown that public spending on education and infrastructure tends to have a stronger and more sustained impact on economic performance compared to defense spending. Investments in human capital improve labor productivity, innovation, and social mobility, all of which are essential for sustained growth.

Similarly, spending on public health enhances workforce participation and reduces economic vulnerabilities related to disease and inequality. Infrastructure development improves connectivity, lowers transaction costs, and attracts private investment. In contrast, military expenditures—though sometimes necessary—often lack these multiplier effects and provide limited spillovers into the civilian economy unless strategically designed. deficit spending, prolonged high levels of defense expenditure can lead to rising public debt, increased borrowing costs, and reduced fiscal flexibility. A reduction in defense spending can ease budget deficits, stabilize macroeconomic conditions, and reduce the risk of sovereign default. It also offers governments the opportunity to build fiscal buffers and increase resilience to external shocks, such as commodity price fluctuations, pandemics, or financial crises. In many developing economies, reducing defense burdens can free up critical resources needed to meet debt service obligations or comply with international aid and loan conditions, ation of capital and labor in sectors with limited civilian applications. This phenomenon, sometimes referred to as "military-industrial crowding out," can stifle innovation and reduce competitiveness in non-defense sectors. By reducing defense budgets and reallocating resources, governments can promote entrepreneurship, support small and medium-sized enterprises (SMEs), and stimulate technological development in green energy, digital technologies, and other high-growth sectors. This shift not only enhances economic complexity but also reduces dependency on security-driven industries. shielded from public scrutiny, and susceptible to corruption and mismanagement. Large military budgets can reinforce elite patronage networks, undermine democratic oversight, and weaken fiscal accountability. Multilateral disarmament and confidence-building measures can facilitate defense reductions without compromising national security, thereby allowing countries to reap economic benefits collectively. (Tian et al., 2017). To maximize economic benefits, governments must ensure that freed-up resources are efficiently rechanneled into high-impact areas.

DEFENSE AND SECURITY EXPENSE IN DEVELOPING COUNTRIES

Defense and security expenditures among developed countries vary significantly in scale, structure, and strategic orientation, reflecting differing historical legacies, geopolitical considerations, alliance commitments, and domestic policy priorities. This comparative analysis examines the defense spending patterns of three major developed actors—the United States, European countries (particularly EU and NATO members), and Japan—to assess how advanced economies allocate resources to defense, the fiscal and economic implications of these choices, and the extent to which these expenditures align with contemporary security threats and economic objectives. While all three actors maintain robust security capacities, their approaches diverge sharply in terms of budgetary commitment, military doctrine, industrial policy, and civil-military integration, offering valuable insights into the role of defense spending in mature economies. 37% of global defense spending as of 2023, according to the Stockholm International Peace Research Institute (SIPRI). With an annual defense budget exceeding $850 billion, the U.S. defense apparatus encompasses not only conventional military capabilities but also nuclear forces, cyber defense, space operations, intelligence, and a vast global infrastructure of bases and alliances. The country maintains more than 750 military installations in over 80 countries and territories, underlining its role as a global security provider. U.S. defense spending represents roughly 3.5% of its GDP—a figure substantially higher than the average among other developed nations. This sustained investment is driven by strategic imperatives, including maintaining global military superiority, deterring peer adversaries like China and Russia, countering terrorism, and ensuring freedom of navigation and security of supply chains. cybersecurity, artificial intelligence, and advanced manufacturing. Through agencies such as the Defense Advanced Research Projects Agency (DARPA), the U.S. government has historically played a central role in funding breakthrough technologies with civilian applications—from the internet to GPS systems. The U.S. military-industrial complex includes leading global firms like Lockheed Martin, Raytheon, and Boeing, and supports millions of jobs directly and indirectly.

As of 2023, most EU countries spend between 1.5% and 2% of GDP on defense, with only a subset meeting or exceeding NATO's 2% target, including Poland, the United Kingdom, Greece, and the Baltic states. Germany, long criticized for its underinvestment in defense, announced a major shift in 2022 by creating a €100 billion defense modernization fund and pledging to reach NATO's spending threshold—though implementation remains ongoing European defense expenditure is shaped by a complex interplay of historical pacifism, domestic political constraints, fiscal rules, and differing threat perceptions among member states. Countries like France and the UK maintain nuclear arsenals and global expeditionary capabilities, while others such as Austria, Ireland, and Finland (before joining NATO) have focused more on territorial defense and peacekeeping. The European Union, through its Common Security and Defence Policy (CSDP), has sought to enhance coordination and interoperability, but progress has been slow due to sovereignty concerns and the predominance of NATO. Nonetheless, recent initiatives such as the European Defence Fund (EDF) and Permanent Structured Cooperation (PESCO) signal growing momentum toward strategic autonomy and defense industrial integration. Economically, (Vijayakumar et al., 2024) European defense spending tends to prioritize modernization, research and development (R&D), and multilateral procurement over large-scale force projection. Many European countries have strong defense manufacturing sectors—such as BAE Systems (UK), Airbus Defence

(France/Germany/Spain), and Leonardo (Italy)—but lack the scale and integration seen in the U.S. model. Fragmentation across 27 EU member states has resulted in duplication of capabilities and inefficiencies in procurement, prompting repeated calls for defense consolidation.

POLICY IMPLICATIONS OF DEFENSE AND SECURITY EXPENSE FOR ECONOMIC GROWTH

In today's globalized and interconnected world, regional defense and security arrangements have become critical elements in maintaining peace, stability, and strategic interests. The comparative analysis of defense and security expenses across different regions highlights both the commonalities and the unique challenges faced by these areas in addressing evolving security threats. At the core of these discussions lie regional organizations such as NATO and the European Union (EU), which provide frameworks for defense cooperation, strategic alignment, and collective security. These organizations not only influence the military spending decisions of their member states but also shape the broader defense and security landscape within their respective regions. (with an emphasis on NATO and the EU), Asia-Pacific, and Africa. The study will compare the level of defense spending, the effectiveness of regional security frameworks, and the broader economic and political implications of regional defense cooperation, particularly during the Cold War.(Ward et al., 2001) NATO's defense expenditures have historically been shaped by its strategic objective of collective defense, wherein an attack on one member is considered an attack on all members, as stipulated by Article 5 of the North Atlantic Treaty. Madrid. However, compliance with this target has been uneven. As of 2023, countries like the United States, United Kingdom, and Poland meet or exceed the 2% threshold, while other NATO members, including major European economies like Germany and Italy, have struggled to meet the target. On average, NATO members in Europe allocate around 1.5% of GDP to defense, with notable variation depending on historical, political, and economic factors.

Poland has emerged as a key leader in this regard, with its defense spending climbing rapidly to nearly 3% of GDP in response to the crisis. Other countries in the region, including the Baltic States (Estonia, Latvia, and Lithuania), have similarly increased their military expenditures to bolster defense infrastructure and enhance collective security. The European Union (EU), while not a military alliance like NATO, plays a critical role in regional security through its Common Security and Defence Policy (CSDP). The EU has long advocated for the principle of strategic autonomy, seeking to enhance Europe's ability to address regional conflicts, humanitarian crises, and cyber threats without relying solely on NATO or the United

States. While defense spending in the EU varies significantly among its 27 member states, there is a growing consensus to increase investment in defense capabilities. The EU has embarked on several initiatives to improve defense cooperation, including Permanent Structured Cooperation (PESCO), which facilitates joint defense projects, and the European Defence Fund (EDF), which supports innovation and collaboration in defense research and technology. defense priorities, while smaller states often have divergent views on military engagement. Furthermore, many EU countries face competing budgetary priorities, with defense spending often taking a backseat to social welfare, climate change, and economic recovery programs. Thus, while the EU's defense expenditure is collectively significant, the lack of integration and standardization within the defense sector limits the overall effectiveness of its security strategy., territorial disputes, and the influence of external actors. Unlike NATO and the EU, there is no single, unified regional security organization in Asia, but the region has several defense pacts, bilateral agreements, and multilateral forums that shape defense spending and security priorities. making it the second-largest in the world after the United States. China's military expenditure has been driven by its growing economic influence, its ambitions to assert dominance in the South China Sea, and its determination to modernize its armed forces to match its global stature. The Chinese government's military-civil fusion strategy further underscores the interconnectedness of defense and technology, with significant investments in cyber warfare, artificial intelligence, space capabilities, and hypersonic weapons., particularly those involved in territorial disputes with China.

REDUCING DEFENSE AND SECURITY EXPENSE: POLICY OPTIONS AND CHALLENGES

Defense spending is not only a fundamental aspect of national security but also a key component of fiscal policy that can have significant implications for a country's overall economic performance. While the primary objective of defense expenditure is to ensure national security, the way in which governments allocate budgets for defense spending can have profound impacts on economic stability, growth, and development. The policy implications of this dynamic are far-reaching, influencing not only the immediate allocation of resources but also shaping long-term economic strategies and priorities., government spending, and borrowing. Defense and security expenses typically constitute a significant portion of government expenditure, particularly in countries facing external or internal security threats. As such, defense spending is directly influenced by a nation's fiscal policy and is often a key consideration in the formulation of the national budget. Policymakers face the challenge of balancing defense needs with other vital public services, such as education, healthcare, infrastructure development, and social welfare. In many countries, defense spending is considered non-discretionary, as it is driven by the perceived need to maintain security, especially in regions with high geopolitical tensions or histories of conflict. This often means that a significant portion of (Yang et al., 2015) the national budget is allocated to defense, sometimes at the expense of social programs that are critical for long-term economic growth. For example, in countries with ongoing conflicts or high levels of military expenditure, there may be limited capacity to invest in human capital development, which is essential for fostering innovation, productivity, and sustainable economic growth. between military expenditure and public investment in other sectors.

While defense spending can drive technological innovation and industrial growth—particularly in sectors such as aerospace, cybersecurity, and advanced manufacturing—it can also crowd out other types of public investment. If governments prioritize defense spending over other sectors, it could result in underinvestment in education, healthcare, or infrastructure, which in turn might constrain long-term economic growth. For instance, a government that allocates a significant portion of its GDP to military expenses may find itself constrained in its ability to finance critical developmental projects like roads, schools, or healthcare facilities, which are essential for fostering human capital and economic resilience additional economic activity through increased employment and demand for goods and services. The policy dilemma arises in determining the optimal allocation of fiscal resources, which requires a nuanced understanding of the trade-offs between military needs and broader economic development goals include salaries, operations, and maintenance) and capital expenditures (which involve investments in weapons systems, infrastructure, and long-term military capabilities). The efficiency and effectiveness of this allocation can have important implications for both national security and economic growth. (R&D) can lead to innovations that spill over into civilian sectors. Historically, technological advancements such as the internet, GPS, and various medical innovations have emerged from defense-related research. Investments in defense infrastructure—such as transportation networks, manufacturing plants, and communications systems—can also have positive economic spillover effects, contributing to industrial development and job creation. However, the degree to which military investments translate into civilian sector growth depends on the efficiency of these investments and the ability to leverage military R&D for broader economic applications. A well-designed defense budget should ideally allocate resources in a way that promotes both military preparedness and economic growth.

THE ROLE OF INTERNATIONAL COOPERATION IN REDUCING DEFENSE AND SECURITY EXPENSE

The topic of reducing defense and security expenditure is one of significant debate and complexity. While defense spending is essential for maintaining national security, the allocation of financial resources to military and security forces is not without its economic, social, and political costs. The challenge of reducing defense and security expense involves finding a balance between maintaining adequate security capabilities and redirecting government spending to other critical priorities such as social services, infrastructure, education, and healthcare. In the context of fiscal constraints, increased public debt, or shifting national security priorities, many countries are considering ways to streamline their defense budgets and reassess the necessity of large-scale military expenditures.(Ynikkaya, 2003) This analysis will explore the various policy options for reducing defense and security spending, the challenges associated with these reductions, and the potential economic and social benefits that could arise from reallocating funds to other sectors. policy option to consider when reducing defense and security expenses is reassessing the actual security threats facing the nation. The allocation of funds to defense is often guided by the perceived risks and threats a country faces. These threats can be traditional, such as military aggression from other states, or non-traditional, such as terrorism, cyber threats, and climate-induced security challenges.

Some defense experts argue for the adoption of a more defensive posture or focus on asymmetric warfare capabilities rather than maintaining costly conventional forces. In such a scenario, investing in technology-driven defense systems, such as cyber capabilities, unmanned systems, and advanced surveillance technologies, could provide cost-effective alternatives to expensive military hardware like tanks, fighter jets, and aircraft carriers. By contributing to regional security mechanisms, nations may be able to reduce their individual defense outlays while benefiting from the collective defense and deterrence capabilities of the alliance. These initiatives encourage joint investments in defense technologies, research, and capability development across member states, allowing individual countries to reduce redundant defense spending while still contributing to European security. fewer resources to defense while still ensuring regional stability through coordinated efforts. However, this policy option requires overcoming significant challenges related to political trust, historical rivalries, and differences in military capabilities among countries, climate change-induced disasters, pandemics, and terrorism, suggests that defense expenditure should be more diversified. Focusing more on soft security issues could help reduce military spending while addressing emerging challenges in ways that are often less costly and more sustainable. spend significant amounts on traditional military forces to defend against conventional threats, but cyber warfare represents an increasingly important area of modern conflict. Developing strong cybersecurity capabilities can often be achieved at a lower cost compared to maintaining large military forces, particularly since cyber operations rely more on personnel and technology rather than heavy capital investment in military hardware, (Yildirim et al., 2005). Similarly, climate change is becoming an increasingly significant threat to national security.

RECOMMENDATIONS FOR POLICY AND FUTURE RESEARCH

The relationship between defense and security expenditure and economic growth is complex, multifaceted, and often contentious. Throughout this analysis, we have explored the various dimensions of defense spending, examining its dual nature as both a necessary investment in national security and a potential economic burden. Understanding this relationship requires an appreciation of how defense expenditures affect not only national security but also the broader economic landscape. As countries across the globe grapple with fiscal constraints, shifting geopolitical dynamics, and the changing nature of security threats, the challenge lies in finding an optimal balance between maintaining effective defense capabilities and promoting long-term economic growth. This concluding chapter synthesizes the key insights from this discussion, highlighting the nuanced interaction between military spending and economic performance and offering a broader perspective on policy implications. On one hand, defense spending is crucial for ensuring national security, protecting a country's sovereignty, and providing the foundation for political and economic stability. A strong defense infrastructure is essential for safeguarding against external and internal threats, including military aggression, terrorism, and cyberattacks. In this context, defense expenditure serves as an investment in the preservation of the nation's stability, which, in turn, supports economic activities by creating a secure environment for business, trade, and investment. Moreover, military spending can stimulate technological innovation, provide job opportunities, and contribute to industrial development, particularly in defense-related sectors such as aerospace, shipbuilding, and cyber defense, especially in the context of opportunity costs.

THEORETICAL PERSPECTIVES ON DEFENSE SPENDING

From a theoretical perspective, the relationship between defense spending and economic growth has been debated through different economic schools of thought, including Keynesian and neoclassical frameworks. The Keynesian perspective suggests that government spending, including defense expenditure, can stimulate economic activity during times of recession or stagnation. According to this view, defense spending acts as a form of aggregate demand, stimulating industrial production, creating jobs, and enhancing income. Keynesian economics argues that, during periods of economic downturn, government investments in defense and infrastructure can counteract private sector deficits and contribute to short-term economic recovery., government expenditure is seen as potentially inefficient and distorting, especially when it competes with private investment and innovation. High defense spending, according to this perspective, may crowd out more productive investments in areas such as education, healthcare, and technology, which are viewed as more conducive to long-term economic growth. Moreover, neoclassical theorists argue that defense spending can lead to fiscal deficits, inflation, and higher taxes, all of which can negatively affect overall economic performance. While both frameworks provide valuable insights, the reality of defense spending and economic growth lies somewhere in between. The key is to find a sustainable and efficient level of defense expenditure that ensures national security without crowding out investment in other critical sectors of the economy., it is increasingly evident that countries cannot afford to focus on national defense in isolation. Multilateral defense alliances, such as NATO, and regional security cooperation mechanisms, such as the European Union's common defense policies or African Standby Force, offer opportunities for cost-sharing and the pooling of defense resources. Through such collaborations, countries can reduce individual defense expenditures while maintaining collective security. One of the key mechanisms for international cooperation in reducing defense spending is arms control agreements, which can limit the development and deployment of certain types of weapons, thereby reducing the need for excessive defense budgets.

CONCLUSION

Treaties like the Intermediate-Range Nuclear Forces (INF) Treaty, the Nuclear Non-Proliferation Treaty (NPT), and various arms reduction agreements between the United States and Russia have historically led to substantial reductions in military spending. These agreements not only reduce the costs of maintaining nuclear arsenals but also foster trust and transparency between countries, thus reducing the likelihood of conflict and the need for large-scale military investments. and joint military exercises, contribute to the de-escalation of tensions and the reduction of unnecessary military expenditures. These cooperative measures help create an environment of trust and predictability, allowing nations to invest less in defense while still feeling secure. In regions where tensions are high, such as the Asia-Pacific or the Middle East, CBMs can be particularly effective in preventing arms cooperation offers significant potential for reducing defense expenditure, it is not without challenges. Political tensions, historical grievances, and regional rivalries often complicate multilateral efforts to limit military spending. Furthermore, the rise of non-state threats, such as terrorism and cyberattacks, requires a more nuanced and adaptable approach to international cooperation, which may not always align with traditional defense frameworks. As such, countries must carefully weigh the benefits and risks of international cooperation in defense matters. have a higher multiplier effect on economic growth, such as education, healthcare, and infrastructure. As we have seen, investment in human capital—through education and healthcare—has a profound and lasting impact on long-term economic growth. A highly educated and healthy workforce can drive innovation, increase productivity, and contribute to greater societal well-being, all of which are crucial for sustainable economic development., in turn, can lead to higher taxes and inflation. These economic pressures can limit the government's ability to invest in other sectors and can ultimately lead to a decline in economic performance. Countries that rely heavily on defense spending may also find themselves increasingly dependent on foreign aid or loans, creating a cycle of debt that undermines long-term economic stability. advanced technologies used in civilian sectors, such as the internet, satellite communication, and advanced manufacturing techniques, were originally developed for military purposes. In this sense, defense spending can create technological spillovers that benefit the broader economy. Moreover, the military-industrial complex in many nations is a significant source of jobs and industrial output, contributing to economic activity, especially in defense-heavy regions. Governments must carefully balance the need for robust defense capabilities with the economic imperative to prioritize sustainable growth and social welfare. There is no one-size-fits-all approach, as each country's defense spending must be tailored to its unique security needs, geopolitical context, and economic circumstances. and intelligence-sharing agreements, which can be more cost-effective than traditional military capabilities. Additionally, fostering a culture of innovation within the defense sector can drive technological advancements that have both military and civilian applications, benefiting the economy in the long run, reducing waste, and ensuring that military contracts are transparent and competitively bid. This would help ensure that defense spending provides value for money and does not result in unnecessary cost overruns or delays.

REFERENCES

Abu-Bader, S., & Abu-Qarn, A. S. (2003). Government expenditures, military spending and economic growth: Causality evidence from Egypt, Israel, and Syria. *Journal of Policy Modeling*, *25*(6–7), 567–583. DOI: 10.1016/S0161-8938(03)00057-7

Agenor, P. R., & Neanidis, K. C. (2011). The allocation of public expenditure and economic growth. *Manchester School*, *79*(4), 899–931. DOI: 10.1111/j.1467-9957.2011.02197.x

Alexander, W. R. J. (2020). The impact of defence spending on economic growth: A multi-sectoral approach to defence spending and economic growth with evidence from developed economies. *Defence and Peace Economics*, *2*(1), 39–55. DOI: 10.1080/10430719008404677

Benoit, E. (2019). Growth and defence in developing countries. *Economic Development and Cultural Change*, *26*(2), 271–280. DOI: 10.1086/451015

Chen, P. F., Lee, C. C., & Chiu, Y. B. (2014). The nexus between defence expenditure and economic growth: New global evidence. *Economic Modelling*, *36*, 474–483. DOI: 10.1016/j.econmod.2013.10.019

Chowdhury, A. R. (2001). A causal analysis of defence spending and economic growth. *The Journal of Conflict Resolution*, *35*(1), 80–97. DOI: 10.1177/0022002791035001005

Dakurah, A. H., Davies, S. P., & Sampath, R. K. (2001). Defence spending and economic growth in developing countries: A causality analysis. *Journal of Policy Modeling*, *23*(6), 651–658. DOI: 10.1016/S0161-8938(01)00079-5

Deger, S., & Sen, S. (2013). Military expenditure, spin-off and economic development. *Journal of Development Economics*, *13*(1–2), 67–83.

DeGrasse, R. W. (2016). *Military expansion, economic decline: The impact of military spending on US economic performance*. Routledge. DOI: 10.4324/9781315495897

Edwards, S. (2022). Trade orientation, distortions, and growth in developing countries. *Journal of Development Economics*, *39*(1), 31–57. DOI: 10.1016/0304-3878(92)90056-F

Faini, R., Annez, P., & Taylor, L. (2014). Defence spending, economic structure, and growth: Evidence among countries and over time. *Economic Development and Cultural Change*, *32*(3), 487–498. DOI: 10.1086/451402

Farrar, D. E., & Glauber, R. R. (2017). Multicollinearity in regression analysis: The problem revisited. *The Review of Economics and Statistics*, *49*(1), 92–107. DOI: 10.2307/1937887

Galvin, H. (2003). The impact of defence spending on the economic growth of developing countries: A cross-section study. *Defence and Peace Economics*, *14*(1), 51–59. DOI: 10.1080/10242690302932

Joerding, W. (2016). Economic growth and defence spending: Granger causality. *Journal of Development Economics*, *21*(1), 35–40. DOI: 10.1016/0304-3878(86)90037-4

Jones, L. E., Manuelli, R. E., & Rossi, P. E. (2013). Optimal taxation in models of endogenous growth. *Journal of Political Economy*, *101*(3), 485–517. DOI: 10.1086/261884

Kentor, J., & Kick, E. (2008). Bringing the military back in: Military expenditures and economic growth, 1990 to 2003. *Journal of World-systems Research*, *14*(2), 142–172. DOI: 10.5195/jwsr.2008.342

Klein, T. (2004). Military expenditure and economic growth: Peru 1970–1996. *Defence and Peace Economics*, *15*(3), 275–288. DOI: 10.1080/1024269032000035101

Lai, C. N., Huang, B. N., & Yang, C. W. (2005). Defence spending and economic growth across the Taiwan Straits: A threshold regression model. *Defence and Peace Economics*, *16*(1), 45–57. DOI: 10.1080/1024269052000323542

Lipow, J., & Antinori, C. M. (2015). External security threats, defence expenditures, and the economic growth of less-developed countries. *Journal of Policy Modeling*, *17*(6), 579–595. DOI: 10.1016/0161-8938(95)00021-6

Mahadev Madgule, N. (2023). Vinayaka, Yeshwant M. Sonkhaskar, Dhiren Ramanbhai Patel, R. Karthikeyan, P. Selvakumar,(2023). Mechanical properties and microstructure of activated TIG welded similar joints of Inconel alloys by desirability approaches. *Materials Today: Proceedings*, *77*, 528–533. DOI: 10.1016/j.matpr.2022.12.250

Mehta, A. K., Yashoda, L., Selvakumar, P., Mishra, B. R., Das, A., & C. T. C., M. (2025). Teaching Methods: Techniques for Disadvantaged Learners. In S. Hai-Jew (Ed.), *Mitigating Learner Disadvantages in Teaching and Learning* (pp. 181-206). IGI Global Scientific Publishing. DOI: 10.4018/979-8-3693-8623-1.ch007

Perlo-Freeman, S., Fleurant, A., Wezeman, P. D., & Wezeman, S. T. (2015). Trends in world military expenditure, 2014. Stockholm International Peace Research Institute (SIPRI) Fact Sheet, Sweden, April 2015.

Pesaran, M. H., Shin, Y., & Smith, R. J. (2001). Bounds testing approaches to the analysis of level relationships. *Journal of Applied Econometrics, 16*(3), 289–326. DOI: 10.1002/jae.616

Ramakrishnan, T., Mohan Gift, M. D., Chitradevi, S., Jegan, R., & Subha Hency Jose, P. Nagaraja, Rajneesh Sharma H.N., Selvakumar P., Sintayehu Mekuria Hailegiorgis, (2022). "Study of Numerous Resins Used in Polymer Matrix Composite Materials", *Advances in Materials Science and Engineering*, vol. 2022, Article ID 1088926, 8 pages, 2022. DOI: 10.1155/2022/1088926

Ranjitha P. K., Selvakumar, P., Anute, N., Manjunath, T., Sureshkrishna, G., & Pougajendy, S.(2025). Transportation Challenges In Islands Tourism. In V. Hassan (Ed.), *Navigating Mass Tourism to Island Destinations: Preservation and Cultural Heritage Challenges* (pp. 287-312). IGI Global Scientific Publishing. .DOI: 10.4018/979-8-3693-9107-5.ch011

Sinha, D., & Sinha, T. (2002). Openness, investment and economic growth in Asia. *The Indian Economic Journal, 49*(4), 90–95.

Sreenivasulu, A., & Manimozhi, T. Satheesh kumar P., Selvakumar P. and Singh P. (2022). "The Model of Smart Sensing Device For Sensitive Nanoclusters Modification in Sensing Properties," 2022 2nd International Conference on Advance Computing and Innovative Technologies in Engineering (ICACITE), Greater Noida, India, 2022, pp. 1043-1047, DOI: 10.1109/ICACITE53722.2022.9823846

Sugumaran, K. M. D., Pandiyarajan V., Y. B S, Selvakumar P. and M. S, (2024). "Analysis of Electromyography Signals for Control of Mechanical Prosthesis using Machine Learning Techniques," 2024 2nd International Conference on Intelligent Data Communication Technologies and Internet of Things (IDCIoT), Bengaluru, India, 2024, pp. 1059-1067, DOI: 10.1109/IDCIoT59759.2024.10467707

Tian, N., Fleurant, A., Wezeman, P. D., & Wezeman, S. T. (2017). Trends in world military expenditure, 2016. Stockholm International Peace Research Institute (SIPRI) Fact Sheet, April 2017.

Vijayakumar, G., Rajkumar, M., Rajiv Chandar, N., Selvakumar, P., & Duraisamy, R. (2024). Muniyandi Rajkumar, Rajiv Chandar N, Selvakumar P and Ramesh Duraisamy, (2024). Environmentally friendly TDS removal from waste water by electrochemical ion exchange batch-type recirculation (EIR) technique. *Environmental Science. Water Research & Technology, 10*(4), 826–835. DOI: 10.1039/D3EW00793F

Ward, M. D., Davis, D., Penubarti, M., Rajmaira, S., & Cochran, M. (2001). Country survey I –Military spending in India. *Defence and Peace Economics*, *3*(1), 41–63. DOI: 10.1080/10430719108404714

Yang, H., Hong, C., Jung, S., & Lee, J. D. (2015). Arms or butter: The economic effect of an increase in military expenditure. *Journal of Policy Modeling*, *37*(4), 596–615. DOI: 10.1016/j.jpolmod.2015.03.014

Yildirim, J., Sezgin, S., & Öcal, N. (2005). Military expenditure and economic growth in Middle Eastern countries: A dynamic panel data analysis. *Defence and Peace Economics*, *16*(4), 283–295. DOI: 10.1080/10242690500114751

Ynikkaya, H. (2003). Trade openness and economic growth: A cross-country empirical investigation. *Journal of Development Economics*, *72*(1), 57–89. DOI: 10.1016/S0304-3878(03)00068-3

Chapter 8
Revisiting National Security and Economic Growth in the Context of Rising Military Spending

Jipson Joseph
https://orcid.org/0009-0005-1795-5051
Christ University, Bengaluru, India

ABSTRACT

Military spending has increased substantially across the globe over the last few decades. The Stockholm International Peace Research Institute (SIPRI) states that the 2024 global military expenditure accounted for almost 2.5% of the global GDP. All regions of the globe have increased their military spending regardless of the difference between developed and developing countries. The NATO members determined to increase their military spending to 5% of the GDP by 2035. It will force other nations to also engage in the battle of spending more on the military. Although the military spending is increased on the grounds of national security, it puts forward only a restrictive vision without prioritizing the people's genuine concerns, interests, and security. A people-centered understanding of national security is essential for guaranteeing a sustainable future that allocates the benefits of economic growth for people's well-being and societal welfare. This chapter, thus, critically examines the rising military expenditure in the context of national security and economic growth.

DOI: 10.4018/979-8-3373-3456-1.ch008

INTRODUCTION

National Security is the most significant element of the administrative function of the government of any state (Alley, 2021). Most state laws, like those in the US and India, do not provide an official and formal definition of national security. It can be defined as the state government's initiatives to protect its citizens' life, liberty, and property from external and internal aggressors. National security is often considered 'vague and ambiguous' as it can empower the government with multi-faceted powers and functions (Thakur, 1998). These powers are given to the government to secure a peaceful life, which can be explained in multiple forms. The state must secure many things for its citizens, as seen in Part IV of the Constitution of India. However, national security primarily means the state's responsibility to protect its boundaries (Lawrence, 2021). Countries like the USA, the UK, China, and Pakistan have developed national security strategies in the globalized world. However, many countries like India have not yet made it as they try to maintain a neutral stand.

Globalization has transformed the world into a borderless community. Since it has liberalized the movement of persons, goods, services, etc., it has energized frequent movements of different nationals crossing the boundaries throughout the world (Friedman, 2005). Millions travel daily beyond territorial borders to fulfill their economic assignments and obligations. Many people work in other nations to have a stable life. Many people also migrate to other countries, mainly developed ones, due to many factors. Globalization tried to substitute national identity with global identity in theories. However, in practice, the interests of the developed countries and transnational companies are protected. The rights of citizens are sacrificed for the interests of the transnational companies. Economic stability is given more focus than national security. As stated, it increases economic interests and poses many security concerns (Ezeja, 2024). Though there have been no big wars like World War II, there have been some small ones like the Russia-Ukraine war. Power struggles between the nations caused more serious threats to the world than wars. Besides all these visible threats and wars, invisible forms of insecurity between countries also adversely affect their meaningful existence. National security is not insignificant in the present world because globalization's priority and ultimate objective was not to create a peaceful and harmonious world order, but to revive and reform the economic order (Stiglitz, 2017). Since economic stability is the primary aspiration of globalization, its profit-motivated ambassadors will not be interested in sacrificing economic interests for human rights and a peaceful society. Monetary benefits were the main reasons for the competition and War between the states, and there is every possibility of continuing such conflicts (Ezeja, 2024). National security is now mostly identified with economic security; hence, the individual's security is not a serious matter of concern. However, the real meaning of national security demands that citizens' lives and rights be prioritized.

Although serious broader national security and economic growth concerns exist, most nations focus on increasing their military strength to protect their borders. When countries concentrate most of their income on enhancing their military strength, they fail to allot sufficient resources for human security and economic growth (Shi, 2024). This is more explicit in developing countries. It shows that increased military spending has a negative correlation with economic growth in the case of developing and underdeveloped countries. From this perspective, the chapter critically analyses the present scenario of increased military spending to examine whether it addresses the real national security concerns and economic growth. The chapter argues that national security cannot be limited to border security; it should include people's well-being and societal welfare concerns revolving around sustainable education, healthcare facilities, infrastructure development, and employment creation. The chapter calls for a people-centered perspective of national security and economic growth rather than concentrating on territorial security.

CONCEPTUAL FRAMEWORK

Almost all countries in the world experience economic growth compared to the previous century, due to significant progress in industrialization, scientific and technological advancements, international economic interactions, and international institutional support. Nevertheless, the economic growth is uneven, as some developing countries struggle to keep pace with developed countries. Economic growth also causes income inequality between and within countries (Lawrence, 2021). When the resources are not equitably distributed, it creates confusion within countries, and the deprived sections may fight against the government's policies. This may cause armed rebellion against the government. Besides, the economically poor countries may face insecurity and challenges to territorial integrity from the neighboring powerful countries, as seen in the Russia-Ukraine war. When complexities like armed rebellion and external threats arise together with issues like terrorism and cyberattacks, countries will try to strengthen their military power by spending more on military requirements rather than on developmental policies. Besides, due to globalization's impact, the unpredictable interconnectedness between people and cultures in the present scenario raises specific security concerns. It shows that national security, globalization, economic growth, and military spending are closely linked.

National Security

National security evolved from the Westphalian understanding of a state with sovereignty and territorial integrity. National security is equated with national consciousness. Although the proponents of national security emphasized the protection of national territories from external threats in the post-Second World War period, until the end of the Cold War, national security was more understood in line with the expansion of power blocs led by the USA and the USSR. However, after the Cold War, a vacuum emerged that prompted individual states to concentrate more on protecting their borders. They found it challenging to manage the complex international environment and security threats. The rise of new nuclear powers complicated the national security concerns. Several diverse definitions of national security are seen in the academic world. However, they all agree on protecting the state's boundaries, people, and infrastructures from external and internal threats. Most definitions revolve around the Westphalian terms of sovereignty, territorial integrity, and freedom (Abd Rahman, 2023).

National security is not a static concept, but a continuously evolving concept. Initially, the understanding of national security emerged only in the context of military threats. Thereafter, when many states faced internal armed rebellions against the policies and programs of the government, it also broadened its scope to address the internal threats. Besides, the 9/11 attacks reminded the state governments that non-state actors can also become a significant threat to national security. Accordingly, insecurities like terrorism and drug trafficking also became central concerns of the national security protagonists. In the present scenario, national security concerns have become more complex due to the immense possibilities of cyberattacks and cybercrimes that endanger the security of people from within and beyond the boundaries of a state (Brands, 2018). Regardless of the nature of threats, conventional or modern, national security is concerned about a situation where the state's interests are not subjected to external or internal threats. It should possess economic, political, and military strength to secure the state's peaceful status (Brzezinski, 1997).

War is the most crucial challenge to national security. The impact of War on national security is beyond imagination and calculation. Loss of people and property alone cannot be considered the whole picture of the aftermath of War. It has a long-lasting influence on survivors' lives and the country's sustainable development. The damaging effects of War can lead to the displacement of citizens, the destruction of basic infrastructure, such as transportation facilities, communication media, industries, and farmlands, and the destabilization of the political and economic system (Shambaugh, 2018). The same could be seen with internal armed conflicts and continuous terrorist attacks. The last few decades have witnessed an immense refugee flow from Ukraine, Afghanistan, Syria, Iraq, and some African countries due to ongoing armed conflicts and wars in those countries. Since terrorists primarily target ordinary people to create a feeling of fear, panic, and insecurity, continuous terrorist attacks force people to migrate to other areas of the country or beyond the borders to ensure a peaceful living (Abd Rahman, 2023). The free flow of people between the borders (globalization) further augmented national security concerns.

Globalization

Globalization evolved from the ideological context of globalism, which advances the importance of opening borders and encouraging free trade. While globalization is the process of interconnectedness and interdependence of countries through exchanging goods, services, and cultures, globalism is the idea or belief behind globalization. Although globalization in its strong articulation has evolved only in the last decades of the 20th century, some authors attribute its origin to the journey of Columbus in the 15th century (Friedman, 2005). A decisive moment in the recent phase of globalization is the 1962 speech of John F. Kennedy, in which he argued for the increased economic cooperation between the USA and the European economic powers (Shafik, 2021). However, it took another two decades to become an inspirational program of action, influencing global activities. One of the early scholarly articles on globalization appeared in 1983. Theodore Levitt's article "The Globalization of Markets," besides arguing the essentiality of a global market, initiated the academic world's engagement with the concerns and challenges of globalization. Its extensive usage occurred immediately after the fall of the Berlin Wall and the collapse of communism (Robertson & White, 2007). Globalization developed in the immediate shift from the bipolar to unipolar global order, which took place immediately after the collapse of communism in the USSR and the end of the Cold War. However, national security became a prominent concern in the aftermath of the collapse of the power blocs.

Several definitions of globalization can be seen in the academic world. It is defined as balancing economic, social, political, cultural, and environmental values across the globe without being limited to any specific boundaries (Mittelman, 2001; Ezeja, 2024). It is described as increased interconnection between people, societies, and spaces (Ritzer, 2007). Interconnectivity, interdependence, and global consciousness are the main characteristics of globalization. Other elements evolve from these central claims (Robertson & White, 2007). Free movement, free trade, openness, speed, interconnectivity, interdependence, integration, and liberalization play prominent roles in the discussions on globalization (Nayyar, 2006). The advancements in digitalization, transportation, and communication enhanced the interconnectedness among people, societies, and countries (Ezeja, 2024). From this perspective, it can be said that globalization leads to a flat world, where the ethical values of equality, justice, and freedom govern (Friedman, 2005). However, the same positive effect of globalization raises concerns on national security, as the increased interconnection and free movement of people and goods can cause security threats, "by facilitating the opportunity for unethical and illegal practices to operate in a fairly unregulated environment" (Asghari, 2017, p.907).

Globalization is often viewed in association with its economic perspective: increased exchanges of goods and services, open market, and free trade. However, Robertson and White (2007) claim that globalization is not unidimensional (economic) but multidimensional. From an economic perspective, globalization emphasizes integrating national markets into the international open market system. From a social and cultural perspective, globalization aims to challenge the sociocultural barriers and promote a global identity and culture. Political globalization advances the importance of international institutions, multinational and transnational corporations, and non-government actors to leverage global governance and policymaking possibilities (MacLean, 2006). It shows that globalization advances a progressive world where the conventional differentiating parameters of financial capacity, trade, culture, societal values, and politics have become thin and insignificant. The increased engagement of international actors in national affairs may cause severe concerns for national security.

The advocates of globalization consider it a suitable mechanism to promote universal brotherhood and a sustainable future. They do not find any harmful effects of globalization (Bhagwati, 2002). However, Stiglitz (2017) argues that the chief proponents of globalization (the IMF, World Bank, and WTO) have become tools for developed countries to promote their interests. They significantly lost their focus on ensuring fairness and justice to developing countries. They prioritized emphasizing the Western nonliberal policies rather than providing a culture of progressive interconnectedness. Since these global institutions and the developed world unreasonably interfere in developing countries' policymaking and decision-making processes because of globalization's interconnectedness, it has become an ongoing challenge to national security. On the one hand, developing countries require economic growth for their sustainable future, and on the other hand, the support from developed countries and international institutions poses specific national security concerns. The rising national security concerns within the context of globalization can be better understood only if we analyze them through the perspective of economic growth.

Economic Growth

Economic growth is considered the most significant concern of the globe in the present century. Even when scholars and international institutions heavily demand to ensure sustainable developmental objectives, many countries and institutions prioritize economic growth at the expense of many other vital concerns. Economic growth is the most relevant sub-area of economics (Acemoglu, 2012). It points to an increase in the percentage of goods and services available in a country within a specific time frame (Drăgoi, 2020). It refers to the proportional increase in the GDP per capita (Colombatto, 2006). The post-Industrial Revolution society prioritized economic growth, which continues to exist and influence the world with an increased rhythm and vigor. During Adam Smith's period, there was no significant financial disparity between the rich and poor countries in the world (Maddison, 2001). However, within a short period, it became explicit due to countries' differential economic growth experiences. Differential growth rates can increase the income per capita gap and the differences in living standards between people and societies. Such a gap can be reduced through a well-designed and sustainable economic growth, as seen in Japan, South Korea, and China (Acemoglu, 2012). Globalization has also allowed national economies to integrate into the international economic landscape and progress toward meaningful growth (Asghari, 2017).

Although there are significant changes concerning the central areas of concern, economic growth and economic development are used interchangeably (Drăgoi, 2020). Both point to the same reality of financial progress in a society. The interconnection between economic growth and national security became a concern among researchers only from the 1970s. The basic assumption of this interconnection is that national security will become challenging in the absence of improvements in the sociopolitical and economic well-being of people (Asghari, 2017). The lack of economic growth and standard of living in a particular country can cause security challenges from both inside and outside. When the economic growth of Sri-Lanka was a complex phenomenon in 2022 due to the mismanagement of the state leaders, the people revolted against the government and overthrew them from power. Mismanagement of finances, shortage of essential goods, and high inflation forced people to form "Aragalaya" (a protest movement) against the government to maintain people's well-being. Furthermore, some countries depend on the wealthier nations due to poor economic growth. For instance, Sri Lanka (before the 2022 protest) and the Maldives depended on China, which tried to expand its political warfare by taking advantage of the situation. The Hambantota port of Sri Lanka had to be given to Chinese Merchants Port Holding for 99 years of lease since the Sri Lankan government failed to repay the loans taken for its construction (Abeyagoonasekera, 2024). Such instances cause the unnecessary involvement of foreign countries in domestic affairs, causing severe security concerns. All these show that significant economic growth is essential for promoting national security. However, with an increase in economic growth, most countries focus on spending more on the military based on national security concerns.

Military Spending

Government spending should focus on the welfare of its citizens and the nation. The government functions with the taxpayers' money. Through direct or indirect taxes, the government collects money from its citizens and institutions to run its daily activities, promote infrastructure development, advance research and innovation, and ensure the country's security. Military spending is one of the core areas of the country's national security concerns. No country is willing to compromise its expenditure on the military, as it is the central force to protect its territories, people, institutions, and values. However, military spending should echo transparency in military contracts (Ali & Solarin, 2020).

Since most military weapon deals are multibillion-dollar businesses, there is a high chance of corruption. It is said that corruption is a common phenomenon in military spending due to the limited number of manufacturers and suppliers and the informal nature of contracts (Transparency International, 2002). Some authors even calculate 15% of the military spending as bribes (D'Agostino et al., 2012). The illegal and unethical interaction between the supplier and the receiver causes severe damage to people's trust in the government. They believe that the government prioritizes their security over personal and political gains. However, many governments find military spending a secure source to satisfy their monetary interests (Mbaku, 2000).

According to the Stockholm International Peace Research Institute (SIPRI, 2025), the military expenditure of the globe increased for the tenth consecutive year in 2024. All the regions point to an increase in their military spending. Both Europe and the Middle East account for rapid growth in military spending. Almost 60% (US$1635 billion) of the total global expenditure on the military in 2024 (US$2718 billion) is spent by the five leading military spenders (the US, China, Russia, Germany, and India). The data also states that the global military expenditure in 2024 accounts for almost 2.5% of the global GDP. It is also noted that more than 100 countries increased their military spending in 2024. The SIPRI (2025) notes that the Russia-Ukraine war caused a severe impact on Europe as it significantly increased military spending beyond the recorded level at the end of the Cold War. Except for Malta, all European countries increased their military spending. Such an increase in Europe also caused an increase in the global military expenditure. Although Myanmar is the poorest country in ASEAN, it accounts for a 66% increase in military spending. It has the highest percentage of increase in Asia and Oceania, mainly due to internal armed conflicts. The data above shows that military spending increases along with wars, warlike situations, terrorist attacks, or internal conflicts.

Military spending is viewed as a burden if the country spends a significant portion of its GDP on enhancing its military. Military spending cannot be considered a needless public expenditure, but it should be within the prudent limits of the country's economic capacity (D'Agostino et al., 2019). Increased military spending from an underdeveloped or developing country has every chance to reduce its commitment toward welfare policies, which are designed to ensure people's security. The increased expenditure on military security points to the failure of the UN and other international institutions. The Universal Declaration of Human Rights (1948) affirmed explicitly in its Article 1 that all human beings "should act towards one another in a spirit of brotherhood." Although the UN charter does not expressly speak about universal brotherhood, it underlines the importance of having a spirit of cooperation and mutual respect. However, when countries and certain categories of people forget these fundamental concerns and prioritize their personal and biased interests, it leads to armed conflicts and wars, demanding more public expenditure on the military. Increased military spending by developing countries will adversely affect their commitment to the people-centered economic development of the country.

LITERATURE REVIEW

Analyzing the data of 112 countries from 1960 to 2000, Brauner (2015) investigates the interconnection between democracy and military spending. The research affirms that democracies spend less than autocracies on the military. He claims that an absolute autocracy spends more than 40% of a full democracy on the military. Such massive spending on the military diverts the autocratic government's attention from people-centered economic growth. Reviewing the data of 59 countries from 1996 to 2016, Ali and Solarin (2020) examined the interrelation between military spending and corruption. They argue that countries with higher corruption rates tend to spend more on the military. They show that the authorities' intention was not to ensure national security but to increase their wealth unethically, causing massive insecurity and burdening the state. Alley (2021) critically analyzes military spending in the context of alliance participation. It states that the military expenditure of junior alliance members is relatively small in deeper alliance treaties compared to shallow alliances. The junior alliance members of deeper alliances can thus concentrate more on people-centered economic growth, as the support of the senior members of the coalition can easily ensure their national security. In the context of NATO's burden-sharing policy, Becker (2021) analyzes the defense spending of its member countries. Most countries prioritize decreasing their military spending as unemployment increases in the post-COVID-19 society. They also spend more on military personnel than on equipment updates. However, Lindgren and Presterud (2023) argue that raising the military labor force cannot be regarded as an effective measure to ensure citizens' aspirations for peace, security, and sovereignty. It only creates tension between labor market policies and defense policies.

Abd Rahman (2023) examines the understanding of national security during and post-Cold War period. Analyzing the relationship between the US and the USSR during the Cold War, and the relationship between the US and China during the post-Cold War period, the author argues that during the Cold War period, national security was restrictively viewed from a military perspective. In contrast, it encompassed various elements like human security, personal security, and community security during the post-Cold War period. da Silva (2023) makes a detailed analysis of the required political accountability concerning military spending. Without proper political accountability, there is every possibility of spending an increased percentage on the military, disregarding other vital concerns and interests of the people. Analyzing the statistics of 150 countries, Shi (2024) examines the impact of an aging population on military spending. The study reveals that the aging population prioritizes social security over military security. Such a prioritization is more explicit and visible in older countries than younger ones. Saeed (2025) explores the impact of military spending on economic growth during peace and interstate violence. During peace times, it does not make a significant impact. However, during the interstate violence times, as the requirement is immediate, it adversely affects economic growth.

The literature analyzed above affirms that various studies have taken place concerning the interplay between national security and economic growth, as well as national security and military spending. Most studies focused on the empirical analysis of the available data to give a clear picture of the current scenario. In line with the studies mentioned above, this chapter examines national security and economic growth within the context of military spending. Compared to previous studies, this chapter uses critical and comparative analysis tools to revisit national security and economic growth when the global spending on the military increases substantially.

SIGNIFICANCE OF THE STUDY

Economic growth was regarded as a prestigious mechanism to ensure people's well-being and societal welfare, especially during the post-Second World War period. However, the Cold War tensions, several wars like Iran-Iraq, India-China, India-Pakistan, Iraq-Kuwait, Israel-Iran, and Russia-Ukraine, internal armed conflicts, and terrorist attacks affirmed that economic growth alone will not suffice to ensure a meaningful personal and societal life. Without assured national security, no society can enjoy the fruits of economic growth. Since the 'freedom from fear' of external threats and armed internal conflicts became a prime concern, countries tried to strengthen their armoury with more advanced weapons, spending millions of dollars on national security. The unimaginable technological growth and the unpredictable expansion of globalization have made it easier for countries to augment their military strength (Abd Rahman, 2023). Any country can guarantee national security by becoming a powerful military force or joining powerful and deeper alliances. The first requires massive spending on the military, whereas the second is based on following the values and mandates of the coalition (Alley, 2021). Since the chapter focuses on military spending, it doesn't engage in the discussions on the impact of the coalition on national security. The SIPRI (2025) states that the world witnessed a steep rise in military spending in 2024. It is calculated that the global military expenditure reached US$2718 billion in 2024, and accounted for the 10th consecutive year of military spending increase. The data shows a rise of 9.3% from 2023. It also notes that military expenditure increased in almost all regions of the globe. However, the impact of military spending on the economy and its growth is a complex point of discussion (D'Agostino et al., 2019). There is no consensus among the researchers and policymakers on whether it positively or negatively influences the economy. Therefore, this chapter examines national security and economic growth concerns in the context of massive military spending using the method of critical analysis.

NATIONAL SECURITY AND GLOBALIZATION: A CRITICAL ANALYSIS

The realist school defines national security from the perspective of power in the global scenario. Since most nations prioritize pursuing power, they concentrate on enhancing their military strength, which is considered the core of national power and international acceptance. National security aspirations evolved from the basic drive for national power (Shi, 2024). It became more vibrant in the era of globalization, as the increasing interconnectedness between people and nations poses a security challenge. This shift primarily occurred in the post-Cold War period. This period has caused tremendous security concerns, like terrorism, illegal migration, drug trafficking, proliferation of weapons of mass destruction, and cyberattacks (Abd Rahman, 2023). National security is often viewed from two perspectives: military national security and non-military national security (Shi, 2024). The military national security concerns prioritize the protection of the borders and the enhancement of military power. The non-military national security revolves around internal security concerns. It specifically focuses on the social security programs, which ensure people's freedom from want, fear, and indignity. However, globalization has narrowed the line between internal and external insecurity. Besides, even when the scholarly world emphasizes incorporating the non-military security threats into the national security framework, policymakers prefer to remain unchanged. This is mainly because there is a specific definitional clarity for military security concerns, while the non-military security areas are vague and complex (Ullman, 1983). Such a scenario is deepened by globalization and its interconnectedness. Since it prioritizes liberalization and economic growth over many other concerns for human progress, it is more concerned about the external threats and financial issues that challenge global economic growth.

Economic Growth and National Security

National security aims to promote a meaningful life for the citizens. Without economic growth, the desired national security objective cannot be achieved. Economic threats, like economic recession, inflation, and trade disputes between countries, can cause significant concerns for the inspiration drive for national security (Abd Rahman, 2023). The economic recession of 2008, which started in the US and spread to other parts of the globe, affirms that many countries had to slow down their efforts for national security and sustainable development goals (SDGs) due to the poor economic conditions. The inflation rate is increasing unpredictably across the globe. Oner (2025) states that inflation results from the government's inadequate financial policies. When the money supply to the market is high compared to the size of the economy, its purchasing power becomes less, adversely affecting the purchasing power as the prices will increase uncontrollably. Such a thing becomes a massive threat to the developing economies compared to the developed ones. While the normal inflation rate should be around 2-3%, the IMF (2025) states that the emerging economies experience an inflation rate of 5.1%. Besides, the present globe experiences enormous financial threats due to the international trade disputes and tariff war between the US and several other countries. The ongoing tensions in international trade can cause severe insecurity to people and the state.

During the Cold War, the US and the USSR prioritized national security and military enhancement over other vital concerns. Many researchers opined that these countries would allocate resources to empowering the military rather than social security programs (Ullman, 1983). Although Ullman predicted it during the intense arms race between the US and the USSR, the situation still exists. The annual budgets of the US, China, the UK, and India underline that their defense budgets are continuously increasing over the years (Shi, 2024). When more funds are allotted to the defense, the state fails to allocate resources for other vital concerns of the economy, negatively affecting its economic growth.

Sustainable Economic Growth

Sustainable economic growth is the predominant concern of the globe in the aftermath of the Brundtland Report of 1987. The report insisted that the developmental aspirations of the present generation should not endanger the environmental concerns of the future generation. It termed this progressive developmental vision as sustainable development. Sustainable economic growth evolves from the theoretical background of sustainable development, which calls for a development that should promote the global social, economic, and environmental sustainability. Economic growth cannot merely be understood as a financial problem, which is measured based on the calculation of GDP. It should be situated in a larger framework of social and environmental concerns. Economic growth cannot be understood as an outcome of market interactions only. It is influenced by the positive efforts of socially oriented policies (Tansel, 2020). An economic system should incorporate social justice and environmental protection to effectively function (Horodecka, 2024). Although the sustainability paradigm has evolved as "limits to growth" (WCED, 1987), challenging the economic aspiration, it genuinely focuses on ensuring the well-being of all beings and all generations (Horodecka, 2024). Sustainable economic growth is an economic growth that promotes justice and fairness. Sustainable economic growth is an essential precondition for national security. The examples of developed countries underline that national security evolves along with sustainable economic growth. From the perspective of military spending, sustainable economic growth demands that military expenditure should not become an obstacle to its people's aspirations for well-being.

Economic Security vis-à-vis Human Security

The post-Cold War changed global scenario advanced the human security policy perspective, which underlined the importance of having a people-centered developmental objective. The United Nations Development Program's (UNDP) 1994 Human Development Report (HDR) proposed the human security paradigm with seven essential categories. Economic security is one among them. Without meaningful economic security, people cannot achieve actual security. Economic security is the energizer for people-centered development to achieve the objective of human security. It underlines that people cannot realize freedom from want, fear, and indignity without realizing their life claims. It aims to protect people and communities from various threats, like physical violence, economic deprivation, social exclusion, and environmental degradation. Some researchers have criticized it as unpredictably broad and not explicitly addressing the state's security (Vaïsse, 2018). However, it is a vibrant policy approach as it prioritizes the security of individuals and communities. It brings down the security concerns from the abstract level (state) to the living reality (people) (Thakur, 1998). During the Cold War, individual security was regarded as evolving from the state's security. However, the UNDP's emphasis on the universalism of life claims affirmed individual security as evolving from human existence and human dignity. At the same time, the market forces also became explicitly strong. Accordingly, it is argued that an individual's security should also incorporate their economic well-being. Economic security thus became a vital element of the human security paradigm. National security is a state's commitment to maintain and guarantee its people's economic growth (economic security) and well-being (human security).

People-Centered National Security

Abd Rahman (2023) argues that the economic recession has caused a decrease in spending on national security, raising serious concerns about the country's security. However, the most crucial problem is limiting national security to territorial security and spending more on the military. Should the central point of concern be the territories of a state or its people? It is a complex discussion point. Some people argue that no person can sustainably live without secure state territories. It is true if we look at the insecurities and dangers of the people of Russia, Ukraine, Iran, Palestine, Israel, Ethiopia, and Yemen. However, Nye, Jr. (2011) defines national security, claiming that it should not only focus on protecting the sovereignty and integrity of the state from external threats but also preserve a country's way of life from internal threats. External and internal threats can damage the people's way of life in a particular state. The broadening of national security to encompass people's way of life has necessitated redefining the national security concept to include areas like military, environmental, personal, social, and economic security (Shi, 2024). The people-centered national security approach argues for including both military and non-military threats and considerations. The territories of a state are protected to safeguard its citizens' lives and property. People are the primary concern of the national security drive. However, due to the sidelining of citizens from the central political concerns at the national and international levels, their required importance is somehow lost. This led to the predominance of the abstract entity, 'state,' over the individuals. People's concerns and interests should be prioritized over any biased interests of the authorities. The Social Contract's theoretical foundation underlines that the state is created to protect the rights and interests of people. The state's authority is thus evolved from the people, not vice versa. Hence, the national security efforts should be oriented towards protecting the people, i.e., national security should be people-centered.

ECONOMIC GROWTH IN THE CONTEXT OF RISING MILITARY SPENDING

The military is an essential component of the state's national security drive. Upgradation of the military with the latest equipment is crucial for modernizing the military, integrating new technologies, and enhancing its capabilities. Although military expenditure is often regarded as an effective mechanism to examine a state's military capability, researchers argue that focus must be given to the quality of military equipment (Olsson, 2022). Spending more on increasing the quantity of equipment without focusing on its quality may not augment the military capability. Instead of making a country powerful in national security, it merely causes an economic burden without giving many positive effects. Systematic studies should be conducted on how military spending affects the country's economic landscape. If the military spending limits economic growth, it is disadvantageous to the country's sustainable future. Economic growth in the context of military expenditure is advantageous for industrialized and developed countries, as a good portion of their GDP comes from international weapon deals. Since the primary weapon manufacturing companies are in developed countries, it brings them an economic advantage. However, it negatively influences developing and underdeveloped countries, as they may be forced to make challenging decisions concerning economic growth. They may be forced to either retain or increase the budget for military spending due to the ongoing pressure of national security demands. When countries with less GDP spend more on military empowerment, they cannot sincerely focus on infrastructural development and other vital concerns of their economy (Abd Rahman, 2023). The most important thing for a country is to balance the genuine concerns of economic growth and military spending. People also have diverse opinions concerning military spending and national security. Some argue that military spending augments national security concerns, whereas others feel it has an adverse impact, as it will result in an arms race and confrontations (Yakovlev, 2007).

Positive Relationship

National security always has a positive relationship with economic growth. Economic growth will also be high in a country where people experience significant national security. When national security provides a basic secure setting for people and institutions to increase their economic contributions, it ultimately results in economic growth (Asghari, 2017). The ongoing instances of wars, warlike situations, terrorist attacks, and internal conflicts alienate investors from a country. Since the investors prioritize favorable working conditions, they will not start ventures in countries where security is a question mark.

Analyzing the impact of military expenditure on economic growth and FDI in five of seven SAARC (South Asian Association for Regional Cooperation) countries during the 1980-1999 period, Hassan et al. (2003) state that military expenditure has a positive relationship with economic growth. They claim that countries with substantial economic growth can only spend more on the military. However, this may not always be true. For instance, even when the Pakistani economy experienced a severe crisis in the financial year of 2023-2024 and 2024-25, it spent almost US$10.2 billion on the military. It further expanded (20%) the defense budget for the financial year 2025-26, while reducing some other public expenditure concerns. Spending massive resources on the military has every chance of reducing the required spending in other vital fields. It is a fallacy that national security can be easily equated with the empowerment of the military. It requires commitment in different fields that prioritize people-centered security.

The US is the world's largest arms exporting country, followed by France, Russia, China, and Germany. The increased arms production and export increase the military arms production industry's contribution to the country's GDP. Although the military spending of these countries is relatively high, they also earn from the export of the latest arms and equipment upgrades (Yakovlev, 2007). Compared to developing countries, they can easily balance their military expenditure with the revenue from arms dealing. Due to the increased spending on the military and the changing international political landscape, many developing countries have augmented their investments in defence research, technological upgrades, and arms production. For instance, in the last few decades, India has made significant progress in producing Agni, Tejus, Brahmos, and the like, which are highly demanded arms by the developing world. Such attempts will help them ensure technological development, arms production, employment creation, and economic growth rather than depending on other countries.

Negative Relationship

The increased military spending does not benefit any society, as it diverts resources from people's genuine concerns to protecting territories. No one can undermine the state security. However, it cannot override people's aspirations for a dignified life. It cannot be achieved without prioritizing their unique claims. When a state is forced to spend more on the military, it is also forced to neglect other genuine concerns. Besides, the impact of corruption on military spending is comparatively significant, and the cost of military activities and the expense of weapon purchase increase along with corruption. Such an increase adversely affects the economy of the purchasing countries because they need to invest more money than the actual cost (D'Agostino et al., 2012).

The most powerful military alliance in the present world, the North Atlantic Treaty Organization (NATO), decided to increase the military spending of its members to a minimum of 2% of their GDP during its 2014 Wales Summit. They decided to make this specified defense spending for ten consecutive years (NATO, 2014). At the 2023 Vilnius Summit, NATO members reaffirmed this decision and pointed out that it may sometimes require more spending (NATO, 2023). However, the 2024 reports show that due to Russia's invasion of Ukraine, most NATO members increased their military spending substantially. Among the 32 members, except Spain, Slovenia, Luxembourg, Belgium, Canada, Italy, Portugal, Croatia, and Slovakia, all others spent more than 2% of their GDP. Poland led the list with 4.12% of its GDP on military spending (Falkenek, 2024). At the Hague Summit, the members unanimously decided to increase their annual defense spending to 5% of GDP by 2035 to ensure their individual and collective obligations. They plan to spend 5% of GDP on defense empowerment in two ways: 3.5% of the GDP "to resource core defense requirements and to meet the NATO capability targets," and 1.5% of the GDP "to inter alia protect our critical infrastructure, defend our networks, ensure our civil preparedness and resilience, unleash innovation, and strengthen our defense industrial base" (NATO, 2025). Such a massive investment is required for national security and the protection of the member countries of the alliance.

However, the issue of such enormous spending on the defense system of a coalition of 32 members can be understood only when we critically examine it from the perspective of the other 163 countries. Most of these 163 countries are either developing or underdeveloped, and their annual budgets do not comprise 2% of the GDP of NATO members. For instance, 2% of the GDP of the US in 2024 was approximately US$584 billion, and that of the UK was approximately US$73 billion. In contrast, India's total annual budget in 2024 was approximately US$756 billion, and Pakistan's was approximately US$68 billion. The UK's defense spending is more than Pakistan's yearly budget. Although India's annual budget is almost 200 billion dollars more than the US's military spending, it shows a massive difference from the demographic point of view. It affirms that although the earth's resources are supposed to be shared with everyone, some are getting an advantage at the cost of others. According to the UN, there are 152 developing countries, and the UNCDF calculates 45 countries as the least developed countries (LDCs). They are the poorest and weakest segment of the global society, accounting for almost 40% of the global population. They account for just 1.3% of the global GDP and only 1.4% of FDI. It shows that when the highly developed NATO countries focus on increasing their yearly military spending, which accounts for just 12% of the global population, it seems a severe denial of the principles of international justice.

Example of Developing Countries

Developing countries should have prioritized economic development to increase the living standards of their people. However, many focus on expanding their military power without paying attention to developmental projects. Developing countries' failure to balance economic development and military spending causes serious developmental concerns. Without due care on infrastructure development and other progressive measures, no country can progress towards a sustainable future. D'Agostino et al. (2012) state that if the developing countries reduce their military spending, it increases their collective economic performance and indirectly reduces the chances of corruption. Ali and Solarin (2020) affirm that the increased military expenditure raised the percentage of corruption in African countries, which harmed their economic performance.

Many international institutions and developed countries provide financial assistance to developing countries. However, some countries use foreign aid to fuel war-related efforts, such as purchasing more weapons (Omitoogun, 2003). It again connects foreign aid, military spending, and corruption. Without clearly furnishing the details of the expenditure of foreign assistance to the beneficiaries, the country's corrupt leaders spend a significant part on military spending. Both accountability and transparency become crucial concerns in such a scenario. Many developed countries are aware of this unethical mode of behavior. However, without focusing on the genuine implementation and monitoring process, they seem happy with the diverted spending of funds. Most developing countries purchase military weapons and equipment from developed countries. Accordingly, the given fund comes back to them, increasing their GDP.

Restricted Vision of National Security

When the chapter speaks of the restricted vision of national security, it has many implications. Firstly, national security is traditionally defined in the context of territorial security. Even when armed internal conflicts and cyberattacks are included in national security, they are understood as attempts to encroach on the country's territorial integrity. National security should prioritize people's security, which demands a dignified living. It should incorporate people's genuine concerns and interests, as without ensuring their freedom from want, fear, and indignity, no state can claim that it guarantees security to its people.

While presenting the 2021 budget to Congress, the Brazilian President, Jair Bolsonaro, proposed a 49% increase in the defense budget, even above the resources allotted for education. Although the proposed budget had to be changed due to severe pressure from the public, media, and the international community, the proposal poses specific questions on our understanding of national security (da Silva, 2023). Why do we associate national security with military security or territorial security? Why are national leaders not more concerned about improving education, healthcare, and basic infrastructure to ensure human security? A country cannot achieve meaningful economic growth if it does not explicitly focus on allotting more resources for education, healthcare, environmental protection, and infrastructure development. Governments should go beyond the restrictive national security vision to include other vital elements of human flourishing. Such a progressive vision will help them to achieve a people-centered security and ensure a sustainable future for the global community (UNDP, 1994).

When Russia initiated war against Ukraine, Putin said that they aimed to "denazify" and demilitarize Ukraine. According to him, if Russia fails to demilitarize Ukraine, it will threaten Russia's national security concerns (Shi, 2024). Although the story of the power blocs of the Cold War ended, its ramifications still continue to exist. The military alliance, NATO, is seen as a threat to Russia, China, and many other countries. They observe the expansion of NATO with caution and prejudice. Although the NATO members claim that they want to ensure peace and order in the global society and security for their members, NATO's existence and expansion cause insecurities across the globe.

One of the complex issues with national security is that its range depends on the national leaders. The leaders of a nation can restrictively or elaborately define national security or national security threats. When national security is restrictively interpreted from the perspective of the state authorities to include only external offline and online attacks and severe internal conflicts, it will not become a burden for the people. However, if they interpret them to include criticism against the state leaders or government policies, it will cause trouble for people. National security threats cannot include criticism against the government and its policies.

A POLICY PERSPECTIVE

Military spending is part of the public expenditure. When governments make agreements to expand their military strength by purchasing the latest weapons and other accessories, they should be made available to the public for scrutiny and verification. If the government does not disclose the details of such agreements to its citizens, taking advantage of the official secret measures, it becomes a complex question of transparency and accountability. Such a disclosure should not become a challenge to national security. However, within the limits of national security concerns, it should be willing to disclose the possible matters to affirm its transparency (Ali & Solarin, 2020). Political accountability is the most essential requirement to reduce unnecessary military spending. When the government is accountable to the public, it prioritizes the public's interests rather than just playing for its political party's interests. Accountability ensures discretion in the decisions (da Silva, 2023).

In a non-democratic setting, political success is always associated with using power (Ali & Solarin, 2020). It uses power through the biased military use for autocratic leaders' personal and political gains. Accordingly, they prioritize spending more on enhancing the military strength. For instance, the Chilean Congress had no control over the government's decisions on military spending. Based on a 1958 enactment, it designated a good percentage of copper export revenue to arms procurement and maintenance. Although there have been widespread protests against it, the system continued until it was replaced in 2020. Accordingly, the Chilean Congress changed the proposed defense budget and allocated those funds to address the COVID-19 emergency (da Silva, 2023). When there is more control on the government by the civic society, it can reduce unnecessary military spending and focus on enhancing people's essential requirements.

Discussions on efficient national security always point to the requirement of good governance. It demands governance based on the rule of law, which provides effective mechanisms for implementation. The government should train and equip appropriate personnel for the successful implementation process. Good governance will also prioritize sustainable economic growth, by which it can efficiently secure its people and their interests. Both public and private sectors will have the potential to pay for the security of their people if the country's good governance focuses on sustainable economic growth (Asghari, 2017). Any country must use its resources for society's most urgent needs. Good governance is the willingness of authorities to realize the real needs of the public and devise policies and programs to support those needs (da Silva, 2023).

CONCLUSION

The globe witnesses unprecedented spending on the military from almost all countries. This is mainly because national security has also become a significant concern in the context of security threats from non-state actors. The increased interconnectedness between nations due to widespread globalization allows state and non-state actors to encroach on the territories of other states and cause insecurities for multiple reasons. Since they use highly enhanced equipment, the state authorities must also prioritize upgrading their arms and military equipment to protect people and territory. When they prioritize military spending, it affects their economic growth. This is more explicit in the developing world, where economic growth is relatively low compared to the developed world. The allocation of more funds to the military poses a restricted vision of national security, as it does not consider a people-centered policy perspective. Although protecting national territories is essential, it cannot be emphasized more than people's genuine needs and claims. The UN and other international institutions and developed countries should devise strategies to promote the UDHR's great aspiration for a universal brotherhood, which the UN Charter also underlines through cooperation and respect between nations. When war occurs, ordinary people on both sides are the primary victims of its consequences. Most wars happen due to the egoistic attitude of some leaders, who prioritize their ego over people's interests. The Westphalian principles of sovereignty and territorial integrity of each country are valid international principles throughout. If the state and non-state actors respect these principles with utmost sincerity, the globe can easily address the questions on national security without spending much on the military. The road to a sustainable future, which the UN repeatedly underlines in its conferences, treaties, and agreements, is not easy to realize if the world is not willing to change its attitude from egoism to altruism, exclusiveness to inclusiveness, and the 'other is a hell' attitude to universal brotherhood.

REFERENCES

Abd Rahman, A. A. (2023). The Concept of National Security in the Period of Cold War and Post-Cold War. *Journal of Law and Sustainable Development, 11*(5), 1–9. https://ojs.journalsdg.org/jlss/article/view/766

Abeyagoonasekera, A. (2024). China's Strategy for Political Warfare in Sri Lanka. *East Asian Policy*, 16(2), 68-81. https://www.worldscientific.com/doi/abs/10.1142/S1793930524000133

Acemoglu, D. (2012). Introduction to Economic Growth. *Journal of Economic Theory, 147*(2), 545–550. DOI: 10.1016/j.jet.2012.01.023

Ali, H. E., & Solarin, S. A. (2020). Military Spending, Corruption, and the Welfare Consequences. *Defence and Peace Economics, 31*(6), 677–691. https://www.tandfonline.com/doi/full/10.1080/10242694.2019.1567181. DOI: 10.1080/10242694.2019.1567181

Alley, J. (2021). Alliance Participation, Treaty Depth, and Military Spending. *International Studies Quarterly, 65*(4), 929–941. DOI: 10.1093/isq/sqab077

Asghari, M. (2017). National Security and Economic Growth. *Iranian Economic Review, 21*(4), 905–924.

Becker, J. (2021). Rusty Guns and Buttery Soldiers: Unemployment and the Domestic Origins of Defense Spending. *European Political Science Review, 13*(3), 307–330. DOI: 10.1017/S1755773921000102

Bhagwati, J. (2002). Coping with Antiglobalization: A Trilogy of Discontents. *Foreign Affairs, 81*(1), 2–7. https://www.jstor.org/stable/20032998. DOI: 10.2307/20032998

Brands, H. (2018). Choosing Primacy: U.S. Strategy and Global Order at the Dawn of the Post-Cold War Era. *Texas National Security Review*, 1(2), 8-33. https://doi.org/DOI: 10.15781/T2VH5D166

Braunder, J. (2015). Military Spending and Democracy. *Defence and Peace Economics, 26*(4), 409–423. https://www.tandfonline.com/doi/full/10.1080/10242694.2014.960245. DOI: 10.1080/10242694.2014.960245

Brzezinski, Z. (1997). *The Grand Chessboard: American Primacy and Its Geostrategic Imperatives*. Basic Books.

Buchholz, K. (2024). The Indian Budget 2024/25. *Statista*. https://www.statista.com/chart/26764/indian-national-budget/

Colombatto, E. (2006). On Economic Growth and Development. *The Review of Austrian Economics, 19*(4), 243–260. https://link.springer.com/article/10.1007/s11138-006-9247-x. DOI: 10.1007/s11138-006-9247-x

D'Agostino, G., Dunne, J. P., & Pieroni, L. (2012). Corruption, Military Spending, and Growth. *Defence and Peace Economics, 23*(6), 591–604. https://www.tandfonline.com/doi/abs/10.1080/10242694.2012.663579. DOI: 10.1080/10242694.2012.663579

D'Agostino, G., Dunne, J. P., & Pieroni, L. (2019). Military Expenditure, Endogeneity, and Economic Growth. *Defence and Peace Economics, 30*(5), 509–524. https://www.tandfonline.com/doi/full/10.1080/10242694.2017.1422314. DOI: 10.1080/10242694.2017.1422314

da Silva, D. L. (2023). Political Accountability and Military Spending. *Defence and Peace Economics, 34*(5), 563–580. https://www.tandfonline.com/doi/full/10.1080/10242694.2022.2129128. DOI: 10.1080/10242694.2022.2129128

Drăgoi, D. (2020). Economic Growth versus Economic Development. *Atlantic Review of Economics*, 4(1), 1-11. https://www.econstor.eu/bitstream/10419/282275/1/100.pdf

Ezeja, I. I. (2024). Globalization and National Security: Unraveling the Multifaceted Nexus. *IDOSR Journal of Arts and Management,* 9(1), 18-24. https://www.idosr.org/globalization-and-national-security-unraveling-the-multifaceted-nexus/

Falkanek, C. (2024). Who's at 2% Percent? Look How NATO Allies Have Increased Their Defense Spending Since Russia's Invasion of Ukraine. *Atlantic Council.* https://www.atlanticcouncil.org/blogs/econographics/whos-at-2-percent-look-how-nato-allies-have-increased-their-defense-spending-since-russias-invasion-of-ukraine/

Friedman, T. L. (2005). *The World is a Flat: A Brief History of the Globalized World in the Twenty First Century.* Allen Lane.

Hassan, M. K., Waheeduzzaman, M., & Rahman, A. (2003). Defense Expenditure and Economic Growth in the SAARC Countries. *The Journal of Political. Social and Economic Studies, 28*(3), 275–293. https://jspes.org/fall2003_hassan.html

Horodecka, A. (2024). Is Economic Development Really Becoming Sustainable? *Forum for Social Economics.* https://www.tandfonline.com/doi/full/10.1080/07360932.2024.2401436

IMF. (2025). Inflation Rate, Average Consumer Prices: Annual Percent Change. https://www.imf.org/external/datamapper/PCPIPCH@WEO/OEMDC/ADVEC/WEOWORLD

Lawrence, P. (2021). The Global and National Inequality Faultlines: The Economic Dimensions of (In)security. *Journal of Global Faultlines*, *8*(1), 23–33. https://www.scienceopen.com/hosted-document?doi=10.13169/jglobfaul.8.1.0023. DOI: 10.13169/jglobfaul.8.1.0023

MacLean, G. A. (2006). Human Security and the Globalization of International Security. *Whitehead Journal of Diplomacy and International Relations,* 7(1), 89-99. https://ciaotest.cc.columbia.edu/olj/shjdir/v7n1/v7n1_07.pdf

Maddison, A. (2001). *The World Economy: A Millennial Perspective*. Development Center. DOI: 10.1787/9789264189980-en

Mbaku, J. M. (2000). *Bureaucratic and Political Corruption in Africa: The Public Choice Perspective*. Kreiger.

NATO. (2014). The Wales Summit Declaration. https://www.nato.int/cps/en/natohq/official_texts_112964.htm

NATO. (2023). The Vilnius Summit Communiqué. https://www.nato.int/cps/en/natohq/official_texts_217320.htm

NATO. (2025). The Hague Summit Declaration. https://www.nato.int/cps/en/natohq/official_texts_236705.htm

Nayyar, D. (2006). Globalization, History, and Development: A Tale of Two Centuries. *Cambridge Journal of Economics*, *30*(1), 137–159. https://academic.oup.com/cje/article/30/1/137/1730040. DOI: 10.1093/cje/bei090

Nye, J. S.Jr. (2011). *The Future of Power*. Perseus Books.

Olsson, P. (2022). Measuring Quality of Military Equipment. *Defence and Peace Economics*, *33*(1), 93–107. DOI: 10.1080/10242694.2020.1851474

Omitoogun, W. (2003). Military Expenditure Data in Africa: A Survey of Cameroon, Ethiopia, Ghana, Kenya, Nigeria, and Uganda. *SIPRI Research Report No. 17*. Stockholm International Peace Research Institute. https://www.sipri.org/publications/2003/military-expenditure-data-africa-survey-cameroon-ethiopia-ghana-kenya-nigeria-and-uganda

Oner, C. (2025). Inflation: Prices on the Rise. *IMF*. https://www.imf.org/en/Publications/fandd/issues/Series/Back-to-Basics/Inflation#:~

Ritzer, G. (2007). Introduction. In Ritzer, G. (Ed.), *The Blackwell Companion to Globalization* (pp. 1–13). Blackwell. DOI: 10.1002/9780470691939.ch

Robertson, R., & White, K. E. (2007). What is Globalization? In Ritzer, G. (Ed.), *The Blackwell Companion to Globalization* (pp. 54–66). Blackwell. DOI: 10.1002/9780470691939.ch2

Saeed, L. (2025). The Impact of Military Expenditures on Economic Growth: A New Instrumental Variables Approach. *Defence and Peace Economics*, *36*(1), 86–101. https://www.tandfonline.com/doi/full/10.1080/10242694.2023.2259651. DOI: 10.1080/10242694.2023.2259651

Shafik, M. (2021). *What We Owe Each Other: A New Social Contract for a Better Society*. Princeton University Press.

Shi, J. (2024). How Population Aging Impacts the Perception of National Security and Military Spending. *SN Social Sciences*, *4*(12), 233. https://link.springer.com/article/10.1007/s43545-024-01031-3. DOI: 10.1007/s43545-024-01031-3

SIPRI. (2025). Unprecedented Rise in Global Military Expenditure as European and Middle East Spending Surges. https://www.sipri.org/media/press-release/2025/unprecedented-rise-global-military-expenditure-european-and-middle-east-spending-surges

Stiglitz, J. (2017). *Globalization and Its Discontents Revisited: Anti-Globalization in the Era of Trump*. Norton.

Tansel, T. B. (2020). The Shape of 'Rising Powers' to Come? The Antinomies of Growth and Neoliberal Development in Turkey. *New Political Economy*, *25*(5), 791–812. https://www.tandfonline.com/doi/full/10.1080/13563467.2019.1584173. DOI: 10.1080/13563467.2019.1584173

Thakur, R. (1998). From National to Human Security. In Harris, S., & Mack, A. (Eds.), *Asia-Pacific security: The Economics-Politics Nexus*. Allen & Unwin.

Ullman, R. H. (1983). Redefining Security. *International Security*, *8*(1), 129–153. https://www.jstor.org/stable/2538489. DOI: 10.2307/2538489

UNDP. (1994). Human Development Report. https://hdr.undp.org/content/human-development-report-1994

Vaïsse, J. (2018). *Zbigniew Brzezinski: America's Grand Strategist*. Harvard University Press.

Yakovlev, P. (2007). Arms Trade, Military Spending, and Economic Growth. *Defence and Peace Economics*, *18*(4), 317–338. DOI: 10.1080/10242690601099679

KEY TERMS AND DEFINITIONS

Cyberattack: Cyberattack is a new form of threat to national security. It targets cyberspace and cyber activities of a country to create confusion and insecurity concerning the functioning of many vital elements.

Economic Security: Economic security refers to a situation of stable income that helps people and society realize their objectives of a dignified life and a sustainable future.

Globalization: Globalization is the process of increasing interconnectedness and interdependence between countries, which occurs through the flow of people, goods, and services. Although it has a history of many centuries, it became more explicit in the last decade of the 20th century with market liberalization.

Human Rights: Human rights are the fundamental and innate claims of people that are universal, interdependent, indivisible, and inalienable. Human rights is a broader framework, which cannot be restricted to security alone. It includes all of humans' fundamental aspirations for a standard of living.

Human Security: Human security is a policy perspective advanced by the UNDP in contrast to the overemphasis on national security. It underlines that the ultimate security rests with the well-being of people.

State Sovereignty: A state's sovereignty refers to its supreme power and authority over internal matters, territorial boundaries, and freedom from external influence.

Sustainability: Sustainability refers to many essential concerns, like environmental protection, economic growth, and social equality. In the context of this chapter, sustainability refers to meeting the economic and security needs of the present generation without compromising the needs of future generations.

Chapter 9
Military Spending on Encrypting Information Used in Customs and Ports as a Trigger for Regional Economic Growth

Gerardo Reyes Ruiz
https://orcid.org/0000-0003-0212-2952
Center for Advanced Naval Studies (CESNAV), Mexico

ABSTRACT

This work presents an approach to the new technologies currently used in Mexican customs and ports. Based on this approach, it is emphasized that National Security is a facilitator for safeguarding the information used and processed in these important national facilities. As a consequence, it is proposed that, to take the first step toward modernizing Mexican customs and ports, proper management of all information is essential. Therefore, proper data encryption must focus on ensuring information security, as without proper management of this information, customs or port modernization cannot be considered. This reasoning is undoubtedly because the primary input of a customs office and a port is precisely the integration of information obtained from products, people, animals, works of art, and hazardous materials that transit through their facilities.

DOI: 10.4018/979-8-3373-3456-1.ch009

INTRODUCTION

Since the beginning of the 21st century, new technologies based on the provision of information have shown significant advances and results in multiple areas of work and knowledge (Vicsek, 2021; Passavanti et al., 2020; Mahr and Huh, 2022). In these contexts, and many others, the Internet of Things (IoT) has been demonstrated to be one of the most effective methods for carrying out this dynamic (Shammar and Zahary, 2020; Pirbhulal et al., 2024). The introduction of new technological tools assisted, precisely, by multiple devices such as smartphones, tablets, MOOCs, SPOCs, smart boards, laptops, online learning tools, dynamic visualizations, virtual laboratories, blended learning and MashUp technologies, among many others, have altered the training process worldwide (Haleem et al., 2022; Alkhudhayr et al., 2019). These technologies are increasingly accessible to people, since through them various benefits can be obtained with their use and learning, such as using applications fully oriented towards information security (Madnick, Huang and Madnick, 2023; Khayyat et al., 2024).

Nowadays, the use of new technologies, almost all of them based on data transmission, is indispensable. Of course, all these technologies have revolutionized the way people -and even businesses- relate to each other. Furthermore, communications are now faster and more efficient (Hitzler, 2021; Andersson, 2018). Due to this technological revolution, the use of multiple mobile devices has reached a considerable level of dependence for people (Chinese Academy of Cyberspace Studies, 2023). In other words, new technologies, especially those focused on mobile devices, have become necessary, almost indispensable, elements for people or businesses to interact with and communicate with each other. Of course, this communication is currently carried out in a more impersonal way, but, above all, in a more efficient way (Harris et al., 2020; Ali et al., 2023). Without a doubt, these new technologies, generally based on mobile devices and data transfer, have also become an indispensable element, especially during and after the COVID-19 pandemic (Wajid and Alam, 2024; Toussaert, 2021; Lee and Trimi, 2021; He, Zhang and Li, 2021). These new technological tools became popular for people to make their online purchases, which turned out to be the safest way to guarantee the most precious thing in life at that time: their health (Valamede, de Oliveira, Munhoz and Akkari, 2022; Katsumata et al., 2022; Chemnad et al., 2022). In this way, the diversity of new technologies and multiple devices became an extremely important means to present a series of technologies innovatively and efficiently (Wang and Wang, 2021; Stocchi et al., 2022; Kalgotra, Gupta and Sharda, 2021).

NATIONAL SECURITY AS AN INCENTIVE FOR CYBERSECURITY

The concepts of security, peace, identity, and other terminologies contextualized in the arena of international political theory have been subject to multiple interpretations (most with evident ideological bias) (Anwar et al., 2018). However, due to the evident lack of conceptual boundaries, security, as a concept, is currently used to attract and stimulate the sponsorship of multiple political projects at the federal and international levels of politics that did not exist in the past (Sussex, Clarke and Medcalf, 2017; Sánchez de la Barquera and Arroyo, 2024; Meerts, 2019). In this sense, Williams (2008) affirmed that security is a powerful political tool to draw attention to priority elements in the competition for governmental attention. On the other hand, Makinda (1998) envisioned security as the preservation of society's norms, rules, institutions, and values. Furthermore, the latter author also asserted that all institutions, principles, and structures associated with society, including its population, must be protected from all types of threats, including, of course, military ones. Therefore, security refers to everything that guarantees a system -or leads it to- a state of protection against potential threats and risks (Weippl and Schrittwieser, 2024). This also generally refers to protecting the confidentiality, integrity, and availability of data (US Department of State, 2024). In other words, security mechanisms should be designed to prevent, to the greatest extent possible, unauthorized access, use, disclosure, interruption, modification, or destruction (Bishop, 2003).

Figure 1. Safety objective (https://www.prakmatic.com)

In this context, the modern concept of National Security dates back to the 17th century, during the Thirty Years' War in Europe and the Civil War in England. In 1648, as a direct consequence of the Peace of Westphalia, the idea was established that the relationship between State and Nation -the balance of power- held sovereign control not only over the internal affairs of a country or region, but also over external security (Phillips, 2023; Janžekovič, 2022; Croxton, 1999). Currently, the definition of National Security is not trivial simply because it addresses multiple concepts, including the following: Power -for example, Political Power or Economic Power- Force -for example, Public Force- Military Force, and National Defense -for example, Diplomacy- (Holmes, 2015). Of course, each of these concepts, in turn, encompasses various terms that are currently attracting the attention of experts (Clarke et al., 2022). In this sense, everything related to a country's National Security policy is determined by multiple factors (Ortiz Arellano, 2021; Bandala López, 2018), including economic needs, geography, external threats, military capabilities, political culture, elite opinion, popular opinion (particularly in democracies), and leaders' perceptions of their country or region's diverse interests, to name a few.

Cybersecurity is defined as the art of protecting networks, devices, and data from unauthorized access or criminal use, and the practice of ensuring the confidentiality, integrity, and availability of information (Cybersecurity & Infrastructure Security Agency, 2024) (see Figure 1). We are currently immersed in a technological era, and this makes us totally vulnerable, as our dependence on technological tools has transformed us into human beings totally dependent on computers and the internet. As a consequence of these vulnerabilities, the main targets have been communications, smart devices, entertainment, transportation, the use of bank cards, the purchase of medicines, merchandise transiting through customs, and, of course, military information, among others. Today, there are many risks related to safeguarding information or data, some of them more serious than others (see Figure 2). Among all these risks, we can mention malware that erases an entire computer system (Akhtar and Feng in 2022 define malware as software that is expressly created to cause damage to a computer or network). Among the main damage, the following can be mentioned: entering a system and altering or stealing files or using a computer to harm one or more users by stealing their bank card information and making unauthorized purchases. In this context, at present there is no guarantee that, even with the best precautions, any of these inconveniences will happen to a person, however, fortunately, there are some measures that can be implemented to minimize these risks.

Figure 2. Types of cyberattacks (Akhtar and Feng, 2022)

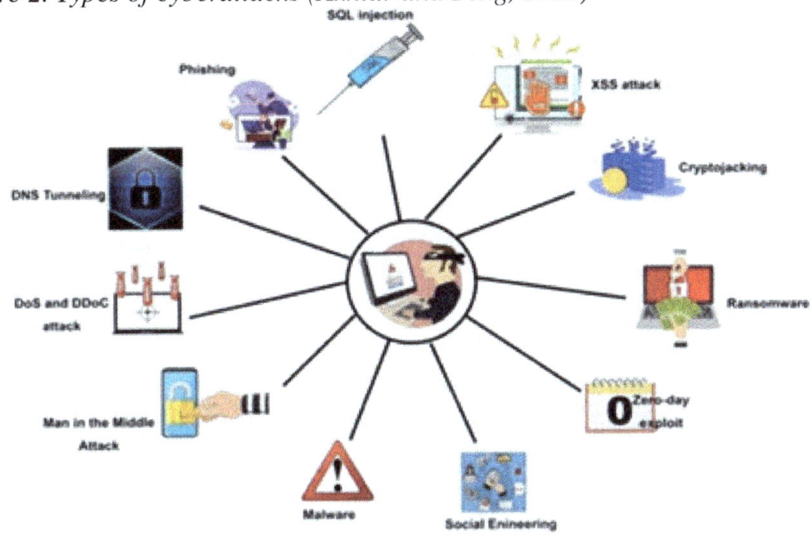

At this point, the following question makes sense: What measures should be taken to improve cybersecurity? Undoubtedly, the answer is not simple because it will depend on multiple factors, and perhaps the most important factor is the financial investment allocated to minimize the risk of a cyberattack, which, unfortunately, is not within everyone's reach. However, the first step to protect against this event is to recognize and subsequently identify the risks. In this scenario, the United States Cyber Defense Agency (America's Cyber Defense Agency, https://www.cisa.gov/), through its agency called the National Coordinator for Critical Infrastructure Security Resilience, recommends that it is essential to identify the following terms to better understand these potential risks:

- **Hacker, attacker, or intruder.** These terms apply to people who deliberately seek to exploit weaknesses in software and computer systems for their benefit. Although their intentions are sometimes benign -generally motivated by curiosity- their actions aim to violate, and even damage, the information on the computer systems they explore. Undoubtedly, the potential outcomes range from curiosity, through the creation of a virus with no negative impact on the owner of the information, to malicious activity such as stealing or altering information.
- **Malicious Code.** This code, also called malware, is a collection of unwanted files or programs intended to cause damage to a computer or compromise data stored on the hard drive. Currently, multiple classifications of malicious code are considered, including viruses, worms, and Trojan horses. In this context,

malicious code has some of the following characteristics: 1) It may require opening an email attachment or being redirected to a specific web page; 2) Some malware spreads without user intervention and is usually launched to exploit any vulnerability in previously installed software; 3) Once a computer has been infected, these computer programs will attempt to locate other computers to harm or infect them; 4) Some malware can spread through email, websites, or networks; 5) Some of these malicious programs give the impression of being one thing, but in reality, all they seek is to damage information, the website, or the network.

- **Vulnerabilities.** These are flaws detected in software, firmware, or hardware that an attacker exploits to perform unauthorized actions on a computer, website, system, or network. These weaknesses can be caused by programming errors in the software, and attackers can then detect them through malware. They then exploit these flaws to harm or infect as many computers as possible with the malware they have designed.

Figure 3. Target of a cyberattack (www.es.vecteezy.com)

For its part, and once the risks of a cyberattack have been recognized, the following cybersecurity practices are recommended to minimize these risks (Cybersecurity Infrastructure Security Agency, 2021): 1) constantly keep software updated; 2) run antivirus software that is, of course, up-to-date; 3) use more secure passwords whenever possible; 4) frequently change default usernames and passwords; 5) implement multi-factor authentication (this is a process that uses at least two components to validate a user's identity or authenticity); 6) install at least one firewall; and; 7) do not trust unexpected emails. However, despite all the precautions, these preventive measures do not guarantee total protection against a cyberattack. This is because malicious code detection relies on signatures (known patterns in the code that can be identified as malware). Therefore, it's worth noting that even the best antivirus software can't guarantee adequate protection against new and advanced threats (such as zero-day exploits and polymorphic viruses).

Figure 4. Preventing cyberattacks (based on Akhtar and Feng, 2022)

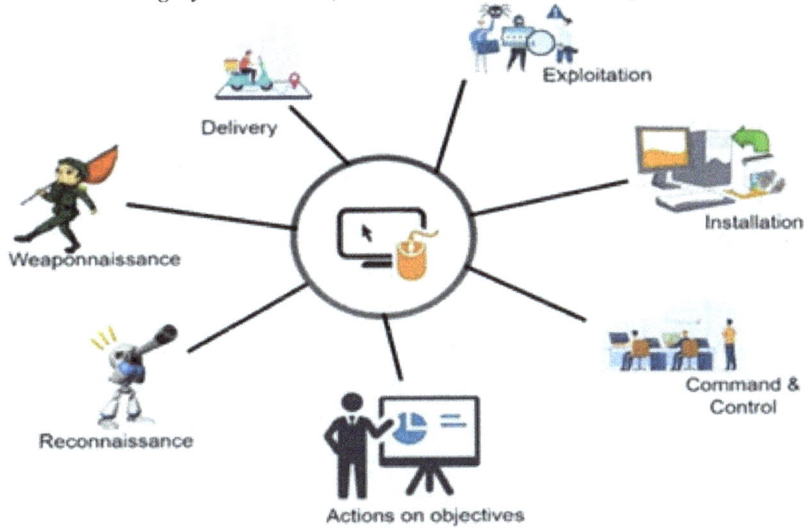

BACKGROUND

Technology, or its very absence, has shaped human information use patterns over the centuries (Wickberg and Gärdebo, 2023; Tanaka, 2022). In recent decades, both computers and the Internet have emerged as indispensable communication networks connecting millions of users across diverse platforms, from desktops to mobile and laptop devices (Kizza, 2023; Kim and Wang, 2021). The concept of technology is often confusing (Agar, 2019), however, Nyamboga and Kemparaju (2002) supported the premise that information technology (IT) is a collective term for various technologies involved in the processing and transmission of information, which may include computing, telecommunications, and microelectronics. In the early 1980s, the American Library Association (1983, p. 183) defined these technologies as “the application of computers and other technologies to the acquisition, organization, storage, retrieval, and dissemination of information.” What should be clear is that IT, such as hardware, software, databases, bulletin boards, and electronic forums, provides effective and innovative means for storing and sharing cutting-edge knowledge (Raudeliuniene, Albats and Kordab, 2021). Furthermore, Pandey and Chakraborty (2002, p. 11) stated that IT is truly efficient for the use of hardware and software for efficient information management, that is, the storage, retrieval, processing, communication, dissemination, and sharing of large volumes of information.

In this context, Emojorho and Adomi (2006) proposed that IT is like a major driver of this era and define it as a set of new technologies and their applications, including all aspects of the use of computers, microelectronic devices, satellites, the Internet, and communication technology. That is, IT encompasses computers, databases (online or offline), information networks (such as the Internet), electronic resources (such as e-books, e-journals, dissertations), software and hardware equipment (such as information infrastructure), and special information services (such as targeted dissemination of information -information encryption-, current affairs awareness services, content services, advertising services, electronic counters, among many others) (Mohsenzadeh and Isfandyari-Moghaddam, 2009).

Recent advances in IT have changed the way people and even organization's function (Chitechi and Otanga, 2020). Much of this dynamic is because personal computers now do the work previously done by people, even more efficiently (Larus, 2024). Computers are now connected to organizations/business networks, and workers share programs, files, and electronic messages. This has allowed remote work to increase and continue to increase, primarily because people now can connect to a company's/institution's computer systems from their homes (Doron, 2022). Of course, the Internet has provided an environment in which information can travel across personal, business, and geographic boundaries. Because of this technological innovation, institutions are making increasingly significant investments in IT, which has gradually become an efficient option for managing organizational knowledge capital (Muthukumar and Hedberg, 2005), because it facilitates both the creation and implementation of knowledge management and, as already mentioned, allows reducing time and space barriers (Rathi, Given and Forcier, 2014). In other words, IT represents a facilitator for the exchange of knowledge and information, mainly because it serves to eliminate barriers and reduce the time and, above all, the effort required to transfer specific knowledge/information (Dang, Le-Hoai and Kim, 2018). Therefore, IT is used, with great success, to connect people with codified knowledge and, above all, to create, share, store, and use important information efficiently (Podrug, Filipovic and Kovac, 2017).

Without a doubt, IT has revolutionized the way people communicate, and consequently, society has been forced to adapt to rapid changes in both the methods and media used, but above all, to the speed with which these changes occur, particularly those focused on communication and services (Danaher and Sætra, 2022). However, IT and rapid scientific and technical progress have imposed incredible pressures on modern societies. Namely, these technologies generate so much information that people are facing, precisely, an information explosion, pollution, and an exponential increase in information (Chew et al., 2023). In this sense, IT is considered an innovation when potential adopters consider it relatively new (García-Avilés, 2020): Kim (2016) stated and envisioned that the development related to IT in recent years has influenced, and will directly influence, the advancement of Internet innovations by seamlessly interconnecting everyday objects such as televisions, refrigerators, light bulbs and multiple household appliances to a universal information network called the Internet of Things (IoT). For its part, IT supports knowledge storage by retaining and organizing an organization's records, experiences, and knowledge so that employees can benefit from them (Dang, Le-Hoai and Kim, 2018). Furthermore, Elizabeth Abraham (2012) proposed that IT capabilities can empower executives to promote a participatory and well-being environment with stakeholders in decision-making, where, in turn, all stakeholders can be informed and, consequently, collaborate in those decisions to raise awareness about their interests.

Because of all the above, data security has become one of the main concerns of all of us connected to the Internet. This is due, among other things, to its rapid growth in recent decades, but above all, to its merging with our lives (Shreyas et al., 2022). Data security ensures that only the intended recipients have access to our information and prohibits any modification or manipulation of the data. To achieve this, several techniques and approaches have been developed over time to guarantee the minimum level of security: Cryptography, using specific -and increasingly efficient- algorithms, is an efficient tool for encrypting any type of information or data set.

WHAT IS CRYPTOLOGY?

The art of cryptography has its origins alongside the art of writing. Humans have always had two inherent needs: (a) to converse and share information, and (b) to communicate selectively (Dewangan, 2020). The rapid development of modern technologies, almost all of them internet-based, has transformed the lives not only of individuals but also of businesses, schools, and government departments that make frequent use of the internet. This exposure has also allowed more illegal users to attack data and destroy information through fake websites, spoofed emails, Trojan horses, and a host of viruses. Of course, the target of these internet-based attacks is computers. Furthermore, some cyber intruders, likely with ulterior motives, target military and government institutions to cause damage and pose potential threats to national security (Tayal et al., 2017). Today, society around the world generates a large amount of information every day, and consequently, information security on the Internet is the main challenge facing new technologies. In this context, Sharma, Yadav and Tiwari (2022) proposed that computer and data security can be achieved with the help of cryptography, mainly because data protection today must consider, at the very least, the confidentiality, authenticity, and integrity of the information. Converting information from a plain text format to another ciphertext format using an encryption key is not as simple as it seems. Furthermore, reverting the ciphertext to its original format becomes infinitely complicated.

Without a doubt, as our electronic networks become increasingly open and interconnected, it is critical to have strong and reliable cryptographic standards and guidelines, algorithms, and encryption methods that provide a foundation for the countless e-commerce transactions taking place around the world, conversations with mobile devices, information handled at customs and ports, military data, and countless other data exchanges (Meirong, 2018). In other words, as we live in the new media age, information has become the most necessary aspect of our lives: We all know that necessary things need to be preserved, and the same goes for information. Therefore, we need to protect and safeguard our information to prevent unauthorized access to it. Consequently, due to all the potential threats in cyberspace, we have undoubtedly had the need to protect our information; this need can be met by cryptography.

The term cryptography refers to "hidden secrets" and deals with encrypting information for secure correspondence. Cryptography originated from the Greek word "kryptos," meaning "hidden" or "secret," and "graphikos," meaning "to study or write": Basically, it is the study or writing of secret codes (Naser, 2021). So, cryptography or cryptology is the practice and study of techniques to ensure secure communication (Paar and Pelzl, 2010). In this way, it can be said, roughly speaking, that cryptography consists of recording a message in such a way that third parties or the public cannot read that private message (Paar, Pelzl and Güneysu, 2024). Thus, cryptography is a technique that involves the use of codes and is used to protect communication so that the person to whom a message or certain information is intended can read and process it correctly: Cryptography uses mathematical techniques to transform data and prevent unauthorized persons from reading or manipulating it, which allows for the exchange of secure messages. However, cryptography is a constantly evolving field that drives research and innovation: the Data Encryption Standard (DES), published by the National Institute of Standards and Technology (2024) in 1977 as the Federal Information Processing Standard (FIPS): https://www

.nist.gov/itl/fips-general-information), was innovative for its time, however, today it would be far below the necessary levels of protection. Therefore, cryptography is a method entirely focused on the protection of information and communications using codes, such that only those for whom the information is intended can read and process it. The taxonomy of cryptography can be established as follows: 1. Symmetric (based on the concept of using the same key to both encrypt and decrypt a message); 2. Asymmetric (based on the use of two different keys, one to encrypt and another to decrypt messages) and 3. Hybrid (uses both symmetric and asymmetric encryption) (Vollala, Ramasubramanian and Tiwari, 2021; Sharma et al., 2022). These types of cryptography include multiple methodologies for encoding information, which would be impossible to describe in this work. However, as an example, some of the most recent methodologies used for encrypting information can be consulted in Tarawneh (2024).

Figure 5. Concept of cryptology (https://www.innovaciondigital360.com)

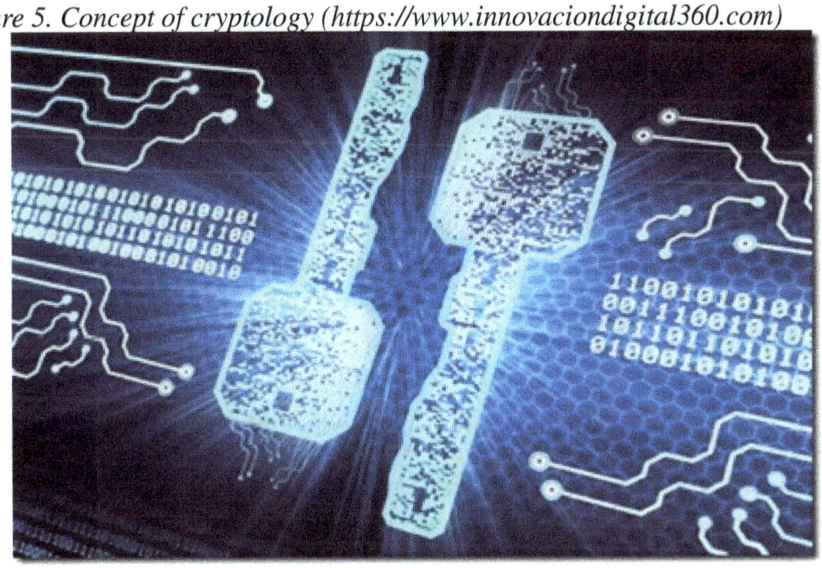

ISSUES, CONTROVERSIES, PROBLEMS

If we start from the fact that every organization, whether public or private, currently has three tools at its disposal to guarantee the security of its information (in the case of SEMAR, this security can cover terms related to National Security): encryption, authentication (the process of validating a user's identity before granting them access to networks, specific accounts, applications, computer systems, among other resources) and authorization (a process that determines the level of access a user has to the resources of a computer system, such as the data, applications and networks they will use). In this regard, the following topics have recently been discussed, or at least have become popular among those specializing in them, related to the updating and modernization of customs, at least in the Latin American context: 1) Technologies for the digital transformation of customs, 2) Traceability of goods, 3) Minimizing customs risks, 4) Technologies for coordinated border management, 5) Smart ports, just to mention a few. For their part, many specialists in the field advocate for the "Comprehensive use of technologies in the smart ports and customs of the future." Without a doubt, this dynamic of updating and modernization is a direct consequence of globalization, the new global economy, and, of course, the enormous advancement of new Information and Communication Technologies (ICTs). All of this has been largely responsible for defining, at least since the beginning of the 21st century, social relations, and especially labor and business relations, around the world.

Of course, technological innovation in customs and ports plays a strategic role not only limited to national security but also impacts economic development through foreign trade. In this context, digital technologies are crucial for industrial and interindustry collaboration and, together with innovation, will represent a new way of thinking and approaching the port and customs ecosystem, not only in a single country or region but even globally. Within this broad scenario of customs and port modernization, transcendental issues also arise, such as the following: a) Technological convergence, b) IoT (Internet of Things) platforms, c) Port interconnection, d) Cloud computing, e) Industry 4.0, f) Multimodality, g) Blockchain technology, just to mention a few. In turn, and about new technologies, some technological developments address the following topics: i) Automation, ii) Robotics, iii) Artificial Intelligence (AI), iv) Augmented Reality, v) Virtual Reality, vi) The Cloud, vii) Big Data, viii) Renewable Energies, ix) Drones, x) 3D Printing, xi) Biometrics, xii) Digitalization, xii) Electronic Identification Means, among many others. Within these topics, undoubtedly, the digitalization of customs and ports can have a significant impact on the global supply chain and improve the efficiency and sustainability of customs and port operations. The benefits for customs and ports include greater efficiency, greater security, greater sustainability, and better quality of service. In other words, both Mexican customs and ports are prepared to play an important role in the global context, especially if we consider, as a first step, substantially improving the service offered to customers transiting through Mexican customs and ports.

Everything outlined in this section is feasible with investment and time. However, the following question becomes very relevant: what do all these strategies, and the use of new technologies aimed at modernizing Mexican customs and ports, have in common? Without a doubt, the information (the use of data) handled in a customs office or port is crucial and even vital to its operation. Therefore, and undeniably, information security must be guaranteed in every customs office and every port. Misuse, falsification, theft of information, poor processing of information, and even incorrect interpretation of information handled in a customs office or port, to cite a few examples, can not only result in economic sanctions but can also escalate into conflicts between companies and even countries.

Figure 6. New technologies in ports and customs (https://portogente.com.br)

SOLUTIONS AND RECOMMENDATIONS

Cyberspace is complex and changing rapidly. Furthermore, thanks to increasing interconnection, it brings us all closer together and keeps us better connected. Of course, this represents new opportunities and, above all, new challenges for Mexico's customs and ports. Therefore, in this section, we must begin with the following questions: What is the main objective of a customs office? And, likewise, what is the main objective of a port? Undoubtedly, the answer to each of these questions leads us to multiple topics, simply because each of these two concepts (Customs and Port) converges and generates a fairly broad range of topics to explore. Beyond National Security, which is undoubtedly associated with these two concepts, we can affirm, at least in this work, that, in essence, both a Customs office and a Port are based on the premise of offering a service to whom? Ultimately, to a large and diverse number of clients. In turn, what is the main objective of providing a service of this nature? The answers are narrow, and ultimately, the main objective of offering a service, in addition to generating profits, is customer satisfaction in an optimal timeframe.

In this context, scientific and technological development, as well as technology transfer, have gradually contributed to multiple advances, which have supported new marketing strategies, some of them entirely oriented towards customer satisfaction (Ramli, 2017; Stonehouse and Snowdon, 2007; Shukla, Dos Santos, Fong and Lu, 2017; Taufique et al., 2014). From this perspective, and without a doubt, one of the main objectives involved in the process of offering a service is, first, to awaken or attract the attention of the potential customer and, subsequently, to determine their level of satisfaction. Therefore, new marketing strategies must take into consideration the entire customer journey, due, among other things, to the fact that throughout this process it is necessary to identify how many and what the main needs are demanded by these customers so that the service is to their liking and in a short period. In other words, it is of utmost importance for the entity to offer a service to identify its customers' main needs; from how to reach them, through to the profitability of the service, and even to knowing whether it can be paid for by the customer or if it is of total interest to them. At this point, it is considered that establishing better strategies for a service, even for each market segment established by specific customers, requires faster, more direct, and efficient interaction. This can be carried out with the support of new technologies (such as virtual reality, augmented reality, or mixed reality): fast because it only depends on the speed of data transmission; direct because it requires interaction with the customer; and efficient because very specific characteristics and information about the service provided can be found, even in real time (Orlosky, Kiyokawa and Takemura, 2017).

In these scenarios, Barnes (1993) already predicted that IT is a strategic resource that can facilitate significant changes in competitive behavior, marketing, and customer service. This is primarily because IT allows a company to achieve distinct competitive advantages. IT is a resource that links the "marketing orientation" and "technological exploitation" of a company that undoubtedly wants to leverage and manage its services correctly and efficiently. Therefore, one of the key factors that will contribute to the future success of service marketing, for both large and small companies, will be the proper exploitation of IT, which will facilitate and optimize the use and management of information. In other words, with these technologies, any company or institution will be redesigning the way it conducts business and markets its services. This is undoubtedly because many marketing-related activities require an organization to constantly monitor business information and the corresponding environments where all its activities are carried out. Consequently, thanks to the constant updating of this information, institutions can make any type of adjustment to their service offerings and, thus, fully satisfy their customers' needs in an optimal timeframe, thereby achieving greater profits. Since IT also deals with information, IT itself can and should facilitate both marketing management and customer service. Therefore, IT can act as a powerful catalyst for improving and promoting customer service satisfaction (Domegan, 1996). For all the reasons discussed in this section, customer satisfaction is considered the main channel that, in turn, motivates ensuring the security of customer information.

Figure 7. Ensuring information is the main objective of ports and customs (https://aduananews.com)

FUTURE DIRECTIONS OF RESEARCH

The SAP Seaport Innovation Summit 2024 (https://www.envisionesl.com/es) and the VI Hemispheric Conference on Logistics, Innovation and Competitiveness (https://portalcip.org/?lang=es, held in Veracruz, Mexico, from January 17-19, 2024) were two international events that showcased the most innovative topics for the modernization of ports and customs around the world, although it should be noted that ports were the priority in both scenarios. However, among a sea of options, it was possible to suggest that some of the topics that caught the attention of experts were the following:

- Single windows and their impact on port logistics,
- Innovation in the offshore industry,
- Technology and security in customs and ports,
- Competitive customs and port management,
- Sustainability and energy efficiency in customs and ports,
- Interconnected ports and smart ports.
- Differences between Port Management Information Systems (PMIS) and Maritime and Port Management Systems,
- Optimizing Ro-Ro Terminal Operations with iPortman's Ro-Ro Solution,
- Future Trends and the Role of Information and Communications Technology (ICT) in Customs, Port, and Logistics Operations,
- Information Hijacking: How Maintenance Is Being Deprived of Asset Health Data,
- Key Steps Toward IoT,
- How to Survive Between Incompatibilities: ROI in AMC Software,
- Solving Aging Assets and a Transitioning Workforce for E&U (Energy and Utilities) Organizations,
- The Importance of HSE for Safer, Compliant, and Sustainable Operations,
- The Quest for Work-Life Balance,
- Blockchain Technology in Port Logistics,
- Implementing Pilot Operations,
- Creating Digital Twins and Smart Ports,
- What Can Companies Do to Improve Processing Times? of Invoices?
- iPortman as an integrated solution for container terminal management (real-time 3D view, robust API, EDI manager),
- Managing warehouses, CFS, and empty yard operations,
- Making berth planning less stressful with smart, automated berth planning solutions,
- RFID: A new paradigm for hybrid applications,
- Expanding the business to new mobile technologies,
- Capturing all port operations and transactions without loss of revenue,
- Low-touch, high-impact technology solution for ports and terminals,
- Simplifying licensing, AMC payment using technologies, and creating an Open Integration Policy,
- Calculating the maximum volume to archive,
- Implementing EAM/CMMS solutions,
- Monitoring port performance,
- Creating technology-driven solutions for rail operations,
- Automation to mitigate port congestion,
- Factual EAM to preserve operations, Efficient ports and terminals,

- IoT for rapid evolution and faster ROI,
- iPortman: Preparing for the ports of the future, and
- Smart ports as a path to the future.

As we can see, all these topics converge toward the search for and creation of spaces for learning, exchanging ideas, and networking around the use of technologies. Undoubtedly, the topic of new technologies is increasingly interesting, such as Artificial Intelligence (AI), especially those that prove to be more innovative and, consequently, interesting to a diverse audience. A demonstration of the interest in these new technologies, primarily related to customs, was seen at the Latin American Confederation of Customs Agents (CLAA), held at the facilities of the Monterrey Institute of Technology and Higher Education (Tec de Monterrey), Mexico City campus, where the first edition of IAduana 2024: Innovation and Security in Foreign Trade was held. This symposium explored both the use and application of AI and cybersecurity. In this scenario, AI can interact with cryptography to ensure a secure cyber environment: Detect and prevent threats; Automate repetitive tasks; Analyze behavior and identify anomalies; Adaptability and continuous learning; Integration with security systems; Rapid and automatic incident response; Predicting future threats; and Resource optimization.

Figure 8. Concept of AI (https://t21.com.mx)

As technological advances have increased, cyber threats have also grown and evolved. Consequently, cryptology faces new challenges and opportunities to secure information: For example, in this area of opportunity, everything from quantum computing to machine learning can be leveraged. In other words, with the imminent advances in the internet and mobile technology, cryptology has become more important than ever. What is clear is that technological advances must offer new tools to strengthen security and guarantee new environments that, in turn, guarantee the security of information against future cyberattacks. The rapid advances in technology have inevitably led to the creation of more complex and sophisticated encryption methods, which have become indispensable tools for protecting information and its confidentiality (such as online financial transactions, online shopping, the management of personal data, social media, and a variety of confidential communications, even those of an international nature). Because of this behavior, data management is now used in everything, and as our dependence on new technologies, communications, and digital storage increases, the role of data protection tools, such as cryptography, will also increase in protecting our data, and their use will become increasingly critical. Thus, the future of cryptology is very promising as researchers work to create cyberattack-resistant encryption and implement new methods to protect data. To achieve this, cryptology must guarantee, at a minimum, the following: i) Detect and prevent threats; ii) Analyze data to verify network intelligence; iii) Automate response and prevention; iv) Ensure continuous improvement and adaptability; and v) Customize digital security based on required needs.

Ultimately, cryptology will continue to play a fundamental role in protecting information in the digital age, whether securing military communications, protecting financial transactions, or safeguarding the privacy of online user information. Therefore, cryptology will remain an indispensable pillar of cybersecurity in an increasingly interconnected world. Thus, future work in cryptology can be considered in the following areas: federated learning for knowledge sharing; neural networks for threat identification; integration of artificial intelligence into IoT devices; merging AI and blockchain to improve security; and quantum cybersecurity, among many others.

Figure 9. Ports and customs of the future (https://www.estrategiaaduanera.mx)

CONCLUSIONS

From the manifestations of ancient hieroglyphics to modern complex computer algorithms, the need to protect our communications and data has driven the development and evolution of cryptography. In the modern world, where information is power, cryptography stands as an indispensable guardian of our privacy and security, especially for all our data handled or transferred online. All the tools and technologies discussed in this paper handle vast amounts of information; however, this information is not unlimited. From this perspective, it is essential to have a repository with ample storage capacity and, of course, one that this repository guarantees its security. Likewise, this repository must be provided with sufficient and necessary computing tools to protect it from any threat, whether internal or external. Of course, these technological tools will generally depend on the budget available to contract or develop the best and most innovative technologies that guarantee data security and protection.

Although the cost of creating and developing some new technologies has decreased exponentially over time, which would be expected to lead to a drop in implementation costs, this trend has not yet been fully verified and may even seem contradictory. For example, one such example is the new cutting-edge technology known as immersive 3D visualization, which is becoming an innovative tool in new product development (NPD) across multiple sectors. This pioneering technology can be integrated into NPD processes or facilitate the understanding of complex information, as well as be used in simulation, planning, and training. However, the desired results will depend on the components implemented; that is, the better the components implemented, the better the results. Of course, this trend can be applied to data protection and security. Thus, proper data management and security will necessarily require the best technological tools to safeguard all information from start to finish.

In the contemporary world, both knowledge and technology have gradually become a strategic asset and the main source of competitive advantage. This is surely because every company/institution develops different products and services, which are reinforced by various innovative technologies whose main objective is to generate profits in the markets or generate value for their services. Undoubtedly, the implementation of a successful and innovative technology requires time and investment; however, it must be the foundation of any update or path toward modernity. On this path toward modernity, Mexican customs and ports must take a first step, which, from the perspective of this work, must be the encryption of all information handled and transferred within or outside their facilities. Because any technological innovation would be meaningless without a guarantee of its functionality or even the discretionary power of its operation or operation. In other words, data encryption at Mexican customs and ports must be in place, from the sending of a simple email to the transfer of documents considered to be of National Security importance.

REFERENCES

Agar, J. (2019). What is technology? Technology: critical history of a concept, by Eric Schatzberg, Chicago and London, University of Chicago Press, 2018, 352 pp. ISBN: 978-0-226-58383-9. *Annals of Science*, *77*(3), 377–382. DOI: 10.1080/00033790.2019.1672788

Akhtar, M. S., & Feng, T. (2022). Malware Analysis and Detection Using Machine Learning Algorithms. *Symmetry*, *14*(11), 2304. DOI: 10.3390/sym14112304

Ali, O., Osmanaj, V., Kwiatek, P., Alryalat, M., Chimhundu, R., & Dwivedi, Y. K. (2023). The impact of technological innovation on marketing: individuals, organizations and environment: a systematic review. *Ekonomska Istrazivanja*, *36*(3), 2210661.. DOI: 10.1080/1331677X.2023.2210661

Alkhudhayr, F., Alfarraj, S., Aljameeli, B., & Elkhdiri, S. (2019). Information Security: A Review of Information Security Issues and Techniques. *2nd International Conference on Computer Applications & Information Security (ICCAIS)*, Riyadh, Saudi Arabia, 2019, pp. 1-6, DOI: 10.1109/CAIS.2019.8769504

American Library Association. (1983). *The ALA Glossary of Library and Information Science*. ALA.

Andersson, G. (2018). Internet interventions: Past, present and future. *Internet Interventions : the Application of Information Technology in Mental and Behavioural Health*, *12*, 181–188. DOI: 10.1016/j.invent.2018.03.008 PMID: 30135782

Anwar, M. A., Rongting, Z., Dong, W., Asmi, F., & Meissner, R. (2018). Mapping the knowledge of national security in the 21st century a bibliometric study. *Cogent Social Sciences*, *4*(1), 1542944. DOI: 10.1080/23311886.2018.1542944

Bandala López, M. A. (2018). Reconceptualización de la Seguridad Nacional: Una aproximación para México. Instotuto de Investigaciones Estratégicas de la Armada de México. https://cesnav.uninav.edu.mx/cesnav/ININVESTAM/docs/docs_analisis/da_24-18.pdf

Barnes, J. G. (1993). New technologies, new markets, and changing marketing practice. *Irish Marketing Review*, *6*, 45–52.

Bishop, M. (2003). What Is Computer Security? *IEEE Security and Privacy*, *1*(01), 67–69. DOI: 10.1109/MSECP.2003.1176998

Chemnad, K., Alshakhsi, S., Almourad, M. B., Altuwairiqi, M., Phalp, K., & Ali, R. (2022). Smartphone Usage before and during COVID-19: A Comparative Study Based on Objective Recording of Usage Data. Informatics, 9. *Informatics (MDPI), 98*(4), 98. DOI: 10.3390/informatics9040098

Chew, X., Alharbi, R., Khaw, K. W., & Alnoor, A. (2023). How information technology influences organizational communication: the mediating role of organizational structure. *PSU Research Review*, DOI: 10.1108/PRR-08-2021-0041

Chinese Academy of Cyberspace Studies. (2023). World Information Technology Development. In *World Internet Development Report 2021*. Springer., DOI: 10.1007/978-981-19-9323-7_3

Chitechi, K. V., & Otanga, D. A. (2020). Current Trends in Information Technology: Which Way for Modern It Experts. *International Journal of Computer Trends and Technology*, *68*(7), 31–36. DOI: 10.14445/22312803/IJCTT-V68I7P105

Clarke, M., Henschke, A., Legrand, T., & Sussex, M. (2022). National Security: Theories, Actors, Issues. In Clarke, M., Henschke, A., Sussex, M., & Legrand, T. (Eds.), *The Palgrave Handbook of National Security*. Palgrave Macmillan., DOI: 10.1007/978-3-030-53494-3_1

Croxton, D. (1999). The Peace of Westphalia of 1648 and the Origins of Sovereignty. *The International History Review*, *21*(3), 569–591. https://www.jstor.org/stable/40109077. DOI: 10.1080/07075332.1999.9640869

Cybersecurity & Infrastructure Security Agency. (2021). *Cyber Essentials Starter Kit*. Recuperado de https://www.cisa.gov/sites/default/files/publications/Cyber%2520Essentials%2520Starter%2520Kit_03.12.2021_508_0.pdf

Cybersecurity & Infrastructure Security Agency. (2024). https://www.cisa.gov/

Danaher, J., & Sætra, H. S. (2022). Technology and moral change: The transformation of truth and trust. *Ethics and Information Technology, 24. Ethics and Information Technology*, *35*(3), 35. DOI: 10.1007/s10676-022-09661-y

Dang, C. N., Le-Hoai, L., & Kim, S. (2018). Impact of knowledge-enabling factors on organizational effectiveness in construction companies. *Journal of Knowledge Management*, *22*(4), 759–780. DOI: 10.1108/JKM-08-2016-0350

de la Barquera, S., & Arroyo, H. (Eds.). (2024). *Diccionario de seguridad y de defensa nacional: 100 claves y conceptos para su análisis y estudio*. Universidad Nacional Autónoma de México, Instituto de Investigaciones Jurídicas.

Dewangan, P. (2020). A Review Paper on Network Security and Cryptography. *International Journal of Scientific Research*, *9*(1), 524–527. https://www.ijsr.net/getabstract.php?paperid=ART20204060

Domegan, C. T. (1996). The adoption of information technology in customer service. *European Journal of Marketing*, *30*(6), 52–69. DOI: 10.1108/03090569610121674

Doron, S. (2022). *The History of Computing: A Very Short Introduction, Very Short Introductions*. Oxford Academic Books., DOI: 10.1093/actrade/9780198831754.001.0001

Elizabeth Abraham, S. (2012). Information technology, an enabler in corporate governance. *Corporate Governance (Bradford)*, *12*(3), 281–291. DOI: 10.1108/14720701211234555

Emojorho, D., & Adomi, A. (2006). An assessment of the use of information technology facilities for academic pursuit. *The Electronic Library*, *24*(5), 706–713. DOI: 10.1108/02640470610707295

García-Avilés, J. A. (2020). Diffusion of Innovation. In Bulck, J. (Ed.), *The International Encyclopedia of Media Psychology*. John Wiley & Sons, Inc., DOI: 10.1002/9781119011071.iemp0137

Haleem, A., Javaid, M., Qadri, M. A., & Suman, R. (2022). Understanding the role of digital technologies in education: A review. *Sustainable Operations and Computers*, *3*, 275–285. DOI: 10.1016/j.susoc.2022.05.004

Harris, B., Regan, T., Schueler, J., & Fields, S. A. (2020). Problematic Mobile Phone and Smartphone Use Scales: A Systematic Review. *Frontiers in Psychology*, *11*, 672. DOI: 10.3389/fpsyg.2020.00672 PMID: 32431636

He, W., Zhang, Z. J., & Li, W. (2021). Information technology solutions, challenges, and suggestions for tackling the COVID-19 pandemic. *International Journal of Information Management*, *57*, 102287. DOI: 10.1016/j.ijinfomgt.2020.102287 PMID: 33318721

Hitzler, P. (2021). A review of the semantic web field. *Communications of the ACM*, *64*(2), 76–83. https://cacm.acm.org/magazines/2021/2/250085-a-review-of-the-semantic-web-field/abstract. DOI: 10.1145/3397512

Holmes, K. R. (2015). What Is National Security? The Heritage Foundation. Index of U.S. Military Strength, 17-26. https://www.heritage.org/sites/default/files/2019-10/2015_IndexOfUSMilitaryStrength_What%20Is%20National%20Security.pdf

Janžekovič, I. (2022). The Balance of Power from the Thirty Years' War and the Peace of Westphalia (1648) to the War of the Spanish Succession and the Peace of Utrecht (1713). *History of European Ideas, 49*(3), 561–579. DOI: 10.1080/01916599.2022.2077401

Kalgotra, P., Gupta, A., & Sharda, R. (2021). Pandemic information support lifecycle: Evidence from the evolution of mobile apps during COVID-19. *Journal of Business Research, 134*, 540–559. DOI: 10.1016/j.jbusres.2021.06.002 PMID: 34565948

Katsumata, S., Ichikohji, T., Nakano, S., Yamaguchi, S., & Ikuine, F. (2022). Changes in the use of mobile devices during the crisis: Immediate response to the COVID-19 pandemic. *Computers in Human Behavior Reports, 5*, 100168. DOI: 10.1016/j.chbr.2022.100168 PMID: 35079660

Khayyat, M. H., Zamzami, N., Zhang, L., Nappi, M., & Umer, M. (2024). Fuzzy-CNN: Improving personal human identification based on IRIS recognition using LBP features. *Journal of Information Security and Applications, 83*, 103761. Advance online publication. DOI: 10.1016/j.jisa.2024.103761

Kim, K. J. (2016). Interacting socially with the Internet of Things (IoT): Effects of source attribution and specialization in human-IoT interaction. *Journal of Computer-Mediated Communication, 21*(6), 420–435. DOI: 10.1111/jcc4.12177

Kim, K. J., & Wang, S. (2021). Understanding the acceptance of the Internet of Things: An integrative theoretical approach. *Aslib Journal of Information Management, 73*(5), 754–771. DOI: 10.1108/AJIM-03-2021-0073

Kizza, J. M. (2023). History of Computing. In *Ethical and Social Issues in the Information Age. Texts in Computer Science*. Springer., DOI: 10.1007/978-3-031-24863-4_1

Larus, J. R. (2024). Evolution of Computing. In Werthner, H. (Eds.), *Introduction to Digital Humanism*. Springer., DOI: 10.1007/978-3-031-45304-5_3

Lee, S. M., & Trimi, S. (2021). Convergence Innovation in the Digital Age and in the COVID-19 Pandemic Crisis. *Journal of Business Research, 123*, 14–22. DOI: 10.1016/j.jbusres.2020.09.041 PMID: 33012897

Madnick, B., Huang, K., & Madnick, S. (2023). The evolution of global cybersecurity norms in the digital age: A longitudinal study of the cybersecurity norm development process. *Information Security Journal: A Global Perspective, 33(3)*, 204-225. DOI: 10.1080/19393555.2023.2201482

Mahr, D., & Huh, J. (2022). Technologies in service communication: Looking forward. *Journal of Service Management, 33*(4/5), 648–656. DOI: 10.1108/JOSM-03-2022-0075

Makinda, S. M. (1998). Sovereignty and Global Security. *Security Dialogue, 29*(3), 281–292. DOI: 10.1177/0967010698029003003

Meerts, C. (2019). Security: Concepts and Definitions. In Shapiro, L., & Maras, M. H. (Eds.), *Encyclopedia of Security and Emergency Management*. Springer., DOI: 10.1007/978-3-319-69891-5_94-2

Meirong, G. (2018). China's cybersecurity legislation, it's relevance to critical infrastructures and the challenges it faces. *International Journal of Critical Infrastructure Protection, 22*, 139–149. DOI: 10.1016/j.ijcip.2018.06.006

Mohsenzadeh, F., & Isfandyari-Moghaddam, A. (2009). Application of information technologies in academic libraries. *The Electronic Library, 27*(6), 986–998. DOI: 10.1108/02640470911004075

Muthukumar, S. L., & Hedberg, J. G. (2005). A knowledge management technology architecture for educational research organizations: scaffolding research projects and workflow processing. *British Journal of Educational Technology, Blackwell Publishing, Oxford, 36 (3)*, 379-395.

Naser, S. M. (2021). Cryptography: From the ancient history to now, it's applications and a new complete numerical model. *International Journal of Mathematics and Statistics Studies, 9*(3), 11–30.

National Institute of Standards and Technology. (2024). https://www.nist.gov/

Nyamboga, C. M., & Kemparaju, T. D. (2002). Information technology in university libraries in Karnataka. *Information Development, 18*(4), 257–265. DOI: 10.1177/026666602321036650

Orlosky, J., Kiyokawa, K., & Takemura, H. (2017). Virtual and augmented reality on the 5g highway. *Journal of Information Processing, 25*(0), 133–141. DOI: 10.2197/ipsjjip.25.133

Ortiz Arellano, E. (2021). Seguridad Nacional del Estado mexicano: Ejes Problemáticos y Factores. *Encrucijada, 38*(38), 94–126. DOI: 10.22201/fcpys.20071949e.2021.38.78088

Paar, Ch., & Pelzl, J. (2010). *Understanding Cryptography. A Textbook for Students and Practitioners*. Springer-Verlag. DOI: 10.1007/978-3-642-04101-3

Paar, Ch., Pelzl, J., & Güneysu, T. (2024). *Understanding Cryptography. From Established Symmetric and Asymmetric Ciphers to Post-Quantum Algorithms*. Springer-Verlag. DOI: 10.1007/978-3-662-69007-9

Pandey, G. P., & Chakraborty, J. (2002). Role of information technology in higher education in the 21st century. *University News*, *40*(8), 11.

Passavanti, R., Pantano, E., Priporas, C. V., & Verteramo, S. (2020). The use of new technologies for corporate marketing communication in luxury retailing: Preliminary findings. *Qualitative Market Research*, *23*(3), 503–521. DOI: 10.1108/QMR-11-2017-0144

Phillips, A. (2023). The Peace of Westphalia. In Bukovansky, M. (Eds.), *The Oxford Handbook of History and International Relations*. Oxford Handbooks Academic., DOI: 10.1093/oxfordhb/9780198873457.013.36

Pirbhulal, S., Chockalingam, S., Shukla, A., & Abie, H. (2024). IoT cybersecurity in 5G and beyond: A systematic literature review. *International Journal of Information Security*, *23*(4), 2827–2879. Advance online publication. DOI: 10.1007/s10207-024-00865-5

Podrug, N., Filipovic, D., & Kovac, M. (2017). Knowledge sharing and firm innovation capability in Croatian ICT companies. *International Journal of Manpower*, *38*(4), 632–644. DOI: 10.1108/IJM-04-2016-0077

Ramli, N. S. (2017). A review of marketing strategies from the European chocolate industry. *Journal of Global Entrepreneurship Research*, *7*(10), 1–17. DOI: 10.1186/s40497-017-0068-0

Rathi, D., Given, L. M., & Forcier, E. (2014). Interorganisational partnerships and knowledge sharing: The perspective of non-profit organisations (NPOs). *Journal of Knowledge Management*, *18*(5), 867–885. DOI: 10.1108/JKM-06-2014-0256

Raudeliuniene, J., Albats, E., & Kordab, M. (2021). Impact of information technologies and social networks on knowledge management processes in Middle Eastern audit and consulting companies. *Journal of Knowledge Management*, *25*(4), 871–898. DOI: 10.1108/JKM-03-2020-0168

Shammar, E. A., & Zahary, A. T. (2020). The Internet of Things (IoT): A survey of techniques, operating systems, and trends. *Library Hi Tech*, *38*(1), 5–66. DOI: 10.1108/LHT-12-2018-0200

Sharma, D. K. (2022). A review on various cryptographic techniques & algorithms. *Materials Today: Proceedings*, *51*(1), 104–109. DOI: 10.1016/j.matpr.2021.04.583

Sharma, P., Yadav, K., & Tiwari, A. K. (2022). A Review Paper on Network Security and Cryptography. *World Journal of Research and Review*, *14*(5), 20–24. https://www.wjrr.org/download_data/WJRR1405012.pdf

Shreyas, M. (2022). A Review Paper on Cryptography. *International Journal of Advanced Research in Science. Tongxin Jishu*, *2*(2), 389–395. https://www.ijarsct.co.in/A2883.pdf

Shukla, M., Dos Santos, R., Fong, A., & Lu, C.-T. (2017). DERIV: Distributed brand perception tracking framework. *Journal of Big Data*, *4*(17), 1–23. DOI: 10.1186/s40537-017-0078-3

Stocchi, L., Pourazad, N., Michaelidou, N., Tanusondjaja, A., & Harrigan, P. (2022). Marketing research on Mobile apps: Past, present and future. *Journal of the Academy of Marketing Science*, *50*(2), 195–225. DOI: 10.1007/s11747-021-00815-w PMID: 34776554

Stonehouse, G., & Snowdon, B. (2007). Competitive advantage revisited: Michael Porter on strategy and competitiveness. *Journal of Management Inquiry*, *16*(3), 256–273. DOI: 10.1177/1056492607306333

Sussex, M., Clarke, M., & Medcalf, R. (2017). National security: Between theory and practice. *Australian Journal of International Affairs*, *71*(5), 474–478. DOI: 10.1080/10357718.2017.1347139

Tanaka, S. (2022). The Old and New of Digital History. *History and Theory*, *61*(4), 3–18. DOI: 10.1111/hith.12284

Tarawneh, M. (2024). *Perspective Chapter: Cryptography-Recent Advances and Research Perspectives*. IntechOpen., DOI: 10.5772/intechopen.111847

Taufique, K. M. R., Siwar, C., Talib, B., Sarah, F. H., & Chamhuri, N. (2014). Synthesis of Constructs for Modeling Consumers' Understanding and Perception of Eco-Labels. *Sustainability (Basel)*, *6*(4), 2176–2200. DOI: 10.3390/su6042176

Tayal, S. (2017). A Review paper on Network Security and Cryptography. *Advances in Computational Sciences and Technology, 10(5)*, 763-770. https://www.ripublication.com/acst17/acstv10n5_10.pdf

Toussaert, S. (2021). Upping uptake of COVID contact tracing apps. *Nature Human Behaviour*, *5*(2), 183–184. DOI: 10.1038/s41562-021-01048-1 PMID: 33479504

US Department of State. (2024). *United States International Cyberspace & Digital Policy Strategy. Towards an Innovative, Secure, and Rights-Respecting Digital Future*. Recuperado de https://www.state.gov/united-states-international-cyberspace-and-digital-policy-strategy/

Valamede, L. S., de Oliveira, G. G., Munhoz, I. P., & Akkari, A. C. S. (2022). Digital Technologies Adoption to Face COVID-19 Pandemic: An Exploratory Approach. In: Iano, Y., Saotome, O., Kemper Vásquez, G.L., Cotrim Pezzuto, C., Arthur, R., Gomes de Oliveira, G. (Eds) Proceedings of the 7th Brazilian Technology Symposium (BTSym'21). BTSym 2021. Smart Innovation, Systems and Technologies, vol 295. Springer, Cham. DOI: 10.1007/978-3-031-08545-1_17

Vicsek, L. (2021). Artificial intelligence and the future of work–lessons from the sociology of expectations. *The International Journal of Sociology and Social Policy*, *41*(7/8), 842–861. DOI: 10.1108/IJSSP-05-2020-0174

Vollala, S., Ramasubramanian, N., & Tiwari, U. (2021). Cryptographic Techniques. In *Energy-Efficient Modular Exponential Techniques for Public-Key Cryptography*. Springer., DOI: 10.1007/978-3-030-74524-0_1

Wajid, R., & Alam, K. (2024). Role of Modern Technology in COVID-19 Care Management. In Alam, K., Daniel, S., Alzahrani, A., & Hassan Almalki, W. (Eds.), *Nursing Practice during COVID-19: Preparation, Education and Support*. Springer., DOI: 10.1007/978-3-031-52110-2_5

Wang, X. V., & Wang, L. (2021). A literature survey of the robotic technologies during the COVID-19 pandemic. *Journal of Manufacturing Systems*, *60*, 823–836. DOI: 10.1016/j.jmsy.2021.02.005 PMID: 33612914

Weippl, E., & Schrittwieser, S. (2024). Introduction to Security and Privacy. In Werthner, H. (Eds.), *Introduction to Digital Humanism*. Springer., DOI: 10.1007/978-3-031-45304-5_26

Wickberg, A., & Gärdebo, J. (2023). Computation, data and AI in Anthropocene history. *History and Technology*, *39*(3-4), 328–346. DOI: 10.1080/07341512.2024.2330724

Williams, P. D. (2008). *Security Studies: An Introduction*. Routledge. DOI: 10.4324/9780203926604

Chapter 10
Human Capital and Economic Growth India's Experience

Raghavender G. Raju
https://orcid.org/0000-0002-2093-1019
Sri Sathya Sai Institute of Higher Learning, India

B. Sai Chintan
SSSIHL, India

ABSTRACT

The building of human capital is critical for economic progress. It has a favorable externality in terms of economic growth. The goal of this research is to demonstrate the importance of human capital in India's economic progress. We utilized the ordinary least square approach to regress Gross Domestic Product upon Public Education & Gross Domestic Capital Formation to emphasize the relevance of human capital on economic growth. As per the regression study, human capital & economic growth has a substantial positive association. Finally, simply investing in education is insufficient. To determine how good, the estimated model is, we ran an in-sample forecast and stability test. The testing has shown positive results. Finally, education should instill human values in students and mould them into men of character and truth. To further understand this, we performed a case study of Sri Satya Sai Institute of Higher Learning to acquire a better knowledge of how integral education works.

DOI: 10.4018/979-8-3373-3456-1.ch010

INTRODUCTION

"The term human capital refers to the economic value of a worker's experience and skills." (Investopedia) The intangible assets like skills, intelligence, education, training are the components of human capital. These attributes such as loyalty and punctuality cannot be quantified or measurable, therefore not present on any reports or statements. The components of human capital contribute to increased productivity and thereby profitability. There is a clear link between human capital and profitability. The more investment in human capital translates to better productivity.

"The knowledge, skills, competencies and other attributes embodied in individuals or groups of individuals acquired during their life and used to produce goods, services or ideas in market circumstances".

-OCED

Human capital can be viewed in individual capacity as well as in a wider capacity as a body, an organization or as society as a whole. Personal human capital speaks to an individual's talents and capabilities. The overall human capital of an economic system is referred to as human capital of an economic. Human capital is among a country's most valuable assets and one of the most critical factors of its economic performance. However, national accounts that focus solely on physical capital frequently fail to account for the influence of human capital. Human capital expenditures are often classified as consumption. Because human capital is subjective, we use education and health spending as proxies for measuring it. Direct investments in education and health care pay off. Education is often acknowledged as a factor in societal and political, political, and cultural evolution. It also aids in economic development, according to many research. Citizens are a country's most precious asset and resource.

As a result, the government must nurture and care for its residents through basic education, which aids in enhancing people's quality of life and, in turn, benefits the nation. No country can be successful in the long run if it does not invest in higher education., which are characterized by large positive externalities. If a person has completed higher education, he is more likely to obtain well-paid jobs than someone who has only completed schooling. When a result, as he earns more money, the standard of living rises, as does his spending and saving habit, which helps the economy thrive. After the investment is made, students and researchers become motivated.

Once they are inspired, they will imagine, which will lead to educational advances and, in turn, economic prosperity. This aim may be realized through the holistic development of people, which can be accomplished through strong educational foundations. Why are certain countries extremely wealthy while others are impoverished? What is the rationale for this? These concerns were raised by a large number of people; it became an intriguing study issue. Human capital accumulation will be one of the answers to this topic. Following WWII, a lot of economists began to consider growth models. In this context, an exogenous growth model was proposed.

Following independence, the government began focusing upon education through five-year plans. By terms of available, quality of instruction and research, enrolment ratios, and other factors, India's higher education sector has progressed dramatically since independence. The number of universities and colleges has expanded in recent years. In the future, we will need to grow significantly.

Factors that Determine Human Capital

- Skills and qualifications
- Education levels
- Work experience
- Social skills - communication
- Intelligence
- Emotional intelligence
- Judgement
- Personality – hard working, harmonious in an office
- Habits and personality traits
- Creativity. Ability to innovate new working practices/products.
- Fame and brank image of an individual. E.g., celebrities paid to endorse a product.
- Geography – Social peer pressure of local environment can affect expectations and attitudes

How to Increase Human Capital

- **Specialization and division of labor.** Division of labor leads to specialization of work. When a worker is assigned a specific job, he acquires deep understanding of the assigned job. Having performed the job repetitively, the worker gains speed and efficiency while eliminating unnecessary elements. This leads to increased specialization of skills. On the flip side, the repetitive nature of the job can cause the onset of fatigue and loss of interest.
- **Education**. Human capital banks on primary levels of education. A literate society is better equipped to take up better and complex jobs.
- **Vocational training.** All skilled professions like plumbing nursing, electrician, require profession specific skills. Vocational training provides relevant skills to the workforce.
- **A climate of creativity**. Human capital enhances productivity by enhancing production. Only a creative brain can think of better and efficient ways of

doing a particular job. Education should stimulate the creativity of the child rather than focusing on remembering data

- **Infrastructure.** A society can be better equipped only when there is access to the required infrastructure. For the growth of human capital, proper transportation, telecommunication, mobile telephone accessibility, and web access are critical.
- **Competitiveness**. Competitiveness helps the economy to maintain its relevance with the dynamic changes in the world. Competition propels innovation. Innovation propels growth and profitability. A state where there is no competition will not find any need to find ways to become better.

Importance of Human Capital

- **Structural unemployment**. Adapting to the ever-changing times is necessary to maintain one's employability. Those who do not possess the skills required for today may find themselves unemployed. The rapid deindustrialization has left many unskilled workers struggling.
- **Quality of employment. One** may be skilled, but the level of skill would make the difference. IN today's economy there is a clear gap between workers with differing skills. Better skills translate to better opportunities and better economic benefits.
- **Economic growth and productivity**. The human capital must be adaptive and well educated. Only a well-educated, adaptive human capital can contribute to growth in long-term.
- **Human capital flight**. Due to the rapid globalization, the flow of human capital to developed nations has increased. Due to better opportunities in those countries, the human capital of the nation could be witnessing a gradual drain. This would directly take a toll on the nation's economy.
- **Limited raw materials**. Some nations possess limited natural resources, which are essential for economic growth. These nations heavily depend on their workforce to act as substitute of these natural resources.
- **Sustainability** "what we leave to future generations; whether we leave enough resources, of all kinds, to provide them with the opportunities at least as large as the ones we have had ourselves (UN, 2012)"

Objective of the Study

The objectives of the study are given below.

- To highlight the role of human capital contribution to Economic Growth.

- To analyses the trends of public expenditure on education in India.
- To estimate the relationship between Human Capital (investment in Education) and economic growth through econometric methodology.
- Case Study on Sri Sathya Sai Institute of Higher Learning(SSSIHL)

EVOLUTION OF INDIA'S EDUCATION POLICY

Currant Scenario

Universities in India After Independence

In India, there has undoubtedly been significant development in the allocation of higher education. India has just 27 universities when it gained independence. However, it has already expanded to roughly 982 universities. The expansion of institutions has aided students' access to higher education. With the increase in numbers, the UGC has attempted to elevate the field's quality. According to reports, India will have the largest group of youth in the world by 2030. As a result, greater emphasis should be placed on educational quality and access.

Table 1. Type-wise Number of Universities as on 31.03.2021 Annual Report 2020-21*

S. No.	Type of University/Institution	Number of Universities/ Institutions (as on 31.03.2021)
1	Central Universities	54
2	State Universities	425
3	State Private Universities	375
4	Institutions established through State Legislation	3
5	Institutions Deemed to be Universities	125
	Total	982

*Universities/Institutions Listed by UGC under section 2(f) of the UGC Act 1956

Figure 1. Type-wise number of universities as on 31.03.2021 (Annual Report 2020-21)*

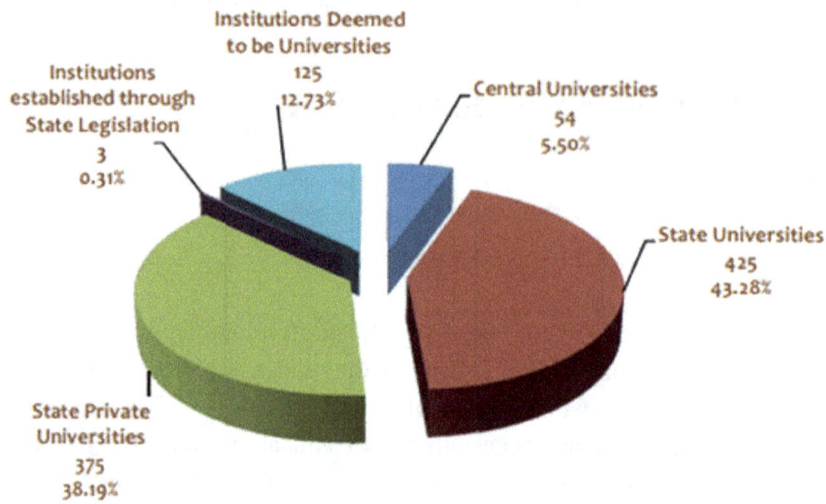

UGC named 54 Central Universities, 425 State Public Universities, 375 State Private Institutions, 3 Institutions created under State Legislature Act, and 125 Institutions Deemed to be Universities for the 2020-21 academic year as of March 31, 2021.

Colleges in India After Independence

In India, the majority of colleges are associated with state or federal universities and offer undergraduate education. Some colleges also provide post-secondary education and research. The affiliating institutions supervise the associated colleges' standards, administer tests, and confer certificates to successful candidates. This college sector is overseen by both public and private entities. Colleges are linked with a university & follow the university's curriculum and examination structure. In addition, certain component colleges are formed and controlled by a specific university. The amount of colleges has grown exponentially, similar to the rise of universities. There were just 578 colleges in 1950-51, but there are now 16,885 affiliated and university colleges. As on 2020-21 data there are 44077 colleges in India. In India, there's many 44077 colleges according to statistics from 2020-21.

Table 2. Year-wise number of colleges (affiliated/constituent) 2010-2011 to 2019-20 Annual Report 2020-21

Year	No. of Colleges
2010-11	32974
2011-12	34852
2012-13	35525
2013-14	36634
2014-15	38498
2015-16	39071
2016-17	40026
2017-18	39527
2018-19	40489
2019-20	42343
2020-21	44077*

* Provisional Figures (Source AISHE Portal 2020-21: Report-List of Institutions)

Figure 2. Growth of colleges (affiliated/constituent): 2010-11 to 2020-21 (Annual Report 2020-21)

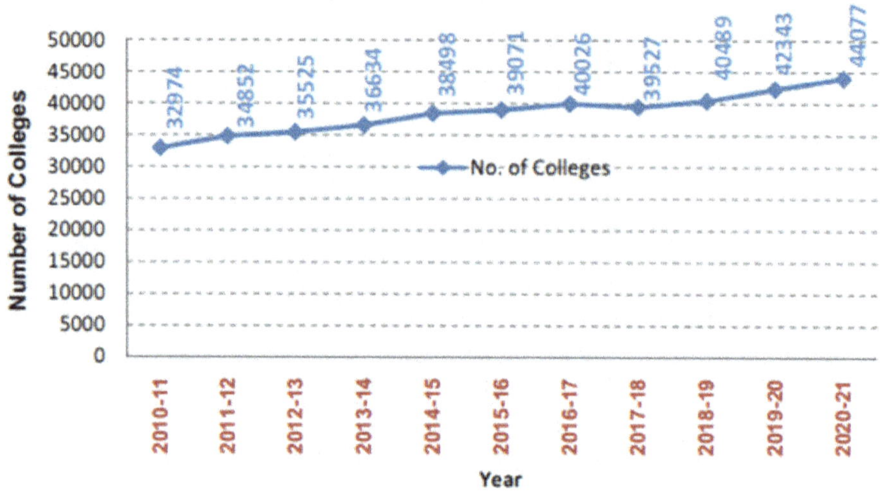

Public Expenditure on Education

Government in a country is responsible for a wholesome development of its citizens. It must make sure that all resources reach at every level in the society. Taxes collected are promised to be spent on the making life of every countryman, a little better. There are several policies that are implemented for various sectors of the country in the name of development. One such is the education sector.

Education is the key to shape young minds who are our prospective citizens. Their minds are innovative and can find creative solutions to many problems. Education chisels one's character. Proper, timely and efficacious spending in education sector would support faster economic development and would also promote human development.

The government invests in education in two ways: one is through centrally sponsored schemes and second through state funded schemes. There are many policies focusing on education of the girl child, rural children and many more. However, the efforts do not seem to be enough. When gauged quantitatively, it captures a picture which indicates towards a meagre interest of the government of the country.

There are children who aspire to study, gain knowledge and attain a stage where they can break out from the shackles of narrow mindedness of the society. They understand the importance of education to bring their family out of poverty and other unprivileged status. Unfortunately, there are many children who have not seen a classroom in their lives a few because of poor financial conditions of the family and some others because of the discrimination based on caste. Many have to dropout to look after their younger siblings or help parents on fields or in household work.

The other major issue is regarding the resource allocation for the education sector. Be it the teacher student ratio, the classroom facilities or the other infrastructure related resources, all seem to remain disproportionately allocated among rural and urban educational institutions. There are many rural schools which had to be closed down due to poor maintenance of the school building. A few other were closed because of lack of teachers for children in the school.

Figure 3. Public expenditure on education (Annual Report 2020-21)

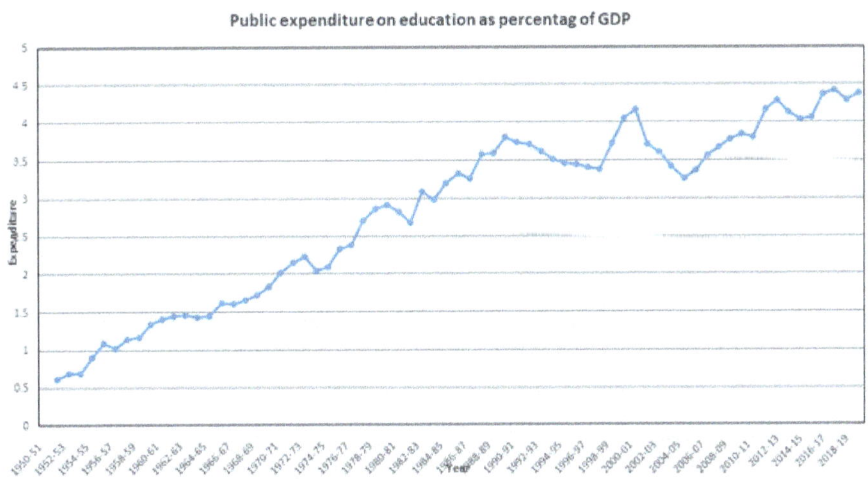

The above graph briefs about the Government spending a percentage of GDP on education sector in the country. The graph captures the data for a span of almost past 69 years. It is evident from the graph that there has not more than even 5% of GDP spent on education. In the year 1950 – 51, the public expenditure has been only 0.5% which could barely reach 1% by the year 1956 – 57. In the first decade, between 1952 and 1961, the average expenditure was 1.01 percent of GDP. And between 1962 and 1971, the next decade spending climbed to 1.62 percent of GDP. Gradually, the expenditure trend picked up, but the growth still remained flat. According to the Kothari committees, expenditures have been steadily increasing during these past few years. The spending climbed to 2.46 between 1972 and 1981.

The trend is also indicative of the mindset of government regarding spending on education sector. If we see the 5-year plans implemented till NITI Aayog, education has not been an issue of immediate concern. Malnutrition and poverty were focused upon more and education lagged behind.

There is a slight growth in public spending in the years 1990 to 93 and then from 1999 to 2008. The reason may be the LPG policy i.e. the Liberalization, Privatization and Globalization, which brought MNCs to India and hence demanded for an educated set of employees. Hence the shifted of focus from other concerns to education.

It can also be observed that the spending has been consistent in the initial years. This has caused slow growth. Roughly from the year 1971, the public spending in education sector took a small leap and continued to consistently increase the percentage of spending till the year 1989. Post which the spending trend remained consistent. However, the spending percentage declined from 1992 until 1999. The average on this decade (1990-2000) can be seen around 3.6%. From the year 1999, the spending picked up again and grew consistently until 2002 and faced another fall till the year 2005. And the trend continued in this decade (2000-2010) also the average value was same compare to the last decade 3.6%. The new government was trying to take the right step in this area which can be seen in this graph, from the last decade which shows that the average value has increased to 4.2% which can be said that this is the highest average compared in the last 7 decades.

So, as is evident from the graph, the public spending on education sector has been like a roller coaster ride. A repetitive pattern of growth and stagnancies has given us assumptions regarding the focus of the government on the education sector. After India gained independence, education sector has drawn the maximum share of the social sector spending of the government, but faced a dire paucity of public spending.

The other facet of this lacuna is related to the state government spending. There may be sanction of finances from the central government, however, the state governments fail to utilize the funds in an efficient manner. This has directly affected the lives of aspiring young minds.

Thus, public spending is not just regarding availability of funds for education it is also about the lack of facilities and infrastructure for education.

REVIEW OF LITREATURE

Based on the current literature, we have highlighted three key studies. The first research project focuses on the importance of human capital to economic growth. The second research looks at India's public education spending patterns. The third research uses econometric techniques to quantify the link between Human Capital (educational investment) and economic growth.

The Role of Human Capital Contribution to Economic Growth

A study by Haldar and Mallik (2010) ascertained whether Human capital may have a role in economic development. With the help of time series analysis of investment in physical capital and human capital. The augmentation of physical capital has been viewed as the go-to method of boost to economic growth in the short term with the technical progress bearing fruit in the long term. To solve the exogenic nature of this theory an element of human capital accumulation was introduced by Romer and Lucas in the endogenous models of growth. The argument was that the human capital paid dividends for the investment made through health, nutrition and sanitation. A nation's human capital is its workforce along with varied skills, knowledge and abilities. Human capital formation is the augmenting of the above traits. All the investments made in helping the augmentation process are termed as human capital development. For the existence of such a workforce, health and nutrition of the workforce becomes a matter of primacy. The study tried to establish a relation between the investments in health and education and per capita GNP growth. It concluded such investments have a significant positive impact on per capita GNP growth in the long run. It was also observed that the opening up of the economy in 1991, has also led to significant growth post that period.

A working paper was published by Mehdi and Chaudhry (2015) delving upon the "Human capital potential of India's future workforce". Policymakers at home, like others, have shown concern towards the capabilities and capacities of the workforce to make themselves employable. In a bid to achieve this goal, the then central government of 2015 unveiled the "Ministry of Skill Development and Entrepreneurship. The National Policy for Skill Development and Entrepreneurship 2015" was formulated with the aim of upskilling and reskilling the workforce entering the market by 2022.The paper bats for looking at a broader picture in a broader timeline; India's workforce will overtake China by 2030 and reach a peak by 2050, and the policy needs to look at transforming India into knowledge economy from the current unskilled and semi-skilled oriented policies. Given the wide timeline available, the vision needs to supersede any economic or political cycle. To move from the current trademark of cheap labor to knowledge economy oriented workforce, the underlying infrastructure in education and health needs a relook. The early days of a childhood makes an impact on the potential of the child and thereby his/her employability. The paper argues that the employment crisis in interrelated with the the insufficient educational and health facilities. Early interventions in childhood through education and health routes will not only lead developing better health and productivity but also better mental, critical and cognitive capacities. In its conclusion, the need to shift from sector specific skills to flexible ability to adapt is emphasized. The policy on human capital needs to recognize the importance and primacy of education and health in childhood stages. Soft skills development needs to be part of the learnings right from childhood.

Dr. Sushma Shukla (2017) published a paper on the relation between human capital and economic growth in India. Behind the economic growth of any country, the important resources in the form of natural, economic, financial, technological capitals play the catalyst role along with social and political dimensions. The paper focuses on deciphering how human capital affects India's economic growth. . The expenditure on healthcare is considered as a proxy variable for human capital. The other variables included secondary School enrollment, and Gross capital formation. Using neoclassical Solow production function and multiple linear regression models, the paper decided on the results using the data from 1995 to 2014. The study found that the economic growth was highly impacted by secondary School enrollment. The study also found a strong positive relation between human capital growth and economic growth. Healthcare expenditure and education expenditure need a fillip in order to facilitate human capital growth. This is necessary for growth to remain sustainable in the longer run.

Javid Ahmad Kha (2018) authored a paper to ascertain the impact that human capital can project on economic growth in the Indian context. Human capital is one of the drivers of the economy and investment in human capital is of prime importance. This paper views health and education as the two components of human capital. Using regression models, the impact of each variable on economic growth is sought to be found. The first two models used a single component to find their individual impact on economic growth, and the final model used human capital, which included both the factors of health and education, as a single component to find its total impact. With respect to the education component, the study showed that the investments made in the education sector positively contributed to enrolment ratios which in turn were having a positive impact on the growth. The investment in the healthcare sector led to increased life expectancy which is a positive indicator for the economy and its growth. Overall, the paper concluded that there is an undeniable impact of human capital on economic growth.

An empirical analysis was carried out by Parika and Singh (2020) on the effects that human capital has on Indian economic growth. A country in possession of a healthy and well educated workforce benefits through sustained economic growth. India, being one of the fastest growing economies and a major global economy, needs to decide the necessity and impact of human capital augmentation. Johansen Cointegration and FMOLS techniques and Granger's causality test are the empirical methods employed in the study. Real Gross Domestic Product and the Human Capital Index are considered as a proxy for economic prosperity and human capital respectively. The data utilized in this study are annual time series data for the period 1980 to 2017. The study found the results on two bases. In the shorter run, human and physical capital were mainly affected by economic output, and, in the long run, human and physical capital affect economic performance.

The Trends of Public Expenditure on Education in India

Chandra (2010), in his research, speaks about the possibility of public investment expenditure in education leading to economic growth. Many benefits of public investment in education reap in the long term. Education is deemed as a harbinger of health and sanitation in the general population of a country. Due to higher levels of education, a society tends to possess an effective workforce and a responsible citizenry. Education also translates to better health and lower mortality rates. All of these factors add up to better economic output. He speaks about the economic theory of 'ripple effect'. The investment in education acts as the stimulus which begets many positive externalities in the economy. He used the time series data of government expenditure on education and economic growth to find the relation between both of them. The methods of study employed included Granger Causality test within an error-correction framework. The study found that there was a strong unidirectional causality from economic growth to expenditure on education, and a moderate causality from education expenditure to economic growth.

Tamang (2022), in his paper on the Impact of Education Expenditure on India's Economic Growth, attempts to examine the relationship between education spending and growth levels in India. The previous works on this topic had led to mixed results. With the usage of time series from 1980-2008, an econometric model was constructed. The neoclassical models developed by Robert Solow (1957) and Romer (1990) had determined the relation between the two variables - education and economic growth. Several empirical studies undertaken too supported this theory. However, two studies from India showed results which were not exactly in line with the already existing conclusions. A study was conducted by Gounden

(1967), in which the investments in education through public expenditure did not pay handsome dividends making it an unfavorable investment. Ansari and Singh (1997) conducted a study to find the relation between public expenditure on education and growth with the help of time series data from 1951 to 1987. In the conclusion of the study, they could not find any relation between the two variables in the long run. To clear the air amidst such differing findings, this paper had sought to find the relation between education expenditure and economic growth. Unit root test and cointegration test were conducted using the time series data from 1980 to 2008. Co-integration of variables was found confirming the presence of a relation in the long term. A 1% level of physical capital per worker may result in a 0.28 percent gain in GDP per worker, whereas a 1% rise in government education spending per worker can result in a 0.11 percent increase in GDP per worker. This confirmed the investments in human capital bear impact on long term growth.

In a study by Kumar and Choudhary (2016), the linkage between education expenditure and economic growth was sought to be defined. Education takes precedence over any factor in transforming an economy to a highly skilled one with an able and skilled workforce. Education empowers the human's cognitive, technical, analytical and interpretive skills. These traits define the skill capacity of an economy. Apart from these economic standpoints, the values and culture imbibed form the human standpoints. The tertiary education builds on the foundational knowledge. Specialized streams, core disciplines pave the way for an information based society. Education takes limelight due to the fact that mere increase in capital and labor would not be enough to derive the optimal growth, the quality of the human capital that operationalizes the other components of capital would play a major role. Population growth in itself would not prove to be a contributor. Education reinforces the workforce with the necessary abilities. The developed economies are propelled by these intangible forces. Schultz devised the following hypothesis: "Some important increases in national income are a consequence of additions to the stock of this form of capital" as a means to measure the costs and benefits of education. The factor of education could be the unseen reason behind the growth of the economy. In the Indian scenario, due to the presence of such education, high tech industries have taken shape. With the usage of data from 1951-52 to 2013-14 The traditional linear regression approach was used in this study. GDP was used as a proxy for economic growth, whereas total government education spending was used as a proxy for the knowledge economy. The data revealed that government education spending and GDP have a favorable association.

Gadbade and Kokate (2021) authored a paper discussing the public expenditure on education in India with focus on state wise and central expenditures. Historically, a significant share of the total social sector expenditure of the govt was allocated to the education sector. However, on the flip side, this sector also has also been highly underfunded when compared to the actual needs. Over the past few years, expenditure on education in many countries has improved. This study focuses on the spending on education incurred by both state and central governments- their mix and future prospects. The study ascertained that expenditure by state governments has been on a downhill, with the central government gradually boosting its spending on these sectors. Notwithstanding these trends, 77% of the expenditure on the education sector is financed by state governments on an average. During the 2000-01 to 2018-19 of the study period, education expenditure as a percentage of state GDP has declined.

A research paper by Zoran (2022) discussed The Impact of Public Education Spending on European Union and BRICS Economic Growth. As the world economies move towards transforming themselves into Knowledge economies, knowledge assumes much importance. Knowledge acts the catalyst role in the development and progress of an economy. Education attracted significant financing and resources right from the industrial revolution. The education system we see today was shaped by the vision behind those investments. This becomes necessary as the education system enables a country to skill and equip its workforce to power its economic output. Consequently, any investment in education and training for skilling of workforce across domains and dimensions translated to contribution to the upping of economic growth. In this process, new methods, knowledge and technologies are discovered, which differentiate an economy from others. Such economies benefit from the added advantage through these resources augmented. The European Union's and BRICS' investments in education, as well as the trends, are reviewed in this study. According to the study, there is a positive relationship between public education spending and the country's gross domestic product.

Ojha (2017) authored a paper involving, a multisectoral neo-classical type CGE model, The model took account of public expenditure on education as a means to develop human capital which facilitates able and relevantly skilled workforce. The study sought to find the impact that an increase in the public expenditure on education backed by a upside in direct tax rates will have on economic growth. The results suggested despite the fiscal constraints on government spendings, an increase in public education expenditure will lead to faster economic growth. Another suggestion made is that focus needs to be maintained on secondary education albeit the cost of higher education. In order to reap maximum benefits of economic growth, investment in physical capital and investment in human capital need to go hand in hand.

To Estimate the Relationship between Human Capital (Investment in Education) and Economic Growth through Econometric Methodology

Qadri and Waheed (2014) presented a time series analysis to ascertain the relationship between human capital and economic growth. The human capital has been a well-known contributor to economic growth in both exogenous and endogenous models of growth. However, the constituents of the human capital remained to be contended. In general, education and health related indicators have been considered as elements of human capital. This paper relied upon the data from 1978-2007 of Pakistan. The author presented data with comparisons drawn along with other Southeast Asian nations. The public expenditure in health and education as a percentage of GDP have been historically low with the health expenditure being always less than one percent of GDP. Comparisons have also been drawn along the education lines wherein the gross enrolment rate of Bangladesh exceeds Pakistan figures. To find the relation between the two indicators, health adjusted education indicator was taken as a proxy for human capital. The findings backed up prior research on the favorable impact of human capital on economic growth. The health adjusted education indicator was found to be a major contributor to economic growth, thereby the education and health sectors needed undivided focus and attention to foster economic growth in the long term.

In a research paper by Dewan Muktdair-Al-Mukit (2012), the relation between Public Expenditure on Education and Economic Growth was studied in the Bangladesh context. As Amartya Sen (1999) said, education has both intrinsic and instrumental value. Amidst the contrary views of education being an enabler of growth, and fiscal policies affecting long run growth, emerging economies like Bangladesh have continued to increase public financing in education in a bid to transform the masses from poverty, prepare a future ready workforce and to accomplish social welfare in society at large. This is duly reflected in the yearly expenditure on education from 2000-2009, which has constantly been between 2-2.5 percentage of GDP. To prove this an econometric model was modelled with usage of time series data from 1995-2009. The results derived exhibited that there was a relative growth of 0.34% in GDP per capita for a rise of 1% in education expenditure. This study concluded that the investments in education sector prove to be contributing to the economic growth.

As similar study was conducted by Muhammad Afzal et al. (2011), in the Pakistan's context. Education is said to serve as a base for the economic prosperity of a nation. With a mix of educational and agricultural reforms, economic prosperity and improvement in socio-economic avenue have been achieved in the subcontinent as well as in the other Asian nations. Due to multiple reasons like the zamindari system, low tax net, corruption and other reasons, the expenditure on education has remained abysmally low over the years. Due to lack of concrete evidence, there are doubts with respect to the efficacy of education in bolstering economic growth. In an attempt to answer such questions, this study looked at the linkages between Real Gross domestic product and education, and between Real Gross domestic product and different levels of education. Time series data from 1970–1971 to 2008–2009 pertaining to labor force, physical capital and education real gross domestic product was used for modelling a ARDL model of cointegration. According to the findings, there is a two-way causal relationship between economic growth and education, as well as between all levels of education & economic growth.

Barik and Das (2019) authored a paper to discuss the higher education system in India and the impact it has had historically on the economy. Historically human resource development and higher education have been in tandem in their evolution and growth. Achievement of full potential, productivity, skill development has been some of the dimensions of study of these two factors. Economic growth and nation building are linked with a comprehensive education system. Financial, natural and human resource capacity building are the essential components of a nation's growth story. These capacities lead to organizing the workforce comprising skilled, unskilled, and semi-skilled components. This paper compares the economic performance of India with its peers in the Asian continent. A detailed examination of economic growth and the evolution of higher education system in India is undertaken in a chronological manner. Furthermore, an assessment of the measures and steps taken recently is taken. In its conclusion, the authors remark that the impact of higher education on economic growth is visible and there is a causal relation between the two variables. Given the demographic setup and being a developing economy, the higher education setup bears a positive impact. Due to effective corrective measures taken over the past decades, the realization of what the author calls a 'knowledge economy' has been possible.

EMPIRICAL ANALYSIS

In this section we present the results of our analysis performed in this study by using several techniques, in accordance with the objectives of the study to analyze the impact of Human Capital on Economic Growth in India. Then we look on some of the other analysis like stability test, forecasting and Granger Causality test.

Regression Model

Before performing a regression analysis, it is imperative to do our stationarity tests, "using the Augmented Dickey-Fuller (ADF) test". We conclusively found out after performing the ADF test that all of our variables, that is, LNGDP, LN PE, LNCF, is not stationary and it is denoted by (I1) in the table.

Table 3. Unit root tests

S.No	Variable	Stationary at levels	First order stationary	Inference
1	LNGDP	0.9680	0.0001	I(1)
2	LNPE	0.4015	0.0001	I(1)
3	LNCF	0.9266	0.0001	I(1)

Author's Calculation

Let us now have a look at the coefficient of our model, which is nothing but the estimates of the model:

lnGDP = f(lnPE + lnCF),

where,

lnGDP is the Gross Domestic Product, a dependent variable that is a function of independent variables,

lnPE is the Public Expenditure on Education, with additionally,

lnCF is the Gross Capital Formation

$$D(lnGDP) = 0.07 + 0.11D(lnPE(-3)) + 0.20D(lnCF(-1)) + 0.07DUM$$

$$(6.51) \qquad (1.82) \qquad (4.76)$$

R-square 0.53

Adjusted R- square 0.51

Durbin-Watson stat 1.84

F-statistic 19.75

The variable lnGDP represents the intercept, which as we can see from the results obtained, is 0.07 as the estimated value. This indicates that when all the independent variables take the value 0, the dependent variable, lnGDP, will have the value of 0.07 on an average.

Moving further to lnPE, which is at lag-3, the coefficient value is 0.11, which basically talks about slope. This means that when Public Expenditure increases by 1 unit, our GDP will also increase by 0.11 units. There is a positive relationship between both these variables.

As can be seen from the coefficient of Gross Capital Formation, our results indicate that 0.20 as the estimated value which means that when capital formation increases by 1 unit, our GDP will increase by 0.20 units, thus proving a positive relationship.

Looking at the dummy variable, when the value coefficient is 1, our GDP will increase by 0.07 units. We have taken 1 dummy variable which gives value for the following years, 1965, 1970, 1973, 1975, 1980, 2000, and 2009, whereas the other years showing null.

Moving on to the significant aspect, the t-statistic talks about the significance of the independent variable. The standard convention for t-statistics is that, higher the t-stat, more significant is the independent variable. For GDP, we have 6.51 and the corresponding p-value is 0.0001, which is lesser than the set alpha. If we know by default that alpha is at 5% significance level, we can say that H0 is rejected, and H1 is accepted, and that the variable is significant.

For Public Expenditure, the t-statistic is at 1.82 and for Gross Capital Formation, the t-statistic is at 4.76, where the corresponding p-value is 0.001. It can be seen that the p-value is lesser than 0.05, when alpha is at 5%, so this variable is significant.

The value for multiple R-squared is at 0.53, which means 53%. This could be interpreted in such a way that all the changes in the independent variables together are able to explain only 53% of the dependent variable.

The main thing to be noted is that we are not supposed to get carried away by the multiple R-squared because of the simple reason that Multiple R-square can increase even if insignificant variables are added to the model.

Thus, adjusted R-squared takes into account only significant variables and throws out the explanatory power, that is, goodness of fit.

We have adjusted R-squared at 0.51, that is, 51%, so we can say that changes in all the independent variables together are able to explain changes in the dependent variable up to 51% which is very good enough.

The standard error of regression, which represents the overall error of a model, is 0.02. The most basic criteria for any model to be termed as, "good", is that the error should be as minimal as possible, and in our case that is the result, so it is acceptable.

When we come to F-statistic, it talks about the overall significance of the model. Higher the F value and lower the P-value will conclude that the model is a very good model. We have P-value as 0.001, which is lesser than 0.005, so we can conclude that all independent variables together are significant and the F-statistic value is at 19.2, which is also very good.

According to the acceptable range for Durbin-Watson Statistics, our result of 1.84 falls into the acceptable range of DW statistics, so we can say that there is no auto correlation among the errors.

Granger Causality Tests

This test is given by Angel Granger, where the null hypothesis states that:

A) Public Expenditure does not Granger cause GDP
B) Public Expenditure does not Granger Cause Public Expenditure

The alternate hypothesis states that:

A) Public Expenditure does cause GDP
B) GDP causes Public Expenditure

We will first evaluate the statement A, where the correspondence f-value is at 4.42, which is very good and associated P-value is at 0.002, and it is lesser than 0.05 (alpha at 5%). So we reject H0 (null) and accept H1(alternate), that is, Public Expenditure causes GDP. That is, changes in the public expenditure leads to changes in GDP.

Looking at statement B, the corresponding f-value is very good which is at 42.38, and as we already know that higher the f-value, the corresponding p-value will be lower. Since we have the P-value as 0.005, which is far lesser than 0.05 (alpha at 5), we reject the H0 (null) and accept the H1 (alternate). This means that the changes in GDP leads to changes in public expenditure.

In-Sample Forecasting

Figure 4. In-sample forecasting statistics

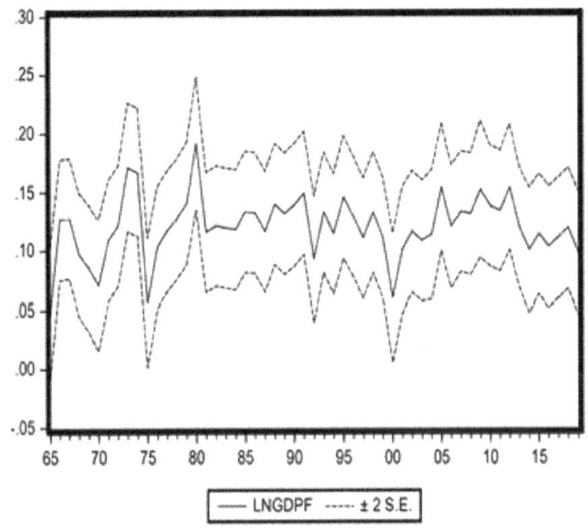

Forecast: LNGDPF	
Actual: D(LNGDP)	
Forecast sample: 1961 2019	
Adjusted sample: 1965 2019	
Included observations: 55	
Root Mean Squared Error	0.024429
Mean Absolute Error	0.019636
Mean Abs. Percent Error	18.62245
Theil Inequality Coefficient	0.097976
Bias Proportion	0.000000
Variance Proportion	0.153974
Covariance Proportion	0.846026
Theil U2 Coefficient	0.576485
Symmetric MAPE	17.07237

Figure 5. The actual and forecasted Ln GDP

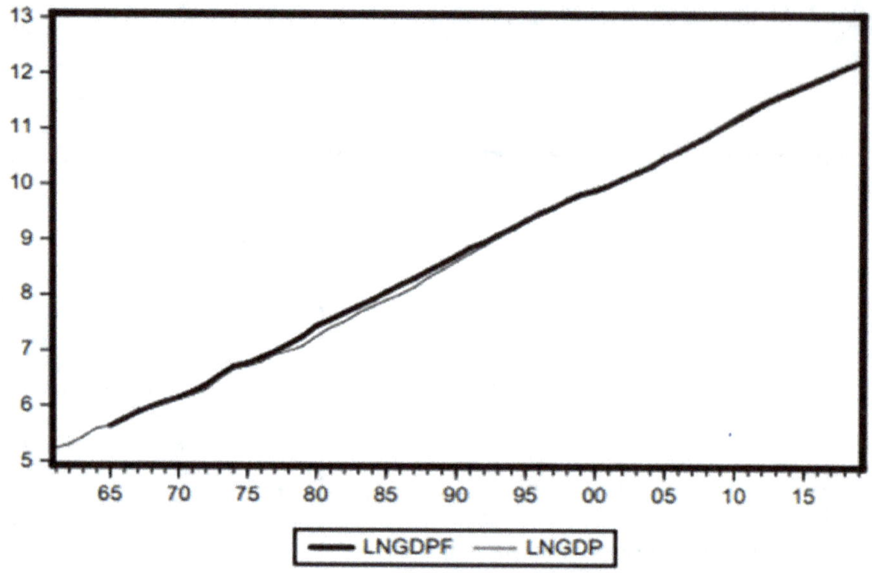

Coming to the in-sample forecasting, we have two primary criteria's, that is, the Root Mean Squared Error (RMSE), and the Theil Inequality Coefficient. The Root Mean Squared error (RMSE) says that, lower the error, the better the model is. Our version of the model of the RMSE is showing 0.02, which is very minimal and hence we can conclude that our model is good.

Theil's inequality coefficient says that if the v statistic value is closer to zero, we can conclude that forecasting method which is the simplest method. If Theil's inequality coefficient is closer to 1, then we can conclude that there is no difference between the actual forecasted methods and the NAVE forecasting method. The value for the co-efficient is 0.09, which is closer to 0, hence we can conclude that forecasted model is better than the NAVe forecasting method.

In terms of the in-sampling forecast, we have fitted the values to understand the model, and get apprehend if the results are good. Thus, we will consider the standard error as the band width and see if all the fitted values are falling in this band width are between -2 & +2. Looking at our graph, we can safely say that it is very much falling within the range.

The criteria for the fitted (lnGDPF) and actual (lnGDP) is, if you want to consider the model as good, then the fitted value should be closer to the actual values and looking at the graph, we can clearly say that the fitted values are closer to actual values, rather fall in-line with the actual values.

Stability Tests

Figure 6. Stability tests statistics

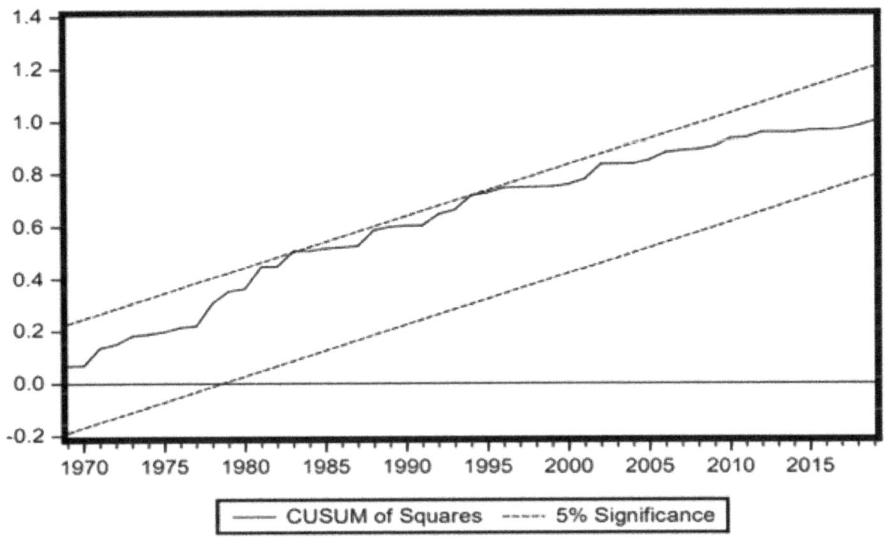

Figure 7. The recursive residuals

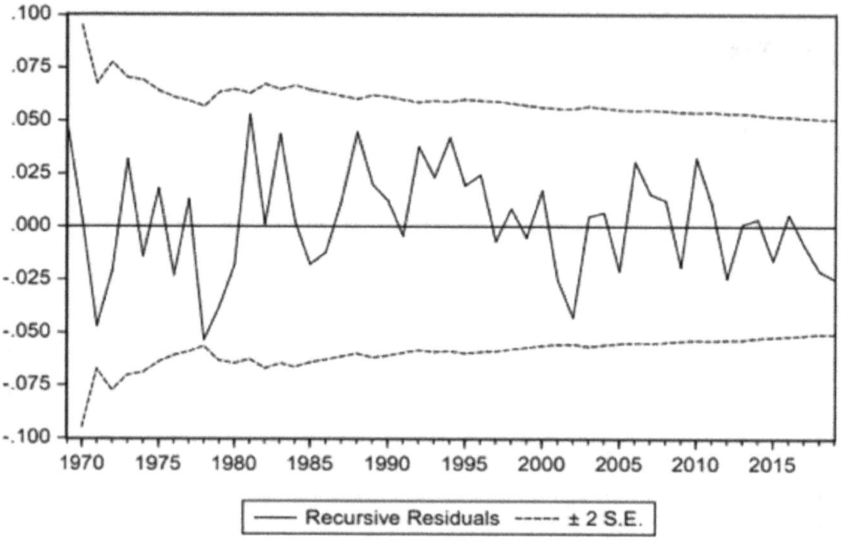

This is one of the diagnostic checking criterias. Under stability test, we will see if the model built is stable. We will interpret coefficients in the long-term to see the stability. For this purpose, we have used recursive residuals test, and the CUSUM test.

We check CUSUM to see if there are any stabilities. We set the significant level and in our own model, it is by default set at 5%. We also have the CUSUM of square test, where we have the band width of -0.2 to +0.2, so if the CUSUM band width falls in this range, we can conclude that the model we built is a stable model, and the co-efficients are good to go in long run.

Residual Test: We plot the recursive residual at the zero lin. Standard errors between -2 and +2 at each point. If the residuals are falling within this range, we can say that our model is stable. As we can see from the graph, the standard error residuals are falling within the range. We can thus conclude that our models are stable in the long-run.

A Case Study On Sri Sathya Sai Institute of Higher Larning (SSSIHL)

Figure 8. SSSIHL administrative building

"**A college** which does not confer the knowledge of the Spiritual Reality to the students who are engaged in the pursuit of various material studies, is as barren as the sky without the moon, or a heart without peace, or a nation without reference to law". Sathya Sai Baba

Sri Sathya Sai Institute of Higher Learning (Deemed to be University), was established on 22 November 1981, at Prashanthi Nilayam, Andhra Pradesh, India. Currently the Institute comprises 4 campuses: (i) Prasanthi Nilayam campus, (ii) Brindavan campus, (iii) Nandigiri campus; (iv) A dedicated Women's Campus as Anantapur campus.

The Institute requires mandatory residential stay at the campus on the lines of the ancient gurukula system. Each campus possesses well equipped computer labs, science labs, libraries and hostels. The Sri Sathya Sai International Centre for Sports and Sri Sathya Sai Hillview stadium are world class outdoor and indoor stadiums respectively.

During its inception, the Institute was given a clear direction by the founder chancellor to impart spiritual education and secular education as the two components of education imparted with spiritual uplift and character developments as the ultimate goals. He envisioned the Institute to be based on the gurukula system of the yore, where students and teachers resided together. The student's education was meant to be not restricted just to the class hours, rather, the entire day was filled with multiple activities to achieve holistic development.

The student, as Bhagawan said, was meant to be "self-reliant, contented and enterprising heroes of action and self-sacrifice, for the purpose of serving humanity." The education imparted needed to be holistic to create "professionally sound, socially responsible and spiritually aware" individuals.

In a bid to realize these lofty goals, the Sri Sathya Sai Value Based Integral System of Education was designed. The system incorporates Intellectual, Physical, Cultural, Devotional and Service as the five dimensions of the system on the base of the gurukula education system. "The five human values of Truth, Right Conduct, Peace, Love and Non-Violence are the undercurrent". In the end, after a stay of 3/2/5 years, the student would be socially responsible, spiritually aware and professionally sound.

The life at SSSIHL bears resemblance to that of Nalanda and Taksha hila. All students live a simple life, in an environment which is conducive for inner peace. The students live the life of a brahmachari adhering to the rules and regulations. Education includes both worldly knowledge like sciences and management as well as the atmic knowledge of Vedas. The institute encourages all the students to learn Vedam to stay rooted in our ancient lifestyle. This in no way impedes the scientific zeal of the institute. The Institute involves itself in research in many contemporary topics like medicine, biotechnology, mathematics and chemistry. The balance is achieved through kindling interest in students' hearts rather than imposing.

This framework is operationalized throughout the day and the year. Typically, the day of a student of SSSIHL starts at 5 a.m. Similar to the ancient gurukula system, the day commences with prayers in the brahma muhurta period. Exercises and yoga are means of keeping the body and mind in good shape. Only a healthy body can house a sound mind. All students sweat out in the early morning breezes through exercises, yoga and games. The spacious fields across campuses provide ample space and equipment for these activities. Post the physical activities and personal ablutions, the breakfast is served. The menu of the meals is regularly revised in order to provide wholesome nutrition while maintaining the balance of tastes.

The college hours commence with a prayer congregation. The Sarva Dharma prayer which is chanted during these sessions reflects the oneness of God that the Institute and its Founder Chancellor believe in. Along with this, the morning prayer congregation acts host to multiple talks and music programs by students, and bhajan sessions.

The college hours continue up to 4:30 p.m. with a lunch break for an hour in between. Post the classes, students have free time which can be used for completing the daily chores and other activities. In the evening, a bhajan session takes place with all students in attendance. Dinner is served after bhajans, after which, students spend time with their studies. The day ends with a night prayer at 10:15 p.m.

The daily schedule, although routine in nature, allows the student to develop a sense of discipline and composure. Punctuality is of prime importance in the institute. To keep up with multiple activities, the students adapt to efficiently managing their time to accommodate for everything.

The hostels host the students for their entire tenure at the institute. The rooms were designed and built spaciously to accommodate 8-10 people in a single room. The students learn to share resources and live together harmoniously. All students recline on beds spread on the floor like in the ancient times. The room is cleaned and maintained completely by its residents alone. Through this student get to learn the value of labour and work. Due to the big number of residents in a single room, one must adapt himself to live and work in a harmonious way. There would be no scope for isolation and detachment from the rest.

Another striking feature of the hostels is that the hostel is run and maintained by the students themselves. The hostels rest on the philosophy of "Each lives for the other and all live for god". On the lines of gurukula system, the students themselves perform various activities which are necessary to keep the schedule moving. Each students becomes part of what is called a 'department'.

The hostel quietly functions with all these departments functioning in the background. Each department is vital for a smooth functioning of the hostel. Each individual is essential to keep the department running. Like in a society, the hostel needs all of its students to perform their roles for smooth sailing. This circular system quietly embeds a sense of responsibility and empathy in the students. Everyone understands the necessity for an orderly living place where rules and regulations are voluntarily abided. The need for enforcement is substituted by the awareness of responsibilities. The lessons for life are learnt at SSSIHL are akin to the Vedic gurukula system where the student performed activities like the above mentioned.

SUMMARY AND CONCLUSION

Until 1960, Human Capital was not accorded significant weight in terms of economic progress. Physical capital was given more attention and concentrate. Many economists were aware of the importance of Human Capital when Schultz highlighted it in 1961. Schultz, Becker, Mincer (1984), and others, among others, have emphasized its importance as the most significant factor of human capital. Education, health, in-service training, and other factors all contribute to human capital. Education helps directly to economic growth through supplying the high-quality people required for manufacturing and development. Education not only conveys knowledge, but it also alters people's self-perceptions and aspirations. Education has the potential to change people's attitudes about "employment, consumption, preferences for family planning, saving proclivities, economic rationality, approach toward social duty, and other economic issues."

Evolution of India's education policy can be stated back to Vedic period where it was guru shishya Parampara. It was more focused not only on knowledge but a holistic development of an individual. During medieval period, we saw the invasion of India by Mughals, where they tried to destroy Indian culture by destroying Nalanda and TakshaSheela. There were very few who also emphasized on Indian culture like Akbar. Delhi, Agra, Jaunpur, and a few more are eminent educational centers during that period. During pre-independence slowly the Indian lifestyle and customs were gradually being influenced by the British. Only those who served the British were allowed to study so that they can serve the British government. Lord Macaulay was the main person to transform the Indian education style to English British style. By the time British left India in 1947 the state of Indian Economy was very bad but in 1949 The University Education Commission was formed. After which there were many policies came in to picture where there were very significant changes happened the most prominent policy was of National Education Policy (2020) in which the aims are to transform the nation into a vibrant knowledge society, with equitable access to education. There were many significant changes happened in the area of Teacher Availability and Training, Technology, Examination Structure. The most attractive thing in this policy was that they emphasised more on holistic development by bringing some value based education not only education but with more advanced technologies, which can be termed as "Vedas to Metaverse".

In grounds of access, quality of instruction and research, enrolment ratios, and other factors, "India's higher education system" have progressed dramatically since independence.

As of 31.03.2021, there were 982 universities, up from 27 in 1947. In addition, the count of colleges has expanded from 578 in 1950-51 to 16,885 associated and university institutions now. There are 44077 colleges according to statistics from 2020-21. In India, there are "central, state, private, and deemed universities". India has the most open universities in the world. Higher education provides a person with a great deal in life. More education benefits a person both psychologically and physically. It aids him in extending his ideas and carrying out his goals. As a result, the government must increase its investment in the education sector. The government-appointed education committees have recommended that education expenditures be at least 6% of GDP. At the moment, the government spends well over 4% of GDP but it is not sufficient.

We sought to scientifically analyses the highlight and role of human capital contribution to Economic Growth in this study, as well as the trend in public education spending at the time. Then to estimate the relationship between Human Capital (investment in Education) and economic growth through econometric methodology. At last we want to see how values are important in education so for that we are looking on a case Study on Sri Sathya Sai Institute of Higher Learning(SSSIHL).

For this study we used annual time series data which is garnered for all models starting from 1961 to 2019. Where our sample size was 59 observations of each variable used in the study. We used Public expenditure on education as a proxy to Human Capital and Gross domestic Capital Formation is a proxy of Physical Capital. GDP = f (PE+CF). We have also taken 8 Dummy periods on 1965, 1970,1973,1975,1980,2000,2009.

We employed Time Series statistics for the empirical analysis. Using GDP as a dependent variable with Public Expenditure on Education (PE) & Gross Domestic Capital Formation (CF) for independent variables, the standard Ordinary Least Square (OLS) approach was applied. Using the Unit Root test, the entire variable became stationary. We used public education spending as a proxy for evaluating human capital. For this study, we used 59 years of time - series data set from 1961 to 2019.

All 59 observations are regarded to be a solid and thorough sample period, as they span the last six decades of the economy. The link is estimated using a statistically significant equation that follows economic theory. These findings led us to accept this concept. Then we verified the model's stability and performed in-sample forecasting. The coefficients of “Root Mean Squared Error (RMSE) & Theil's Inequality” were both significant.

Then, to see if there was a link between human capital and economic growth, we utilized the Granger causality test. We discovered and observed that both GDP and Education cause or are caused by each other in a bidirectional manner. The return is assured because the relationship is bidirectional. So spending may be raised without anxiety.

Finally, we attempted to conduct a “case study of Sri Satya Sai Institute of Higher Learning “in order to gain a better understanding of how integral education works. We discovered that it is more or less similar to the vedic gurukula education system, in which students are trained for all-round holistic development.

Baba once said “Spiritual education is not a distinct and separate discipline; it is part and parcel of all types and levels of education. In fact, it is the very foundation on which a lasting edifice can be built. Secular and spiritual educations are like the two halves in the seeds of pulses; the germ that sprouts are in between; it is fed by both”.

Finally, to sum up the importance of the education here we quote the Chinese proverb which highlights the education:

"If you are planning for a year, grow rice and vegetables;
If you are planning for decades, grow trees.
But, if you are planning for centuries, educate children."

To add to the proverb,

If you are Planning for sustained and all round development for centuries,
Don't merely educate children but mould them into men of character and faith.

Currently, the new education strategy emphasizes holistic development; nevertheless, it would be beneficial if the Indian government attempted to emphasize a value-based education system from the ground up.

REFERENCES

Afzal, M., Rehman, H., Farooq, M., & Sarwar, K. (2011). Education and economic growth in Pakistan: A cointegration and causality analysis. *International Journal of Educational Research, 50*(5-6), 321–335. DOI: 10.1016/j.ijer.2011.10.004

Chandra, A. (2010). Does Government Expenditure on Education Promote Economic Growth? An Econometric Analysis. *Munich Personal RePEc Archive*, (25480), 1–12.

Dewan, M.-A.-M. (2012). Public Expenditure on Education and Economic Growth: The Case of Bangladesh. *IJAR-BAE, 1*(4), 10–18.

Gadbade, Gunwant Bapu, Kokate, Chandrakant Namdevrao (2021). View of Public Expenditure on Education An Interstate Analysis of India. *Pularch's Journal of Archaeology of Egypt/Egyptology* 18(4). ISSN 1567-214x

Haldar, S. K., & Girijasankar, M. (2010). Does human capital cause economic growth? A case study of India. *International Journal of Economic Sciences and Applied Research, 3*(1), 7–25.

Khan, J. (2018). Human capital Development and Economic Growth in India. Research review. *International Journal of Multidisciplinary, 3*(7), 484–488.

Kumar, N., & Choudhary, P. (2016). The Relationship between Education Expenditure and Economic Growth in India. *J Adv Res Appl Math Stat, 1*(2), 119–123.

Mehdi, A., & Chaudhry, D. (2015). Human capital potential of India's future workforce, Working Paper, No. 308, *Indian Council for Research on International Economic Relations (ICRIER),* New Delhi.

Mincer, J. (1984). Human capital and economic growth. *Economics of Education Review, 3*(3), 195–205. DOI: 10.1016/0272-7757(84)90032-3

Ojha, V. (2017). The Impact of Public Education Expenditure on Economic Growth and Income Distribution in India. *Business Analyst, 37*(2), 9–37.

Parika, A., & Singh, B. P. (2020). How Does Human Capital Affect Economic Growth in India? An Empirical Analysis. MPRA Paper *102428*. University Library of Munich.

Qadri, F., & Waheed, A. (2014). Human capital and economic growth: A macroeconomic model for Pakistan. *Economic Modelling, 42*, 66–76. DOI: 10.1016/j.econmod.2014.05.021

Romer, P. (1990). Human capital and growth: Theory and evidence. *Carnegie-Rochester Conference Series on Public Policy*, *32*, 251–286. DOI: 10.1016/0167-2231(90)90028-J

Shukla, S. (2017). Human capital and economic growth in India. *International Journal of Current Research*, *9*(11), 61628–61631.

Subhalaxmi Barik, & Das, D. S. (2019). Higher Education System In India And Its Impact On The Economy. *Think India Journal, 22*(10), 7301–7308. https://thinkindiaquarterly.org/index.php/think-india/article/view/12106

Tamang, P. (2022). The Impact of Education Expenditure on India's Economic Growth. *Journal of International Academic Research*, *11*(3), 14–20.

Zoran, T., 2022. Analysis of the Impact of Public Education Expenditure on Economic Growth of European Union and BRICS. *Economic Analysis*, 48(1-2, 19-38), pp.19-37.

ADDITIONAL READING

Alataş, S. (2016). The Effect of Human Capital on Economic Growth: A Panel Data Analysis. 14(27), pp.539-555.

Dae-Bong, K. (2009). Human Capital and its measurement. *OECD World Forum*, pp.1-15.

Gundlach, E. (1997). Human capital and economic development: A macroeconomic assessment. *Inter Economics*, *32*(1), 23–35. DOI: 10.1007/BF02929817

Hanushek, E. A. (2013). Economic growth in developing countries: The role of human capital. *Economics of Education Review*, *37*, 204–212. DOI: 10.1016/j.econedurev.2013.04.005

Holden, L., & Biddle, J. (2017). The Introduction of Human Capital Theory into Education Policy in the United States. *History of Political Economy*, *49*(4), 537–574. DOI: 10.1215/00182702-4296305

Hussain Ansari, T. (2022). *An Analysis of Public Expenditure on Education in India.* World Wide Journal of Multidisciplinary Research and Development.

Jayaram, N. "Higher Education in India." Asian universities: Historical perspectives and contemporary challenges (2004): 85.

Kaul, S. (2006). *Higher education in India: seizing the opportunity*. The Indian Council for Research on International Economic Relations.

Kouton, J. (2018). *Education expenditure and economic growth: Some empirical evidence from C^ote d'Ivoire*. ENSEA.

Kumar, D. (2020). Trends and Growth of Public Expenditure on Education in India: An analysis. *IJEMMASSS*, *2*(3), 109–117.

Lin, T.-C. (2004). The role of higher education in economic development: An empirical study of Taiwan case. *Journal of Asian Economics*, *15*(2), 355–371. DOI: 10.1016/j.asieco.2004.02.006

Mercan, M., & Sezer, S. (2014). The Effect of Education Expenditure on Economic Growth: The Case of Turkey. *Procedia: Social and Behavioral Sciences*, *109*, 925–930. DOI: 10.1016/j.sbspro.2013.12.565

Motkuri, V. and E. Revathi (2020 18 Sept). Private and Public Expenditure on Education in India: Trend over last Seven Decades, CESS-RSEPPG Research Brief #2, Research Cell on Education (RSEPPG), Centre for Economic and Social Studies, Hyderabad.

Pelinescu, E. (2015). The impact of human capital on economic growth. *Procedia Economics and Finance*, *22*(1), 184–190. DOI: 10.1016/S2212-5671(15)00258-0

Raghavender Raju, G. (2010, Apr). *Education and Economic Development in India*, The Asian Economic Review. *The Indian Institute of Economics*, *52*(1), 157–168.

Raju, R. G. (2010). Education as Investment: India Ranks Low. *Eternal India*, *2*(5), 139 151.

Schütt, F. (2022). *The Importance of Human Capital for Economic Growth*. IWIM.

Son, H. (2010). Human Capital Development. *ADB Economics Working Paper*, (225), pp.1-36.

Suwandaru, A., Alghamdi, T., & Nurwanto, N. (2021). Empirical Analysis on Public Expenditure for Education and Economic Growth: Evidence from Indonesia. *Economies*, *9*(4), 146. DOI: 10.3390/economies9040146

Tanuka Endow, A. (2008). Public Expenditure on Education in India: Recent Trends and Outcomes. *Research Consortium on Educational Outcomes and Poverty*, *8*(18), 1–51.

Viswanath, J. (2009). K. L. N. Reddy, and Vishwanath Pandit. "Human Capital Contributions to Economic Growth in India: An Aggregate Production Function Analysis.". *Indian Journal of Industrial Relations*, 473–486.

Wilson, R. A., & Briscoe, G. "The impact of human capital on economic growth: a review." Impact of Education and Training, Third Report on Vocational Training Research in Europe: background report. Luxembourg: Office for Official Publications of the European Communities, Cedefop Reference series 54 (2004).

Compilation of References

Abbas, S., & Wizarat, S. (2018). Military expenditure and external debt in South Asia: A panel data analysis. *Peace Economics, Peace. Science & Public Policy, 24*(3).

Abd Rahman, A. A. (2023). The Concept of National Security in the Period of Cold War and Post-Cold War. *Journal of Law and Sustainable Development, 11*(5), 1–9. https://ojs.journalsdg.org/jlss/article/view/766

Abdel-Khalek, G., Mazloum, M. G., & El Zeiny, M. R. M. (2020). Military expenditure and economic growth: The case of India. *Review of Economics and Political Science, 5*(2), 116–135. DOI: 10.1108/REPS-03-2019-0025

Abeyagoonasekera, A. (2024). China's Strategy for Political Warfare in Sri Lanka. *East Asian Policy*, 16(2), 68-81. https://www.worldscientific.com/doi/abs/10.1142/S1793930524000133

Abu-Bader, S., & Abu-Qarn, A. S. (2003). Government expenditures, military spending and economic growth: Causality evidence from Egypt, Israel, and Syria. *Journal of Policy Modeling, 25*(6–7), 567–583. DOI: 10.1016/S0161-8938(03)00057 7

Acemoglu, D. (2012). Introduction to Economic Growth. *Journal of Economic Theory, 147*(2), 545–550. DOI: 10.1016/j.jet.2012.01.023

Acocella, N. (1992). The multinational firm and the theory of industrial organization. In Del Monte, A. (Ed.), *Recent developments in the theory of industrial organization* (pp. 232–251)., DOI: 10.1007/978-1-349-11771-0_10

Afzal, M., Rehman, H., Farooq, M., & Sarwar, K. (2011). Education and economic growth in Pakistan: A cointegration and causality analysis. *International Journal of Educational Research, 50*(5-6), 321–335. DOI: 10.1016/j.ijer.2011.10.004

Agar, J. (2019). What is technology? Technology: critical history of a concept, by Eric Schatzberg, Chicago and London, University of Chicago Press, 2018, 352 pp. ISBN: 978-0-226-58383-9. *Annals of Science*, *77*(3), 377–382. DOI: 10.1080/00033790.2019.1672788

Agenor, P. R., & Neanidis, K. C. (2011). The allocation of public expenditure and economic growth. *Manchester School*, *79*(4), 899–931. DOI: 10.1111/j.1467-9957.2011.02197.x

Ahmed, Z., Wang, Z., & Ali, S. (2019). Investigating the non-linear relationship between urbanization and CO2 emissions: An empirical analysis. *Air Quality, Atmosphere & Health*, *12*(8), 945–953. DOI: 10.1007/s11869-019-00711-x

Aizenman, J., & Glick, R. (2006). Military expenditure, threats, and growth. *The Journal of International Trade & Economic Development*, *15*(2), 129–155. DOI: 10.1080/09638190600689095

Akar, G., Saritas, T., & Kizilkaya, O. (2021). The Impact of Human Development on Economic Growth: An Application on Transition Economies. *Business and Economics Research Journal*, *12*(2), 307–318. DOI: 10.20409/berj.2021.323

Akbota, A., & Baek, J. (2018). The environmental consequences of growth: Empirical evidence from the Republic of Kazakhstan. *Economies*, *6*(1), 19. DOI: 10.3390/economies6010019

Akhtar, M. S., & Feng, T. (2022). Malware Analysis and Detection Using Machine Learning Algorithms. *Symmetry*, *14*(11), 2304. DOI: 10.3390/sym14112304

Al Jazeera. (2025). *US approves sale of 20 F-16 fighter jets worth $5.58bn to Philippines*. AlJazeera. https://www.aljazeera.com/news/2025/4/2/us-approves-sale-of-20-f-16-fighter-jets-worth-5-58bn-to-philippines

Alenda-Demoutiez, J. (2022). From economic growth to the human: Reviewing the history of development visions over time and moving forward. *Third World Quarterly*, *43*(5), 1038–1055. DOI: 10.1080/01436597.2022.2042680

Alexander, W. R. (1990). The impact of defence spending on economic growth: A multi-sectoral approach to defence spending and economic growth with evidence from developed economies". *Defence and Peace Economics*, *2*(1), 39–55. DOI: 10.1080/10430719008404677

Ali, H. E., & Abdellatif, O. A. (2015). Military expenditures and natural resources: Evidence from rentier states in the Middle East and North Africa". *Defence and Peace Economics*, *26*(1), 5–13. DOI: 10.1080/10242694.2013.848574

Ali, H. E., & Solarin, S. A. (2020). Military Spending, Corruption, and the Welfare Consequences. *Defence and Peace Economics, 31*(6), 677–691. https://www.tandfonline.com/doi/full/10.1080/10242694.2019.1567181. DOI: 10.1080/10242694.2019.1567181

Ali, O., Osmanaj, V., Kwiatek, P., Alryalat, M., Chimhundu, R., & Dwivedi, Y. K. (2023). The impact of technological innovation on marketing: individuals, organizations and environment: a systematic review. *Ekonomska Istrazivanja, 36*(3), 2210661.. DOI: 10.1080/1331677X.2023.2210661

Alkhudhayr, F., Alfarraj, S., Aljameeli, B., & Elkhdiri, S. (2019). Information Security: A Review of Information Security Issues and Techniques. *2nd International Conference on Computer Applications & Information Security (ICCAIS)*, Riyadh, Saudi Arabia, 2019, pp. 1-6, DOI: 10.1109/CAIS.2019.8769504

Alley, J. (2021). Alliance Participation, Treaty Depth, and Military Spending. *International Studies Quarterly, 65*(4), 929–941. DOI: 10.1093/isq/sqab077

Alptekin, A., & Levine, P. (2012). Military Expenditure and Economic Growth: A Meta analysis. *European Journal of Political Economy, 28*(4), 636–650. DOI: 10.1016/j.ejpoleco.2012.07.002

American Library Association. (1983). *The ALA Glossary of Library and Information Science*. ALA.

Amir-ud-Din, R., Sajjad, F. W., & Aziz, S. (2020). Revisiting arms race between India and Pakistan: A case of asymmetric causal relationship of military expenditures. *Defence and Peace Economics, 31*(6), 721–741. DOI: 10.1080/10242694.2019.1624334

Andersson, G. (2018). Internet interventions: Past, present and future. *Internet Interventions : the Application of Information Technology in Mental and Behavioural Health, 12*, 181–188. DOI: 10.1016/j.invent.2018.03.008 PMID: 30135782

Ando, S. (2009). The impact of defence expenditure on economic growth: Panel data analysis based on feder model". *International Journal of Economic Policy Studies, 4*(1), 141–154. DOI: 10.1007/BF03405719

Antonakis, N. (1997). Military expenditure and economic growth in Greece, 1960-90. *Journal of Peace Research, 34*(1), 89–100. DOI: 10.1177/0022343397034001007

Anwar, M. A., Rongting, Z., Dong, W., Asmi, F., & Meissner, R. (2018). Mapping the knowledge of national security in the 21st century a bibliometric study. *Cogent Social Sciences, 4*(1), 1542944. DOI: 10.1080/23311886.2018.1542944

Army Recognition. (2025). *Singapore confirms the purchase of eight more F-35A fighter jets to complement earlier F-35B acquisition*. Global Defense News Army Recognition Group. https://armyrecognition.com/news/aerospace-news/2025/singapore-confirms-the-purchase-of-eight-more-f-35a-fighter-jets-to-complement-earlier-f-35b-acquisition

Arthur, G. (2024). *Brunei defense budget surges by 32%, with focus on intel, targeting*. Defense News. https://www.defensenews.com/global/asia-pacific/2024/03/07/brunei-defense-budget-surges-by-32-with-focus-on-intel-targeting/

Arthur, G. (2025). *Japan passes record defense budget, while still playing catch-up*. Defense News. https://www.defensenews.com/global/asia-pacific/2025/01/16/japans-passes-record-defense-budget-while-still-playing-catch-up/

Arthur, G. (2025). *Singapore raises defense budget, readies new military acquisitions*. Defense News. https://www.defensenews.com/global/asia-pacific/2025/03/07/singapore-raises-defense-budget-readies-new-military-acquisitions/

Asghari, M. (2017). National Security and Economic Growth. *Iranian Economic Review*, *21*(4), 905–924.

Asia Maritime Transparency Initiative. (2024). *Chinese power projection*. Center for Strategic and International Studies. https://amti.csis.org/chinese-power-projection/

Asia Maritime Transparency Initiative. (2025). *Vietnam Island Tracker*. Center for Strategic and International Studies. https://amti.csis.org/island-tracker/vietnam/

Atesoglu, H. S. (2009). Defense spending and aggregate output in the United States. *Defence and Peace Economics*, *20*(1), 21–26. DOI: 10.1080/10242690701775533

Azam, M., Khan, F., Zaman, K., & Rasli, A. M. (2016). Military expenditures and unemployment nexus for selected South Asian countries. *Social Indicators Research*, *127*(3), 1103–1117. DOI: 10.1007/s11205-015-0993-7

Aziz, N., & Asadullah, M. N. (2017). Military Spending, Armed Conflict, and Economic Growth in Developing Countries in the Post-Cold War Era. *Journal of Economic Studies (Glasgow, Scotland)*, *44*(1), 47–68. DOI: 10.1108/JES-01-2015-0021

Aziz, N., & Khalid, U. (2019). Armed conflict, military expenses and FDI inflow to developing countries. *Defence and Peace Economics*, *30*(2), 238–251. DOI: 10.1080/10242694.2017.1388066

Backhouse, R. E., & Fontaine, P. (2010). Introduction: History of Economics as History of Social Science. In *History of Political Economy* (Vol. 42, pp. 1–21). Duke University Press., DOI: 10.1215/00182702-2009-070

Backhouse, R. E., & Fontaine, P. (2010). *The History of the Social Sciences since 1945*. Cambridge University Press. DOI: 10.1017/CBO9780511845260

Baiashvili, T., & Gattini, L. (2020). *Impact of FDI on economic growth: The role of country income levels and institutional strength*. Economics EIB Working Paper 2020/02, European Investment Bank. ISBN 978-92-861-4573-5

Ball, N. (1983). Military Expenditure, Economic Growth, and Socio-economic Development in the Third World. *Iberoamericana–Nordic Journal of Latin American and Caribbean Studies, 12*(1-2).

Ball, N. (1983). Military expenditure and socio-economic development. *International Social Science Journal, 35*(95), 411–429.

Bandala López, M. A. (2018). Reconceptualización de la Seguridad Nacional: Una aproximación para México. Instotuto de Investigaciones Estratégicas de la Armada de México. https://cesnav.uninav.edu.mx/cesnav/ININVESTAM/docs/docs_analisis/da_24-18.pdf

Bardhan, P. (2004). *Scarcity, conflicts, and cooperation: Essays in the political and institutional economics of development*. MIT Press. https://www.amazon.com/Scarcity-Conflicts-Cooperation-Institutional-Development/dp/0262524295

Barnes, J. G. (1993). New technologies, new markets, and changing marketing practice. *Irish Marketing Review, 6*, 45–52.

Barro, R. J. (1991). Economic Growth in a Cross-Section of Countnes. *The Quarterly Journal of Economics, 106*(2), 407–443. DOI: 10.2307/2937943

Barro, R. J. (2001). Human Capital and Growth. *The American Economic Review, 91*(2), 12–17. DOI: 10.1257/aer.91.2.12

Batchelor, P., Dunne, J. P., & Saal, D. S. (2000). Military spending and economic growth in South Africa. *Defence and Peace Economics, 11*(4), 553–571. DOI: 10.1080/10430710008404966

Becker,G.(2017).*EconomicTheory*(2nded.).Routledge.DOI:10.4324/9781351327688

Becker, G. S., Murphy, K. M., & Tamura, R. (1990). Human Capital. Fertility, and Economic Growth. *Journal of Political Economy, 98*(5, Part 2), 12–37. DOI: 10.1086/261723

Becker, J. (2021). Rusty Guns and Buttery Soldiers: Unemployment and the Domestic Origins of Defense Spending. *European Political Science Review, 13*(3), 307–330. DOI: 10.1017/S1755773921000102

Becker, J., & Dunne, J. P. (2023). Military spending composition and economic growth. *Defence and Peace Economics, 34*(3), 259–271. DOI: 10.1080/10242694.2021.2003530

Becker, R., Enders, W., & Lee, J. (2006). A stationarity test in the presence of an unknown number of smooth breaks. *Journal of Time Series Analysis, 27*(3), 381–409. DOI: 10.1111/j.1467-9892.2006.00478.x

Beckley, M., Gvosdev, N., Fiddler, C., Vaughn, S., Park, J., & Matsuda, T. (2025). *Strengthening US alliances in the Indo-Pacific*. Foreign Policy Research Institute. https://www.fpri.org/article/2025/03/strengthening-us-alliances-in-the-indo-pacific/

Begum, R. A., Raihan, A., & Said, M. N. M. (2020). Dynamic impacts of economic growth and forested area on carbon dioxide emissions in Malaysia. *Sustainability (Basel), 12*(22), 9375. DOI: 10.3390/su12229375

Behera, L. K. (2013). *Indian defence industry: Issues of self-reliance* (IDSA Monograph Series No. 21). Institute for Defence Studies and Analyses.

Behera, L. K., & Nayak, P. M. (2021). India's Defence Expenditure: A Trend Analysis. *Strategic Analysis, 45*(5), 395–410. DOI: 10.1080/09700161.2021.1965343

Benhabib, J., & Spegel, M. M. (1992). The Role of Human Capital and Political Instability in Economic Development, unpublished manuscript. New York University, May 1992.

Benoit, E. (1973). Defense and Economic Growth in Developing Countries. US: Boston: Health and Co., Lexington Books.

Benoit, E. (1973). *Defence and Economic Growth in Developing Countries*. Lexington Books.

Benoit, E. (1978). Growth and defence in LDCs. *Economic Development and Cultural Change, 26*, 271–280. DOI: 10.1086/451015

Berckman, L., Chavali, A., Hardin, K., Sloane, M., & Dronamraju, T. (2024). *2025 aerospace and defense industry outlook.* Deloitte Insights. https://www2.deloitte.com/us/en/insights/industry/aerospace-defense/aerospace-and-defense-industry-outlook.html

Berthelemy, J. C., Herrera, R., & Sen, S. (1995). Military expenditure and economic development: An endogenous growth perspective. *Economics of Planning, 28*(2), 205–233. DOI: 10.1007/BF01263638

Besley, T., & Persson, T. (2011). *Pillars of prosperity: The political economics of development clusters*. Princeton University Press., https://www.degruyter.com/document/doi/10.1515/9781400840526/html

Bhagwati, J. (2002). Coping with Antiglobalization: A Trilogy of Discontents. *Foreign Affairs*, *81*(1), 2–7. https://www.jstor.org/stable/20032998. DOI: 10.2307/20032998

Bhagwati, J. (2019). *The Promise of India: How Prime Ministers Nehru to Modi Shaped the Nation (1947–2019)*. Penguin Random House India Private Limited.

Bhattacharyya, R. (2018). Relationship Between Military Expenditure, Economic Growth, and Social Expenditure in India, China, and Bangladesh. In *Handbook of Research on Military Expenditure on Economic and Political Resources* (pp. 285–306). IGI Global.

Bils, M., & Klenow, P. (2000). Does schooling cause growth? *The American Economic Review*, *90*(5), 1160–1183. DOI: 10.1257/aer.90.5.1160

Bishop, M. (2003). What Is Computer Security? *IEEE Security and Privacy*, *1*(01), 67–69. DOI: 10.1109/MSECP.2003.1176998

Bisht, I. S. (2025). *Fincantieri, TKMS join forces to offer submarine to Philippine Navy*. The Defense Post. https://thedefensepost.com/2025/04/18/fincantieri-tkms-submarines-philippines/

Biswas, B., & Ram, R. (1986). Military expenditures and economic growth in less developed countries: An augmented model and further evidence". *Economic Development and Cultural Change*, *34*(2), 361–372. DOI: 10.1086/451533

Blanco, J., & Aznar, J. (2004). *Introducción a la Economía. Teoría y Práctica*. Editorial Mcgraw-Hill.

Bögenhold, D. (2021). Economics in the Social Science Spectrum: Evolution and Overlap with Different Academic Areas. *Atlantic Economic Journal*, *49*(4), 335–347. DOI: 10.1007/s11293-022-09739-4

Borlaug, N. (2007). Feeding a hungry world. *Science*, *318*(5849), 359. DOI: 10.1126/science.1151062 PMID: 17947551

Bran, A. C. (2023). Does Military Spending Spur Economic Growth? An Empirical Approach. *Proceedings of the International Conference on Business Excellence*, Vol. 17(1), pp. 178-187. DOI: 10.2478/picbe-2023-0020

Brands, H. (2018). Choosing Primacy: U.S. Strategy and Global Order at the Dawn of the Post-Cold War Era. *Texas National Security Review*, 1(2), 8-33. https://doi.org/DOI: 10.15781/T2VH5D166

Braunder, J. (2015). Military Spending and Democracy. *Defence and Peace Economics, 26*(4), 409–423. https://www.tandfonline.com/doi/full/10.1080/10242694.2014.960245. DOI: 10.1080/10242694.2014.960245

Brian. (2025). *Singapore strengthens cyber defence with new SAF commands.* CyberCover.sg. https://cybercover.sg/2025/singapore-strengthens-cyber-defence-with-new-saf-commands/

Brooks, S. G., Ikenberry, J. G., & Wohlforth, W. C. (2013). Don't come home, America: The case against retrenchment". *International Security, 37*(3), 7–51. DOI: 10.1162/ISEC_a_00107

Brooks, S. G., & Wohlforth, W. C. (2008). *World out of Balance: International Relations and the Challenge of American Primacy*. Princeton University Press.

Brzezinski, Z. (1997). *The Grand Chessboard: American Primacy and Its Geostrategic Imperatives*. Basic Books.

Buchholz, K. (2024). The Indian Budget 2024/25. *Statista.* https://www.statista.com/chart/26764/indian-national-budget/

Budhathoki, P. B., Dahal, A. K., & Bhattarai, G. (2024). Does the military expenditure hurt the economic growth? *Journal of Business and Management Review, 5*(3), 189–204.

Bueger, C. (2015). What is maritime security? *Marine Policy, 53*, 159–164. DOI: 10.1016/j.marpol.2014.12.005

Cappelen, Å., Gleditsch, N. P., & Bjerkholt, O. (1984). Military spending and economic growth in the OECD countries". *Journal of Peace Research, 21*(4), 361–373. DOI: 10.1177/002234338402100404

Carment, D., Prest, S., & Samy, Y. (2009). *Security, development and the fragile state: Bridging the gap between theory and policy*. Routledge. https://www.taylorfrancis.com/books/mono/10.4324/9780203873977/security-development-fragile-state-david-carment-stewart-prest-yiagadeesen-samy

Case, K., Fair, R. C., & Oster, S. E. (2019). *Principles of Microeconomics* (Global Edition 13th). Pearson.

Cavatorta, E., & Smith, R. P. (2017). Factor Models in Panels with Cross-sectional Dependence: An Application to the Extended SIPRI Military Expenditure Data. *Defence and Peace Economics, 28*(4), 437–456. DOI: 10.1080/10242694.2016.1261428

Cevik, S., & Ricco, J. (2018). No buck for the bang: Revisiting the military-growth nexus. *Empirica, 45*(4), 639–653. DOI: 10.1007/s10663-017-9380-8

Chakraborty, S. (2018). The Impact of Military Spending on Economic Development: A Study of the Indian Economy. In *Handbook of Research on Military Expenditure on Economic and Political Resources* (pp. 182–191). IGI Global. DOI: 10.4018/978-1-5225-4778-5.ch010

Chandra, A. (2010). Does Government Expenditure on Education Promote Economic Growth? An Econometric Analysis. *Munich Personal RePEc Archive*, (25480), 1–12.

Chandy, L. (2023). *Economic Development in an Era of Climate Change*. Carnegie Endowment for International Peace.

Chang, H.-C., Huang, B.-N., & Yang, C. W. (2011). Military expenditure and economic growth across different groups: A dynamic panel Granger-causality approach. *Economic Modelling, 28*(6), 2416–2423. DOI: 10.1016/j.cconmod.2011.06.001

Chan, S., & Mintz, A. (Eds.). (1992). *Defense, welfare and growth: Perspectives and evidence*. Routledge. DOI: 10.4324/9780203203590

Chemnad, K., Alshakhsi, S., Almourad, M. B., Altuwairiqi, M., Phalp, K., & Ali, R. (2022). Smartphone Usage before and during COVID-19: A Comparative Study Based on Objective Recording of Usage Data. Informatics, 9. *Informatics (MDPI), 98*(4), 98. DOI: 10.3390/informatics9040098

Cheng, I. (2025). Mindef signs contract to acquire two more Invincible-class submarines. *The Straits Times*. https://www.straitstimes.com/singapore/mindef-signs-contract-to-acquire-two-more-invincible-class-submarines

Cheng, M., Chung, L., Tam, C., Yuen, R., Chan, S., & Yu, I. (2012). "*Tracking the Hong Kong Economy*". Occasional Paper, 3, 1-30.

Chen, P. F., Lee, C. C., & Chiu, Y. B. (2014). The nexus between defence expenditure and economic growth: New global evidence. *Economic Modelling, 36*, 474–483. DOI: 10.1016/j.econmod.2013.10.019

Cheung, Y.-W., & Chinn, M. (1997). Further investigation of the uncertain unit root in GNP. *Journal of Business & Economic Statistics, 15*(1), 68–73. DOI: 10.1080/07350015.1997.10524688

Chew, X., Alharbi, R., Khaw, K. W., & Alnoor, A. (2023). How information technology influences organizational communication: the mediating role of organizational structure. *PSU Research Review*, DOI: 10.1108/PRR-08-2021-0041

Chimits, Ch. (2024). *European Economic Security: Current practices and further development.* European Parliament Coordinator: Policy Department for External Relations. Directorate General for External Policies of the Union. PE 754.449-April 2024. Recuperado de https://www.europarl.europa.eu/RegData/etudes/IDAN/2024/754449/EXPO_IDA(2024)754449_EN.pdf

ChinaPower Project. (2025). *How much does China spend on its military?* Center for Strategic and International Studies. https://chinapower.csis.org/military-spending

Chinese Academy of Cyberspace Studies. (2023). World Information Technology Development. In *World Internet Development Report 2021.* Springer., DOI: 10.1007/978-981-19-9323-7_3

Chitadze, N. (2011). *Geopolitics.* Universal.

Chitadze, N. (2024). *World Politics.* International Black Sea University.

Chitechi, K. V., & Otanga, D. A. (2020). Current Trends in Information Technology: Which Way for Modern It Experts. *International Journal of Computer Trends and Technology, 68*(7), 31–36. DOI: 10.14445/22312803/IJCTT-V68I7P105

Choi, Y., Kim, H., & Lee, Y. (2022). Economic Consequences of the COVID-19 Pandemic: Will It Be a Barrier to Achieving Sustainability? *Sustainability (Basel), 14*(3), 1629. Advance online publication. DOI: 10.3390/su14031629

Chowdhury, A. R. (1991). A causal analysis of defense spending and economic growth. *The Journal of Conflict Resolution, 35*(1), 80–97. DOI: 10.1177/0022002791035001005

Christopoulos, D., & León-Ledesma, M. (2010). Smooth breaks and non-linear mean reversion: Post-Bretton Woods real exchange rates. *Journal of International Money and Finance, 29*(6), 1076–1093. DOI: 10.1016/j.jimonfin.2010.02.003

Chugh, S. K. (2017). *Modern Macroeconomics* (MIT Press). USA: The MIT Press.

Churchill, S. A., & Yew, S. L. (2018). The effect of military expenditure on growth: An empirical synthesis. *Empirical Economics, 55*(3), 1357–1387. DOI: 10.1007/s00181-017-1300-z

Clarke, M., Henschke, A., Legrand, T., & Sussex, M. (2022). National Security: Theories, Actors, Issues. In Clarke, M., Henschke, A., Sussex, M., & Legrand, T. (Eds.), *The Palgrave Handbook of National Security.* Palgrave Macmillan., DOI: 10.1007/978-3-030-53494-3_1

CNBC. (2025). *Global military spending hits $2.46 trillion in 2024: IISS Report.* CNBC. https://www.cnbctv18.com/world/global-military-spending-hits-2-46-trillion-dollars-in-2024-us-india-russia-ukraine-defence-budget-19571050.htm

Cohen, D. (2006). *Globalization and its enemies.* MIT press. DOI: 10.7551/mitpress/3311.001.0001

Cohn, T. H., & Hira, A. (2020). *Global political economy: Theory and practice.* Routledge. DOI: 10.4324/9781003056881

Cole, B. D. (2024). *The evolution of China's naval strategy.* The National Bureau of Asian Research – Strategic Space. https://strategicspace.nbr.org/the-evolution-of-chinas-naval-strategy/

Collier, P., & Hoeffler, A. (2002). *Military Expenditure — Threats, Aid, and Arms Races.* Policy Research Working Paper Series 2927. The World Bank.

Collier, P. (2006). War and military spending in developing countries and their consequences for development. *The Economics of Peace & Security Journal, 1*(1), 10–13. DOI: 10.15355/epsj.1.1.10

Colombatto, E. (2006). On economic growth and development. *The Review of Austrian Economics, 19*(4), 243–260. DOI: 10.1007/s11138-006-9247-x

COMECSO. (2025). Sitio web del Consejo Mexicano de Ciencias Sociales. https://www.comecso.com/

Constantinescu, M. (2023). Measuring economic resilience for the CEE and Black Sea countries in the framework of comprehensive defence. *Security and Defence Quarterly, 44*(4), 55–83.

Cooper, J. (1998). The Military Expenditure of the USSR and the Russian Federation, 1987–97. *SIPRI Yearbook, 1999*, 243–259.

Cooper, J. (2022). *Implementation of the Russian Federal Budget During January-July 2022 and Spending on the Military.* SIPRI Background Paper. DOI: 10.55163/STMI3484

Cowan, R., & Foray, D. (1995). Quandaries in the economics of dual technologies and spillovers from military to civilian research and development. *Research Policy, 24*(6), 851–868. DOI: 10.1016/0048-7333(94)00802-7

Croxton, D. (1999). The Peace of Westphalia of 1648 and the Origins of Sovereignty. *The International History Review, 21*(3), 569–591. https://www.jstor.org/stable/40109077. DOI: 10.1080/07075332.1999.9640869

Cybersecurity & Infrastructure Security Agency. (2021). *Cyber Essentials Starter Kit*. Recuperado de https://www.cisa.gov/sites/default/files/publications/Cyber%2520Essentials%2520Starter%2520Kit_03.12.2021_508_0.pdf

Cybersecurity & Infrastructure Security Agency. (2024). https://www.cisa.gov/

Cypher, J. M. (2007). From military Keynesianism to global-neoliberal militarism. *Monthly Review (New York, N.Y.), 59*(2), 37–50. https://search.proquest.com/openview/d68c9a0da01fd2c21277facab55146dd/1.pdf?pq-origsite=gscholar&cbl=48155. DOI: 10.14452/MR-059-02-2007-06_4

d'Agostini, G., Dunne, J. P., & Pieroni, L. (2012). Corruption, military spending and growth". *Defence and Peace Economics*, *23*(2), 591–604. DOI: 10.1080/10242694.2012.663579

d'Agostino, G., Dunne, J. P., & Pieroni, L. (2016). Government spending, corruption and economic growth". *World Development*, *84*, 190–205. DOI: 10.1016/j.worlddev.2016.03.011

d'Agostino, G., Dunne, J. P., & Pieroni, L. (2018). Military Expenditure, Endogeneity and Economic Growth. *Defence and Peace Economics*, *30*(5), 509–524. DOI: 10.1080/10242694.2017.1422314

Dakurah, A. H., Davies, S. P., & Sampath, R. K. (2001). Defense spending and economic growth in developing countries: A causality analysis". *Journal of Policy Modeling*, *23*(6), 651–658. DOI: 10.1016/S0161-8938(01)00079-5

Danaher, J., & Sætra, H. S. (2022). Technology and moral change: The transformation of truth and trust. *Ethics and Information Technology, 24*. *Ethics and Information Technology*, *35*(3), 35. DOI: 10.1007/s10676-022-09661-y

Dang, C. N., Le-Hoai, L., & Kim, S. (2018). Impact of knowledge-enabling factors on organizational effectiveness in construction companies. *Journal of Knowledge Management*, *22*(4), 759–780. DOI: 10.1108/JKM-08-2016-0350

Dangwal, A. (2024). Cash-strapped Indonesia OKs third & final batch of Rafale fighters after struggling to buy Mirage-2000s. *EurAsian Times*. https://www.eurasiantimes.com/cash-strapped-indonesia-oks-third-final-batch-of-rafale-fighters/

Das, K. (2019). Terrorism, Military Expenditure, and Foreign Capital Inflow: An Empirical Study for India. In *The Impact of Global Terrorism on Economic and Political Development* (pp. 279–291). Emerald Publishing.

Datta, K. (2019). Military expenditure and economic growth relationship revisited in some South Asian countries: with special reference to India. In *National Security: Breakthroughs in Research and Practice* (pp. 810–835). IGI Global. DOI: 10.4018/978-1-5225-7912-0.ch041

de la Barquera, S., & Arroyo, H. (Eds.). (2024). *Diccionario de seguridad y de defensa nacional: 100 claves y conceptos para su análisis y estudio*. Universidad Nacional Autónoma de México, Instituto de Investigaciones Jurídicas.

Defence Security Asia. (2025). Regional skies on fire: Rafale, F-35B, Gripen E/F and F-15EX to ignite Southeast Asia's arms race. *Defence Security Asia*. https://defencesecurityasia.com/en/regional-skies-on-fire-rafale-f-35b-gripen-e-f-and-f-15ex-to-ignite-southeast-asias-arms-race/

Deger, S. (1986). Economic development and defense expenditure". *Economic Development and Cultural Change*, *35*(1), 179–196. DOI: 10.1086/451577

Deger, S., & Sen, S. (1983). Military expenditure, spin-off and economic development. *Journal of Development Economics*, *13*(1-2), 67–83. DOI: 10.1016/0304-3878(83)90050-0

Deger, S., & Sen, S. (1995). Military expenditure and developing countries. In Hartley, K., & Sandler, T. (Eds.), *Handbook of Defence Economics* (Vol. 1, pp. 275–307). Elsevier.

Deger, S., & Sen, S. (1995). Military expenditure and developing countries. In Hartley, K., & Sandler, T. (Eds.), *Handbook of defense economics* (Vol. 1, pp. 275–307). Elsevier., https://www.sciencedirect.com/science/article/pii/S1574001305800134 DOI: 10.1016/S1574-0013(05)80013-4

Deger, S., & Smith, R. (1983). Military expenditure and growth in less developed countries. *The Journal of Conflict Resolution*, *27*(2), 335–353. DOI: 10.1177/0022002783027002006

Deger, S., & Smith, R. (1985). Military expenditure and development: The economic linkages. *IDS Bulletin*, *16*(4), 49–54. DOI: 10.1111/j.1759-5436.1985.mp16004010.x

DeGrasse, R. W. (2016). *Military expansion, economic decline: The impact of military spending on US economic performance*. Routledge. DOI: 10.4324/9781315495897

Desli, E., & Gkoulgkoutsika, A. (2021). Military spending and economic growth: A panel data investigation". *Economic Change and Restructuring*, *54*(3), 781–806. DOI: 10.1007/s10644-020-09267-8

Desli, E., Gkoulgkoutsika, A., & Katrakilidis, C. (2017). Investigating the dynamic interaction between military spending and economic growth. *Review of Development Economics, 21*(3), 511–526. DOI: 10.1111/rode.12268

Dewangan, P. (2020). A Review Paper on Network Security and Cryptography. *International Journal of Scientific Research, 9*(1), 524–527. https://www.ijsr.net/getabstract.php?paperid=ART20204060

Dewan, M.-A.-M. (2012). Public Expenditure on Education and Economic Growth: The Case of Bangladesh. *IJAR-BAE, 1*(4), 10–18.

Dhanya, D. (2025). *Indonesia set to acquire F-15EX fighter jets: Here's what you need to know*. Tempo.co. https://en.tempo.co/read/1998518/indonesia-set-to-acquire-f-15ex-fighter-jets-heres-what-you-need-to-know

Dogan, N. (2016). Agriculture and environmental Kuznets curves in the case of Turkey: Evidence from the ARDL and bounds test. *Zemedelská Ekonomika, 62*(12), 566–574. DOI: 10.17221/112/2015-AGRICECON

Domegan, C. T. (1996). The adoption of information technology in customer service. *European Journal of Marketing, 30*(6), 52–69. DOI: 10.1108/03090569610121674

Dorn, F., Potrafke, N., & Schlepper, M. (2024). European Defence Spending in 2024 and Beyond: How to Provide Security in an Economically Challenging Environment. EconPol POLICY REPORT. *CESifo Research Network*, 35 p.

Doron, S. (2022). *The History of Computing: A Very Short Introduction, Very Short Introductions*. Oxford Academic Books., DOI: 10.1093/actrade/9780198831754.001.0001

Doval, A. (2022). Tackling adversaries through strong and effective national security policies. In BlueKraft Digital Foundation (Ed.), *Modi@20: Dreams meet delivery* (pp. [insert page numbers]). Rupa Publications.

Dragoi, D. (2020). Economic growth versus economic development. *Atlantic Review of Economics (ARoEc)*, 4(1), 1-11. https://hdl.handle.net/10419/282275

Drăgoi, D. (2020). Economic Growth versus Economic Development. *Atlantic Review of Economics*, 4(1), 1-11. https://www.econstor.eu/bitstream/10419/282275/1/100.pdf

Drezner, D. W. (2013). Military primacy doesn't pay (nearly as much as you think)". *International Security, 38*(1), 52–79. DOI: 10.1162/ISEC_a_00124

Dritsakis, N. (2004). Defense spending and economic growth: An empirical investigation for Greece and Turkey". *Journal of Policy Modeling*, *26*(2), 249–264. DOI: 10.1016/j.jpolmod.2004.03.011

Duman, N. (2024). *Understanding China's pursuit of power in the South China Sea* (Doctoral dissertation, San Francisco State University). https://scholarworks.calstate.edu/downloads/nc580w80b

Dunne, P., & Coulomb, F. (2008). Peace, War and International Security: Economic Theories. In *Contributions to Conflict Management, Peace Economics and Development*, 6, 13-36. Bingley: Emerald (MCB UP). DOI: 10.1016/S1572-8323(08)06002-5

Dunne, J. P. (2013). Military Keynesianism: An assessment. In Jain, L. C. (Ed.), *Cooperation for a Peaceful and Sustainable World: Part 2* (pp. 117–129). Emerald Group Publishing Limited., DOI: 10.1108/S1572-8323(2013)00020.2011

Dunne, J. P., & Mohammed, N. A. (1995). Military spending in sub-saharan africa: Some evidence for 1967-85. *Journal of Peace Research*, *32*(3), 331–343. DOI: 10.1177/0022343395032003006

Dunne, J. P., & Nikolaidou, E. (2012). Defence spending and economic growth in the EU15". *Defence and Peace Economics*, *23*(6), 537–548. DOI: 10.1080/10242694.2012.663575

Dunne, J. P., & Smith, R. P. (2020). Military expenditure, investment and growth". *Defence and Peace Economics*, *31*(6), 601–614. DOI: 10.1080/10242694.2019.1636182

Dunne, J. P., Smith, R. P., & Willenbockel, D. (2005). Models of Military Expenditure and Growth: A Critical Review. *Defence and Peace Economics*, *16*(6), 449–461. DOI: 10.1080/10242690500167791

Dunne, J. P., & Tian, N. (2015). Military expenditure, economic growth and heterogeneity". *Defence and Peace Economics*, *26*(1), 15–31. DOI: 10.1080/10242694.2013.848575

Dunne, J. P., & Tian, N. (2016). Military expenditure and economic growth, 1960–2014. *The Economics of Peace and Security Journal*, *11*(2), 50–56. DOI: 10.15355/epsj.11.2.50

Dunne, J., & Tian, N. (2020). *Military Expenditures and Economic Growth*. Oxford Research Encyclopedia of Politics., DOI: 10.1093/acrefore/9780190228637.013.1929

Dunne, J., & Uye, M. (2010). Military Spending and Development. In Tan, A. (Ed.), *The Global Arms Trade: A Handbook* (pp. 293–305). Routledge.

Dunne, P., & Nikolaidou, E. (2001). Military expenditure and economic growth: A demand and supply model for Greece, 1960-96. *Defence and Peace Economics, 12*(1), 47–67. DOI: 10.1080/10430710108404976

Dunne, P., Nikolaidou, E., & Vougas, D. (2001). Defence spending and economic growth: A causal analysis for Greece and Turkey. *Defence and Peace Economics, 12*(1), 5–26. DOI: 10.1080/10430710108404974

Dunne, P., & Tian, N. (2013). Military expenditure and economic growth: A survey. *The Economics of Peace and Security Journal, 8*(1), 5–11. DOI: 10.15355/epsj.8.1.5

Easterlin, R. A. (2013). Happiness and Economic Growth: The Evidence. *Discussion Paper Series (University of Southern California)*, IZA DP No. 7187. Recuperado de https://docs.iza.org/dp7187.pdf

Edwards, S. (2022). Trade orientation, distortions, and growth in developing countries. *Journal of Development Economics, 39*(1), 31–57. DOI: 10.1016/0304-3878(92)90056-F

Eldessouki, A., & Al Midfa, N. (2024, Sep 16). Malaysia's strategic hedging toward China and the United States. *TRENDS Research & Advisory*. https://trendsresearch.org/insight/malaysias-strategic-hedging-toward-china-and-the-united-states/

Elizabeth Abraham, S. (2012). Information technology, an enabler in corporate governance. *Corporate Governance (Bradford), 12*(3), 281–291. DOI: 10.1108/14720701211234555

Elliott, G., Rothenberg, T. J., & Stock, J. H. (2012). *Efficient tests for an autoregressive unit root (No. t0130)*. National Bureau of Economic Research.

Elveren, A. Y. (2025). *Heterodox economics of military spending*. Taylor & Francis. https://books.google.com/books?hl=en&lr=&id=FU1NEQAAQBAJ&oi=fnd&pg=PP1

Emojorho, D., & Adomi, A. (2006). An assessment of the use of information technology facilities for academic pursuit. *The Electronic Library, 24*(5), 706–713. DOI: 10.1108/02640470610707295

Energy Institute. KPMG, & Kearney. (2024). *Statistical Review of World Energy 2024 (73rd ed.)*. Energy Institute. https://assets.kpmg.com/content/dam/kpmg/az/pdf/2024/Statistical-Review-of-World-Energy.pdf

Engle, R. F., & Granger, C. W. (2017). Co-integration and error correction: Representation, estimation, and testing. *Econome J Econom Soc, 55*(2), 251–276.

Erickson, A. S. (2024). Essence of distinction: The ends, ways, and means of China's military maritime quest. *Frontiers in Political Science*, *6*, 1448241. https://www.frontiersin.org/journals/political-science/articles/10.3389/fpos.2024.1448241/full. DOI: 10.3389/fpos.2024.1448241

Escudé, G. J. (2021). Karl Marx's Theory of Capitalism Exposition, Critique, and Appraisal. *MPRA*, Paper No. 113685, 1-590. https://mpra.ub.uni-muenchen.de/113685

European Parliament. (2025). *Defence: How the EU is boosting its security*. European Parliament. https://www.europarl.europa.eu/topics/en/article/20190612STO54310/defence-how-the-eu-is-boosting-its-security

Ezeja, I. I. (2024). Globalization and National Security: Unraveling the Multifaceted Nexus. *IDOSR Journal of Arts and Management,* 9(1), 18-24. https://www.idosr.org/globalization-and-national-security-unraveling-the-multifaceted-nexus/

Faini, R., Annez, P., & Taylor, L. (1984). Defense spending, economic structure, and growth: Evidence among countries and over time". *Economic Development and Cultural Change*, *32*(3), 487–498. DOI: 10.1086/451402

Falkanek, C. (2024). Who's at 2% Percent? Look How NATO Allies Have Increased Their Defense Spending Since Russia's Invasion of Ukraine. *Atlantic Council*. https://www.atlanticcouncil.org/blogs/econographics/whos-at-2-percent-look-how-nato-allies-have-increased-their-defense-spending-since-russias-invasion-of-ukraine/

FAO. (2017). *Food and Agriculture Organization of the United Nations. The future of food and agriculture, trends and challenges*. FAO, FAO.

Farrar, D. E., & Glauber, R. R. (2017). Multicollinearity in regression analysis: The problem revisited. *The Review of Economics and Statistics*, *49*(1), 92–107. DOI: 10.2307/1937887

Farrell, H., & Newman, A. L. (2019). Weaponized interdependence: How global economic networks shape state coercion. *International Security*, *44*(1), 42–79. DOI: 10.1162/isec_a_00351

Fatehi-Sedeh, K., & Safizadeh, M. H. (1989). The association between political instability and flow of foreign direct investment. *Management International Review*, 4–13.

Førrisdahl, M. B. (2024). *Cooperation and struggle: A comparative analysis of Vietnam and the Philippines in the South China Sea disputes* (Master's thesis, Norwegian University of Science and Technology). https://ntnuopen.ntnu.no/ntnu-xmlui/handle/11250/3141959

Fourcade, M., Etienne, O., & Yann, A. (2015). The Superiority of Economists. *The Journal of Economic Perspectives*, *29*(1), 89–114. DOI: 10.1257/jep.29.1.89

Frederiksen, P. C., & Looney, R. E. (1983). Defense expenditures and economic growth in development countries: Some further empirical evidence". *Armed Forces and Society*, *9*(4), 633–645. DOI: 10.1177/0095327X8300900406

Friedman, T. L. (2005). *The World is a Flat: A Brief History of the Globalized World in the Twenty First Century*. Allen Lane.

Furuya, K. (2023). The Japan Coast Guard's role in realizing a Free and Open Indo-Pacific. *Pacific Forum*. https://pacforum.org/publications/pacnet-4-the-japan-coast-guards-role-in-realizing-a-free-and-open-indo-pacific/

Gadbade, Gunwant Bapu, Kokate, Chandrakant Namdevrao (2021). View of Public Expenditure on Education An Interstate Analysis of India. *Palarch's Journal of Archaeology of Egypt/Egyptology* 18(4). ISSN 1567-214x

Galvin, H. (2003). The impact of defence spending on the economic growth of developing countries: A cross-section study. *Defence and Peace Economics*, *14*(1), 51–59. DOI: 10.1080/10242690302932

Gannon, J. A. (2021). *Use Their Force: Interstate Security Alignments and the Distribution of Military Capabilities*. University of California.

García-Avilés, J. A. (2020). Diffusion of Innovation. In Bulck, J. (Ed.), *The International Encyclopedia of Media Psychology*. John Wiley & Sons, Inc., DOI: 10.1002/9781119011071.iemp0137

Gavilanes, R., & Michael, J. (2020). Military Expenditure and Economic Growth: The South American Case. *MPRA*, Artículo No. 98508. https://mpra.ub.uni-muenchen.de/98508/

Gilpin, R. (1988). The theory of hegemonic war. *The Journal of Interdisciplinary History*, *18*(4), 591–613. https://www.jstor.org/stable/204816. DOI: 10.2307/204816

Giraldo Martinez, G. A., Flórez Zuluaga, J. A., Morante Granobles, D. F., & Escobar Soto, J. F. (2023). Efectos económicos de la inversión en investigación y desarrollo en defensa y su impacto en la productividad en países desarrollados. *Revista Facultad de Ciencias Económicas*, *31*(1), 13–29. DOI: 10.18359/rfce.6223

GlobalData. (2025, May 25). South Korea spent $222 billion on defence from 2021–2025. Asia Pacific Defence Reporter. https://asiapacificdefencereporter.com/south-korea-spent-222-billion-on-defence-from-2021-2025/

Glynn, J., Perera, N., & Verma, R. (2007). Unit root tests and structural breaks: A survey with applications. *Journal of Quantitative Methods for Economics and Business Administration*, *3*(1), 63–79.

Godard, G. (2024). *South Korea as the New International Defence Industrial Powerhouse: Implications for Europe(Briefing Paper No. 2/2024).* European Institute for Asian Studies. https://eias.org/wp-content/uploads/2024/07/South-Korea-as-the-New-International-Defence-Industrial-Powerhouse-Implications-For-Europe.pdf

Gonzales, J. T. (2023). Implications of AI innovation on economic growth: A panel data study. *Journal of Economic Structures*, *12*(1), 13. DOI: 10.1186/s40008-023-00307-w

Gonzalo, J., & Lee, T. H. (2018). Pitfalls in testing for long run relationships. *Journal of Econometrics*, *86*(1), 129–154. DOI: 10.1016/S0304-4076(97)00111-5

Green, D. J. (2016). *The third option for the South China Sea: The political economy of regional conflict and cooperation.* Springer. https://books.google.com/books?hl=en&lr=&id=tMs6DQAAQBAJ&oi=fnd&pg=PR5

Green, D. R., & Anderson, J. H. (2024). *Confronting China: US defense policy in an era of great power competition.* Bloomsbury Publishing. https://www.torrossa.com/it/resources/an/5868699

Grossman, G., & Krueger, A. B. (1991) Environmental impacts of a North American free trade agreement. National Bureau of Economic Research 1991. working paper 3914, NBER: Cambridge, MA, USA.

GSDN. (2025). *Increased U.S. military presence in the Indo-Pacific: Global implications.* Global Strategic & Defense News. https://gsdn.live/increased-u-s-military-presence-in-the-indo-pacific-global-implications/

Guild, J. (2024). *Indonesia's Scorpene submarine deal with France, explained.* The Diplomat. https://thediplomat.com/2024/04/indonesias-scorpene-submarine-deal-with-france-explained/

Guo, Z., Jiang, Y., & Yu, H. (2013). Defence expenditure, budget deficits, and income distribution in India (1970–2009). In *Cooperation for a Peaceful and Sustainable World Part 2* (pp. 25–37). Emerald Group Publishing Limited. DOI: 10.1108/S1572-8323(2013)00020.2006

Gupta, D., & Sriram, K. (2018). Impact of security expenditures in military alliances on violence from non-state actors: Evidence from India. *World Development*, *107*, 338–357. DOI: 10.1016/j.worlddev.2018.03.004

Gupta, S., De Mello, L., & Sharan, R. (2001). Corruption and military spending. *European Journal of Political Economy, 17*(4), 749–777. DOI: 10.1016/S0176-2680(01)00054-4

Güriş, B. (2019). A new nonlinear unit root test with Fourier function. *Communications in Statistics. Simulation and Computation, 48*(10), 3056–3062. DOI: 10.1080/03610918.2018.1473591

Gürler, M., & Özsoy, Ö. (2019). Exploring the relationship between life expectancy at birth and economic growth in 56 developing countries. *Journal of Global Health Reports, 3*, e2019001. DOI: 10.29392/joghr.3.e2019001

Ha, D. T., & Tien, T. N. (2024). Vietnam - India oil and gas cooperation: From "Strategic Partnership" to "Comprehensive Strategic Partnership". *International Journal of Religion, 5*(7), 212–225. DOI: 10.61707/mk4k8805

Haider, A., Jabeen, S., Rankaduwa, W., & Shaheen, F. (2023). The Nexus between Employment and Economic Growth: A Cross-Country Analysis. *Sustainability (Basel), 15*(15), 11955. DOI: 10.3390/su151511955

Haldar, S. K., & Girijasankar, M. (2010). Does human capital cause economic growth? A case study of India. *International Journal of Economic Sciences and Applied Research, 3*(1), 7–25.

Haleem, A., Javaid, M., Qadri, M. A., & Suman, R. (2022). Understanding the role of digital technologies in education: A review. *Sustainable Operations and Computers, 3*, 275–285. DOI: 10.1016/j.susoc.2022.05.004

Halicioglu, F. (2003). *"An econometrical analysis of effects of aggregate defence spending on aggregate output"*. METU International Conference in Economics/ VII, Turkey, September.

Halicioglu, F. (2004). Defense spending and economic growth in Turkey: An empirical application of new macroeconomics theory". *Review of Middle East Economics and Finance, 2*(3), 34–43. DOI: 10.2202/1475-3693.1028

Hansen, B., & Phillips, P. C. B. (2010). Estimation and inference in models of cointegration: A simulation study. *Advances in Econometrics, 8*, 225–24.

Hanushek, E. A., & Wößmann, L. (2010). Education and Economic Growth. In Peterson, P., Baker, E., & McGaw, B. (Eds.), *International Encyclopedia of Education* (Vol. 2, pp. 245–252). Elsevier. DOI: 10.1016/B978-0-08-044894-7.01227-6

Harris, B., Regan, T., Schueler, J., & Fields, S. A. (2020). Problematic Mobile Phone and Smartphone Use Scales: A Systematic Review. *Frontiers in Psychology, 11*, 672. DOI: 10.3389/fpsyg.2020.00672 PMID: 32431636

Hartley, K., & Sandler, T. (Eds.). (1990). *The economics of defence spending: An international survey*. Routledge.

Harvey, R. (2024). *Fossil fuel use, emissions hit records in 2023, report says*. Reuters. https://www.reuters.com/business/environment/fossil-fuel-use-emissions-hit-records-2023-report-says-2024-06-19/

Harvey, D. (2017). The 'new' imperialism: Accumulation by dispossession. In Resnick, S., & Wolff, R. (Eds.), *Karl Marx* (pp. 213–237). Routledge., DOI: 10.4324/9781315251196-10

Harvey, D., & Mills, T. (2002). Unit roots and double smooth transitions. *Journal of Applied Statistics, 29*(5), 675–683. DOI: 10.1080/02664760120098739

Hassan, M. K., Waheeduzzaman, M., & Rahman, A. (2003). Defense Expenditure and Economic Growth in the SAARC Countries. *The Journal of Political. Social and Economic Studies, 28*(3), 275–293. https://jspes.org/fall2003_hassan.html

Hauenstein, M., Smith, M., & Souva, M. (2021). Democracy, External Threat and Military Spending. *Research & Politics, 8*(4), 1–13. DOI: 10.1177/20531680211049660

Heo, U. (1998). Modeling the defense-growth relationship around the globe. *The Journal of Conflict Resolution, 42*(5), 637–657. DOI: 10.1177/0022002798042005006

Heo, U. (2000). The defense-growth nexus in the United States revisited. *American Politics Quarterly, 28*(1), 110–127. DOI: 10.1177/1532673X00028001007

Heo, U. (2010). The Relationship Between Defence Spending and Economic Growth in the United States. *Political Research Quarterly, 63*(4), 760–770. DOI: 10.1177/1065912909334427

Heo, U., & Ye, M. (2016). Defense spending and economic growth around the globe: The direct and indirect link. *International Interactions, 42*(5), 774–796. DOI: 10.1080/03050629.2016.1149067

He, W., Zhang, Z. J., & Li, W. (2021). Information technology solutions, challenges, and suggestions for tackling the COVID-19 pandemic. *International Journal of Information Management, 57*, 102287. DOI: 10.1016/j.ijinfomgt.2020.102287 PMID: 33318721

Hirshleifer, J. (1987). *Economic behaviour in adversity*. University of Chicago Press.

Hitzler, P. (2021). A review of the semantic web field. *Communications of the ACM*, *64*(2), 76–83. https://cacm.acm.org/magazines/2021/2/250085-a-review-of-the-semantic-web-field/abstract. DOI: 10.1145/3397512

Hobbes, T. (1651). *Leviathan: Or the matter, forme, & power of a common-wealth ecclesiastical and civil.* Project Gutenberg. https://www.gutenberg.org/files/3207/3207-h/3207-h.htm

Holmes, K. R. (2015). What Is National Security? The Heritage Foundation. Index of U.S. Military Strength, 17-26. https://www.heritage.org/sites/default/files/2019-10/2015_IndexOfUSMilitaryStrength_What%20Is%20National%20Security.pdf

Honrada, G. J., Ranjbar, D., & Mukan, S. (2023). Regional democratization: A comparative analysis of EU and US efforts in Central Asia and Southeast Asia. *Journal of International Students*, *19*(2), 277–306. https://e-journal.uum.edu.my/index.php/jis/article/view/16476

Hoong, L. W. (2024). Malaysia will strengthen territorial defence while keeping diplomatic channels open in South China Sea. *The Straits Times*. https://www.straitstimes.com/asia/se-asia/malaysia-will-strengthen-territorial-defence-while-keeping-diplomatic-channels-open

Horodecka, A. (2024). Is Economic Development Really Becoming Sustainable? *Forum for Social Economics*. https://www.tandfonline.com/doi/full/10.1080/07360932.2024.2401436

Hossain, M. S. (2025). Surging arms stockpile in Southeast Asia: Preparation for war? Modern Diplomacy. https://moderndiplomacy.eu/2025/02/22/surging-arms-stockpile-in-southeast-asia-preparation-for-war/

Hou, N. (2010). *Arms race, military expenditure and economic growth in India* (Doctoral dissertation, University of Birmingham).

Htwe, T. M. (2025). China's strategic influence and rivalries in Southeast Asia: BRIC and China's geopolitical strategy. In Sabir, A. R., & Fatima, A. M. (Eds.), *Changing the global political economy: BRICS countries and alternative relations strategies* (pp. 119–146). IGI Global., https://www.igi-global.com/chapter/chinas-strategic-influence-and-rivalries-in-southeast-asia/365241

Ibn-Mohammed, T., Mustapha, K. B., Godsell, J., Adamu, Z., Babatunde, K. A., Akintade, D. D., Acquaye, A., Fujii, H., Ndiaye, M. M., Yamoah, F. A., & Koh, S. C. L. (2021). A critical analysis of the impacts of COVID-19 on the global economy and ecosystems and opportunities for circular economy strategies. *Resources, Conservation and Recycling*, *164*, 105169. DOI: 10.1016/j.resconrec.2020.105169 PMID: 32982059

Ikenberry, G. J. (2011). *Liberal Leviathan: The Origins, Crisis, and Transformation of the American World Order*. Princeton University Press. DOI: 10.2307/j.ctt7rjt2

IMF. (2025). Inflation Rate, Average Consumer Prices: Annual Percent Change. https://www.imf.org/external/datamapper/PCPIPCH@WEO/OEMDC/ADVEC/WEOWORLD

India Today. (2025, Mar 25). *Despite US forces being stretched thin, South China Sea activity grows: Report.* India Today. https://www.indiatoday.in/world/story/despite-us-forces-being-stretched-thin-south-china-sea-activity-grows-report-glbs-2698939-2025-03-25

International Crisis Group. (2024). *Asia in flux and US-China military competition.* Crisi Group. https://www.crisisgroup.org/asia/north-east-asia/china-united-states/asia-flux-and-us-china-military-competition

International Institute for Strategic Studies. (2024). Asia-Pacific regional security assessment 2024: Key developments and trends. IISS. https://www.iiss.org/publications/strategic-dossiers/asia-pacific-regional-security-assessment-2024/

International Trade Administration. (2024, Jan 8). Thailand - Defense and Security. U.S. Department of Commerce. https://www.trade.gov/country-commercial-guides/thailand-defense-and-security

Invezz. (2024, Oct 11). Rising tensions in South China Sea threaten global trade routes. https://invezz.com/news/2024/10/11/rising-tensions-in-south-china-sea-threaten-global-trade-routes/

Isfat, M., & Raihan, A. (2022). Current practices, challenges, and future directions of climate change adaptation in Bangladesh. *Int J Res Publ Rev*, *3*(5), 3429–3437.

Islam, M. M., Khan, M. K., Tareque, M., Jehan, N., & Dagar, V. (2021). Impact of globalization, foreign direct investment, and energy consumption on CO2 emissions in Bangladesh: Does institutional quality matter? *Environmental Science and Pollution Research International*, *28*(35), 48851–48871. DOI: 10.1007/s11356-021-13441-4 PMID: 33929670

Ismail, S. (2017). Military expenditure and economic growth in South Asian countries: Empirical evidences. *International Journal of Economics and Financial Issues*, *7*(3), 318–325.

Jaafar, W. S. W. M., Maulud, K. N. A., Kamarulzaman, A. M. M., Raihan, A., Sah, S. M., Ahmad, A., Saad, S. N. M., Azmi, A. T. M., Syukri, N. K. A. J., & Khan, W. R. (2020). The Influence of forest degradation on land surface temperature—A case study of Perak and Kedah, Malaysia. *Forests*, *11*(6), 670. DOI: 10.3390/f11060670

Jalil, A., Abbasi, H. K. N., & Bibi, N. (2016). Military expenditures and economic growth: Allowing structural breaks in time series analysis in the case of India and Pakistan. *Quality & Quantity*, *50*(4), 1487–1505. DOI: 10.1007/s11135-015-0217-x

Jana, S. K., Karmakar, A. K., & Maiti, A. (2018). Military Expenditure in India: Trends and Its Relation With GDP and Education Expenditure. In *Handbook of Research on Military Expenditure on Economic and Political Resources* (pp. 367–381). IGI Global.

Janžekovič, I. (2022). The Balance of Power from the Thirty Years' War and the Peace of Westphalia (1648) to the War of the Spanish Succession and the Peace of Utrecht (1713). *History of European Ideas*, *49*(3), 561–579. DOI: 10.1080/01916599.2022.2077401

Jebli, M. B., & Youssef, S. B. (2017). The role of renewable energy and agriculture in reducing CO2 emissions: Evidence for North Africa countries. *Ecological Indicators*, *74*, 295–301. DOI: 10.1016/j.ecolind.2016.11.032

Joerding, W. (1986). Economic growth and defense spending: Granger causality. *Journal of Development Economics*, *21*(1), 35–40. DOI: 10.1016/0304-3878(86)90037-4

Jones, D. M., & Jenne, N. (2022). Hedging and grand strategy in Southeast Asian foreign policy. *International Relations of the Asia-Pacific*, *22*(2), 205–235. DOI: 10.1093/irap/lcab003

Jones, L. E., Manuelli, R. E., & Rossi, P. E. (2013). Optimal taxation in models of endogenous growth. *Journal of Political Economy*, *101*(3), 485–517. DOI: 10.1086/261884

Kaldor, M. (1976). The military in development. *World Development*, *4*(6), 459–482. DOI: 10.1016/0305-750X(76)90032-2

Kalgotra, P., Gupta, A., & Sharda, R. (2021). Pandemic information support lifecycle: Evidence from the evolution of mobile apps during COVID-19. *Journal of Business Research*, *134*, 540–559. DOI: 10.1016/j.jbusres.2021.06.002 PMID: 34565948

Kamisuna, T. (2025, Apr 14). Japan's maritime cooperation in Southeast Asia. International Institute for Strategic Studies. https://www.iiss.org/online-analysis/online-analysis/2025/04/japans-maritime-cooperation-in-southeast-asia/

Kanbur, R. (2002). Economics, Social Science and Development. *World Development, 30*(3), 477–486. DOI: 10.1016/S0305-750X(01)00117-6

Kania, E. B., & Laskai, L. (2021). Myths and realities of China's military-civil fusion strategy. Center for a New American Security. https://s3.us-east-1.amazonaws.com/files.cnas.org/documents/Myths-and-Realities-of-China's-Military-Civil-Fusion-Strategy_FINAL-min.pdf

Kapetanios, G., Shin, Y., & Snell, A. (2003). Testing for a unit root in the nonlinear STAR framework". *Journal of Econometrics, 112*(2), 359–379. DOI: 10.1016/S0304-4076(02)00202-6

Kates, S. (2020). *Classical Economic Theory and the Modern Economy*. Edward Elgar Publishing. DOI: 10.4337/9781786433572

Katsumata, S., Ichikohji, T., Nakano, S., Yamaguchi, S., & Ikuine, F. (2022). Changes in the use of mobile devices during the crisis: Immediate response to the COVID-19 pandemic. *Computers in Human Behavior Reports, 5*, 100168. DOI: 10.1016/j.chbr.2022.100168 PMID: 35079660

Kentor, J., & Kick, E. (2008). Bringing the military back in: Military expenditures and economic growth, 1990 to 2003. *Journal of World-systems Research, 14*(2), 142–172. DOI: 10.5195/jwsr.2008.342

Khalid, M. A., & Mustapha, A. B. (2014). Long-run relationships and causality tests between military expenditure and economic growth in India. *The Economics and Finance Letters, 1*(6), 49–58. DOI: 10.18488/journal.29/2014.1.4/29.4.49.58

Khalid, U., Okafor, L. E., & Aziz, N. (2020). Armed conflict, military expenditure and international tourism. *Tourism Economics, 26*(4), 555–577. DOI: 10.1177/1354816619851404

Khan, J. (2018). Human capital Development and Economic Growth in India. Research review. *International Journal of Multidisciplinary, 3*(7), 484–488.

Khan, M. W. A., Panigrahi, S. K., Almuniri, K. S. N., Soomro, M. I., Mirjat, N. H., & Alqaydi, E. S. (2019). Investigating the dynamic impact of CO2 emissions and economic growth on renewable energy production: Evidence from FMOLS and DOLS tests. *Processes (Basel, Switzerland), 7*(8), 496. DOI: 10.3390/pr7080496

Khatter, P. (2025). *Union Budget: 2025–26, government continues modernization efforts and enhancement of indigenisation in defence sector*. Ernst & Young LLP.

Khayyat, M. H., Zamzami, N., Zhang, L., Nappi, M., & Umer, M. (2024). Fuzzy-CNN: Improving personal human identification based on IRIS recognition using LBP features. *Journal of Information Security and Applications*, *83*, 103761. Advance online publication. DOI: 10.1016/j.jisa.2024.103761

Kim, D. J. (2022). *Compound containment: A reigning power's military-economic countermeasures against a challenging power*. University of Michigan Press., https://library.oapen.org/handle/20.500.12657/53689 DOI: 10.3998/mpub.11622137

Kim, K. J. (2016). Interacting socially with the Internet of Things (IoT): Effects of source attribution and specialization in human-IoT interaction. *Journal of Computer-Mediated Communication*, *21*(6), 420–435. DOI: 10.1111/jcc4.12177

Kim, K. J., & Wang, S. (2021). Understanding the acceptance of the Internet of Things: An integrative theoretical approach. *Aslib Journal of Information Management*, *73*(5), 754–771. DOI: 10.1108/AJIM-03-2021-0073

Kim, S. K. (2024). Challenges to the capacity-building of Maritime Domain Awareness (MDA) in East Asia: What is at stake? *Ocean Development and International Law*, *55*(3), 395–416. DOI: 10.1080/00908320.2024.2405501

Kindleberger, C. P. (1970). *Power and money*. Springer. https://books.google.com/books?hl=en&lr=&id=6DiuCwAAQBAJ&oi=fnd&pg=PA3

Kindleberger, C. P. (1988). *International capital movements*. Cambridge University Press.

Kirchner, E. (2024). Geo-economic and geopolitical developments in EU–Asia security relations. *Asia Europe Journal*, *22*(3), 333–349. DOI: 10.1007/s10308-024-00706-z

Kirikkaleli, D., & Kalmaz, D. B. (2020). Testing the moderating role of urbanization on the environmental Kuznets curve: Empirical evidence from an emerging market. *Environmental Science and Pollution Research International*, *27*(30), 38169–38180. DOI: 10.1007/s11356-020-09870-2 PMID: 32617821

Kizza, J. M. (2023). History of Computing. In *Ethical and Social Issues in the Information Age. Texts in Computer Science*. Springer., DOI: 10.1007/978-3-031-24863-4_1

Klein, T. (2004). Military expenditure and economic growth: Peru 1970–1996. *Defence and Peace Economics*, *15*(3), 275–288. DOI: 10.1080/1024269032000035101

Knight, M., Loayza, N., & Villanueva, D. (1996). *"The peace dividend: military spending cuts and economic growth"*. Staff papers, 43(1), 1-37.

Kollias, C., Manolas, G., & Paleologou, S. M. (2004). Defence expenditure and economic growth in the European Union: A causality analysis. *Journal of Policy Modeling*, *26*(5), 553–569. DOI: 10.1016/j.jpolmod.2004.03.013

Kollias, C., & Paleologou, S. (2019). Military Spending, Economic Growth and Investment: A Disaggregated Analysis by Income Group. *Empirical Economics*, *56*(3), 935–958. DOI: 10.1007/s00181-017-1379-2

Kollias, C., & Paleologou, S. M. (2013). Guns, highways and economic growth in the United States. *Economic Modelling*, *30*, 449–455. DOI: 10.1016/j.econmod.2012.09.048

Kraska, J. (2011). *Maritime Power and the Law of the Sea: Expeditionary Operations in World Politics*. Oxford University Press. DOI: 10.1093/acprof:oso/9780199773381.001.0001

Kruse, R. (2011). A new unit root test against ESTAR based on a class of modified statistics. *Statistische Hefte*, *52*(1), 71–85.

Kuik, C.-C. (2024, Jul 8). Tilting toward Beijing? Malaysia's relations with China after Li Qiang's visit. Carnegie Endowment for International Peace. https://carnegieendowment.org/posts/2024/07/malaysias-relations-with-china-after-li-qiangs-visit?lang=en

Kumar, G. (2017). Countries military expenditures: Definitions and determinants. *Economic Affairs*, *62*(4), 647–654. DOI: 10.5958/0976-4666.2017.00078.X

Kumar, N., & Choudhary, P. (2016). The Relationship between Education Expenditure and Economic Growth in India. *J Adv Res Appl Math Stat*, *1*(2), 119–123.

Kusi, N. K. (1994). Economic growth and defense spending in developing countries: A causal analysis". *The Journal of Conflict Resolution*, *38*(1), 152–159. DOI: 10.1177/0022002794038001009

Kuzemko, C., Blondeel, M., Bradshaw, M., Bridge, G., Faigen, E., & Fletcher, L. (2025). Rethinking energy geopolitics: Towards a geopolitical economy of global energy transformation. *Geopolitics*, *30*(2), 531–565. DOI: 10.1080/14650045.2024.2351075

Kynacou, G. A. (1991). Level and Growth Effects of Human Capital. A Cross-Country Study of the Convergence Hypothesis, unpublished manuscript, New York University, June 1991.

Lai, C. N., Huang, B. N., & Yang, C. W. (2005). Defence spending and economic growth across the Taiwan Straits: A threshold regression model. *Defence and Peace Economics*, *16*(1), 45–57. DOI: 10.1080/1024269052000323542

Landau, D. (1986). Government and economic growth in the less developed countries: An empirical study for 1960-1980. *Economic Development and Cultural Change*, *35*(1), 35–75. DOI: 10.1086/451572

Lariosa, A.-M. (2025, May 23). Philippine Navy to open new bases in Subic Bay, Mindanao. Naval News. https://www.navalnews.com/naval-news/2025/05/philippine-navy-to-open-new-bases-in-subic-bay-mindanao/

Larus, J. R. (2024). Evolution of Computing. In Werthner, H. (Eds.), *Introduction to Digital Humanism*. Springer., DOI: 10.1007/978-3-031-45304-5_3

Lawrence, P. (2021). The Global and National Inequality Faultlines: The Economic Dimensions of (In)security. *Journal of Global Faultlines*, *8*(1), 23–33. https://www.scienceopen.com/hosted-document?doi=10.13169/jglobfaul.8.1.0023. DOI: 10.13169/jglobfaul.8.1.0023

Lee, S. M., & Trimi, S. (2021). Convergence Innovation in the Digital Age and in the COVID-19 Pandemic Crisis. *Journal of Business Research*, *123*, 14–22. DOI: 10.1016/j.jbusres.2020.09.041 PMID: 33012897

Leitão, N. C. (2021). Testing the role of trade on carbon dioxide emissions in Portugal. *Economies*, *9*(1), 22. DOI: 10.3390/economies9010022

Lendon, B. (2025, Apr 30). World's military spending rises at highest rate in nearly four decades, report says. CNN. https://edition.cnn.com/2025/04/30/world/world-military-spending-report-sipri-intl-hnk-ml

Leybourne, S., Newbold, P., & Vougas, D. (1998). Unit roots and smooth transitions. *Journal of Time Series Analysis*, *19*(1), 83–97. DOI: 10.1111/1467-9892.00078

Liang, X., Tian, N., Lopes da Silva, D., Scarazzato, L., Karim, Z. A., & Guiberteau Ricard, J. (2025, Apr). *Trends in world military expenditure, 2024*. Stockholm International Peace Research Institute. DOI: 10.55163/AVEC8366

Li, C. P. (2023). An analysis of the US Indo-Pacific strategy in US-China competition. *American Journal of Chinese Studies*, *30*(1), 43–59. https://www.jstor.org/stable/45474900

Lim, D. (1983). Another look at growth and defense in less developed countries. *Economic Development and Cultural Change*, *31*(2), 377–384. DOI: 10.1086/451326

Linh, N. T. (2024). Vietnam and the South China Sea. In Nguyen, T. H. (Ed.), *Security dynamics in the South China Sea* (pp. 198–218). Routledge., https://www.taylorfrancis.com/chapters/edit/10.4324/9781032657493-15/vietnam-south-china-sea-thanh-hai-nguyen-thi-linh

Linker, R. (2025). *Weapon Market Outlook 2024 – 2028*. Report Linker. https://www.reportlinker.com/clp/global/663365

Lipow, J., & Antinori, C. M. (2015). External security threats, defence expenditures, and the economic growth of less-developed countries. *Journal of Policy Modeling, 17*(6), 579–595. DOI: 10.1016/0161-8938(95)00021-6

Liu, X. (2025, Mar 5). China plans 7.2% defense budget rise, marking 10th consecutive year of single-digit growth. *Global Times*. https://www.globaltimes.cn/page/202503/1329511.shtml

Liu, X., & Bae, J. (2018). Urbanization and industrialization impact of CO2 emissions in China. *Journal of Cleaner Production, 172*, 178–186. DOI: 10.1016/j.jclepro.2017.10.156

Lobo-Guerrero, L. (2012). *Insuring war: Sovereignty, security and risk*. Routledge. DOI: 10.4324/9780203122075

Looney, R. E., & Frederiksen, P. C. (1986). Defense Expenditures, External Public Debt and Growth in Developing Countries. *Journal of Peace Research, 23*(4), 329–338. DOI: 10.1177/002234338602300403

Lopes da Silva, D. (2023). Political Accountability and Military Spending. *Defence and Peace Economics, 34*(5), 563–580. DOI: 10.1080/10242694.2022.2129128

Lucas, R. E. (1988). On the Mechanics of Development Planning. *Journal of Monetary Economics, 22*, 3–42. DOI: 10.1016/0304-3932(88)90168-7

Maass, R. W., Norrlof, C., & Drezner, D. W. (2014). *"The profitability of primacy"*. International Security, 38(4-Summer), 188-205.

Macharashvili, N. (2025). *Can Europe Defend Itself and Ukraine without U.S. Support?* Gfsis.org. https://gfsis.org/en/can-europe-defend-itself-and-ukraine-without-u-s-support/

MacKinnon, J. G., Haug, A. A., & Michelis, L. (2019). Numerical distribution functions of likelihood ratio tests for cointegration. *Journal of Applied Econometrics, 14*(5), 563–577. DOI: 10.1002/(SICI)1099-1255(199909/10)14:5<563::AID-JAE530>3.0.CO;2-R

MacLean, G. A. (2006). Human Security and the Globalization of International Security. *Whitehead Journal of Diplomacy and International Relations*, 7(1), 89-99. https://ciaotest.cc.columbia.edu/olj/shjdir/v7n1/v7n1_07.pdf

Maddison, A. (2001). *The World Economy: A Millennial Perspective*. Development Center. DOI: 10.1787/9789264189980-en

Madnick, B., Huang, K., & Madnick, S. (2023). The evolution of global cybersecurity norms in the digital age: A longitudinal study of the cybersecurity norm development process. *Information Security Journal: A Global Perspective, 33(3)*, 204-225. DOI: 10.1080/19393555.2023.2201482

Mahadev Madgule, N. (2023). Vinayaka, Yeshwant M. Sonkhaskar, Dhiren Ramanbhai Patel, R. Karthikeyan, P. Selvakumar,(2023). Mechanical properties and microstructure of activated TIG welded similar joints of Inconel alloys by desirability approaches. *Materials Today: Proceedings*, *77*, 528–533. DOI: 10.1016/j.matpr.2022.12.250

Mahr, D., & Huh, J. (2022). Technologies in service communication: Looking forward. *Journal of Service Management*, *33*(4/5), 648–656. DOI: 10.1108/JOSM-03-2022-0075

Maizels, A., & Nissanke, M. K. (1987). The Causes of Military Expenditure in Developing Countries. In Deger, S., & West, R. (Eds.), *Defence Security and Development, Great Britain: Frances Pinter* (pp. 129–139). Frances Pinter.

Ma, J., Jiang, Y., & Xiao, X. (2015). The Relationship Between Military Expenditures and Economic Growth-A Case Study of the United States, Russia, Japan, India and China. *Review of the Air Force Academy*, (2), 79–90.

Makinda, S. M. (1998). Sovereignty and Global Security. *Security Dialogue*, *29*(3), 281–292. DOI: 10.1177/0967010698029003003

Malizard, J. (2015). Does Military Expenditure Crowd Out Private Investment: A Disaggregate Perspective for the Case of France. *Economic Modelling*, *46*(C), 44–52. DOI: 10.1016/j.econmod.2014.10.049

Malufti, F. (2025, Apr 30). *Indonesian Navy seeks SOSUS-like systems to detect foreign submarines*. Naval News. https://www.navalnews.com/naval-news/2025/04/indonesian-navy-seeks-sosus-like-systems-to-detect-foreign-submarines/

Mankiw, N. G. (2012). *Principles of Economics*. South-Western Cengage Learning.

Mansoob Murshed, S., & Mamoon, D. (2010). Not loving thy neighbour as thyself: Trade, democracy and military expenditure explanations underlying India—Pakistan rivalry. *Journal of Peace Research*, *47*(4), 463–476. DOI: 10.1177/0022343310364577

Marimuthu, M., Khan, H., & Bangash, R. (2021). Is the fiscal deficit of ASEAN alarming? Evidence from fiscal deficit consequences and contribution towards sustainable economic growth. *Sustainability (Basel)*, *13*(18), 10045. DOI: 10.3390/su131810045

Markowski, S., Chand, S., & Wylie, R. (2017). Economic growth and demand for military expenditure in the Indo-Pacific Asia region. *Defence and Peace Economics*, *28*(4), 473–490. DOI: 10.1080/10242694.2016.1274059

Matthews, R. (Ed.). (2019). *The political economy of defence*. Cambridge University Press., https://books.google.com/books?hl=en&lr=&id=lLOQDwAAQBAJ&oi=fnd&pg=PR10 DOI: 10.1017/9781108348058

Mavrotas, G. (2011). Security and development: Delving deeper into the nexus. In Mavrotas, G. (Ed.), *Security and development* (pp. 1–17). Edward Elgar Publishing., DOI: 10.4337/9781781007037.00006

Mbaku, J. M. (2000). *Bureaucratic and Political Corruption in Africa: The Public Choice Perspective*. Kreiger.

McKibbin, W., & Roshen, F. (2023). The global economic impacts of the COVID-19 pandemic. *Economic Modelling*, *129*, 106551. DOI: 10.1016/j.econmod.2023.106551

Meerts, C. (2019). Security: Concepts and Definitions. In Shapiro, L., & Maras, M. H. (Eds.), *Encyclopedia of Security and Emergency Management*. Springer., DOI: 10.1007/978-3-319-69891-5_94-2

Mehdi, A., & Chaudhry, D. (2015). Human capital potential of India's future workforce, Working Paper, No. 308, *Indian Council for Research on International Economic Relations (ICRIER),* New Delhi.

Mehta, A. K., Yashoda, L., Selvakumar, P., Mishra, B. R., Das, A., & C. T. C., M. (2025). Teaching Methods: Techniques for Disadvantaged Learners. In S. Hai-Jew (Ed.), *Mitigating Learner Disadvantages in Teaching and Learning* (pp. 181-206). IGI Global Scientific Publishing. DOI: 10.4018/979-8-3693-8623-1.ch007

Meirong, G. (2018). China's cybersecurity legislation, it's relevance to critical infrastructures and the challenges it faces. *International Journal of Critical Infrastructure Protection*, *22*, 139–149. DOI: 10.1016/j.ijcip.2018.06.006

Mia, M. R., Tao, J. L., & Anderson, C. D. (2024). The South China Sea dispute and regional response. Quest Journal of Management and Social Sciences, 6(1), 74–86. https://nepjol.info/index.php/qjmss/article/view/67377

Miller, R. C. (2018). *International political economy: Contrasting world views*. Routledge.

Mincer, J. (1984). Human capital and economic growth. *Economics of Education Review*, *3*(3), 195–205. DOI: 10.1016/0272-7757(84)90032-3

Mintz, A., & Huang, C. (1990). Defense expenditures, economic growth, and the "peace dividend". *The American Political Science Review*, *84*(4), 1283–1293. DOI: 10.2307/1963264

Modern Diplomacy. (2025, Feb 22). *Surging arms stockpile in Southeast Asia: Preparation for war?* Modern Diplomacy. https://moderndiplomacy.eu/2025/02/22/surging-arms-stockpile-in-southeast-asia-preparation-for-war/

Mohsenzadeh, F., & Isfandyari-Moghaddam, A. (2009). Application of information technologies in academic libraries. *The Electronic Library*, *27*(6), 986–998. DOI: 10.1108/02640470911004075

Moon, Y. J., & Hio Gum, K. (2006). A Model for the Value of Intellectual Capital. *Canadian Journal of Administrative Sciences*, *23*(3), 253–269. DOI: 10.1111/j.1936-4490.2006.tb00630.x

Mukhopadhyay, P., Sinha, M., & Sengupta, P. P. (2018). Public Expenditure on Defence and Economic Development: A Comparative Study on India and China. In *Handbook of Research on Military Expenditure on Economic and Political Resources* (pp. 170–181). IGI Global.

Mulligan, C. B., & Sala-I-Martin, X. (1992). Some Empirical Evidence on Two-Sector Models of Endogenous Growth. unpublished manuscript, University of Chicago, June 1992.

Murdoch, J. C., Pi, C. R., & Sandler, T. (1997). The Impact of Defense and Non-defense Public Spending on Growth in Asia and Latin America". *Defence and Peace Economics*, *8*(2), 205–224. DOI: 10.1080/10430719708404876

Murphy, K. M., & Topel, R. H. (2013). Some Basic Economics of National Security. *The American Economic Review*, *103*(3), 508–511. DOI: 10.1257/aer.103.3.508

Muthukumar, S. L., & Hedberg, J. G. (2005). A knowledge management technology architecture for educational research organizations: scaffolding research projects and workflow processing. *British Journal of Educational Technology, Blackwell Publishing, Oxford, 36 (3)*, 379-395.

Nair, P. (2009). An Evaluation of India's Defence Expenditure. *Economic and Political Weekly*, 40–46.

Nan, H. (2025, May 7). *China's military-civil fusion: A challenge to the US military-industrial complex?* ThinkChina. https://www.thinkchina.sg/technology/chinas-military-civil-fusion-challenge-us-military-industrial-complex

Narang, R. K. (2024, Sep). *Military–civil technology fusion (MCTF) for making India Atmanirbhar: Global drone hub @2030* (MP-IDSA Monograph Series No. 87). Manohar Parrikar Institute for Defence Studies and Analyses.

Naser, S. M. (2021). Cryptography: From the ancient history to now, it's applications and a new complete numerical model. *International Journal of Mathematics and Statistics Studies*, *9*(3), 11–30.

National Institute of Standards and Technology. (2024). https://www.nist.gov/

NATO. (2014). The Wales Summit Declaration. https://www.nato.int/cps/en/natohq/official_texts_112964.htm

NATO. (2023). The Vilnius Summit Communiqué. https://www.nato.int/cps/en/natohq/official_texts_217320.htm

NATO. (2025). The Hague Summit Declaration. https://www.nato.int/cps/en/natohq/official_texts_236705.htm

Nayyar, D. (2006). Globalization, History, and Development: A Tale of Two Centuries. *Cambridge Journal of Economics*, *30*(1), 137–159. https://academic.oup.com/cje/article/30/1/137/1730040. DOI: 10.1093/cje/bei090

Nelson, R. R., & Phelps, E. S. (1966). Investment in Humans, Technological Diffusion, and Economic Growth. *The American Economic Review*, *56*, 69–75.

Neu, C. R., & Wolf, Ch.Jr. (1994). *The Economic Dimensions of National Security*. RAND Corporation., https://www.rand.org/pubs/monoFigure_reports/MR466.html

Newman, N. (2024). *Journalism, Media, and Technology Trends and Predictions 2024*. USA: Reuters Institute for the Study of Journalism with the support of the Google News Initiative (GNI).

Nguyen, A. T., Lu, S. H., & Nguyen, P. T. T. (2021). Validating and forecasting carbon emissions in the framework of the environmental Kuznets curve: The case of Vietnam. *Energies*, *14*(11), 3144. DOI: 10.3390/en14113144

Nicholson, W., & Snyder, Ch. (2016). *Microeconomic Theory: Basic Principles and Extensions* (12th ed.). Cengage Learning.

Nikolov, B. (2025, Apr 21). *Philippines receives India's game-changing BrahMos missile system*. Bulgarian Military. https://bulgarianmilitary.com/2025/04/21/philippines-receives-indias-game-changing-brahmos-missile-system/

Nondo, C., & Kahsai, M. S. (2020). The impact of energy intensity, urbanisation, industrialisation, and income on CO2 emissions in South Africa: An ARDL bounds testing approach. *African Journal of Economic and Sustainable Development*, *7*(4), 307–330. DOI: 10.1504/AJESD.2020.106826

Novales, A., Fernández, E., & Ruiz, J. (2022). *Economic Growth. Theory and Numerical Solution Methods*. Springer. DOI: 10.1007/978-3-662-63982-5

Nyamboga, C. M., & Kemparaju, T. D. (2002). Information technology in university libraries in Karnataka. *Information Development*, *18*(4), 257–265. DOI: 10.1177/026666602321036650

Nye, J. S.Jr. (2011). *The Future of Power*. Perseus Books.

Öcal, N. (2003). Are the military expenditures of India and Pakistan external determinants for each other: An empirical investigation. *Defence and Peace Economics*, *14*(2), 141–149. DOI: 10.1080/10242690302917

Odugbesan, J. A., & Adebayo, T. S. (2020). The symmetrical and asymmetrical effects of foreign direct investment and financial development on carbon emission: Evidence from Nigeria. *SN Applied Sciences*, *2*(12), 1–15. DOI: 10.1007/s42452-020-03817-5

Ojha, V. (2017). The Impact of Public Education Expenditure on Economic Growth and Income Distribution in India. *Business Analyst*, *37*(2), 9–37.

Oktafian, I. (2024, Sep 23). *Indonesia to launch cyber force as fourth branch of military*. Jakarta Globe. https://jakartaglobe.id/news/indonesia-to-launch-cyber-force-as-fourth-branch-of-military

Olsson, P. (2022). Measuring Quality of Military Equipment. *Defence and Peace Economics*, *33*(1), 93–107. DOI: 10.1080/10242694.2020.1851474

Omitoogun, W. (2003). Military Expenditure Data in Africa: A Survey of Cameroon, Ethiopia, Ghana, Kenya, Nigeria, and Uganda. *SIPRI Research Report No. 17*. Stockholm International Peace Research Institute. https://www.sipri.org/publications/2003/military-expenditure-data-africa-survey-cameroon-ethiopia-ghana-kenya-nigeria-and-uganda

Oner, C. (2025). Inflation: Prices on the Rise. *IMF*. https://www.imf.org/en/Publications/fandd/issues/Series/Back-to-Basics/Inflation#:~

Orlosky, J., Kiyokawa, K., & Takemura, H. (2017). Virtual and augmented reality on the 5g highway. *Journal of Information Processing*, *25*(0), 133–141. DOI: 10.2197/ipsjjip.25.133

Ortiz Arellano, E. (2021). Seguridad Nacional del Estado mexicano: Ejes Problemáticos y Factores. *Encrucijada*, *38*(38), 94–126. DOI: 10.22201/fcpys.20071949e.2021.38.78088

Ortiz, C., Alvarado, R., & Salinas, A. (2019). The effect of military spending on output: New evidence at the global and country group levels using panel data cointegration techniques". *Economic Analysis and Policy*, *62*, 402–414. DOI: 10.1016/j.eap.2018.10.004

Oztuna, A. (2024). *Assessing the Chinese naval infrastructure changes in the South China Sea using geospatial intelligence* (Master's thesis). Johns Hopkins University. https://jscholarship.library.jhu.edu/items/ffda3520-ef96-4dab-afd5-2ee3f712d41e

Paar, Ch., & Pelzl, J. (2010). *Understanding Cryptography. A Textbook for Students and Practitioners*. Springer-Verlag. DOI: 10.1007/978-3-642-04101-3

Paar, Ch., Pelzl, J., & Güneysu, T. (2024). *Understanding Cryptography. From Established Symmetric and Asymmetric Ciphers to Post-Quantum Algorithms*. Springer-Verlag. DOI: 10.1007/978-3-662-69007-9

Palm, F., Smeekes, S., & Urbain, J. (2006). *Bootstrap Unit Root Tests: Comparison and Extensions*. Maastricht: METEOR, Maastricht University School of Business and Economics. METEOR Research Memorandum No. 015.

Pandey, G. P., & Chakraborty, J. (2002). Role of information technology in higher education in the 21st century. *University News*, *40*(8), 11.

Parameswaran, P. (2024). Southeast Asia and US–China competition: Realities, responses, and regional futures. In Khoo, N. K. S., Nicklin, G., & Tan, A. C. (Eds.), *Indo-Pacific security: US–China rivalry and regional states' responses* (pp. 115–129). World Scientific., https://books.google.com/books?hl=en&lr=&id=3_L3EAAAQBAJ&oi=fnd&pg=PA115 DOI: 10.1142/9781800614857_0008

Parika, A., & Singh, B. P. (2020). *How Does Human Capital Affect Economic Growth in India? An Empirical Analysis*. *MPRA Paper 102428*. University Library of Munich.

Parkin, M. (2018). *Microeconomics* (13th ed.). Pearson.

Passavanti, R., Pantano, E., Priporas, C. V., & Verteramo, S. (2020). The use of new technologies for corporate marketing communication in luxury retailing: Preliminary findings. *Qualitative Market Research*, *23*(3), 503–521. DOI: 10.1108/QMR-11-2017-0144

Perlo-Freeman, S., Fleurant, A., Wezeman, P. D., & Wezeman, S. T. (2015). Trends in world military expenditure, 2014. Stockholm International Peace Research Institute (SIPRI) Fact Sheet, Sweden, April 2015.

Perlo-Freeman, S., Ismail, O., & Solmirano, C. (2010). Military expenditure. In *SIPRI Yearbook 2009* (pp. 179–211). Stockholm International Peace Research Institute.

Perlo-Freeman, S., Solmirano, C., & Wilandh, H. (2013). Global developments in military expenditure. *SIPRI Yearbook*, *2013*, 127–134.

Perron, P. (1989). The great crash, the oil price shock, and the unit root hypothesis". *Econometrica*, *57*(6), 1361–1401. DOI: 10.2307/1913712

Perron, P. (1997). Further evidence on breaking trend functions in macroeconomic variables". *Journal of Econometrics*, *80*(2), 355–385. DOI: 10.1016/S0304-4076(97)00049-3

Pesaran, M. H., Shin, Y., & Smith, R. J. (2001). Bounds testing approaches to the analysis of level relationships. *Journal of Applied Econometrics*, *16*(3), 289–326. DOI: 10.1002/jae.616

Pesaran, M. H., & Timmermann, A. (2005). Small sample properties of forecasts from autoregressive models under structural breaks. *Journal of Econometrics*, *129*(1–2), 183–217. DOI: 10.1016/j.jeconom.2004.09.007

Peter, G. Peterson Foundation. (2025, May 5). The United States spends more on defense than the next 9 countries combined. https://www.pgpf.org/article/the-united-states-spends-more-on-defense-than-the-next-9-countries-combined

Phillips, A. (2023). The Peace of Westphalia. In Bukovansky, M. (Eds.), *The Oxford Handbook of History and International Relations*. Oxford Handbooks Academic., DOI: 10.1093/oxfordhb/9780198873457.013.36

Pieroni, L. (2009). Military expenditure and economic growth. *Defence and Peace Economics*, *20*(4), 327–339. DOI: 10.1080/10242690701589876

Piętak, Ł. (2014). Review of theories and models of economic growth. *Comparative Economic Research*, *17*(1), 45–60. DOI: 10.2478/cer-2014-0003

Pirbhulal, S., Chockalingam, S., Shukla, A., & Abie, H. (2024). IoT cybersecurity in 5G and beyond: A systematic literature review. *International Journal of Information Security*, *23*(4), 2827–2879. Advance online publication. DOI: 10.1007/s10207-024-00865-5

Podrug, N., Filipovic, D., & Kovac, M. (2017). Knowledge sharing and firm innovation capability in Croatian ICT companies. *International Journal of Manpower*, *38*(4), 632–644. DOI: 10.1108/IJM-04-2016-0077

Porter, T. M., & Ross, D. (2003). *The Modern Social Sciences*. Vol. 7 of The Cambridge History of Science. Cambridge: Cambridge University Press.

Powell, R. (1993). Guns, butter, and anarchy. *The American Political Science Review*, *87*(1), 115–132. DOI: 10.2307/2938960

Pradhan, R. P. (2010). Defense spending and economic growth in China, India, Nepal and Pakistan: Evidence from cointegrated panel analysis. *International Journal of Economics and Finance*, *2*(4), 65–74. DOI: 10.5539/ijef.v2n4p65

Pradhan, R. P., Arvin, M. B., Norman, N. R., & Bhinder, H. K. (2013). Military expenditure and economic growth: Using causality, cointegration and missing variables. *International Journal of Computational Economics and Econometrics*, *3*(3-4), 164–186. DOI: 10.1504/IJCEE.2013.058496

PRS Legislative Research. (2025). *Demand for Grants 2025-26 Analysis: Defence*. https://prsindia.org

Qadri, F., & Waheed, A. (2014). Human capital and economic growth: A macroeconomic model for Pakistan. *Economic Modelling*, *42*, 66–76. DOI: 10.1016/j.econmod.2014.05.021

Rafiq, S., Salim, R., & Apergis, N. (2016). Agriculture, trade openness and emissions: An empirical analysis and policy options. *The Australian Journal of Agricultural and Resource Economics*, *60*(3), 348–365. DOI: 10.1111/1467-8489.12131

Rahman, M. M., & Alam, K. (2021). Exploring the driving factors of economic growth in the world's largest economies. *Heliyon*, *7*(5), e07109. DOI: 10.1016/j.heliyon.2021.e07109 PMID: 34136687

Raifu, I. A., & Aminu, A. (2023). The effect of military spending on economic growth in MENA: Evidence from method of moments quantile regression. *Future Business Journal*, *9*(1), 7. DOI: 10.1186/s43093-023-00181-9

Raisová, M., & Ćurþová, J. (2014). Economic growth-supply and demand perspective. *Procedia Economics and Finance, 15*, 184–191. DOI: 10.1016/S2212-5671(14)00476-6

Raju, M. H., & Ahmed, Z. (2019). Effect of military expenditure on economic growth: Evidences from India Pakistan and China using cointegration and causality analysis. *Asian Journal of German and European Studies*, *4*(1), 3. DOI: 10.1186/s40856-019-0040-6

Ramakrishnan, T., Mohan Gift, M. D., Chitradevi, S., Jegan, R., & Subha Hency Jose, P. Nagaraja, Rajneesh Sharma H.N., Selvakumar P., Sintayehu Mekuria Hailegiorgis, (2022). "Study of Numerous Resins Used in Polymer Matrix Composite Materials", *Advances in Materials Science and Engineering*, vol. 2022, Article ID 1088926, 8 pages, 2022. DOI: 10.1155/2022/1088926

Ramli, N. S. (2017). A review of marketing strategies from the European chocolate industry. *Journal of Global Entrepreneurship Research*, *7*(10), 1–17. DOI: 10.1186/s40497-017-0068-0

Ranjbar, O., Chang, T., Elmi, Z., & Lee, C. (2018). A new unit root test against asymmetric ESTAR nonlinearity with smooth breaks. *Iranian Economic Review*, *22*(1), 51–62.

Ranjitha P. K., Selvakumar, P., Anute, N., Manjunath, T., Sureshkrishna, G., & Pougajendy, S.(2025). Transportation Challenges In Islands Tourism. In V. Hassan (Ed.), Navigating MassTourism to Island Destinations: Preservation and Cultural Heritage Challenges (pp. 287-312). IGI Global Scientific Publishing. .DOI: 10.4018/979-8-3693-9107-5.ch011

Raska, M. (2024). Reimagining defense innovation: Defense AI in Singapore. In Borchert, H., Schütz, T., & Verbovszky, J. (Eds.), *The very long game* (pp. 22–27). Springer., DOI: 10.1007/978-3-031-58649-1_25

Rathi, R. (2025, Apr 17). *Island Defence: Assessing Taiwan's Military Capabilities*. Modern Diplomacy. https://moderndiplomacy.eu/2025/04/17/island-defence-assessing-taiwans-military-capabilities/

Rathi, D., Given, L. M., & Forcier, E. (2014). Interorganisational partnerships and knowledge sharing: The perspective of non-profit organisations (NPOs). *Journal of Knowledge Management*, *18*(5), 867–885. DOI: 10.1108/JKM-06-2014-0256

Raudeliuniene, J., Albats, E., & Kordab, M. (2021). Impact of information technologies and social networks on knowledge management processes in Middle Eastern audit and consulting companies. *Journal of Knowledge Management*, *25*(4), 871–898. DOI: 10.1108/JKM-03-2020-0168

Raza, S. A., Shahbaz, M., & Paramati, S. R. (2017). Dynamics of military expenditure and income inequality in Pakistan. *Social Indicators Research*, *131*(3), 1035–1055. DOI: 10.1007/s11205-016-1284-7

Rebelo, S. (1991). Long-Run Policy Analysis and Long-Run Growth. *Journal of Political Economy*, *99*(3), 500–521. DOI: 10.1086/261764

Reiter, D. (Ed.). (2017). *The sword's other edge: Trade-offs in the pursuit of military effectiveness*. Cambridge University Press. DOI: 10.1017/9781108241786

Repnikov, A. (2024). *Defense Expenditures and Economic Growth of Countries of the World: Determinants and Channels of Interrelations*. Ideas. file:///D:/nchitadze/Downloads/48-58+Article+Repnikova%20(3).pdf

Reserve Bank of India. (2025). Major heads of expenditure of the central government. Government of India. https://rbi.org.in/scripts/PublicationsView.aspx?id=21190

Retter, L. (2019). *Relationships between the economy and national security. Analysis and considerations for economic security policy in the Netherlands*. Santa Monica, Calif., and Cambridge, UK: the RAND Corporation. https://www.rand.org/pubs/research_reports/RR4287.html

Reuters (2023). *Russia Plans Huge Defense Spending Hike in 2024 as War Drags*. Bloomberg. https://www.reuters.com/business/aerospace-defense/russia-plans-hugedefence-spending-hike-2024-bloomberg-2023-09-22/ (дата обращения: 16.03.2024).

Ritzer, G. (2007). Introduction. In Ritzer, G. (Ed.), *The Blackwell Companion to Globalization* (pp. 1–13). Blackwell. DOI: 10.1002/9780470691939.ch

Riveros Gavilanes, J. M. (2020). Military Expenditure and Economic Growth: The South American Case. *MPRA*, Paper No. 98508. https://mpra.ub.uni-muenchen.de/98508

Roberts, B. (2011). Exploitation, appropriation, and subsumption. *Rethinking Marxism*, *23*(3), 341–351. DOI: 10.1080/08935696.2011.583005

Romer, P. M. (1990). Human Capital and Growth. Theory and Evidence. *Carnegie-Rochester Conference Series on Public Policy*, *32*, 1990. DOI: 10.1016/0167-2231(90)90028-J

Rosenberg, D. (2002). The rise of China: Implications for security flashpoints and resource politics in the South China Sea. In Dent, C. M. (Ed.), *The rise of China in Asia: Security implications* (pp. 229–261). Routledge.

Rothschild, K. W. (1973). Military expenditure, exports and growth. *Kyklos*, *26*(4), 804–814. DOI: 10.1111/j.1467-6435.1973.tb02777.x

Rothwell, J. T., Cojocaru, A., Srinivasan, R., & Kim, Y. S. (2024). Global evidence on the economic effects of disease suppression during COVID-19. *Humanities & Social Sciences Communications*, *11*(78), 1–14. DOI: 10.1057/s41599-023-02571-4

Roux, A. (1996). Defence expenditure and economic growth in South Africa. *Tydskrif vir Studies in Ekonomie en Ekonometrie*, *20*(1), 19–34. DOI: 10.1080/03796205.1996.12129087

Rueschemeyer, D., & Evans, P. B. (1985). The state and economic transformation: Toward an analysis of the conditions underlying effective intervention. In Evans, P. B., Rueschemeyer, D., & Skocpol, T. (Eds.), *Bringing the state back* (pp. 44–77). Cambridge University Press., DOI: 10.1017/CBO9780511628283.004

Saeed, L. (2023). The Impact of Military Expenditures on Economic Growth: A New Instrumental Variables Approach. *Defence and Peace Economics*. DOI: 10.1080/10242694.2023.2259651

Sakwa, R. (2025). *The Culture of the Second Cold War*. Anthem Press. DOI: 10.2307/jj.24751871

Samuelson, P. A., & Nordhaus, W. D. (1948). *Economics*. McGraw-Hill Education.

Sandler, T., & George, J. (2016). Military expenditure trends for 1960–2014 and what they reveal. *Global Policy*, *7*(2), 174–184. DOI: 10.1111/1758-5899.12328

Sangfor Technologies. (2025, Mar 7). *Cybersecurity in Malaysia: AI investments on the rise*. Sangfor. https://www.sangfor.com/blog/cybersecurity/cybersecurity-malaysia-ai-investments-rise

Sari, M. I. (2025, Apr 5). *Indonesia's defence strategy is in urgent need of a refresh.* East Asia Forum. https://eastasiaforum.org/2025/04/05/indonesias-defence-strategy-is-in-urgent-need-of-a-refresh/

Sarwar, S., Alsaggaf, M. I., & Tingqiu, C. (2019). Nexus Among Economic Growth, Education, Health, and Environment: Dynamic Analysis of World-Level Data. *Frontiers in Public Health*, *7*, 307. DOI: 10.3389/fpubh.2019.00307 PMID: 31709219

Sasidhar, M. (2024). Balancing Defence and Diplomacy: A Deep Strategic Analysis of India's Military Expenditure and Its Impact on Global Peace *SSRN* 5240582.

Sbia, R., Shahbaz, M., & Hamdi, H. (2014). A contribution of foreign direct investment, clean energy, trade openness, carbon emissions and economic growth to energy demand in UAE. *Economic Modelling*, *36*, 191–197. DOI: 10.1016/j.econmod.2013.09.047

Schmidt, J. D. (2004). *Rethinking the nexus between development theory and IR: From old divisions to new encounters*(Working Paper No. 107). Research Center on Development and International Relations, Aalborg University. https://vbn.aau.dk/files/33748899/DIR_wp_107.pdf

Schoeni, D. E. (2016). Defense offsets and public policy: Beyond economic efficiency. *The Air Force Law Review*, *76*, 95–135. https://heinonline.org/hol-cgi-bin/get_pdf.cgi?handle=hein.journals/airfor76&section=4

Schumpeter, J. A. (1954). *A History of Economic Analysis*. Oxford University Press.

Schumpeter, J. A. (2021). *The Theory of Economic Development (Routledge Classics)* (1st ed.). Routledge. DOI: 10.4324/9781003146766

Schwartz, R. A. (2023). *Undermining the state from within*. Cambridge University Press. DOI: 10.1017/9781009219907

SEDEMA. (2025). Glosario. Definiciones. Recuperado de http://data.sedema.cdmx.gob.mx:9000/datos/glosario-definicion/Econom%C3%ADa

Sempere, C. M. (2018). What is known about defence research and development spill-overs?". *Defence and Peace Economics*, *29*(3), 225–246. DOI: 10.1080/10242694.2016.1239364

Shafer, D. M. (1994). *Winners and losers: How sectors shape the developmental prospects of states*. Cornell University Press.

Shafik, M. (2021). *What We Owe Each Other: A New Social Contract for a Better Society*. Princeton University Press.

Shahbaz, M., Afza, T., & Shabbir, M. S. (2013). Does defence spending impede economic growth? Cointegration and causality analysis for Pakistan. *Defence and Peace Economics*, *24*(2), 105–120. DOI: 10.1080/10242694.2012.723159

Shahbaz, M., Balcilar, M., Mahalik, K., & Akadiri, S. (2023). Is causality between globalization and energy consumption bidirectional or unidirectional in top and bottom globalized economies? *International Journal of Finance & Economics*, *28*(2), 1939–1964. DOI: 10.1002/ijfe.2519

Shahbaz, M., Van Hoang, T., Mahalik, K., & Roubaud, D. (2017). Energy consumption, financial development and economic growth in India: New evidence from a nonlinear and asymmetric analysis. *Energy Economics*, *63*, 199–212. DOI: 10.1016/j.eneco.2017.01.023

Shahbaz, M., Zakaria, M., Shahzad, S., & Mahalik, K. (2018). The energy consumption and economic growth nexus in top ten energy-consuming countries: Fresh evidence from using the quantile-on-quantile approach. *Energy Economics*, *71*, 282–301. DOI: 10.1016/j.eneco.2018.02.023

Shah, S. A., He, C., Makhijani, H. B., & Shah, M. (2015). Arms race, economic growth, and government expenditure: Empirical investigation for India and Pakistan. *Journal of Economics and Sustainable Development*, *6*(6), 23–30.

Shammar, E. A., & Zahary, A. T. (2020). The Internet of Things (IoT): A survey of techniques, operating systems, and trends. *Library Hi Tech*, *38*(1), 5–66. DOI: 10.1108/LHT-12-2018-0200

Sharma, D., & Phulli, K. (2020). Forecasting and Analyzing the Military Expenditure of India Using Box-Jenkins ARIMA Model. *arXiv preprint arXiv:2011.06060.*

Sharma, D. K. (2022). A review on various cryptographic techniques & algorithms. *Materials Today: Proceedings*, *51*(1), 104–109. DOI: 10.1016/j.matpr.2021.04.583

Sharma, P., Yadav, K., & Tiwari, A. K. (2022). A Review Paper on Network Security and Cryptography. *World Journal of Research and Review*, *14*(5), 20–24. https://www.wjrr.org/download_data/WJRR1405012.pdf

Shi, J. (2024). How Population Aging Impacts the Perception of National Security and Military Spending. *SN Social Sciences*, *4*(12), 233. https://link.springer.com/article/10.1007/s43545-024-01031-3. DOI: 10.1007/s43545-024-01031-3

Shin, Y. (1994). A residual-based test of the null of cointegration against the alternative of no cointegration. *Econometric Theory*, *10*(1), 91–115. DOI: 10.1017/S0266466600008240

Shivam. (2025, Apr 29). *Top Military Spenders of 2024–25: India's Position in the Global Military Expenditure Race*. Adda247. https://currentaffairs.adda247.com/top-military-spenders-of-2024-25-indias-position-in-the-global-military-expenditure-race/

Short, J. R. (2025). *Hedging and Conflict in the South China Sea*. Taylor & Francis., DOI: 10.4324/9781003537298

Shreyas, M. (2022). A Review Paper on Cryptography. *International Journal of Advanced Research in Science. Tongxin Jishu, 2*(2), 389–395. https://www.ijarsct.co.in/A2883.pdf

Shukla, M., Dos Santos, R., Fong, A., & Lu, C.-T. (2017). DERIV: Distributed brand perception tracking framework. *Journal of Big Data, 4*(17), 1–23. DOI: 10.1186/s40537-017-0078-3

Shukla, S. (2017). Human capital and economic growth in India. *International Journal of Current Research, 9*(11), 61628–61631.

Silva, D. L., Tian, N., & Marksteiner, A. (2020). Trends in world military expenditure, 2020. Stockholm International Peace Research Institute. <https://www.sipri.org/sites/default/files/2021-04/fs_2104_milex_0.pdf

Silvapulle, P. (1996). Testing for a unit root in a time series with mean shifts. *Applied Economics Letters, 3*(10), 629–635. DOI: 10.1080/135048596355826

Singh, R. (2023, May 12). *Vietnam's purchase of Kilo-class submarines and military modernization.* CESCUBE. https://www.cescube.com/vp-vietnam-s-purchase-of-kilo-class-submarines-and-military-modernization

Singh, S. (2025, Mar 25). *Despite US forces being stretched thin, South China Sea activity grows: Report.* India Today. https://www.indiatoday.in/world/story/despite-us-forces-being-stretched-thin-south-china-sea-activity-grows-report-glbs-2698939-2025-03-25

Singh, R. P. (2014). Building advanced defence technology capacity. In Debroy, B., Tellis, A. J., & Trevor, R. (Eds.), *Getting India back on track: An action agenda for reform* (pp. 281–294). Carnegie Endowment for International Peace. DOI: 10.2307/j.ctt1n2ttcb.21

Sinha, D., & Sinha, T. (2002). Openness, investment and economic growth in Asia. *The Indian Economic Journal, 49*(4), 90–95.

SIPRI. (2024). Comunicado de prensa. EMBARGO: https://www.huffingtonpost.es/uploads/files/2024/06/17/Milex%20Press%20Release%20ESP.pdf

SIPRI. (2024). *Sources and methods.* SIPRI. https://www.sipri.org/databases/milex/sources-andmethods

SIPRI. (2025). Sitio web del Stockholm International Peace Research Institute. https://www.sipri.org/

SIPRI. (2025). Unprecedented rise in global military expenditure as European and Middle East spending surges. https://www.sipri.org/media/press-release/2025/unprecedented-rise-global-military-expenditure-european-and-middle-east-spending-surges

SIPRI. (2025). Unprecedented Rise in Global Military Expenditure as European and Middle East Spending Surges. https://www.sipri.org/media/press-release/2025/unprecedented-rise-global-military-expenditure-european-and-middle-east-spending-surges

Sköns, E., Allebeck, A. C., Loose-Weintraub, E., & Stålenheim, P. (1999). Military expenditure. *SIPRI Yearbook*, 269–350.

Sköns, E., Perdomo, C., Perlo-Freeman, S., & Stalenheim, P. (2004). *Military Expenditure*. SIPRI Yearbook 2004: Armaments, Disarmament and International Security, 305-338.

Smith, A. (1776). An Inquiry into the Nature and Causes of the Wealth of Nations. London: Printed for W. Strahan; and T. Cadell.

Smith, A. (1776). *An inquiry into the nature and causes of the wealth of nations*. W. Strahan and T. Cadell. https://www.britannica.com/topic/the-Wealth-of-Nations

Smith, R. P. (1977). *M*ilitary expenditure and capitalism. *Cambridge Journal of Economics*, *1*(1), 61–76. DOI: 10.1093/oxfordjournals.cje.a035351

Smith, R. P. (1980). The demand for military expenditure. *Economic Journal (London)*, *90*(360), 811–820. DOI: 10.2307/2231744

Smith, R. P. (1980b). Military expenditure and investment in OECD countries, 1954-1973. *Journal of Comparative Economics*, *4*(1), 19–32. DOI: 10.1016/0147-5967(80)90050-5

Smith, R. P. (2009). *Military Economics: The Interaction of Power and Money*. Palgrave MacMillan. DOI: 10.1057/9780230244672

South China Sea Strategic Situation Probing Initiative. (2025). *An incomplete report on U.S. military activities in the South China Sea in 2024*. https://www.scspi.org/en/yjbg/incomplete-report-us-military-activities-south-china-sea-2024

Sreenivasulu, A., & Manimozhi, T. Satheesh kumar P., Selvakumar P. and Singh P.,(2022). "The Model of Smart Sensing Device For Sensitive Nanoclusters Modification in Sensing Properties," 2022 2nd International Conference on Advance Computing and Innovative Technologies in Engineering (ICACITE), Greater Noida, India, 2022, pp. 1043-1047, DOI: 10.1109/ICACITE53722.2022.9823846

Srinivas, V. N. (2006). Trends in Defence Expenditure: India, China and Pakistan. *Air Power Journal*, *3*(1), 63–82.

Stålenheim, P., Perdomo, C., & Sköns, E. (2008). Military expenditure. *SIPRI Yearbook*, 175–206.

Steindl, U. M. (2024). Geopolitical instability and escalating conflicts: The impact on East Asian defence innovation systems. *Vienna Journal of East Asian Studies*, *15*(1), 159–186. DOI: 10.30965/25217038-01501008

Stiglitz, J. (2017). *Globalization and Its Discontents Revisited: Anti-Globalization in the Era of Trump*. Norton.

Stocchi, L., Pourazad, N., Michaelidou, N., Tanusondjaja, A., & Harrigan, P. (2022). Marketing research on Mobile apps: Past, present and future. *Journal of the Academy of Marketing Science*, *50*(2), 195–225. DOI: 10.1007/s11747-021-00815-w PMID: 34776554

Stockholm International Peace Research Institute. (2023). *SIPRI Military Expenditure Database*. SIPRI. https://www.sipri.org/databases/milex

Stockholm International Peace Research Institute. (2025, Apr). *Trends in military expenditure 2024* [PDF]. https://www.sipri.org

Stonehouse, G., & Snowdon, B. (2007). Competitive advantage revisited: Michael Porter on strategy and competitiveness. *Journal of Management Inquiry*, *16*(3), 256–273. DOI: 10.1177/1056492607306333

Strangio, S. (2024, Oct 17). *Malaysia's Anwar again says oil and gas exploration will continue*. The Diplomat. https://thediplomat.com/2024/10/malaysias-anwar-again-says-oil-and-gas-exploration-will-continue/

Strangio, S. (2025, Mar 25). *Vietnam island building in South China Sea continuing at 'breakneck pace'*. The Diplomat. https://thediplomat.com/2025/03/vietnam-island-building-in-south-china-sea-continuing-at-breakneck-pace/

Stubbs, R. (2017). *Rethinking Asia's economic miracle: The political economy of war, prosperity and crisis* (2nd ed.). Macmillan International Higher Education., https://link.springer.com/content/pdf/10.1057/978-1-137-55726-1.pdf

Subhalaxmi Barik, & Das, D. S. (2019). Higher Education System In India And Its Impact On The Economy. *Think India Journal, 22*(10), 7301–7308. https://thinkindiaquarterly.org/index.php/think-india/article/view/12106

Sugumaran, K. M. D., Pandiyarajan V., Y. B S, Selvakumar P. and M. S, (2024). "Analysis of Electromyography Signals for Control of Mechanical Prosthesis using Machine Learning Techniques," 2024 2nd International Conference on Intelligent Data Communication Technologies and Internet of Things (IDCIoT), Bengaluru, India, 2024, pp. 1059-1067, DOI: 10.1109/IDCIoT59759.2024.10467707

Sunge, R., Mudzingiri, C., & Mkhize, N. (2024). The COVID-19 pandemic and economic recovery: The mediating role of governance, a global perspective. *Heliyon*, *10*(22), e39869. DOI: 10.1016/j.heliyon.2024.e39869 PMID: 39584076

Sussex, M., Clarke, M., & Medcalf, R. (2017). National security: Between theory and practice. *Australian Journal of International Affairs*, *71*(5), 474–478. DOI: 10.1080/10357718.2017.1347139

Tabelli, V. (2024). Trade and diplomacy through interconnectivity: The Belt and Road Initiative and its mitigating role in the South China Sea (Master's thesis). Charles University. https://dspace.cuni.cz/bitstream/handle/20.500.11956/197719/120483394.pdf?sequence=1

Tamang, P. (2022). The Impact of Education Expenditure on India's Economic Growth. *Journal of International Academic Research*, *11*(3), 14–20.

Tan, W. K. D. (2015). Fueled by wealth, funneled by politics: The dominance of domestic drivers of arms procurement in Southeast Asia (Doctoral dissertation, Naval Postgraduate School, Monterey, CA). https://calhoun.nps.edu/bitstream/handle/10945/47882/15Dec_Tan_Wah%20Kheng%20Dean.pdf?sequence=1

Tanaka, S. (2022). The Old and New of Digital History. *History and Theory*, *61*(4), 3–18. DOI: 10.1111/hith.12284

Tang, C. F., & Tan, B. W. (2015). The impact of energy consumption, income and foreign direct investment on carbon dioxide emissions in Vietnam. *Energy*, *79*, 447–454. DOI: 10.1016/j.energy.2014.11.033

Tansel, T. B. (2020). The Shape of 'Rising Powers' to Come? The Antinomies of Growth and Neoliberal Development in Turkey. *New Political Economy*, *25*(5), 791–812. https://www.tandfonline.com/doi/full/10.1080/13563467.2019.1584173. DOI: 10.1080/13563467.2019.1584173

Tarawneh, M. (2024). *Perspective Chapter: Cryptography-Recent Advances and Research Perspectives*. IntechOpen., DOI: 10.5772/intechopen.111847

Taufique, K. M. R., Siwar, C., Talib, B., Sarah, F. H., & Chamhuri, N. (2014). Synthesis of Constructs for Modeling Consumers' Understanding and Perception of Eco-Labels. *Sustainability (Basel)*, *6*(4), 2176–2200. DOI: 10.3390/su6042176

Tayal, S. (2017). A Review paper on Network Security and Cryptography. *Advances in Computational Sciences and Technology, 10(5)*, 763-770. https://www.ripublication.com/acst17/acstv10n5_10.pdf

Teng, B., Wang, S., Shi, Y., Sun, Y., Wang, W., Hu, W., & Shi, C. (2022). Economic recovery forecasts under impacts of COVID-19. *Economic Modelling, 110*, 105821. DOI: 10.1016/j.econmod.2022.105821 PMID: 35261424

Teng, J. Z., Khan, M. K., Khan, M. I., Chishti, M. Z., & Khan, M. O. (2021). Effect of foreign direct investment on CO2 emission with the role of globalization, institutional quality with pooled mean group panel ARDL. *Environmental Science and Pollution Research International, 28*(5), 5271–5282. DOI: 10.1007/s11356-020-10823-y PMID: 32960445

Thakur, R. (1998). From National to Human Security. In Harris, S., & Mack, A. (Eds.), *Asia-Pacific security: The Economics-Politics Nexus*. Allen & Unwin.

Thomas, A. M. (2021). *Macroeconomics: An Introduction*. Cambridge University Press. DOI: 10.1017/9781108764919

Tian, N., Fleurant, A., Wezeman, P. D., & Wezeman, S. T. (2017). Trends in world military expenditure, 2016. Stockholm International Peace Research Institute (SIPRI) Fact Sheet, April 2017.

Töngür, Ü., Hsu, S., & Elveren, A. Y. (2015). Military Expenditures and Political Regimes: Evidence from Global Data, 1963-2000. *Economic Modelling, 44*, 68–79. DOI: 10.1016/j.econmod.2014.10.004

Toussaert, S. (2021). Upping uptake of COVID contact tracing apps. *Nature Human Behaviour, 5*(2), 183–184. DOI: 10.1038/s41562-021-01048-1 PMID: 33479504

Tran, T. (2024). Does corruption moderate the military spending–informal economy nexus? The empirical evidence from Asian Countries. *International Journal of Social Economics, 51*(11), 1468–1482. DOI: 10.1108/IJSE-06-2023-0454

Trattner, C., Jannach, D., Motta, E., Costera Meijer, I., Diakopoulos, N., Elahi, M., Opdahl, A. L., Tessem, B., Borch, N., Fjeld, M., Øvrelid, L., De Smedt, K., & Moe, H. (2022). Responsible media technology and AI: Challenges and research directions. *AI and Ethics, 2*(4), 585–594. DOI: 10.1007/s43681-021-00126-4

Trebesch, C. (2023). The Ukraine support tracker: which countries help Ukraine and how? *KIEL Working Paper,* No. 2218, 75 p.

Tsitouras, A., & Tsounis, N. (2024). Military Outlays and Economic Growth: A Nonlinear Disaggregated Analysis for a Developed Economy. *Peace Economics, Peace. Science & Public Policy, 30*(3), 341–391. DOI: 10.1515/peps-2024-0010

Tsong, C., Lee, C., Tsai, L., & Hu, T. (2016). The Fourier approximation and testing for the null of cointegration. *Empirical Economics, 51*(3), 1085–1113. DOI: 10.1007/s00181-015-1028-6

Turillazzi, A. (2024). Navigating risk: China's aircraft carrier strategy. *SAIS Europe Journal of Global Affairs,* 27. https://www.saisjournal.eu/article/99-Aina-Turillazzi-Navigating-Risk.cfm

Turker, H. (2023, Aug 24). Maritime chessboard: The geopolitical dynamics of the South China Sea. *Geopolitical Monitor.* https://www.geopoliticalmonitor.com/maritime-chessboard-the-geopolitical-dynamics-of-the-south-china-sea/

Tyebjee, F. F. (2025, Mar 10). Malaysia's unseen, silent underwater warriors. *The Vibes.* https://www.thevibes.com/articles/lifestyle/105719/malaysias-unseen-silent-underwater-warriors

U.S. Department of Defense. (2024, Mar 11). Department of Defense releases the President's Fiscal Year 2025 defense budget [Press release]. https://www.defense.gov/News/Releases/Release/Article/3718698/department-of-defense-releases-the-presidents-fiscal-year-2025-defense-budget/

U.S. Department of Defense. (2025, Mar). Vision statement for a prosperous and secure Southeast Asia. https://www.defense.gov/News/Releases/Release/Article/3973788/us-department-of-defense-vision-statement-for-a-prosperous-and-secure-southeast/

U.S. Department of State. (2025, Jan 20). U.S. security cooperation with the Philippines. Bureau of Political-Military Affairs. https://www.state.gov/u-s-security-cooperation-with-the-philippines/

U.S. Energy Information Administration. (2013). *Contested areas of South China Sea likely have few conventional oil and gas resources.* Eia. https://www.eia.gov/todayinenergy/detail.php?id=10651

U.S. Navy. (2025). *NIWC Pacific enhances India's maritime security capabilities.* America's Navy. https://www.navy.mil/Press-Office/News-Stories/display-news/Article/4196056/niwc-pacific-enhances-indias-maritime-security-capabilities/

Ullman, R. H. (1983). Redefining Security. *International Security, 8*(1), 129–153. https://www.jstor.org/stable/2538489. DOI: 10.2307/2538489

UNDP. (1994). Human Development Report. https://hdr.undp.org/content/human-development-report-1994

UR, R. (2022). Military Expenditure and Economic Growth: Evidence from India and Pakistan. *Research Journal of Humanities and Social Sciences, 13*(1), 12–16.

US Department of Defense. (2025). *Ukraine Events Timeline*. US Department of Defense. https://www.defense.gov/Spotlights/Support-for-Ukraine/Timeline/

US Department of State. (2024). *United States International Cyberspace & Digital Policy Strategy. Towards an Innovative, Secure, and Rights-Respecting Digital Future*. Recuperado de https://www.state.gov/united-states-international-cyberspace-and-digital-policy-strategy/

Vaïsse, J. (2018). *Zbigniew Brzezinski: America's Grand Strategist*. Harvard University Press.

Valamede, L. S., de Oliveira, G. G., Munhoz, I. P., & Akkari, A. C. S. (2022). Digital Technologies Adoption to Face COVID-19 Pandemic: An Exploratory Approach. In: Iano, Y., Saotome, O., Kemper Vásquez, G.L., Cotrim Pezzuto, C., Arthur, R., Gomes de Oliveira, G. (Eds) Proceedings of the 7th Brazilian Technology Symposium (BTSym'21). BTSym 2021. Smart Innovation, Systems and Technologies, vol 295. Springer, Cham. DOI: 10.1007/978-3-031-08545-1_17

Van Veeren, E., Stevens, C., & Senu, A. (2024). Secrecy games, power, and resistance in global politics. *Review of International Studies*, 1–18. https://www.cambridge.org/core/journals/review-of-international-studies/article/secrecy-games-power-and-resistance-in-global-politics/A9F2834F169D66304FD5F39722CFAA0C. DOI: 10.1017/S0260210524000275

Vicarelli, F. (1984). *Keynes: The instability of capitalism*. Palgrave Macmillan., DOI: 10.9783/9781512819892

Vicsek, L. (2021). Artificial intelligence and the future of work–lessons from the sociology of expectations. *The International Journal of Sociology and Social Policy, 41*(7/8), 842–861. DOI: 10.1108/IJSSP-05-2020-0174

VietnamPlus. (2025). *Vietnam eyes 8% growth in 2025 through strategic reforms*. Vietnam Plus. https://en.vietnamplus.vn/vietnam-eyes-8-growth-in-2025-through-strategic-reforms-post319053.vnp

Vijayakumar, G., Rajkumar, M., Rajiv Chandar, N., Selvakumar, P., & Duraisamy, R. (2024). Muniyandi Rajkumar, Rajiv Chandar N, Selvakumar P and Ramesh Duraisamy, (2024). Environmentally friendly TDS removal from waste water by electrochemical ion exchange batch-type recirculation (EIR) technique. *Environmental Science. Water Research & Technology, 10*(4), 826–835. https://di.org/10.1039/D3EW00793F. DOI: 10.1039/D3EW00793F

Vision of Humanity. (2024, May 19). *Navigating tensions, conflict and prosperity in the South China Sea*. Vision of Humanity. https://www.visionofhumanity.org/navigating-tensions-conflict-and-prosperity-in-the-south-china-sea/

Vollala, S., Ramasubramanian, N., & Tiwari, U. (2021). Cryptographic Techniques. In *Energy-Efficient Modular Exponential Techniques for Public-Key Cryptography*. Springer., DOI: 10.1007/978-3-030-74524-0_1

Voumik, L. C., Islam, M. J., & Raihan, A. (2022a). Electricity production sources and CO2 emission in OECD countries: Static and dynamic panel analysis. *Glob Sustain Res, 1*(2), 12–21. DOI: 10.56556/gssr.v1i2.327

VPK. (2025). *Global arms exports in 2024 and for the period 2021-2024*. TimeWeb. https://odkb-csto.org/analytics/?ELEMENT_ID=24011#loaded

Wajid, R., & Alam, K. (2024). Role of Modern Technology in COVID-19 Care Management. In Alam, K., Daniel, S., Alzahrani, A., & Hassan Almalki, W. (Eds.), *Nursing Practice during COVID-19: Preparation, Education and Support*. Springer., DOI: 10.1007/978-3-031-52110-2_5

Wallerstein, I. (1984). *The politics of the world-economy: The states, the movements and the civilizations*. Cambridge University Press., https://books.google.com/books?hl=en&lr=&id=tXmk4Izf4RUC&oi=fnd&pg=PP9

Wang, G. (2019). Marx's monetary theory and its practical value. *China Political Economy, 2*(2), 182–200. DOI: 10.1108/CPE-10-2019-0026

Wang, L., Vo, X. V., Shahbaz, M., & Ak, A. (2020a). Globalization and carbon emissions: Is there any role of agriculture value-added, financial development, and natural resource rent in the aftermath of COP21? *Journal of Environmental Management, 268*, 110712. DOI: 10.1016/j.jenvman.2020.110712 PMID: 32510446

Wang, W., Wei, K., Kubatko, O., Piven, V., Chortok, Y., & Derykolenko, O. (2023). Economic Growth and Sustainable Transition: Investigating Classical and Novel Factors in Developed Countries. *Sustainability (Basel), 15*(16), 12346. DOI: 10.3390/su151612346

Wang, X. V., & Wang, L. (2021). A literature survey of the robotic technologies during the COVID-19 pandemic. *Journal of Manufacturing Systems*, *60*, 823–836. DOI: 10.1016/j.jmsy.2021.02.005 PMID: 33612914

Wang, Z., Rasool, Y., Zhang, B., Ahmed, Z., & Wang, B. (2020b). Dynamic linkage among industrialisation, urbanisation, and CO2 emissions in APEC realms: Evidence based on DSUR estimation. *Structural Change and Economic Dynamics*, *52*, 382–389. DOI: 10.1016/j.strueco.2019.12.001

Ward, M. D., & Davis, D. R. (1992). Sizing up the peace dividend: Economic growth and military spending in the United States, 1948-1996. *The American Political Science Review*, *86*(3), 748–755. DOI: 10.2307/1964136

Ward, M. D., Davis, D., Penubarti, M., Rajmaira, S., & Cochran, M. (1991). Country survey I–military spending in India. *Defence and Peace Economics*, *3*(1), 41–63. DOI: 10.1080/10430719108404714

Ward, M. D., & Mahajan, A. K. (1984). Defence expenditures, security threats, and governmental deficits: A case study of India, 1952–1979. *The Journal of Conflict Resolution*, *28*(3), 382–419. DOI: 10.1177/0022002784028003002

Welch, P. J., & Welch, G. F. (2016). *Economics: Theory and Practice* (11th ed.). Wiley.

Wezeman, S. T. (2020). *Russia's Military Spending: Frequently Asked Questions*. SIPRI. https://www.sipri.org/commentary/topical-backgrounder/2020/russias-militaryspending-frequently-asked questions (дата обращения: 12.02.2024).

Wickberg, A., & Gärdebo, J. (2023). Computation, data and AI in Anthropocene history. *History and Technology*, *39*(3-4), 328–346. DOI: 10.1080/07341512.2024.2330724

Wiesmeth, H. (2022). *Environmental Economics: Theory and Policy in Equilibrium*. Springer. DOI: 10.1007/978-3-031-05929-2

Williams, L. (2025, Mar 5). China's defense budget: The real figures behind the world's second-largest military. *The Rio Times*. https://www.riotimesonline.com/chinas-defense-budget-the-real-figures-behind-the-worlds-second-largest-military/

Williamson, S. (2017). *Macroeconomics (The Pearson Series in Economics)* (6th ed.). Pearson.

Williams, P. D. (2008). *Security Studies: An Introduction*. Routledge. DOI: 10.4324/9780203926604

Winnebeck, J., Sutter, O., Hermann, A., Antweiler, C., & Conermann, S. (2023). The analytical concept of asymmetrical dependency. *Journal of Global Slavery, 8*(1), 1–59. https://brill.com/view/journals/jgs/8/1/article-p1_1.xml. DOI: 10.1163/2405836X-00801002

World Bank. (2017). *Global economic prospects: A fragile recovery* (June 2017). World Bank Group. https://openknowledge.worldbank.org/bitstream/handle/10986/26800/9781464810244.pdf

Wu, X., & Velasco, J. C. (2024). Navigating the Indo-Pacific: Vietnam's hedging strategies amid the geopolitical rivalry between China and the United States. *Asian Perspective, 48*(1), 95–118. DOI: 10.1353/apr.2024.a919883

Xiao, H., Sadler, M., & Quek, K. (2021). Guns and butter in China: How Chinese citizens respond to military spending. *The China Quarterly, 245*, 248–261. DOI: 10.1017/S0305741020000260

Xinhua News Agency. (2024, Dec 27). China launches new-generation amphibious assault ship. Xinhuanet. http://www.news.cn/english/2023-12/27/c_1212345678.htm

Yakovlev, P. (2007). Arms Trade, Military Spending, and Economic Growth. *Defence and Peace Economics, 18*(4), 317–338. DOI: 10.1080/10242690601099679

Yang, H., Hong, C., Jung, S., & Lee, J. D. (2015). Arms or butter: The economic effect of an increase in military expenditure. *Journal of Policy Modeling, 37*(4), 596–615. DOI: 10.1016/j.jpolmod.2015.03.014

Yesilyurt, F., & Yesilyurt, M. E. (2019). Meta-analysis, military expenditures and growth. *Journal of Peace Research, 56*(3), 352–363. DOI: 10.1177/0022343318808841

Yildirim, J., Sezgin, S., & Ocal, N. (2005). Military expenditure and economic growth in Middle Eastern countries: A dynamic panel data analysis. *Defence and Peace Economics, 16*(4), 283–295. DOI: 10.1080/10242690500114751

Ynikkaya, H. (2003). Trade openness and economic growth: A cross-country empirical investigation. *Journal of Development Economics, 72*(1), 57–89. DOI: 10.1016/S0304-3878(03)00068-3

Yu, J. (2025, May 23). *The Evolving Role of U.S. Forces in Korea and Its Implications for the ROK-U.S. Alliance.* RealClearDefense. https://www.realcleardefense.com/articles/2025/05/23/the_evolving_role_of_us_forces_in_korea_1112227.html

Zhang, M. (2025). China–Japan–South Korea trilateral cooperation: Institution building and power politics. Springer Nature. https://books.google.com/books?hl=en&lr=&id=YsE7EQAAQBAJ&oi=fnd&pg=PR5

Zha, W. (2025). Hedging without strategy. *Contemporary Southeast Asia*, *47*(1), 33–66. https://www.jstor.org/stable/27378715?casa_token=7nYaWBFQ0vIAAAAA:LI8Ezs62squC1nGfNdqI66StviFeQNZLDy406Al2Mftp7ypYC5fH4hd7jQFpybQieSV5WWT1rcZitomSkR3Hp1DSNTZiAzOCEm6noAB_RjYchA06Z-afpA. DOI: 10.1355/CS47-1b

Zhu, Z. (2024, Dec). Analysis and Forecasting of India's Defence Expenditure. In *2024 9th International Conference on Modern Management, Education and Social Sciences (MMET 2024)* (pp. 835–843). Atlantis Press.

Zivot, E., & Andrews, D. (1992). *F*urther evidence on the great crash, the oil-price shock, and the unit-root hypothesis. *Journal of Business & Economic Statistics*, *10*(3), 25–44. DOI: 10.1080/07350015.1992.10509904

Zmami, M., & Ben-Salha, O. (2020). An empirical analysis of the determinants of CO2 emissions in GCC countries. *International Journal of Sustainable Development and World Ecology*, *27*(5), 469–480. DOI: 10.1080/13504509.2020.1715508

Zona Militar. (2025, May 21). *The U.S. will upgrade the facilities of a key base for the deployment of the Philippine Navy in the South China Sea.* Zona Militar. https://www.zona-militar.com/en/2025/05/21/the-u-s-will-upgrade-the-facilities-of-a-key-base-for-the-deployment-of-the-philippine-navy-in-the-south-china-sea/

Zoran, T., 2022. Analysis of the Impact of Public Education Expenditure on Economic Growth of European Union and BRICS. *Economic Analysis*, 48(1-2, 19-38), pp.19-37.

About the Contributors

Gerardo Reyes Ruiz. He is an Actuary by training from the Faculty of Sciences-UNAM; he studied a Specialty in Econometrics in the Postgraduate Studies Division of the Faculty of Economics-UNAM; He obtained a Master's and Doctorate in Business Studies (actuarial profile) from the Faculty of Economics and Business of the University of Barcelona, Spain. Later he did a postdoctoral stay at the Center for Economic, Administrative, and Social Studies (CIECAS) of the National Polytechnic Institute (IPN). His work experience has been in public education institutions (UNAM, UAEM, IPN, Centro de Estudios Superiores Navales-CESNAV) where he has taught classes in Bachelor's, Specialty, Master's, and Doctorate degrees. All this accumulated experience allowed him to enter the National System of Researchers (SNI), Social Area, of Mexico (he has the appointment of Level I National Researcher). He is currently attached to the Center for Superior Naval Studies (CESNAV), in Mexico.

***

A. Ranjithkumar is an accomplished political scientist currently serving as Assistant Professor of Political Science at Vel Tech University, Chennai. A respected member of several international editorial boards and academic associations, he brings together rigorous scholarship and a strong commitment to inclusive governance and social transformation. He holds a Ph.D. in Political Science from Pondicherry University and completed his Post-Doctoral Fellowship at Gandhigram Rural Institute, with additional qualifications in Population Studies, Labour Law, and Education. Dr. Ranjithkumar has authored and edited over 10 books and published more than 40 research papers on social justice, Dalit rights, gender issues, and rural development. He has presented and chaired panels at prestigious global platforms, including the IPSA 75th Anniversary Conference in Lisbon and the 28th World Congress of Political Science in Seoul. He has received the ICSSR International

Travel Grant and funding under Vision Viksit Bharat @ 2047, reflecting his active leadership in both research and policy engagement.

Umut Akduğan, has his BA degree in the field of Mathematics Education at Marmara University in 2007. Subsequently, he received his MA degree in the field of Econometrics at Trakya University and PhD degrees in the field of Economics at Istanbul University. The author currently continues his career at Trakya University, Faculty of Economics and Administrative Sciences, Department of Public Finance, since 2017. Dr. Akduğan is interested in Econometrics of Macroeconomic Modelling, Environmental Economics and Fiscal Policy.

Sudhanshu Chandra Founding Faculty, Assistant Professor & Academic Coordinator at Manuu Law School, Maulana Azad National Urdu University Hyderabad. A Central University, Ministry of Education, Govt. of India Established by an Act of Parliament in 1988, Accredited with Grade A+ by NACC, (Gachibowli, Hyderabad-500032, Telangana) He Completed his B.A.LLB(Hons)-Dr. Ram Manohar Lohiya National Law University Lucknow (U.P). LLM-National Law University Jodhpur (Rajasthan), Cleared UGC-NET, Ph.D. in Law from Gautam Buddha University Greater Noida (U.P.) Authored Books- The Effect of Intellectual Property Rights and Conservation on Biodiversity Law in India (Associated Publishing House-2023) ISBN-978-81-965309-8-3, Custodial Violence by Police in India: Analysis of Judicial Decisions 2010-2020 (Associated Publishing House-2023)-ISBN-978-81-965248-0-7. Also taken Copyright of work Custodial Violence by Police in India: Analysis of Judicial Decisions 2010-2020 Registration No-L-124572/2023 Dated-09/06/2023. Copyright of work- "AI-Assisted Patent Opportunity Detector" Registration No-L-159904/2025 Dated -20/01/2025 & taken Design No- 430368-001 Dated - 27/01/2025 Editor/Co-Editor of Books- "The Menace and Implications of Narcotic Drug Abuse and Alcoholism in India: A Socio-Legal Study" (Singhal Law Publication-2022)-ISBN-978-93-93493-75-0. "International Conference on Law & Technology" (Manuu Law School-2025)-ISBN-978-81-983681-0-2. Presented/Published Several Research Papers in International/ National/Scopus/UGC-Care Listed Journals. Judged Several National Moot Court Competitions.

Sachin Chavan is a Professor at the Balaji Institute of International Business, Pune. With a deep understanding of international business dynamics and a passion for teaching, he plays a key role in shaping the academic and professional development of students. His commitment to excellence in education and research contributes to the institute's reputation as a center of academic distinction.

Rajat B. Hubballi is an Assistant Professor in the MBA Department at New Horizon College of Engineering. With a strong academic background, he is pursuing a Ph.D. at Jain University and has cleared KSET. His expertise lies in finance, taxation, FinTech, and AI applications in business. He has presented and published papers in SCOPUS, IEEE, and UGC CARE journals. A resourceful educator, he has also authored books and holds multiple patents in AI-driven business solutions. His research interests include blockchain, cloud accounting, and green finance. He actively contributes to academic events, faculty development programs, and student mentorship.

Sangshaptak Jana has completed P.G. in Economics from Vidyasagar University, Midnapore, West Bengal, India

Jipson Joseph has a PhD in Ethics from DVK Bangalore. Currently, he is a Research Scholar at School of Law, Christ University, Bangalore, India. His research interests are in the fields of ethics, gender studies, constitutional law, human rights, human security, national security, economic sustainability, environmental justice, SDGs, developmental policies, and global poverty. He has published 6 books, co-edited one book, and contributed scholarly articles to many international and national journals and edited volumes including IGI Global Scientific Publishing's edited books.

Lavanya K. is a visionary educator with over 25 years of experience in commerce and management. A published author, patent holder, and seminar leader, she blends academic excellence with innovative, student-centric learning. Her research in fintech and sustainability reflects a commitment to progress, integrity, and meaningful impact in higher education.

T.C. Manjunath was born on 6th February 1967. He did his BE from RV College of Engg. in 1989, ME in Robotics & Automation from LD College of Engg. in 1992 with First Rank and PhD in Systems & Control Engg. from IIT Bombay in the year 2007. He is currently working as the Dean Research R & D and as Professor in the Dept. of Computer Science & Engineering with specialization in IoT, Cyber Security & Blockchain Technology in Rajarajeswari College of Engineering, Bengaluru, Karnataka. He has completed B.E. Degree from R.V. College of Engg., M.E. Govt.'s LD College of Engg., Gujarat Univ., Ahmedabad in First Rank and Ph.D. in Systems and Control Engineering from the Indian Institute of Technology Bombay IIT Bombay He has got a teaching academic, research and administrative experience of more than 35+ years 10 years as Principal, 8 years as HoD rest as faculty and has published more than 1200+ research papers in various national & international journals and conferences, with 175+ patents 50 book-chapters, 25 awards and also published 25 text books in various field of science, engineering and technology, completed projects worth Rs. 9 Crores till date apart from guiding 10 PhD scholars. He is a member of 30 Professional Society Chapters and is a fellow of IE, IETE, AMIEE and a chartered engineer. He got the best research scholar award in 2006 in IIT Bombay amongst all the research scholars of the institute. He has got 10 awards in academics and research activities.

P. Selvakumar is currently an Associate Professor in the Department of Science and Humanities at Nehru Institute of Technology, Coimbatore, Tamil Nadu, India. Prior to joining Nehru Institute of Technology, he held positions as an Assistant Professor in the Department of Science and Humanities various engineering colleges in Coimbatore, Tamil Nadu, India, spanning from 2011 to 2023. Dr.P. Selvakumar's academic and research interests lie primarily in the field of phytochemistry. He has made significant contributions to his field, with an impressive record that includes 30 journal publications, 12 patents, and 20 conference papers. Additionally, he has organized 5 seminars and conferences, further demonstrating his commitment to academic and scientific exchange. Throughout his career, Dr. P.Selvakumar has been recognized for his dedication and excellence in teaching, having been honored with several awards, including the Best Teacher Awards. He holds a prominent position in the academic community, contributing actively to research.

Mikail Pehlivan, has his BA degree in the fields of Public Administration and Public Finance (double major) at Afyon Kocatepe University in 2015. Subsequently, he received his MA and PhD degrees in the field of Public Finance at Istanbul University. The author currently continues his career at Trakya University, Faculty of Economics and Administrative Sciences, Department of Public Finance, since 2017. Dr. Pehlivan is interested in Public Economics, Environmental Economics and Regulation Economics.

Roop Raj is working as Associate Professor in Economics. Raj has done his 10th and 12th education from Jawahar Navodaya Vidyalaya Jhajjar, Haryana, after which he has obtained BA Economics Hons, MA Economics, UGC-NET-JRF Economics, M.Phil Economics and PhD Economics degree. Raj has published 14 book chapters and more than 70 research papers in international journals, most of which have been published by foreign publishers like Springer, Elsevier, Wiley, Emerald etc. Most of the research papers are Scopus, web of Science, SCI indexed and UGC-Care listed. Raj has also registered 17 patents till now, out of which 6 are design patents and 11 are utility patents. Dr. Raj has authored six books in his subject. He has also completed many research oriented training/FDP/orientation/

refresher programmes related to his subject. Dr. Raj has presented his research work in more than 67 national/ international seminars/ Conferences also.

G Raghavender Raju is Currently the Dean of Student Welfare and Heading the Department of Humanities and Social Sciences, Sri Sathya Sai Institute of Higher Learning, Prasanthi Nilayam Campus, Puttaparthi. He is an expert in the areas of Macroeconomics, Monetary Theory & Policy International Economics & Finance. He has guided 4 Ph.Ds, around 100 dissertations, published three books, about ten chapters in edited volumes, around 50 research papers in refereed national and international journals and presented over 50 papers in national and international conferences. He is invited as a Resource Person of Econometrics at various Universities in India.

Gokila S, currently working as an Assistant Professor is pursuing Ph.D in Anna university, chennai. She has published more than 6 articles in Scopus and published multiple national journals and international journals She has completed eight NPTEL courses and awarded elite positions.Her area of interest is Data structures, Machine learning and theory of computation

Guru Basava Aradhya S is a seasoned academician with 17 years of experience in management education. He currently serves as the HoD & Professor at School of Commerce and Management Studies, Geeta University. He holds a Ph.D. in Management and has mentored five Ph.D. scholars. His expertise includes HR, marketing, and business analytics. A prolific researcher, he has published in SCOPUS, ABDC, and UGC CARE journals. He has organized numerous international conferences and contributed to NAAC and NBA accreditations. His industry collaborations include fa culty exchange programs and consultancy projects. Passionate about academia, he actively fosters innovation, research, and student development.

Index

H

I

M

N

P

S

www.ingramcontent.com/pod-product-compliance
Lightning Source LLC
LaVergne TN
LVHW081543300926
849161LV00006B/1504